Springer Texts in Business and Economics

For further volumes:
http://www.springer.com/series/10099

Farrokh Langdana • Peter T. Murphy

International Trade
and Global Macropolicy

 Springer

Farrokh Langdana
Rutgers Business School
Newark, NJ, USA

Peter T. Murphy
Fort Salonga, NY, USA

ISSN 2192-4333
ISSN 2192-4341 (electronic)
ISBN 978-1-4614-1634-0
ISBN 978-1-4614-1635-7 (eBook)
DOI 10.1007/978-1-4614-1635-7
Springer New York Heidelberg Dordrecht London

Library of Congress Control Number: 2013937047

Printed on acid-free paper

Springer is part of Springer Science+Business Media (www.springer.com)

To my wife Mary, and to all my students.
                                    Farrokh Langdana

*To my wife Babette, to my wonderful family,
and to all the students, professors, and
administrators of the unparalleled Rutgers
Executive MBA Program.*
                                    Peter T. Murphy

About the Authors

Dr. Farrokh Langdana is a professor in the Finance/Economics Department at Rutgers Business School, New Jersey. In addition to this volume, he is the author of three research-oriented books—two coauthored with Prof. Richard C.K. Burdekin—and the textbook *Macroeconomic Policy: Demystifying Monetary and Fiscal Policy*, now in its second edition, and several publications pertaining to macroeconomic policy and macro-experimentation.

Dr. Langdana is currently the Director of the globally ranked Executive MBA (EMBA) Program at Rutgers Business School. He teaches Macroeconomic Policy as well as International Trade and Global Macroeconomics in the EMBA Program as well as in the full-time and Flex MBA programs at Rutgers Business School.

In addition to being the recipient of the Warren I. Susman Award for Excellence in Teaching (Rutgers University's highest teaching award), Prof. Langdana has also been awarded the Paul Nadler Award for Teaching Excellence, the Horace dePodwin Research Award, over ten Executive MBA Teaching Excellence Awards and over 20 Rutgers MBA teaching awards. In addition to teaching in the United States, Prof. Langdana has also taught Executive MBA students in China (Beijing and Shanghai), Singapore, France, and in Iceland and has lectured in India.

Please visit Business.Rutgers.edu/Langdanamacro and scroll down for some of Prof. Langdana's blogs. He can be contacted at Langdana@Business.Rutgers.edu

Peter T. Murphy is an operating partner with Dubilier & Company. He currently serves as President and CEO of DC Safety, a leading supplier of safety products to the automotive industry. Mr. Murphy has 25 years of experience as a pioneer and leader in global business, establishing ventures and achieving growth in dozens of countries across Asia, Europe, and the Americas. Mr. Murphy's expertise in strategy and value creation is complemented by his hands-on experience in multiple disciplines, including sales, operations, supply chain, finance, marketing, and technology. His industry experience, in addition to automotive, includes the packaging, apparel, medical equipment, and retail sectors.

Mr. Murphy received his Master's in Business Administration with a concentration in Finance from Rutgers Business School and was awarded the Executive MBA Achievement Award for Highest Academic Achievement in the EMBA Program. He earned his Bachelor of Science in Humanities from Iona College. He has given lectures on international business and global trade to academic and business audiences in Asia and the United States and has taught at the MBA level as an adjunct lecturer at Rutgers Business School.

Peter T. Murphy can be contacted at murphypt@gmail.com

Acknowledgments

The authors are most grateful to the Rutgers Executive MBA classes of 2011 and 2012 for their detailed comments and suggestions pertaining to early drafts of this volume. While a large number of our current and former students provided valuable feedback, we would be gravely remiss if we did not explicitly mention Allison Nagelburg, Dhruti Mistri, Surabhi Sharma, Hong Jing, Saravanan Pillai, Rushab Kamdar, Toshiyo Hayashi, MaryJane Salvato, and Ken LaMontagne for their very significant editorial suggestions.

We doubly thank Sandra Barker (Rutgers EMBA, 2012) for kindly agreeing to be our official, and amazing, proofreader and editor, and that too when the request was made by us at the eleventh hour! Sandra worked night and day, at the end literally by candlelight in the aftermath of Hurricane Sandy, to help bring this work to life. She was also instrumental in recruiting our talented fact-checker, Nancy Nguyen (BA, Rutgers, 2010), whose thorough efforts greatly improved the final product and to whom we are most grateful. Sandra came through yet again by enlisting our two talented illustrators, Castro Desroches and Ricardo Paredes, who delivered wonderful interpretations of the concepts that we outlined. We are most thankful to both for their fine work.

The authors also thank Tia Angelos of Getty Images, Elizabeth Dunn of Duke University, Robert Doane of the MIT Museum and especially Elisa Marquez of AP Images for their gracious assistance in securing many of the photographs which so enhance the appeal of this book. We would furthermore like thank Ralph Foster for permission to include graphs and information from his work in Chap. 13.

Both authors are indebted to Jon Gurstelle, our editor at Springer, for allowing us the time and the flexibility to complete this volume. With Farrokh Langdana dealing with family issues in Bombay and with running the Rutgers EMBA Program in New Jersey, as well as the academic portions of three programs in Asia, and with Peter T. Murphy balancing his responsibilities as CEO of DC Safety with those of raising newborn twins, the book warranted several deadline push-backs, and Jon has indeed been most gracious.

Both authors are particularly grateful to Prof. Barry Karafin, whose uncompromising refusal to "buy" conventional free trade doctrine in our hyper-connected world finally led to very interesting modifications and clarifications to the conventional free trade theory and to Strategic Trade described in this book. The authors are indebted to all past MBA and EMBA students at Rutgers Business School in New Jersey, and in Prof. Langdana's classes in France and in Iceland, for their comments and their arguments, both for and against free trade. Many of the topics of heated discussion presented in the "articles" in this volume have been inspired by these amazing in-class discussions.

Farrokh Langdana dedicates this book to his wife, Mary, for good reason. As most authors would attest, a book is really a multiyear commitment, an intertemporal disruption of any semblance of a normal life, not just for the author, but for the whole family. With that in mind, Farrokh Langdana thanks Mary for all her patience, her suggestions, and all the vigorous debates that sprang from her well-justified skepticism with the political aspects of global trade. Farrokh Langdana also acknowledges stimulating global macroeconomic policy discussions with his son, Christopher, and his soon-to-be daughter-in-law, Lindsey Moffat, for her support. Farrokh thanks his parents, Zarrin and Keki, for imbibing in him a love for books and instilling in him the work ethic necessary to bring this book to life.

Farrokh Langdana also acknowledges two former Executive MBA students who have guest-lectured in his Trade classes and whose insights have helped shape several key topics in this book. Al Porcello, Head, Group Project Methodology and Application Portfolio Management at Novartis, has shared his high-powered analysis pertaining to the intra-service aspects of R&D in pharmaceutical research and in the future of 3D Printing. And Mitchell Rona, Vice President of Operations of SIGMA Corporation and a veteran of US-China iron/steel trade, who has been on the receiving end of many of the US countervailing duties and other trade distortions, provided first-hand "adventures in the world of trade distortions" which were truly eye-opening and extremely valuable.

Peter T. Murphy dedicates this book to his wife, Babette; to his children, Amanda, Tommy, Kara, Megyn, and Quentin; to his parents, Susan and Quentin; and to his sisters, Deborah and Betsy, and their husbands and children, all of whose love and encouragement provides him with a never-ending source of inspiration. He would also like to express his gratitude to the many clients, employees, business partners, and colleagues with whom he has been so fortunate to work over the years, and who have provided him with the opportunity to experience first-hand the global business implications of everything discussed in this text. He would like to single out certain individuals whose friendship, advice, collaboration, and offers of opportunity have been especially meaningful: Leon Rosenberg, Larry Lampl, Mitch Kupinsky, Sidney Chan, Joel Simon, Harvey Feinman, John Lau, Barry Karafin, Suresh Govindaraj, Tom Franco, and Michael Dubilier. He further extends his deep thanks to his professors, administrators, and classmates from the extraordinary Rutgers Executive MBA class of 2010, in which he learned the theory underpinning nearly everything he has practiced in business, and much, much more.

Contents

Chapter 1
Introduction

In this post-financial crisis environment, as the USA and other advanced economies continue to experience sluggish growth (at best), persistent high unemployment, and political agitation for increasingly protectionist and sometimes xenophobic policies, discussions pertaining to free trade are often fraught with emotion, tension, and hysteria.

The goal of this book is to serve an unmet need: to allow business practitioners and students at the M.B.A. and Executive M.B.A. levels to cut through the emotions and superficial "solutions" and gain a thorough understanding of the hard-hitting theoretical models—which we call "Engine Rooms"—that drive trade and global macroeconomics in the real world. A key feature of this volume is the presentation of theoretical models, and the discussion of their implications in the context of real-world applications. The volume is uniquely designed for current and future business leaders who are or will be engaged in the global economy—whether through their supply chains, operations, sales, marketing, or financing—or as is becoming the norm, all of the above. Armed with an understanding of the theoretical underpinnings driving goods, capital, and ideas across national boundaries, these leaders will foresee the effects of trade and macroeconomic policy changes, and will have the tools to make sound, informed decisions for themselves and their global organizations.

Specifically written for a one-semester course, the book's content replicates the unique format of *Macroeconomic Policy: Demystifying Monetary and Fiscal Policy* (Springer) by Farrokh Langdana, Ph.D., in which theory is embedded in a real-world context via specially crafted simulated news articles that serve to reinforce the major takeaways from each chapter. Key passages are lettered (a), (b), etc., and underlined, with the expectation that the reader will explain and discuss the implications of each key passage in light of what was learned.

We are confident that this volume will equip the reader with these so-called "Engine-Rooms," and he or she will emerge with a thorough working knowledge of these important topics.

F. Langdana and P.T. Murphy, *International Trade and Global Macropolicy*,
Springer Texts in Business and Economics, DOI 10.1007/978-1-4614-1635-7_1,
© Springer Science+Business Media New York 2014

1.1 Overview

In the conventional M.B.A. and Executive M.B.A. curricula of highly ranked programs, it is increasingly evident that two areas of discussion are conspicuously absent.

One such area pertains to **International Trade**.

During the protracted global downturn of 2008 which continues to the present, most economies, including that of the USA, have become increasingly protectionist. Exports and imports have taken on normative implications: Exports are "good," whereas imports are "bad" because the common perception is that they cause job losses at home. Accusations of unfair trade abound; the air is rife with allegations of "dumping" and frantic appeals for "anti-dumping duties," and so on. In addition, many governments, intent on ensuring ongoing indigenous innovation, are exploring several forms of "strategic trade" by subsidizing designated "champion" industries with giant doses of tax revenues.[1] It will become clear as we delve into trade theory that such policies are misguided and counterproductive, benefitting at most certain narrow interests. We shall see how the free exchange of goods and services across national boundaries in fact improves the overall welfare of all trading countries. Such outcomes are often counterintuitive. Our readers, as future business leaders and policymakers, require a firm grasp of trade issues in order to make decisions unencumbered by popular but misguided notions, and to explain these decisions to often skeptical audiences.

The other topic that is often conspicuously absent from M.B.A. curricula is **Global Macroeconomic Policy**.

In the current global economy, any strategic executive decisions made in the absence of exchange rate considerations or global capital flows would be seriously inadequate and downright simplistic. With global capital being highly mobile, it is imperative that even domestic monetary and fiscal policies be analyzed in the context of the global economy. For instance, the relentless monetization of US budget deficits by the Federal Reserve over the 2008–2013 period has had huge repercussions for many emerging economies. Among these are overheated asset markets, commodity inflation, and appreciating currencies, with secondary and

---

[1] Even during the time in which this book was written, examples were plentiful: China retaliated for US tariffs on Chinese steel with duties on US poultry products; new American duties on Chinese tires were met with new Chinese duties on American-built automobiles; Brazil threatened the USA with duties in response to American agriculture subsidies and later enacted tariffs on 100 categories of products. Both of the 2012 US candidates for president accused China of being a currency manipulator, which interestingly was the same accusation made by Brazil against the USA to justify its tariffs; currency controls were effected *within the Eurozone* (in Cyprus); India and the USA traded accusations of unfair subsidization in their renewable energy industries; the USA slapped tariffs on Chinese solar panels, to which the Chinese responded with levies on polysilicon, and, not to be left behind in a global boom of xenophobia, Russia banned the adoption of Russian-born babies by US citizens.

tertiary effects following. Understanding these issues puts our reader in a position to anticipate these effects and to take preemptive action.

Each of the areas mentioned above—trade as well as global macroeconomics—would be (at least) a semester's worth of material in a Ph.D.-level economic program. However, at the M.B.A. and Executive M.B.A. level, the prime focus is on the *policy implications and practical applications* of the topics in the above two areas.

In this book, key elements of both these areas have been seamlessly synthesized in one comprehensive International Trade and Global Macroeconomic Policy course. The book, in a sense, mimics the perpetually updated and highly popular course, taught over the last 20 years in Rutgers Business School's Executive M.B.A. program.

The first part of this volume includes topics from International Trade, such as:

- The Ricardian trade theorem
- The effect of trade on wages and employment
- Intra-industry vs. inter-industry trade
- Trade barriers such as tariffs, quotas, and non-tariff barriers
- Strategic trade, dumping, and countervailing duties
- Intellectual property rights violations
- Outsourcing, off-shoring, and the product life cycle
- Innovation and trade policies

The second part addresses vital issues in Global Macroeconomic Policy, such as:

- Non-sustainable budget deficits, capital inflows, and hot capital
- Exchange rate pegs, speculative asset price bubbles, and global contagion
- Long-term balance of payment deficits and their effects on exchange rates
- Global reserve currency
- Challenges in the Eurozone
- The history of the Gold Standard and the possible revitalization of a currency anchor

As we reach the later chapters, we deploy our increasingly comprehensive models to explore contemporary global trade and macroeconomic issues, bringing to bear the tools and knowledge that we have gained in earlier chapters.

In most instances, we refrain from delving deeply into the mathematical derivations underlying the models that we present. We aim to impart a practical understanding, rather than theoretical mastery. There is no shortage of fine textbooks available for the Ph.D. student who seeks a complete set of equations for every trade and macroeconomic theorem covered herein. There is however a severe dearth of texts covering these topics for *you*; the current or future executive who is expected to operate and make decisions in a global business environment from 30,000 ft. It is for you that this book is written.

Part I
International Trade Theory

In Part 1 we build the Ricardian trade model from the ground up, starting with the concepts of absolute and comparative advantage, and proceeding to develop the concepts of production frontiers, indifference curves, and the terms of trade between countries. We will come to examine how free trade yields benefits to *both* trading partners in the two-country model, regardless of the level of absolute wages or nominal prices in either country.

We then progress to the relaxation of the many assumptions that underlie Ricardian trade theory to determine if the advantages of free trade do indeed still hold in these more 'real world' cases. In the process, we review intra-industry trade, which actually accounts for the majority of trade among developed countries.

We finally pull away from the nice clean world of free trade to explore the harsh reality of global trade distortions. Topics include tariffs, quotas, export subsidies (strategic trade) and non-tariff barriers (NTBs). We conclude this section with a review of two powerful critiques of free trade.

The discussion in Part 1 is all based in microeconomic theory. All variables are "real" here, that is, the discussion is in "units" of goods, labor, and capital; there is no money in this section. In Part 2 we shall introduce money and exchange rates in a global macroeconomic setting.

Chapter 2
The Origins of International Trade Theory

Summary We begin this chapter with the traditional definitions of mercantilism and the concept of Adam Smith's absolute advantage (AA). The chapter then launches into perhaps the most vital cog in the demystification of trade and trade-related issues—the notion of comparative advantage (CA), as given to us by David Ricardo. Policymakers and analysts typically confuse absolute advantage with the foundational building block of global trade, comparative advantage, and this causes much confusion in discussions pertaining to global trade.

While most trade textbooks confine the discussion of CA to algebraic expressions and the standard England versus Spain case put forth by Ricardo,[1] we bring the definition and exploration of CA into a present-day context. We explicate the concepts of "opportunity cost" and "factors of production" and discuss the role of "factor intensity" in determining CA.

These concepts are reinforced by the simulated media article exercise at the end of this chapter. In all the cases in this book, the reader/student will be asked to relate the indicated passages in these cases/articles to key concepts covered in the chapter. These exercises highlight the pervasiveness of global trade theory and global macroeconomic policy in our daily business decisions and in our lives in general.

2.1 Mercantilism

From the sixteenth to the eighteenth centuries, **mercantilism** was the policy of Europe's Great Powers as they expanded their empires, and was the universal framework by which international trade was understood. Mercantilism focuses on maximizing exports in order to bring "specie" (precious metals) into the country:

---

[1] David Ricardo explained his theory of comparative advantage using a two-country (England and Portugal), two-commodity (wine and cloth) example. We will examine the two-country, two-commodity model in this chapter.

F. Langdana and P.T. Murphy, *International Trade and Global Macropolicy*,
Springer Texts in Business and Economics, DOI 10.1007/978-1-4614-1635-7_2,
© Springer Science+Business Media New York 2014

The more gold and silver that a country accumulates, the richer it is. Imports are discouraged with heavy tariffs on foreign goods. Trade under mercantilism is a zero-sum game, with winners who win only at the expense of losers.

Huge spikes of inflation driven by increases in the domestic money supply (which accumulates as exports are exchanged for specie) would regularly ravage the countries that pursued mercantilist policies. It was David Hume, in 1752, who first articulated a theory to explain this phenomenon, which evolved over time to be known as the **quantity theory of money**.[2] Simply stated, increasing the amount of specie (money) in the economy does nothing to increase real wealth; instead, it just means that more money is required to trade for the same goods and services as before.

Whereas mercantilism is couched in a historical context here, it must be noted that the inherent spirit of mercantilism—in which exports and imports have normative implications, exports considered "good" and "job-losing" imports considered "bad"—has been alive and well through economic history. In fact, as economies slow down, the age-old spirit of mercantilism often rears its head.

Mercantilism has a dangerously intuitive and popular appeal. Free trade, as we will explicate in this book, unfortunately does not. Free trade is not intuitive; it is not easy to explain, and far less easy to successfully defend, particularly when living in the midst of a deep and enduring economic slowdown.

2.2 Absolute Advantage: Adam Smith

Adam Smith was the first to articulate the possibility that international trade is *not* a zero-sum game and that, in fact, a single-minded reliance on exports is counterproductive. He explained that different countries will use different quantities of resources in producing the same goods. Thus, each country should *specialize* in manufacturing only the good(s) that it can make with the fewest resources. Global output is thus maximized. Then, by trading freely, *each* trading country will end up with a greater quantity of goods than before.

We can see Smith's theory in action with an example. Let's consider a hypothetical world with only two countries:

Say we are given two countries A and B, where Country A is an efficient producer of coffee and Country B is an efficient producer of tea, and each has a

---

[2] David Hume's 1752 essay "Of Money" may be readily found online, including at http://www.econlib.org/library/LFBooks/Hume/hmMPL26.html#Part II, Essay III, OF MONEY. The crux of his argument: "It seems a maxim almost self-evident, that the prices of every thing depend on the proportion between commodities and money, and that any considerable alteration on either has the same effect, either of heightening or lowering the price."

Fig. 2.1 Absolute advantage

	Units of Labor	
	Country A	Country B
Good X Coffee	**2** a**L**x	3 bLx
Good Y Tea	5 aLy	**4** b**L**y

labor force of 100 workers.[3] What does Adam Smith's idea of absolute advantage (AA) tell us about the advantages of specialization and trade?

Let's say that the labor requirements to produce coffee and tea in each country are as follows:

	Number of laborers to produce 1 unit of the good	
	Country A	Country B
Good X: Coffee	Two laborers	Three laborers
Good Y: Tea	Five laborers	Four laborers

We can see that in Country A, only two laborers are needed to produce 1 unit of coffee, whereas three laborers are required in Country B to produce that same unit. However, Country A requires five workers to produce 1 unit of tea, to Country B's four.

The standard notation to indicate the quantity of labor required to produce a unit of goods is given by

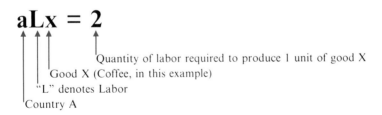

$$aLx = 2$$

Quantity of labor required to produce 1 unit of good X
Good X (Coffee, in this example)
"L" denotes Labor
Country A

The relationships are generally illustrated with a grid as shown in (Fig. 2.1).

---

[3] At this point, we assume that the labor force is identical in Countries A and B and that factors such as transportation costs, infrastructure quality, and labor skills do not complicate matters. Later, as we ratchet-up our sophistication, we will bring in real-world elements, but for now, we concentrate on the pure bedrock theory.

Country A is said to have an **absolute advantage** in X (coffee), as it can make 1 unit of coffee with fewer units of labor than can Country B. Similarly, Country B is said to have an absolute advantage in Y (tea).

Were each country to devote 50 % of its 100 laborers to producing each good, the total global output would be

	Coffee (good X)	Tea (good Y)
Country A	25 units (50 laborers, aLx $=$ 2)	10 units (50 laborers, aLy $=$ 5)
Country B	16.67 units (50 laborers, bLx $=$ 3)	12.5 units (50 laborers, bLy $=$ 4)
Global output	**41.67 units of coffee**	**22.5 units of tea**

However, if each country specializes

	Coffee (good X)	Tea (good Y)
Country A	50 units (100 laborers, aLx $=$ 2)	0
Country B	0	25 units (100 laborers, bLy $=$ 4)
Global output	**50 units of coffee**	**25 units of tea**

We can see that world output of *both goods* is maximized if each country _specializes_. By trading freely, more of both goods are available to consumers in each country.

Of course, under specialization but without trade, Country A's consumers would have no tea, and Country B's consumers would have no coffee. This is why, to make Adam Smith's theory operational, the countries must trade freely with each other. Countries will produce and export those goods in which they have an AA and import the others.

But can we explicitly show that with the maximization of world output, both countries are actually better off? And what does "better off" really mean? And, most importantly, what happens if, say, Country A makes *both* coffee and tea with fewer resources than Country B? What then? The stage is set for the cornerstone model of free trade—the "engine room," if you will. Enter, David Ricardo.

2.3   Comparative Advantage: David Ricardo

The hitch with the theory of absolute advantage comes when we introduce Country C, which is neither the most efficient producer of coffee nor the most efficient producer of tea. Unfortunately for the disadvantaged Country C, it has no place in Adam Smith's theoretical world.

David Ricardo (1772–1823). Warren J. Samuels Portrait Collection, David M. Rubenstein Rare
Book & Manuscript Collection, Duke University

Here, David Ricardo makes his invaluable contribution. In his *Principles of
Political Economy* (1817), Ricardo considers a country's **comparative advantage**
(CA) in producing a given good.

A country has a comparative advantage in the goods and/or services that it makes
more efficiently than another country. To understand *more efficiently*, we must
define the fundamental concept of **opportunity cost**.

Consider Countries A and B from our discussion above.

2.3.1 Opportunity Cost

Opportunity cost, from microeconomic theory, is simply the value of the forgone
option. The opportunity cost of reading this chapter, for example, is the value of all the
activities that were sacrificed for the time it took to read it. The opportunity cost is the
"real" cost in microeconomic terms, as opposed to a cost given in monetary units.

In the example of the two countries cited earlier, we see that for the same labor
required to produce 1 unit of tea (five laborers), Country A could instead produce
2½ units of coffee (two laborers per unit). We can say that the opportunity cost to
Country A of producing 1 unit of tea is 2½ units of coffee.

Similarly, for each unit of tea produced by Country B, which requires 4 units of
labor, it must sacrifice the production of $1\frac{1}{3}$ units of coffee, which requires 3 units of
labor. B's opportunity cost to produce 1 unit of tea is $1\frac{1}{3}$ units of coffee.

	Country A		Country B	
	Units of Labor	Opportunity Cost	Units of Labor	Opportunity Cost
Good X Coffee	2 aLx	**0.4** =aLx/aLy	3 bLx	0.75 =bLx/bLy
Good Y Tea	5 aLy	2.5 =aLy/aLx	4 bLy	**1.33** =bLy/bLx

Fig. 2.2 Opportunity cost. Country A has an absolute advantage producing both goods X and Y, but B is *more efficient* than A, in terms of opportunity cost, at producing good Y

The real "cost" of good X should be measured in terms of the *opportunity cost* of other goods—in this case, good Y—that are given up to produce or consume 1 unit of good X.

The opportunity cost of producing 1 unit of good X in terms of good Y may be computed as the amount of labor required to produce 1 unit of good X divided by the amount of labor required to produce 1 unit of good Y. That is, **how much Y (tea) do we have to give up in order to produce 1 more unit of good X (coffee)**?

So the opportunity cost to Country A of producing 1 unit of good X (coffee) in terms of good Y (tea) is given by

$$\mathbf{\frac{aLx}{aLy}}$$

$\mathbf{aLx}$ *(units of labor required to produce 1 unit of X in A)*

$\mathbf{aLy}$ *(units of labor required to produce 1 unit of Y in A)*

In Fig. 2.2, we see the opportunity costs to Countries A and B of producing each good, in terms of the alternative good. Each Country's CA good is highlighted.

The relative efficiencies of each country in producing its advantaged good are illustrated here.

However, we already know that Countries A and B possess absolute advantages in producing coffee and tea, respectively. What about Country C, which is advantaged in *neither* coffee nor tea?

Let's compare Country C, which we may take to represent a developing country with little infrastructure, to Country A, a relatively advanced country that is a more efficient producer of both goods (Fig. 2.3).

Country C is at an *absolute disadvantage* in producing both X and Y.

However, when we look at the *opportunity costs* to Countries A and C of producing each good, we find something interesting (Fig. 2.4).

For each unit of tea that Country A produces, it must sacrifice the production of 2.5 units of coffee. However, Country C can produce 1 unit of tea and sacrifice only 1.25 units of coffee. We can see that while Country C requires more labor than Country A to produce either good, Country C does enjoy an advantage over Country A in terms of its *relative* efficiency in producing good Y.

Fig. 2.3 Country A has absolute advantage in both goods X and Y

	Units of Labor	
	Country A	Country C
Good X Coffee	**2** aLx	8 cLx
Good Y Tea	**5** aLy	10 cLy

	Country A		Country C	
	Units of Labor	Opportunity Cost	Units of Labor	Opportunity Cost
Good "X" Coffee	2 aLx	**0.4** =aLx/aLy	8 cLx	0.8 =cLx/cLy
Good "Y" Tea	5 aLy	2.5 =aLy/aLx	10 cLy	**1.25** =cLy/cLx

Fig. 2.4 Opportunity cost determines comparative advantage. Country C, at an absolute disadvantage in both goods, is comparatively advantaged in the production of "Y" (tea)

This relationship is given by

$$\frac{cLy}{cLx} < \frac{aLy}{aLx}$$

$$1.25 < 2.5$$

That is, Country C's opportunity cost to produce 1 unit of Y (tea) in terms of X (coffee) is less than that of Country A. While it has no absolute advantage in either good, Country C enjoys a **comparative advantage** in producing good Y.

Similarly, Country A can be said to enjoy a CA in producing good X, as

$$\frac{aLx}{aLy} < \frac{cLx}{cLy}$$

$$0.4 < 0.8$$

It is a mathematical identity given two countries and two goods that each country will be comparatively advantaged in one of the goods.[4] In other words, if we have

---

[4] The exception being identical factor requirements to produce the two goods in each country (aLx = bLx and aLy = bLy). We explore this condition in Chap. 3.

two countries, A and C, and two goods, X and Y, and if Country C has a CA in Y (tea), then this automatically implies that Country A will have a CA in X. In this situation, *while a country may be able to have an absolute advantage in both goods, it cannot have a comparative advantage in both goods.*

We may define comparative advantage as follows:

Given two Countries A and B, producing two goods X and Y, **Country A is said to have a comparative advantage in good X if the opportunity cost of making 1 more unit of X in A (in terms of Y) is less than the opportunity cost of making 1 more unit of X in B (in terms of Y).**

2.4 Factors of Production: Labor and Capital

We have limited our discussion of comparative advantage thus far to the units of labor required to produce a given good. This conforms to Ricardo's original model.[5] However, few industries require only labor to produce goods or even services. Labor (**L**), in fact, is only one of two basic **factors of production** in our application of Ricardo's theorem, the other being capital (**K**). In trade theory, we use the term "capital" to refer to a country's nonhuman productive assets, including plant and equipment, buildings, and infrastructure.

A country's gross fixed capital investment accumulates as a result of profitable enterprises and continued reinvestment of some portion of profits. Some countries make much more efficient use of capital than do others. Typically, as a country advances in technological sophistication, its employment of capital becomes increasingly efficient.

We will use labor in most of our early examples because it is simpler to conceive, since people are discrete units and more adaptable to movement between industries than capital assets, which are often specialized to a particular purpose.

We fully incorporate capital into our discussions in Chap. 4.[6]

---

[5] Ricardo's model essentially held that the ratio of capital to labor was the same across industries in a given country. This has the effect of rendering capital as an irrelevant factor. Further, under the "labor theory of value" prevalent in Ricardo's day and to which he subscribed, the value of capital was determined by the amount of labor that went into creating it – therefore, we might say that capital was essentially a pass-through input representing additional, stored labor. The Ricardian model of trade was later expanded to explicitly include two distinct inputs, most thoroughly by Hecksher and Ohlin (see Chap. 5); we employ a two-input model as our basic framework.

[6] As noted our basic Ricardian model assumes only two factors of production, labor (L) and capital (K). We discuss the relaxing of this assumption in Chap. 5.

2.4.1 Factor Intensity

We have defined "**aLy**" as the quantity of labor required to produce 1 unit of good Y in Country A. Similarly, "**aKy**" would represent the quantity of *capital*[7] required to produce 1 unit of good Y in Country A:

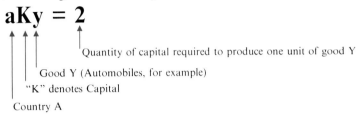

We use the term **factor intensity** to refer to the quantity of a given factor required to produce 1 unit of a good. Thus, "**aKy**" represents the capital *factor intensity* of good Y in Country A, "**bLx**" represents the labor factor intensity of good X in Country B, etc.

2.5 Ricardo's Simplifying Assumptions

This is a good place to note that David Ricardo, in order to simplify his explication of the basic premise of comparative advantage, made certain assumptions. Our Ricardian trade model initially incorporates these assumptions:

1. There are only two countries and two commodities.
2. There are only two factors of production, labor (L) and capital (K).[8]
3. There is perfect competition in all industries (including the factor market and the finished goods market).
4. Labor is all of the same level of skill and efficiency within each country.
5. Labor and capital are perfectly mobile within a country (and thus always able to fill any production need within that country) but cannot shift between countries.
6. There is free trade that involves no trade barriers or frictional transaction costs.
7. There are no transportation costs. Also, while not explicitly stated by Ricardo, it is implied that there are no environmental or infrastructure costs.
8. Production operates with constant returns to scale ("constant costs").

---

[7] Capital here is assumed to be quantifiable into discrete units. We can conceive of a "unit" of capital to represent a set of productive assets of a given value.

[8] Please refer to footnote 5.

9. Both countries have identical technology, and technology is fixed, i.e., there is no technological change.
10. Each country fully utilizes all resources (labor and capital are fully employed).

We will relax some of these simplifying assumptions as we proceed in our analysis and will strip away all those that still remain in Chap. 5. We will find Ricardo's theory just as robust with these assumptions removed.

Simulated News Articles

At the end of this and the following chapters, we present a series of simulated news articles which serve to reinforce the key takeaways from the chapter. Key passages are lettered (a), (b), etc., and underlined. Explain and discuss the implications of each key passage in light of what you have learned in the chapter.[9]

Article 2.1. Trade Minister Makes Controversial Speech

Bryan McCausland, *Boston Trade Dispatch*

The Trade Minister of Athabaltic, Dr. Giles Mellonovich, made what some considered a speech "giving away" jobs to neighboring Carpatia. "The man has gone mad—this is a gigantic give-away of national employment to Carpatia! What about us?" cried Nadia Koznan of the Athabaltic Metalworkers Union.

Others, such as Professor Boris Koleslawsky of the University of Lower Kresnow, were somewhat sanguine. "Ah, the spirit of David Ricardo lives on—David is smiling on us today from his place in International Trade heaven," he sighed dreamily, clutching his worn leather coat tighter around him as the biting wind raced through Stanislink Square.

Some crucial and controversial excerpts of the Mellonovich speech are presented here:

"My fellow Athabaltics, now that our neighbor Carpatia has emerged from her dark period of economic difficulties and (a) has embraced democracy, the free market, and the world community, I see a whole new and great chapter in the development of our beloved country."

"I proclaim that we look carefully at our two biggest sectors of employment—electronics design and manufacturing. In electronics we are giants—our exceptional universities have created some of the brightest engineers and scientists, and

---

[9] The assignment is to "click on" the underlined passage—your answer should provide, in a few sentences, whatever context and explanations are necessary in order to clarify its meaning to one not as versed as you in international trade theory!

our best and brightest graduates head directly for electronics internships as their first preference nowadays. Manufacturing, while once the mainstay of Athabaltic, is something that we have to reexamine very carefully—we have to reevaluate our support for this sector in light of the teachings of the great David Ricardo and Adam Smith."

(b) "I remember the Green declaration of last year, when this country wanted less pollution, and cleaner air and water. I also see that our children shun the lower paying manufacturing jobs. And I now see that the workers in neighboring (c) Carpatia are willing and able to do excellent manufacturing. In fact, if you remember, Carpatia was a manufacturing giant before it had its 'troubles' about 30 years ago. They have the skills, they have the hungry workers who are happy to do manufacturing work, and we have well-trained scientists and engineers who will be only too happy to sell them higher-end electronics products and buy their less complex manufactured goods from them. (d) We have a huge amount of resources, in both people and equipment, invested in the manufacturing sector, which could produce more output for our great country if it were better deployed to those areas where we are strongest."

(e) "Consequently. I propose a national policy that will allow some of our big manufacturing companies to transfer manufacturing jobs to Carpatia and set up operations there."

Fred Simplemodelz, President of the Steel Tubing and Sheet Metal Workers Association of Lower Metrovia, roared, "This is one great Betrayal! He is selling off the jobs of the ones who work the hardest! What sense does this make? (f) We can make both electronics and manufacturing with fewer workers than those people in Carpatia! Why bother with them at all!?"

We went back to Prof. Koleslawsky's office, where he sat sipping a cup of tea while conferring with the eminent economist Dr. Pytor Murphysboro. "You see, the Trade Minister has his hands full. (g) Trade is not intuitive. It never has been. But trade is inevitable. It's like water flowing downhill: It will find a way to flow. Nobody—nobody can stop it!"

"Yes, yes, bravo!" exclaimed Dr. Murphysboro, hungrily gulping down his lunch. "Someday I will tell you why I started a label factory in China!"

On this enigmatic and philosophical note, we headed to our favorite corner in the square to stand in line for the giant homemade mustard-infused hot dogs created by the great hot dog vendor known as Ivan the Great. Now his is one job that no Carpatian can do!

Hints and Solutions

Article 2.1

(a) We will see in the next few chapters that one fundamental aspect of free trade is that it is endogenous—entirely market driven. Centralized planning, favored by nondemocracies, and overly regulated markets are not conducive to either free trade or the benefits thereof.

(b) Through trade, countries typically move "up" over time from agriculture and mining raw materials to basic manufactures, to increasingly complex manufacturing, to engineering and design, and finally to services and "knowledge" work. Progress along this path is typically accompanied by improved quality of life and better environmental stewardship. We will explore this phenomenon in later chapters.

(c) Carpatia, by virtue of a historic tradition of excellence in manufacturing, may easily have a comparative advantage in it.

(d) This illustrates the concept of opportunity cost. The factors employed in manufacturing would be better deployed to electronics, where Athabaltic has a comparative advantage.

(e) Athabaltic is making a conscious decision to "go global" and engage in trade with Carpatia, much like Premier Deng Xiaoping's monumental decision to crack open the door and allow China to trade with the world in 1979. While controversial in party circles at the time, the results 30 years later speak for themselves.

(f) Fred is clearly referring to the fact that Athabaltic may have an absolute advantage over Carpatia in both electronics as well as manufacturing.

(g) It is not indeed. The notion of opportunity costs driving comparative advantage is not for the faint of heart.

Chapter 3
The Ricardian Trade Model

Summary This chapter develops the basic Ricardian trade model and its foundations. The discussion begins by developing the production possibilities frontier out of our earlier discussion of opportunity costs, and powers through the constant-cost model of free trade, before arriving at the conventional model of increasing costs and imperfectly substitutable inputs. Along the way we are introduced to the role of consumer tastes and preferences as manifested in "indifference curves", which are fully explained. As we stated in our introduction, this book is written for business practitioners and policymakers, not Ph.D. students, and so we keep our discussion at a high level and do not include deep microeconomic detail or delve into the mathematical calculations underlying the theory.

However, we strongly believe that a full-fledged and multifaceted defense of free trade is only possible if the reader truly understands the fundamental bedrock theory that drives Ricardo's famous result. The reason that so many misperceptions about trade persist is that the results are often counterintuitive. For example, can permitting low-level manufacturing jobs to move overseas benefit the majority of consumers in the home country? Emphatically, yes! However, this is difficult to conceive, much less explain, without a solid grounding in the underlying theory. To develop one's inner personal conviction, there is no substitute to "seeing" indifference curves of both countries drifting upward with free trade.

At the end of the chapter, we transition to a series of very practical and non-theoretical trade-related issues to "wake up" the theoretical models and bring them into a real-world context. These practical insights are provided by several simulated media articles that raise questions such as "Why should we trade with Country B? Their standard of living is below ours. They will simply drag us down!" Or, "It just makes sense to make what we need in our Country A. This way we keep our jobs and our money right here at home. It's a no-brainer!" Once again the reader will be required to critically evaluate all the underlined passages in the articles by applying

F. Langdana and P.T. Murphy, *International Trade and Global Macropolicy*,
Springer Texts in Business and Economics, DOI 10.1007/978-1-4614-1635-7_3,
© Springer Science+Business Media New York 2014

material from the current as well as the preceding chapter. The trade skeptic, who presses the most common anti-trade arguments, will be a recurring presence throughout this and later chapters, and the reader should be able to recognize and quickly refute the skeptic's popular misconceptions.

3.1 The Production Possibilities Frontier

The journey into the main "engine room" of free trade, the Ricardian trade model, begins with a very necessary overview of some essential microeconomic building blocks, starting with the **production possibilities frontier (PPF)**.

We begin with a two-country, two-good world, where labor is the only factor of production. Given factor intensity (aLx, aLy), we can plot a production frontier, which shows all maximum possible combinations of goods that can be produced given the total endowment of factor resources available in the country.

In Fig. 3.1, we plot the **PPF** for each country. We assume a total endowment of 10 units of labor in Country A and 12 units of labor in Country B (Fig. 3.2).

We chose a total endowment of labor in each country equal to **aLx * aLy** and **bLx * bLy** simply for convenience, as this yields nice integers for our illustrative purposes.

Regardless of the total endowment of labor chosen for Country A, the slope of the production possibilities frontier will remain the same and be computed as $-$ **(aLx/ aLy)**.[1] This ratio has tremendous significance as it represents the opportunity cost (as defined earlier) of making one more unit of good X in Country A (in terms of Y).

The fundamental takeaway at this point is that the *slope* of the PPF always—always—represents this opportunity cost. If Country A has a "flatter slope" relative to Country B, the implication then is that the opportunity cost of producing good X in Country A is lower than the opportunity cost of producing good X in Country B. Therefore, A has a comparative advantage in X (which also implies that B has a comparative advantage in Y).

Fig. 3.1 Labor factor intensity in A and B for goods X and Y

	Units of Labor	
	Country A	*Country B*
Good X	2	3
Electronics	aLx	bLx
Good Y	5	4
Toys	aLy	bLy

---

[1] The intuition for the negative slope here comes from the fact that this ratio measures a trade-off of one good for the other. We will generally speak of "aLx/aLy" without the sign, for convenience, unless we are drawing graphs.

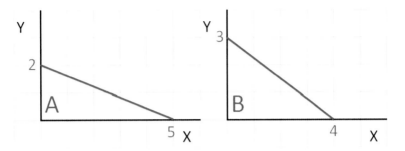

Fig. 3.2 PPFs for Countries A and B producing goods X and Y

A country's PPF will generally expand outward (from the origin) over time as it grows in productivity, develops resources, and thus is able to produce more goods and services.

It is important to note that for the moment, we have assumed **constant costs**; that is, each additional unit of X and Y cost the same to produce as the last regardless of the total output. This is what makes the production possibilities frontiers appear as simple, straight lines. However, this condition is rarely satisfied in the real world, where constraints on production efficiency and resources result in varying costs-per-unit depending on output.

3.2   The Production Possibilities Frontier with Increasing Costs

The linear models above assume constant costs of production regardless of the quantity of units produced.

From microeconomic theory, we know that most goods are associated with a nonlinear production function, where output beyond a certain, efficient level becomes increasingly costly as resources are strained beyond their limit to produce the marginal unit.[2]

The difference between constant costs and **increasing costs** manifests itself in the PPF, which becomes nonlinear.

Most trade diagrams use the increasing costs model for the PPF, as this is more reflective of real-world experience. In macroeconomic trade theory, we are generally examining entire industries, rather than individual firms, and in the aggregate, industries generally operate near the trough of the curve depicted in Fig. 3.3.

The production possibilities frontier identifies the limits of *production* in a given country. Our next microeconomic building block relates to *consumption* choices.

---

[2] Since we are considering an entire industry within each country, we ignore the decreasing costs area of the average cost curve and assume that we start in the efficient range, which implies an increasing-costs model. The increasing-costs area is represented by all points on the curve to the right of "peak efficiency". (Fig. 3.3)

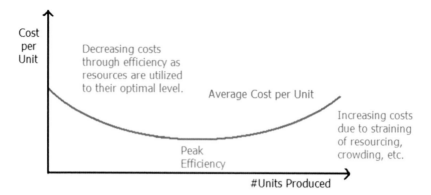

Fig. 3.3   Average cost curve

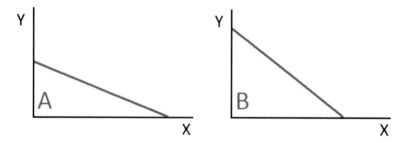

Fig. 3.4   Production possibilities frontier—**constant costs** (linear production frontier)

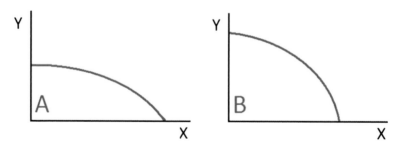

Fig. 3.5   Production possibilities frontier—**increasing costs** (nonlinear production frontier). With an increasing costs, the PPF assumes the concave shape seen here

3.3   Indifference Curves

As stated, the production possibilities frontier tells us how much of each good we can produce, given our resources. But where along that frontier should we produce? Should we make only coffee and no tea? A 50–50 mix? How do we decide?

3.3.1 Consumer Preferences

Unless production in our country is determined by central planners,[3] domestic producers will orient themselves to produce as much of each good as consumers are willing and able to purchase.

So, how do we know what consumers want to buy?

Let's keep within a two-good world model, where there is only food and clothing.[4] And let's say that these goods are somehow quantifiable into "units"; perhaps a unit of food is a typical day's supply of food, and a unit of clothing is an "average" sort of outfit that one might wear on a given day. We are of course assuming away a lot here, but this simple example applies more generally once these assumptions are eased.

When we consider consumer preferences, there are two core rules that drive microeconomic theory:

1. **More is better**[5]

   From a consumer's standpoint, for any good that is useful or desired, **more is better**. Ten units of food are better than 1, and 20 are better than 10.

2. **More is better at a declining rate**

   If we have no food, we would give up quite a significant amount of clothing to obtain a single unit of food. Once we have a reasonable supply of food, we would trade less clothing to obtain each additional unit—our need is not as desperate as before. And if we are stocked to the ceilings with an endless supply of food, then we really wouldn't give up much clothing at all to obtain another food unit.

   Likewise, if we have no clothing, we'd give up a large number of units of food to obtain that first article of clothing. And, as our one outfit would get pretty dirty if we didn't have a second one to wear while we wash it, we'd give up a pretty substantial amount of food to obtain the second unit of clothing—less than we would give up to obtain the first, but still quite a lot. However, once our wardrobe is sufficient, we might not sacrifice that much food to obtain another unit of clothing. And if we have filled every closet in our house with one outfit after another of every possible style and color, we would not really sacrifice much food at all to obtain another ensemble.

---

[3] That central planning is rare enough today to be relegated to a footnote is significant. Only 30 years prior to the publication of this volume, a significant portion of the world operated under strict central-planning regimes. While central planners have made something of a comeback in certain sectors of the advanced democracies in the wake of the recent global economic crisis, full-scale top-down planning is today limited to North Korea and a handful of others.

[4] We relax all these seemingly simplistic assumptions, like that of a two-good, two-factor world in Chap. 5. We also introduce real-world complications such as transportation costs, labor skills, trade distortions, etc., in later chapters. Nevertheless, the fundamental results obtained by implementing the simplified model at this time will not be compromised by these later refinements.

[5] Students of microeconomics will recognize this as the "non-satiation" assumption. For the formulation "(1) More is better, and (2) More is better at a declining rate" the authors are grateful to their dear friend Dr. Peter Parks (1960–2012).

Units of clothing that we already own	Quantity of food that we would give up to obtain one more unit of clothing	Comments
0	4	"It's raining, I'm cold, and I need something to wear!"
1	2	"It'd sure be nice to have a second outfit"
2	1.5	
3	1.1	
4	0.9	
5	0.6	"I've got a week's worth of clothing; I don't need much more"
6	0.5	
7	0.4	
8	0.3	
9	0.3	
10	0.25	"I don't know what I'm going to do with all these outfits"
11	0.15	
12	0	"Another article of clothing is the last thing that I need"

Fig. 3.6 Diminishing marginal utility, food versus clothing

These two rules are the essence behind the theory of **diminishing marginal utility**. More of any good or service is better, but each additional unit adds less utility (which we might consider satisfaction or happiness) than the one before.

Keeping those two rules in mind, we can draw up a hypothetical set of trade-offs between food and clothing. Our table (Fig. 3.6) shows how many units of food we'd give up to obtain one additional unit of clothing, depending on how much clothing we already own.

The relationship works in reverse as well. If we have no food, we would give up quite a lot of clothing to obtain a meal! To keep our example simple, we'll assume a symmetrical relationship—we would give up 4 units of clothing to obtain the first unit of food, and so on—the reverse of the table in Fig. 3.6.[6]

3.3.2 Indifference Curves

With these facts in mind, we draw a graph (Fig. 3.7) illustrating the trade-offs that we are willing to make between food and clothing, based on our needs and preferences.

Here we see the relationship in graphical form. From point **A** to point **B**, starting with only 1 unit of clothing, we'd be willing to sacrifice 2 units of food to obtain an

---

[6] The relationship need not be symmetrical (and rarely if ever is, in practice). Typically, units of one good are more or less valued relative to the other across the range of quantities. We use a symmetrical relationship here for simplicity.

Fig. 3.7 Indifference curve

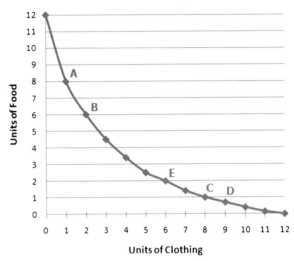

additional outfit. But to get from point **C** to point **D**, where we already have 8 units of clothing, we would only sacrifice about 1/3 of a unit of food to get our hands on yet another ensemble to throw into our crowded closet.

The relationship works in reverse as well. We see that if we have only 1 unit of food, at point **C**, and want to obtain a second, we would give up 2 units of clothing to obtain it, moving from point **C** to point **E**.

What we have actually drawn here is an **indifference curve**. The curve is a function of our preferences as expressed by how much of each good we would sacrifice to obtain an additional unit of the other. This curve shows all points where we have maximized our satisfaction between food and clothing. It is called an indifference curve because at any point along the line, we have obtained the same maximum overall level of satisfaction. So, we are *indifferent* between the points (A, B, C, D, or E, or any point in between) at which we consume.

The slope and convexity of this curve illustrate our relative preferences for one good over another across the spectrum of quantities that we examined. Our preferences may be "averaged" with those of all other consumers in the economy to derive an aggregate indifference curve reflective of the country as a whole.

Theoretically, there are an infinite number of indifference curves, all shaped similarly, which represent the combination of goods that we would consume if our incomes permitted.

We may represent the consumer preference relationship by an infinite series of indifference curves extending to higher and higher levels of overall utility.

In Fig. 3.8 we see that consumption anywhere on indifference curve IC2 yields higher overall satisfaction (utility) compared to consumption on indifference curve IC1, and consumers achieve even higher utility at any point on indifference curve IC3.

Fig. 3.8 Consumer
preferences as represented
by indifference curves

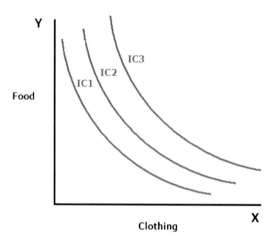

Fig. 3.9 Consumer
preferences as represented
by indifference curves,
with budget constraint

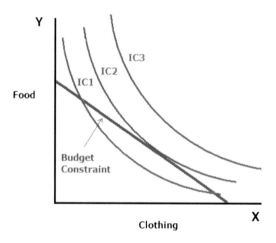

Consumers will always choose the highest possible indifference curve; the
limitation will be their budget.

Unlike utility, which changes depending on the quantity of a particular good that
we acquire, we assume that the *price* of an item does not change no matter how
much of it we buy. Therefore, our budget constraint will have a constant slope and
may be represented on this graph showing all possible combinations of food and
clothing given our available income (Fig. 3.9).

In microeconomics, we would draw the "budget constraint" line to find the point
where our preferences meet our available income. That point will be the point at
which we consume goods X and Y.

We can see that our budget constraint is shaped very much like our production
possibilities frontier. The reason for this is that the prices of goods X and Y are

Fig. 3.10 Consumer preferences as represented by indifference curves, constant-costs PPF

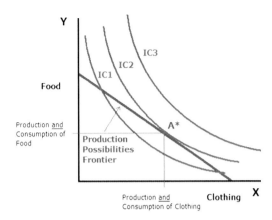

determined by their costs of production; therefore, the trade-offs we discussed with respect to the PPF are reflected in the budget constraint, which simply shows the price relationship between the two goods.

On a national level, the PPF and the budget constraint are therefore identical (one may also think of this in terms of national income accounting, where gross national income equals gross national product—every expenditure for one party is income to another, by mathematical identity).[7]

We have finally arrived at the method by which we know where to find the point of consumption on the PPF. **Production *and* consumption** will occur at the point where the highest possible indifference curve is tangent to (meets) the production possibilities frontier. We see an example of this, under constant costs, in Fig. 3.10 above.

In Fig. 3.11, we see an example under increasing costs.

The points of consumption and production, denoted $\mathbf{A}^*$ and $\mathbf{B}^*$ in Figs. 3.10 and 3.11, are known as points of **autarky**. Under autarky, a country does not indulge in any global trade or meaningful global economic interaction.[8] Such a country may consume only what it is capable of producing itself; it is said to produce and consume at its autarky point.

The model serves equally well with a PPF representative of increasing costs. In this case, the PPF will be concave to the origin as described previously. Production and consumption will occur at the point where the highest possible indifference curve is tangent to the PPF.[9]

---

[7] We will explore national income accounting in detail in Chap. 7.

[8] Presently, North Korea would perhaps be the singular poster-child for a country operating under autarky.

[9] Students of microeconomics will recognize that at the tangency point, the rate at which consumers are "willing" to substitute X for Y (the slope of the indifference curve, also known as the rate of marginal substitution) is equal to the rate at which producers are "able and willing" to transform X to Y (also known as the marginal rate of transformation), given by the slope of the PPF at the tangency point.

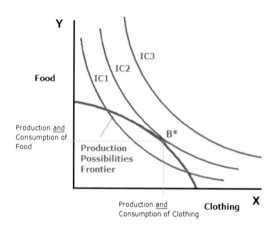

Fig. 3.11 Consumer preferences as represented by indifference curves, increasing costs PPF

As tastes and preferences change, the shape and slope of the indifference curve will shift, based on shifting consumer attitudes about how much of each good they would trade off for an extra unit of the other good. The slope (overall angle, not the convexity) of the indifference curve may be relatively steep, which indicates in our example that we would generally give up a lot more food to obtain an additional unit of clothing than we would give up clothing to obtain food. Or, the indifference curve may be more horizontal, meaning that we'd surrender a lot of clothing to obtain an additional unit of food. The convexity (inward curvature) of the indifference curve might shift as well, depending on shifting attitudes about how much less each additional unit of a good is valued than the last.

In this volume, given our applications-driven objective, we abstract from formal mathematical derivations of these curves. The important points to know are that:

1. Consumer preferences are represented by indifference curves.
2. Indifference curves vary in shape and slope (but are always downward sloping and generally convex to the origin[10]).
3. Production and consumption will occur where the highest possible indifference curve meets the production possibilities frontier.

Our simplistic model so far has assumed a closed economy where all production and consumption occurs domestically. We will now expand our model to incorporate trade.

---

[10] To clarify any confusion on "convex" versus "concave" in our terminology: PPFs are concave to the origin, i.e., bulging upward from the origin; indifference curves are convex to the origin, i.e., bulging inward toward the origin, or, if you prefer, shaped like a slide running down and then increasingly to the right.

3.4   Ricardo's Theory in Practice: The Ricardian Two-Step Trade Model

Given a world with two countries, A and B, making two goods, X and Y, both endowed with L units of labor that are identical, with constant costs,[11] where:

- A has a comparative advantage in X, but does not trade. It produces and consumes X and Y at A^*_X and A^*_Y, respectively (in Fig. 3.12).
- B has a comparative advantage in Y, but does not trade. It produces and consumes X and Y at B^*_X and B^*_Y, respectively.

Neither country trades; both are operating under autarky.

Note that we can visually infer that A does indeed have a CA in X (and therefore B in Y) by simply observing the slopes of the PPF lines in Fig. 3.12. The "flatter" line in A means that aLx/aLy for A is less than bLx/bLy in B, thus implying that the opportunity cost of producing X in A is less than the opportunity cost of producing X in B. Ergo, A has a comparative advantage in X.

We will now see how implementing Ricardo's theorem, in two steps, helps both countries.

Ricardo's Two-Step Theorem

1. **Countries must specialize in the goods/services in which they have a comparative advantage.**
    As discussed, specialization increases global output of both X and Y.
    Country A specializes 100 % in good X. Production of good Y ceases, and Country A's production of X moves all the way to the Y-intercept at the right in Fig. 3.12 above, from A^*_X to A^P_X.

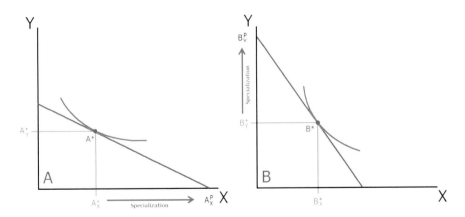

Fig. 3.12   Countries A and B producing and consuming under autarky

---

[11] In the next section, we will relax the "constant-costs" assumption and move to an increasing costs model.

Country B specializes 100 % in good Y. Production of good X ceases, and Country B's production of good Y moves from $\mathbf{B^*_Y}$ to $\mathbf{B^P_Y}$.

2. **Countries must then trade freely.**

Through trade, each country now has access to not only its own production, but the other country's production as well. Thus, the production frontier for each country is now global in scope.

However, this second part of Ricardo's 2-step theorem raises a host of questions. If both countries were to indeed trade freely, at what ratio of exchange between goods would this trade take place? What would the volume of exports and imports be for each country?

3.4.1   The Global Terms of Trade

We will use relative prices as a proxy for the opportunity costs in our production function. Prices incorporate all the costs of production and are translatable between countries. Relative prices give us a quantifiable measure of the trade-off at every point on each country's PPF.

We assume frictionless transactions and are unconcerned with currency, as we are analyzing ratios of exchange, rather than specific figures. The discussion at this point is in "real" terms, with relative prices expressed in terms of ratios only.[12]

The price ratio of 1 unit of X to 1 unit of Y is given by $\mathbf{Px/Py}$. We call this ratio of exchange between two goods the *trading price ratio*, expressed as $(\mathbf{Px/Py})$. Within Country A, we denote this ratio as $(\mathbf{Px/Py})_A$. We refer to the *global* trading price ratio as $(\mathbf{Px/Py})^{TT}$, where "TT" represents "terms of trade." This global trading price ratio is referred to as the **Global Terms of Trade**.[13]

According to Ricardo, global trade takes place endogenously at $(\mathbf{Px/Py})^{TT}$ such that

$$\left(\frac{\mathbf{Px}}{\mathbf{Py}}\right)_A < \left(\frac{\mathbf{Px}}{\mathbf{Py}}\right)^{TT} < \left(\frac{\mathbf{Px}}{\mathbf{Py}}\right)_B$$

Where

Px = price of X
Py = price of Y
$(Px/Py)_A$ = price of X divided by price of Y in Country A (trading price ratio in A)
$(Px/Py)_B$ = price of X divided by price of Y in Country B (trading price ratio in B)
$(Px/Py)^{TT}$ = Global Terms of Trade

---

[12] Currencies will enter into the analysis in the latter part of the book in the Global Macroeconomics section.

[13] The "Global Terms of Trade" is also called the International Terms of Trade. We use "Global" throughout for consistency.

Fig. 3.13 Factor intensity of goods X and Y in countries A and B

	Units of Labor	
	Country A	Country B
Good X	2	4
Food	aLx	bLx
Good Y	5	3
Clothing	aLy	bLy

Before we delve into the intuition driving the compound inequality above, a quick review of the budget line and the slope of the production possibilities frontier is in order.

If national income for a country is given as "**Inc**", and Px and Py are the prices of X and Y in that country (the only goods produced), then we have

$$\textbf{Inc} = \textbf{PxX} + \textbf{PyY}$$

Where

X = total quantity produced of good X
Y = total quantity produced of good Y
Px, Py = prices of goods X and Y (in local currency)[14]

If we say that in our hypothetical world, factor intensity in A and B is as given in Fig. 3.13, that (to keep our example simple) labor is the only input, and that A and B are endowed with 10 and 12 units of labor respectively, we can draw the PPF for Country A as shown in Fig. 3.14.[15]

We see in the figure that Country A can produce 5 units of X, or 2 units of Y, or various combinations in between. Whatever Country A's national income may be, it will be distributed accordingly. For example, if Country A's national income is 100, then Px = 20 and Py = 50.

From our equation above, we can see that if Country A produces only good X, then

$$\textbf{Inc} = \textbf{PxX} + \textbf{PyY}$$
$$= (20)(5) + (50)(0) = 100$$

---

[14] For any currency or common unit of exchange, as we are interested in the ratio of the two prices, not their absolute level. It may be convenient, however, to think of prices as being in local currency.

[15] The assumption of one input (here, labor) is made to maintain simplicity at this stage of our discussion. Relaxing this assumption (which may alternatively be given as a fixed ratio of labor to capital across industries) brings us to the PPF with increasing costs, which we examine later in this chapter.

Fig. 3.14 Production
Possibilities Frontier (PPF)
for Country A

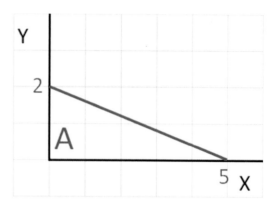

Alternatively, if Country A produces only good Y, then

$$\textbf{Inc} = \textbf{PxX} + \textbf{PyY}$$
$$= (20)(0) + (50)(2) = 100$$

We see that the intercepts on the X and Y axes of the graph are Inc/Px
($100/20 = 5$) and Inc/Py ($100/50 = 2$). The slope of the PPF then works out to be

$$\text{Slope of PPF} = -\frac{\left(\frac{\text{Inc}}{\text{Py}}\right)}{\left(\frac{\text{Inc}}{\text{Px}}\right)} = -\left(\frac{\textbf{Px}}{\textbf{Py}}\right)$$

Thus, for Country A, the slope of its PPF is $-(\textbf{Px/Py})_A$. It will also be equal to
$-(aLx/aLy)$:

$$-\left(\frac{\text{Px}}{\text{Py}}\right)_A = -\left(\frac{20}{50}\right) = -0.4$$
$$-\left(\frac{aLx}{aLy}\right) = -\left(\frac{2}{5}\right) = -0.4$$

Similarly, for Country B, the slope of its PPF is $-(Px/Py)_B$, equal to
$-(bLx/bLy)$, as we see in Fig. 3.15.

Again, we can assign any national income to Country B; for simplicity's sake,
we'll say that national income is 1,200 units.[16] Country B can produce 3 units of X,
or 4 units of Y. Thus, the price for good X in Country B would be 400 ($= 1,200/3$),
and the price for good Y in Country B would be 300 ($1,200/4$). So we can calculate
the slope of B's PPF as follows

---

[16] Again, any figure here for national income will serve the same purpose; we are interested in
price ratios, not nominal prices.

Fig. 3.15 PPF for Country B

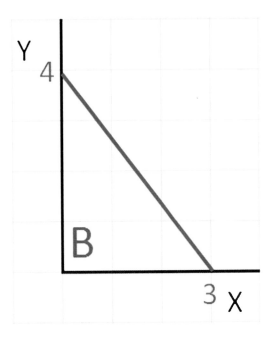

$$-\left(\frac{Px}{Py}\right)_B = -\left(\frac{400}{300}\right) = -1.33$$

$$-\left(\frac{bLx}{bLy}\right) = -\left(\frac{4}{3}\right) = -1.33$$

The intuition behind the negative slope of the trading price ratio is that it represents an *opportunity cost* ratio, i.e. how much good Y must be *given up* (in other words, *subtracted*) to produce 1 additional unit of good X; thus, the negative sign.

Going back to Ricardo's inequality,

$$\left(\frac{Px}{Py}\right)_A < \left(\frac{Px}{Py}\right)^{TT} < \left(\frac{Px}{Py}\right)_B$$

We examine the PPF of Country A, which today specializes in only good X, as shown in Fig. 3.16.

Production takes place at the lower-right corner with Country A specializing in only good X (food), producing a quantity of $A^P{}_X$. However, as "Man does not live on bread alone,"[17] consumers in Country A will require access to some quantity of good Y (clothing). Let's now perform a simple experiment: If A were to attempt to make some amount of Y at home, what would the cost of this be, in terms of output sacrificed of X?

---

[17] Matthew 4:4. Source: The Holy Bible, New International Version 1984, Biblica, Inc

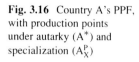

Fig. 3.16 Country A's PPF, with production points under autarky (A^*) and specialization (A_X^P)

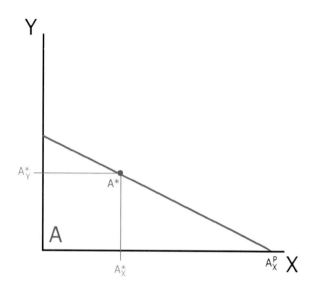

Very simply, given the fact that the slope of Country A's PPF is −0.4, this implies that A can make 0.4 units of Y domestically by giving up 1 unit of X. That, after all, is A's opportunity cost of making X in terms of Y: To make 1 more unit of X, A would have to give up 0.4 units of Y. So by sacrificing 1 unit of X, A now can produce 0.4 units of Y.

However, what if Country A were to obtain a better deal from Country B? If B offered A more than 0.4 units of Y in return for 1 unit of X, then A would certainly grab such an offer. But what amount of Y would B be willing to trade in return for 1 unit of X?

Today Country B is specializing in producing only good Y (clothing). Production takes place at the upper-left corner at B^P_Y in Fig. 3.18. We know that since the slope of B's PPF is −1.33, this means that for B to produce any X at home, it must sacrifice 1.33 units of Y. So if by trading with Country A, Country B can obtain 1 unit of X for anything less than 1.33 units of Y, it's a good deal for B!

We can see the outlines of a deal shaping up here: Country A will be happy to give up 1 unit of X to obtain anything more than 0.4 units of Y, and Country B will be happy to give up anything less than 1.33 units of Y to obtain 1 unit of X. Thus, any exchange ratio where Country B gives Country A between 0.4 and 1.33 units of Y in return for 1 unit of X will be satisfactory to both parties.

In Fig. 3.17, the red arrows represent trading price ratios offering Country A more units of Y in return for 1 of X than the 0.4 units that it currently obtains under autarky. In essence, any of the red arrows in the diagram are "better deals" for Country A, as each of the arrows offers A more Y in exchange for 1 unit of X, compared to A's cost of converting X to Y at home.

Country A will logically and endogenously trade with some other country or countries (Country B in this case) given any of the red arrows in Fig. 3.17 as it

Fig. 3.17 Preferential terms
of trade for Country A. A will
trade 1 unit of X for any
amount of Y greater than 0.4

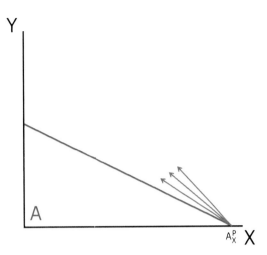

Fig. 3.18 Preferential terms
of trade for Country B. B will
be happy to give up anything
less than 1.33 units of Y to
obtain 1 unit of X

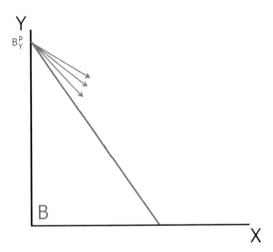

would be more advantageous to trade at these prices than to make Y at home. Each
of the red arrows is "steeper" than $(Px/Py)_A$, which is the slope of the PPF. This
explains why trade will indeed take place when a "steeper" global trading line
becomes available, or $(Px/Py)_A < (Px/Py)^{TT}$.

Similarly, let's examine Country B's PPF. Country B specializes only in producing Y and is now producing $B_P{}^Y$ units of Y and zero units of X. The slope of its
PPF is -1.33. This implies that if Country B wants to make X at home, it must give
up 1.33 units of Y to obtain 1 unit of X.

For Country B to receive a "better deal" from Country A, Country B would need
to obtain anything better than 1 unit of X for 1.33 units of Y (indicated by the red
arrows in Fig. 3.18). Naturally, if such a deal were available, it would make sense

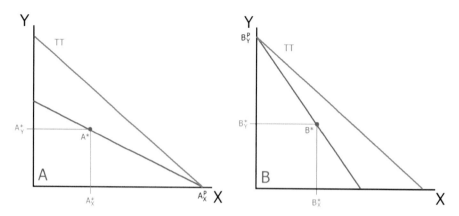

Fig. 3.19 Global terms of trade (green line) from the perspective of countries A and B

for Country B to trade with Country A rather than for B to attempt to make X at home. In other words, Country B will trade if a "flatter," or less steep, global trading line becomes available, or $(PX/PY)^{TT} < (Px/Py)_B$.

Graphically, we can represent this relationship with a global production frontier that runs from $\mathbf{B^P_Y}$ to $\mathbf{A^P_X}$. This global production frontier is called the **Global Terms of Trade (TT)** line (Fig. 3.19).

Result: World production is greater with trade than it is under autarky. In Fig. 3.20, A^* and B^* are the autarky points, described earlier in this chapter, and we can see that both countries' production functions (which are now identical) have expanded beyond what was possible without trading.

Given that both countries now have "better deals" available to each of them, thanks to the other country's ability to make either X or Y more efficiently (i.e., with lower opportunity cost in terms of the other good), at which point will consumption now take place?

Keeping in mind that consumers strive to attain the highest possible indifference curve, we see that consumption in each country occurs where the consumption indifference curve is tangent to the Global TT line, at $\mathbf{A^C}$ and $\mathbf{B^C}$. We see that **each country can now consume on a higher indifference curve,** and both countries can consume outside of their domestic production possibilities frontiers. **Both countries are better off with free trade.**

And we can also observe that both countries now consume more of both goods X and Y than they could have under autarky[18]:

---

[18] This is not always the final result, as sometimes consumers, given the opportunity, may reduce their consumption of one item to obtain more of another. The final point of consumption will depend on the shape of the indifference curve (consumer preferences) and the availability of the consumption bundle outside the domestic PPF, thanks to specialization and free trade.

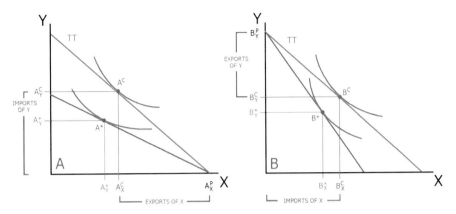

Fig. 3.20 Production and consumption in A and B with trade and full specialization. A and B now export some of the good in which they have CA, and import their disadvantaged good

Country A consumes at $\mathbf{A}^C{}_X$ and $\mathbf{A}^C{}_Y$, higher for both goods than its consumption at $\mathbf{A}^*{}_X$ and $\mathbf{A}^*{}_Y$ under autarky.

Country B consumes at $\mathbf{B}^C{}_X$ and $\mathbf{B}^C{}_Y$, significantly higher consumption than at $\mathbf{B}^*{}_X$ and $\mathbf{B}^*{}_Y$ under autarky.

Finally, we see that both countries now **export** part of their production of their comparatively advantaged good and **import** all of their consumption of their comparatively disadvantaged good. Country A consequently exports $\left(\mathbf{A}^P{}_X - \mathbf{A}^C{}_X\right)$ of good X and imports all of its consumption $\mathbf{A}^C{}_Y$ of good Y from B, while Country B exports $\left(\mathbf{B}^P{}_Y - \mathbf{B}^C{}_Y\right)$ of Y and imports all of its X from A. *(Note that the graphs are not to scale; in a two-country world, A's imports must equal B's exports, and vice versa.)*

3.5 Ricardo with Increasing Costs

The constant-costs model implies *full specialization* in the comparatively advantaged good. Under increasing costs, due to diminishing marginal returns beyond a certain point of production, a good becomes so expensive to produce that full specialization makes no economic sense. In this case, specialization will occur but will generally not be complete; some of the disadvantaged good will still be produced in each country.

Given two Countries A (with CA in good X) and B (with CA in good Y), under autarky, we begin with A and B originally producing and consuming goods X and Y at $\mathbf{A}^*$ and $\mathbf{B}^*$, respectively, in Fig. 3.21.

When we open the two countries to trade, Country A will begin to specialize in good X, and Country B will begin to specialize in good Y. A's production will move from its starting point at $\mathbf{A}^*$ toward full production of X (to the right) along its PPF, and B's production will move (to the left) from $\mathbf{B}^*$ toward full production of Y.

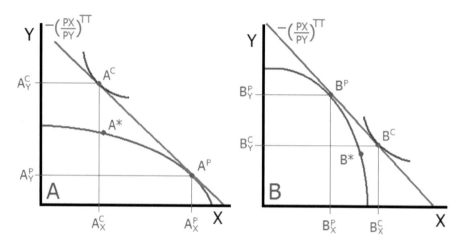

Fig. 3.21 Production and consumption in A and B under increasing costs. Specialization is now incomplete with each country still producing some of its comparatively disadvantaged good

Under increasing costs, the trade-off of X for Y shifts along the PPF curve, and now without full specialization, we must concern ourselves with that trade-off.

When both countries have reached a point on their respective PPF *where the slopes of their PPFs are equal*, the maximum possible world production has been reached. Trade will stabilize at those points. This occurs at $\mathbf{A^P}$ and $\mathbf{B^P}$. Keep in mind that global trade is driven by differences in opportunity costs—the slopes of the PPF lines—and once the slopes are equalized, there is a freeze in further specialization.

The Global Terms of Trade line will reflect this maximum possible world production relationship.[19] Graphically, the Global Terms of Trade line will be the tangent line to the points where the slopes of A and B's PPFs are equal. (These are points $\mathbf{A^P}$ and $\mathbf{B^P}$ in our example.)

The Global Terms of Trade (TT) line is denoted as $-(\mathbf{PX/PY})^{\mathbf{TT}}$ in Fig. 3.21. (Note that while it is included in this figure, the "–" sign is sometimes omitted for notational convenience.)

3.5.1   Results

- Both countries, as a whole, are better off with specialization and free trade.
- Consumers in both countries can now consume more of *both goods*.

---

[19] The Global Terms of Trade line can also be thought of (and is, by mathematical identity) the global production possibilities frontier (global PPF).

- Under increasing costs, the production shift toward the comparatively advantaged good *stops short of full specialization* due to the diminishing marginal returns of specialization beyond a certain point. Both countries will still produce *some* of the disadvantaged good.
- *Both* countries are no longer forced to consume only what they can produce at home. Both final consumption points are now located outside the autarkic domestic production possibilities frontier.

3.6   Benefits of Trade for Countries with the Same PPFs

Accepting the benefits of trade as we have outlined above, one may still wonder whether countries with *identical* factor endowments and comparative advantages can still benefit through trade.

In fact, even for countries with the same factor endowments and PPFs (and thus, the same comparative advantages), free trade is beneficial.

This is because no two countries will have identical **tastes**. Trade allows each country to consume on a higher indifference curve than would be possible otherwise, increasing the overall welfare of both countries.

The graphs in Figs. 3.22 and 3.23 illustrate how each country can consume more of its preferred good than was possible to produce under autarky.

In Fig. 3.22, we see that while Country A and Country B enjoy identical factor endowments and production possibilities sets, they each have different preferences, represented by their respective indifference curves. Under autarky, each will produce and consume a different mix of goods.

We can see that the slopes of the countries' respective PPFs, represented by their trading price ratios (the green lines $-[Px/Py]_A$ and $-[Px/Py]_B$), are different as a result.

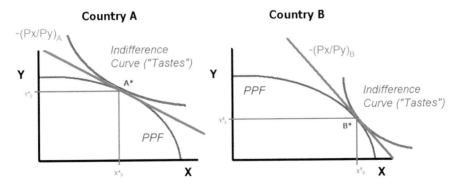

Fig. 3.22 Autarky, increasing costs model. A and B have *identical PPFs, different tastes* (Note: Figure not to scale)

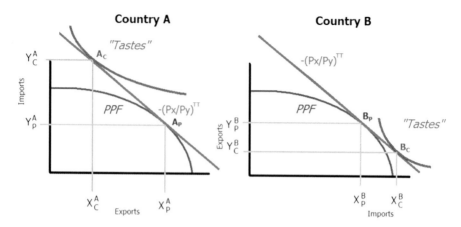

Fig. 3.23 Trade, increasing costs model. A and B have *identical PPFs, different tastes* (Note: Figure not to scale)

With trade, the trading price ratios of each country will converge into one global trading price ratio, represented by the Global Terms of Trade line in each graph in Fig. 3.23.

Each country's set of preferences now intersects the Global TT line at a higher indifference curve than was possible under autarky. Each country now enjoys more consumption of the mix of goods that it prefers.

Trade also facilitates the flow of innovation between countries, which increases productive efficiency and expands the PPF of both countries over time faster than was possible under autarky.

3.7 Intra-Industry Trade

We have seen how trade can benefit countries with different factor endowments (and thus, the same production possibilities frontier and comparative advantage). We have also seen how even two countries with identical factor endowments but different tastes can benefit from trade.

But can countries with identical factor endowments *and identical tastes* benefit from trade?

The answer, as it turns out, is an emphatic yes!

Given two countries with the same factor endowments (and thus, the same PPF and CA), and identical tastes (identical indifference curves), trade may still be beneficial if their industries exhibit increasing returns to scale.

The countries will engage in **intra-industry trade**—each producing different components of products for the same industry. This allows for a much higher degree of specialization in component part production than would have been possible

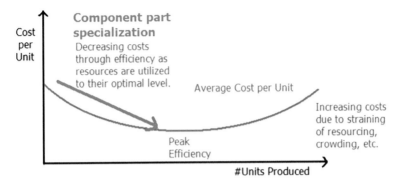

Fig. 3.24 Output volume and average cost per unit. Intra-industry trade involves component specialization, with decreasing costs

under autarky. As each country is free to focus on specific components, economies of scale are reached that are otherwise impossible given limited resources.

Unlike the increasing costs model (which is appropriate for entire *industries*), with its concave-shaped PPF, intra-industry trade involves a much higher level of specialization, and the economic groupings involved will be smaller—not entire industries but groups of firms or even single firms. These groupings will be operating on the downward-sloping portion of the average cost curve (depicted in Fig. 3.24), and will benefit with lower average production costs as quantities increase. This effect is known as **increasing internal returns to scale**,[20] and produces a *convex-shaped PPF* for intra-industry trade.

Internal economies of scale allow highly efficient, narrowly focused producers to crank out only specialized components such as aircraft tail sections in every production shift, with all the manufacturing processes set up for just that one part. This means that the tail sections can be produced very efficiently, and the average cost drops as more and more are produced. Factors that can contribute to internal returns to scale include large "setup" costs for production runs that may be amortized over greater and greater quantities, product-specific research and development expenditures, efficient robotics, and highly specialized labor.

---

[20] *Increasing external returns to scale* occur when an entire industry's average cost decreases with increased industry output. This happens as industries grow to attract pools of suppliers and labor with increasingly specialized skills. This effect is seen in the IT industry in Silicon Valley, California, or in Bangalore, India. Ricardian theory assumes that entire industries are *already* operating at their optimal cost-per-unit (at the trough of the average cost curve in Fig. 3.24), implying that all possible external economies of scale have already been achieved. This is the condition that creates the concave-shaped PPF for entire industries. Note that "economies of scale" is synonymous with and often used in place of "returns to scale" for both internal and external returns to scale.

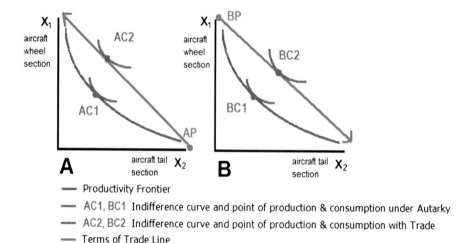

Fig. 3.25 Intra-industry trade benefits both A and B

With intra-industry trade, rather than exchanging goods X and Y, the two countries are exchanging component parts of good X, which we might consider X_1, X_2, and so on. In Fig. 3.25, good X is a complex, modern aircraft like the Boeing 787 Dreamliner, which incorporates parts manufactured in dozens of countries. Countries A and B have identical factor endowments—and thus identical PPFs—*and* identical tastes.

Note that the PPFs for both A and B are the opposite of the concave frontiers described earlier; here we have the long "tails" extending toward either axis.

Without trade, each country's production of the aircraft is limited by the amount of component parts they can produce, given their resources. In Fig. 3.25, we see Countries A and B initially producing and consuming at **AC1** and **BC1,** respectively, under autarky.

We now posit that Country A specializes in X_2 (aircraft tail sections), producing at point **AP**, and B specializes in X_1 (aircraft wheel sections), producing at point **BP**. A global trade line running between these two points, representing open bilateral trade between these fully specialized producers and depicted by the green terms of trade line in the figures, now becomes possible. Countries A and B now consume at **AC2** and **BC2.**

We see that with each country fully specializing in different components, the terms of trade line is pushed out beyond what is possible under autarky. This results in more components overall, and one can infer more production of aircraft for both countries!

We will return to the concept of intra-industry trade in Chap. 5.

Articles

Article 3.1. Trade Pacts Spawns Conflict

Zarrin Daruvalla, *International Trade Biweekly*

It has been only 10 days since Teutonia signed the free-trade pact with neighboring Salso, and already the air is rife with—take your pick—jubilation, euphoria, conflict, and despair. We spent the better part of the week randomly interviewing citizens from a wide range of professions in both countries, and the results are truly amazing. In this article, we have grouped together some of the more vocal skeptics and disbelievers of the free-trade pact. We follow with the responses from the proponents of the pact between technology-savvy Teutonia and manufacturing juggernaut Salso, in the Hints and Solutions section of this article.

At Teutonia Business School, we run into graduate student Rudi Schlossburger, chewing frantically on his late lunch at the university cafeteria. (a) "You know, I have a problem with the 'whole country being better off' assumption according to Ricardo—I studied economics even though I am a physicist," he adds shyly, slicing into his wiener schnitzel. "You know, when you look out the window, free trade always seems to create unemployment for many people—I am afraid that (b) we will see this happening in manufacturing and assembly as all those jobs soon move to Salso!"

Eva Mellonbaum, owner of the local patisserie, also takes us by surprise. "Guess what? I know as much about economics as I do about chocolate éclairs! I have a degree in economics—that is how I now efficiently run this #1 ranked pastry shop in the city!" she says as she proudly points to the ratings posted on her wall, as my staff and I desperately hope that she will substantiate the announcement with a free sampling of all her delights. Eva adds, "I always had a problem with 'more is better.' (c) According to the theory, the higher the curves—what are they called, indifference curves?—the better. I disagree! More is not always better. I mean, how many iPods and laptops and Blackberries can I buy? And if the more is better assumption is wrong, then Poof! The whole thing crashes!" She then mercifully offers us two free pastries each. I love my job!

We then trot over to Won Ching Lee's martial arts school to speak to a profusely sweating Won wearing a "Bad Guys Fear Won" T-shirt. (d) "Look, Salso has a lower standard of living than us. If we do free trade, Bang! Our standard will fall to their level! Who needs that?" he exclaims, nimbly sidestepping a frontal attack from a roaring 250 lb. student and nonchalantly throwing him over his back onto a sack of blankets. (e) "And besides, the wages in Salso are 1/10th our wages—hey, no brainer! All of our jobs will fly there in a nanosecond! I don't need an economics degree to see that!" he roars, as he dodges a screaming sword-waving student, deftly flinging her over his back onto another sack of blankets. We hastily decide to try another, somewhat less exciting location.

Next we talk to Father Alfredo Episcolo of the Salso High School, who intones that he is well aware of how free trade is supposed to work. "But I never understood the mechanism. (f) <u>Who will ensure that Country A trades in X and Country B in Y?</u> (g) <u>And Country A only makes X—I mean, how unrealistic is that?</u> And did you know that Ricardo made a host of some (h) <u>amazingly restrictive assumptions?</u> I wonder if our great leaders knew that before signing their Free Trade Treaty!" He then apologizes as he had a crisis on his hands. Should he replace the age-old clock on the tower, recently refurbished by Dr. Robert Braunstein, with a new digital version from Taiwan? Tradition or technology? Ah, the perils of high command.

On the way back, even my cameraman decides to chime in, such is the intensity of this debate. "Look," explains Amit Verma, "I hear the speeches, and I read the theory—but give me a break! (i) <u>How will all the workers making, say, Y in Country A suddenly switch over to making X—I mean, could you and I stop being reporters and suddenly become programmers tomorrow if, say, our country does indeed have a Comparative Advantage in programming?</u> I mean, come on! Who comes up with stuff like this?"

With this sobering thought, we climb back into the train and head for home. What if my job suddenly became the "Y job" in Country A? What if I ended up on the "wrong side" of free trade? What if my industry suddenly found itself to be in comparative disadvantage? But no dire thoughts now—instead it's time to swing by Eva's #1 ranked pastry place on my way home; in the evenings she puts all her day-old pastries on sale. Now, the economics of *that* are incontrovertible!

Hints and Solutions

Article 3.1

(a) In the following chapter, we will see that while the whole country is better off with trade, all individuals are not—at least not immediately following free trade. As you may infer, workers in the product/service that has comparative advantage will indeed be better off, but many workers in the comparatively disadvantaged industry will be worse off. And these workers will demand protection in the form of tariffs, quotas, etc.

(b) The inference here is that Teutonia does not have a comparative advantage in manufacturing or assembly and that Salso does. However, by definition, Teutonia will have a comparative advantage in some *other* goods and/or services. Remember, it is *comparative* advantage that drives trade, not absolute advantage.

(c) Eva is right—after all, how many of her pastries could one eat? But the key here is to define X and Y as desirable goods in the right context. X could be innovations leading to more health care, cleaner air, better quality of life, less dependence on nonrenewable energy resources, etc. Moreover, the shape and convexity of indifference curves incorporate the trade-offs, including saturation points, among various goods. The rarity of aesthetics among the many billions of people on the planet is evidence enough that in the aggregate, greater consumption possibilities are always preferred.

(d) On the contrary, free trade raises *both* countries to higher indifference curves—both countries are better off, because both consume more.

(e) No aspect of free-trade theory is driven by *absolute* wages! Instead, trade is driven by aLx/aLy and bLx/bLy, that is, by the differences in opportunity costs. There could be a remote tribe in the middle of the Sahara Desert whose wages may be the lowest in the world, but the opportunity cost of making anything there would be prohibitive given the absence of infrastructure, water, power grids, etc. We will further explore the effect of trade on wages when we cover the Stolper–Samuelson theorem in the next chapter.

(f) This is the beauty of specialization and free trade. It is endogenously driven—automatically, by market forces. In a later chapter, we discuss strategic trade that is engineered to varying degrees by central planning. But for now, unfettered trade is driven purely by market forces.

(g) Yes, full specialization may seem unrealistic, but if one examines free trade for the individual states in America, we can easily observe nearly full specialization. State A could be in mostly agriculture, while State B could be in IT, and State C could be in aerospace. In any event, with increasing costs, we see how full specialization never occurs, and both A and B will make *some quantity* of both goods, X and Y.

(h) Ricardo's model assumes a world of perfect competition, no frictional transaction costs, unfettered trade, and transportation and communication costs embedded in the opportunity costs of each good. This is not now nor ever has been the real world. However, the model is very useful in illustrating the intuition and concepts behind trade in a straightforward and concise manner. We strip away all these assumptions in later chapters—and find that even with the assumptions dropped, Ricardo still lives—in fact, the model generates even more sophisticated and realistic results.

(i) This is indeed a valid point. Russell Roberts, in his brilliant book, <u>The Choice: A Fable of Free Trade and Protectionism</u>, illustrates very poignantly that the shift from X to Y, for example, is certainly not an overnight shift but instead a generational shift.[21] Parents tell their kids that the future of industry X that had employed several generations of their family in the past now looks uncertain with trade and that they should perhaps consider entering industry Y for their future.

---

[21] Russell Roberts, *The Choice: A Fable of Free Trade and Protectionism*, Prentice Hall, 3rd Edition, 2006. Roberts brilliantly employs the device of a benevolent ghost – adapted from the Jimmy Stewart movie *It's a Wonderful Life* – to explicate the advantages of free trade in this parable written for the lay reader.

Chapter 4
Factor Intensity

Summary This chapter begins with a thorough discussion of the Heckscher–Ohlin theorem and the notions of "factor intensity" and "factor abundance" and then moves to the US–China–Eurozone situation.

Next in line is the Stolper–Samuelson factor-price equalization theorem followed by the powerful Mundell Hypothesis.

With these analytical additions to the basic Ricardian model, we emerge from this chapter with a clear view of how trade benefits each country overall and how these benefits are distributed among its producers and consumers.

Once again, in typical fashion, we present articles that feature challenging criticisms made by trade skeptics, in this case focusing on the interaction between high-skilled labor and capital-abundant countries (USA, Japan, Western Europe) and low/medium-skilled labor-abundant, capital-scarce countries (developing Asia and Central Europe).

4.1 Heckscher–Ohlin Theorem (HOT)

Heckscher and Ohlin[1] integrated the notion of **factor abundance** with the fact that different goods and services employ different levels of **factor intensities**. Simply stated, the Heckscher–Ohlin theorem (HOT) demonstrates that a country has a comparative advantage in the good that employs its **abundant factor** *intensely*.

We begin by defining the first component of the HOT theorem, **factor abundance**, and follow with a discussion of **factor intensity**.

---

[1] Eli Heckscher (1879–1952) and Bertil Ohlin (1899–1979) developed this model at the Stockholm School of Economics. It was first put forth in published form in 1933.

F. Langdana and P.T. Murphy, *International Trade and Global Macropolicy*,
Springer Texts in Business and Economics, DOI 10.1007/978-1-4614-1635-7_4,
© Springer Science+Business Media New York 2014

Fig. 4.1 Country A is
labor-abundant

$$\left(\frac{W}{R}\right)^A < \left(\frac{W}{R}\right)^B$$

Fig. 4.2 Country B is
labor-scarce

$$\left(\frac{W}{R}\right)^B > \left(\frac{W}{R}\right)^A$$

(a) **Factor abundance**

Country **A** is defined to be labor abundant if the ratio of labor to capital in **A**, denoted $(L/K)^A$, is greater than the ratio of labor to capital in **B**, denoted $(L/K)^B$. It must be noted that factor abundance is a *relative* definition—as are virtually all the definitions in trade theory. In other words, while Europe may have more workers relative to Sri Lanka, the latter would still be considered the labor-abundant country when one compares its labor/capital ratio to that of Europe. Sri Lanka may have fewer workers than Europe, but it has significantly less capital. Europe may have more workers but disproportionally more capital, rendering Europe's labor/capital ratio lower than Sri Lanka's.

In other words, $(L/K)^{\text{Sri Lanka}} > (L/K)^{\text{Europe}}$.

Since "labor" and "capital" are not quantifiable definitions, with "capital" being particularly difficult to measure, and "labor" comprising workers with a range of skills, we use **relative prices** to measure abundance.

If the supply of labor in a given country is high, the wage (returns to labor) in that country will be lower, as there are more people for employers to choose from. If the supply of labor is scarce, the wage will be higher. Similarly, if capital in a country is scarce, the returns to capital will be relatively high. And, if capital is plentiful, the returns to capital will be lower. We use the term **rents** synonymously with returns to capital.[2]

If we represent wages as (**W**) and rents as (**R**), we can say that

Country A is labor abundant if: $(W/R)^A < (W/R)^B$. (Fig. 4.1)

Where: **W** = Wages (returns on Labor)
        R = Rents (returns on Capital)

If Country A is endowed with an abundant supply of labor, wages, relative to rents, will be low. When comparing countries' endowments of capital and labor, we use the wage/rent ratio in each country as the determinant of relative abundance or scarcity of each factor.

By mathematical identity, if Country A is labor abundant, it is capital scarce. And, if we are talking about only two countries and their *relative* abundance, by definition if Country A is labor abundant, then Country B is labor scarce (Fig. 4.2).

---

[2] We use the term *rents* in its economic sense, meaning the returns to any productively employed capital.

$$\left(\frac{R}{W}\right)^B < \left(\frac{R}{W}\right)^A$$

Fig. 4.3   Country B, being labor-scarce, is by mathematical identity capital-abundant

Country A   **Country B**

$$\frac{aLx}{aKx} > \frac{aLy}{aKy} \quad and \quad \frac{bLx}{bKx} > \frac{bLy}{bKy}$$

Fig. 4.4   Factor intensity. Good X is labor-intensive

Country A   **Country B**

$$\frac{aKx}{aLx} < \frac{aKy}{aLy} \quad and \quad \frac{bKx}{bLx} < \frac{bKy}{bLy}$$

Fig. 4.5   Factor intensity. Good Y is capital-intensive

Flip the ratios, and we see that if Country B is labor scarce, by mathematical identity, it is capital abundant (Fig. 4.3).

Factor abundance answers the question: "Where does comparative advantage come from?" It comes precisely from factor abundance.

We now turn to defining the second component of HOT: "factor intensity."

(b) **Factor intensity**

Once again, we have two countries, A and B, making two goods, X and Y. There are two inputs, labor and capital. Let good X be apparel, and let good Y be jet engines.

In this case, good X (apparel) is defined as being **labor intensive** if, **in both Countries A and B**, the *ratio of labor to capital* employed in the manufacture of apparel (**X**) is greater than the *ratio of labor to capital* employed in the manufacture of jet engines (**Y**). We see this depicted in Fig. 4.4.

Conversely, jet engines are **capital intensive** as they will employ more capital relative to labor irrespective of where they are produced, be it in Country A or B. This is simply the "flip side" of the relationship shown in Fig. 4.4 (see Fig. 4.5).

Intensity shows us which goods and services most heavily utilize which factors. With factor abundance known, intensity answers the question: "In which goods and services will I have comparative advantage?" The answer? Those goods that employ the abundant factor intensely.

In Chap. 2, we were simply given that Country A had a CA in X and Country B in Y. Now, we are in a position to determine what *drives* the comparative advantage of a country—where does it "come from?" Thanks to HOT, once we identify factor abundance, we marry this with a good or service that employs the abundant factor intensively, and, voila, we have arrived at the determination of comparative advantage for that particular country.

We now transition, finally, to the welfare of the factors of production. What happens to wages? How will the wages of high-skilled labor fare vs. those of low-skilled labor? What happens to employment in the country as a whole and in specific sectors? We are now in a position to address some of the most pressing and controversial issues pertaining to trade.

4.2   Stolper–Samuelson Theorem (SST)

In 1941, economists Wolfgang Stolper and Paul Samuelson built on the work of Heckscher and Ohlin by analyzing how the benefits of trade are distributed within a trading country.

SST simply states that

Trade will benefit a country's abundant factor relative to its scarce factor.

In Fig. 4.6, we present a labor-abundant Country A and its supply and demand for labor and capital.

Country A is given to be labor abundant. It initiates policies to deploy the Ricardian trade theorem, by specializing in good X (textiles), which employs labor intensively. (Good Y is avionics, which employs capital intensively).

As Country A begins to specialize in X, the demand for labor increases, and the curve shifts to the right in Fig. 4.6 from blue to green, denoted by ①.

The labor demand adjustments are mitigated somewhat by the reduced demand for capital-intensive good Y (avionics). As Country A shuts down its avionics plants and labs, many of the workers making avionics are displaced, thereby resulting in a slight leftward shift in demand for labor, denoted by ② in Fig. 4.6. The final net increase in labor demand is seen in the shift from the original blue curve to the red curve.

These effects work in reverse on capital. As the capital-intensive avionics labs are shut down, the attendant demand for capital drops from the blue to the green demand-for-capital curve, denoted by ①. Finally, the labor-intensive textile industry would indeed need some capital as it expands, which accounts for the rightward shift in demand for capital denoted by ②. The net drop in capital demand is therefore from the blue to the red curve.

Result: Trade has increased the demand for labor in A, its abundant factor, and this has benefitted this factor in the form of higher employment and ultimately higher wages (which are determined by the intersection of the labor supply and labor demand curves).

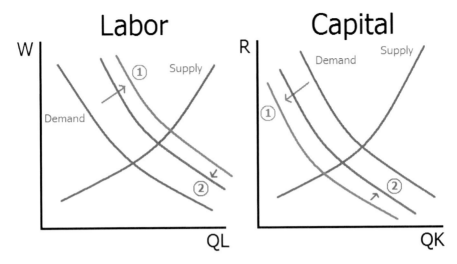

Fig. 4.6 Supply and Demand for labor and capital in Country A, which is labor-abundant and capital-scarce. **W** = wages, **R** = rents (returns to capital), **QL** = quantity of labor, **QK** = quantity of capital. Here we see the Stolper-Samuelson theory in action for labor-abundant Country A

So, we can see that a labor-abundant country which opens up to trade will see its wages increase. The abundant factor (workers here in Country A) will be better off, and the scarce factor (owners of capital in Country A) will indeed be worse off in the immediate aftermath of trade. Likewise, a capital-abundant country which opens up to trade will see its returns to capital go up, and its wages go down.

It is important to note that the definition of abundance means that the factor that benefits will represent the majority of the country's productive base. Thus, the country's overall welfare will be increased through trade, and this is what we mean by the "whole country" being "better off" in the Ricardian trade model.

It is also important to note that when we speak of a capital-abundant country benefitting from trade in capital-intensive goods, the growth from trade will benefit the workers in those industries (as well as the owners of capital) and will open up opportunities in those industries that did not exist before.

We can infer from the SST that over time, the ratios of wages to rents will tend toward equality between trading countries, as the returns to each country's abundant factor grow. For example, as the demand for labor-abundant Country A's textiles and toys generates higher wages, the relative price of labor to capital will increase. The reverse is true for capital-abundant Country B, where the price (in the form of rents) of capital relative to wages will increase as the demand for its high-tech goods rises. It is important, as always, to remember that this has nothing to do with *absolute* wages or rents—it is the *ratio* of one to the other *within each country* that will tend toward parity over the very long term.

4.3   The Six Steps to Increase the Overall Welfare of a Country

We may now combine what we have learned so far about Ricardo's comparative advantage, the Heckscher–Ohlin theorem, and the Stolper–Samuelson theorem into a comprehensive outline of how a country may increase its overall welfare through trade:

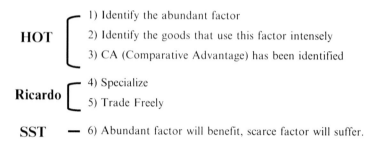

Result: The country as a whole is better off!

Goods and services are not the only things that can move between countries. The factors of production can move as well. This could result in an increase in the supply of a given factor which depresses returns—for example, a flood of labor that depresses wages overall. How does trade theory account for this possibility?

4.4   The Mundell Hypothesis

Robert Mundell, the Nobel Prize-winning Canadian economist, did pioneering work on a host of economic topics. Among his many contributions was a key insight into cross-border trade:

Trade in outputs serves as a substitute for the movement of factors of production.

Labor and capital will be attracted to countries where the returns on these factors are highest. Given poor, labor-abundant Country A, and wealthy, capital-abundant Country B (where wages are higher than in Country A since labor is scarce in Country B), labor will be attracted to move to Country B to seek higher returns.

Robert Mundell's Hypothesis shows that while labor can move from Country A to Country B in the form of workers migrating (Fig. 4.7), labor can also go from A to B *embedded in the labor-intensive products* which are produced by the labor in A (Fig. 4.8).

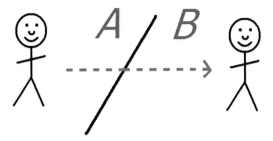

Fig. 4.7 Labor migrates from A to B

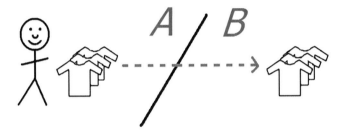

Fig. 4.8 Labor migrates from A to B in the form of the labor value *embedded in the products* exported by A into B

When products are manufactured in A, the labor employed to produce them "goes into" the products; it is part of their value. When goods move from A to B, the labor component of their value moves with them. B's demand for the goods that are produced in A leads to a higher demand for labor in A. The returns to labor (wages) in A increase, thanks to the Stolper–Samuelson theorem. In other words, the effect on A's wages is similar irrespective of whether labor emigrates to B, or the labor-intensive good is exported to B! Thus, without a single person crossing a border, labor can "immigrate" from A to B "within" the goods that are produced in A!

Thus, with free trade, A's abundant factor—its workers—will gain higher wages without emigrating. And in doing so, the workers from Country A (and the citizens of Country B) would not have to endure the inevitable social/political/emotional stresses that typically accompany any large-scale movement of labor from one country to another.

Similarly, capital will naturally flow to areas where its returns are higher. Given that B is capital abundant, there will be a tendency for B to move its capital into A, where capital is scarce, to generate higher rents. However, under free trade, capital can move in the form of the outputs produced in B. This will tend to increase the returns to capital in B and serve to keep B's capital at home where it is still earning the high returns through trade that it would have sought by locating overseas.

The Mundell Hypothesis has been a key theorem underlying many global free-trade treaties. It was crucial in getting NAFTA[3] approved—the logic was that Mexican workers would be induced to stay in Mexico if free trade were possible between the USA and Mexico. It was also implemented in the expansion of the European Union (EU) and the Eurozone, in that the ensuing free trade and the accompanying common currency would stem the flow of workers from labor-abundant Central Europe to Western Europe.

Articles

Article 4.1. Town Hall Tempest in Gettysburg

Anne Ryan, *Gettysburg Global Sentinel*

It seemed like the Battle of Gettysburg was being fought all over again at the Gettysburg Town Hall, where the fourth round of national debates on the free-trade pact with Habano was being hotly discussed.

Paul Coffey, president of the Pennsylvania Welders Guild, patiently proclaimed, (a) "The wages in Habano are about 25 % of our wages—there is going to be that 'giant sucking sound'[4] as all our blue-collar jobs go there, mark my words! It is simply Un-American to do this to us!"

Professor William Ryan of Gettysburg College, looking the part in his rumpled tweed jacket with multiple pens protruding from his pocket, patiently tried to get a word in. "Look, I am as American as the next guy—hey, I was in the Marines! (b) But rest assured that the blue collar jobs are not going to be driven by the absolute wage differential! This is one of my points in my bestseller, *109 Things in Economics that Everyone Should Know.*"

---

[3] The North American Free Trade Agreement of 1994 removed most trade restrictions and tariffs among the United States, Canada, and Mexico.

[4] Independent presidential candidate H. Ross Perot famously evoked this image in 1992, referring to the drain of jobs from the USA to Mexico that would supposedly ensue should trade barriers between the USA and Mexico be removed. Trade protectionism was a major element of the Perot platform. Perot's statement from the first presidential debate of 1992 is worth quoting in full as it captures many elements of anti-trade sentiment: "To those of you in the audience who are business people, pretty simple: If you're paying $12, $13, $14 an hour for factory workers and you can move your factory South of the border, pay a dollar an hour for labor, hire young – let's assume you've been in business for a long time and you've got a mature work force – pay a dollar an hour for your labor, have no health care – that's the most expensive single element in making a car – have no environmental controls, no pollution controls and no retirement, and you don't care about anything but making money, there will be a giant sucking sound going south."

"Not true!" shrieked Esmeralda Tuffey, chairperson of the American Women Welder's Union. (c) "There is a theorem that says that the wages will be equal—I think it is in your book, Professor!"

But before the professor could respond, Vito Gonzales, the elderly spokesperson of the union, took the floor and in his deep, sad voice mourned the loss of the cities and towns. "I see empty towns where mills once stood. I see empty malls. (d) I see entire neighborhoods lying in ruins where once company towns stood—the jobs are gone. Is this what you call the benefits of free trade?!" The crowd roared with delight and then suddenly rushed off to prevent Esmeralda from choking some poor graduate student from Gettysburg College who seemed to agree with Professor Ryan.

Once again Paul Coffey took the floor. (e) "I have just one question for the professor. Does it not make sense to make it all at home so we get the jobs AND the money...because...." He could not finish. The crowd roared. Four metalworkers lifted Paul Coffey and carried him away over their shoulders, shouting "Coffey for President!" Prof. Ryan finally restored some order. "I can tell you this. (f) Around the beginning of the twentieth century, almost 80 % of this country was in agriculture. Now we have barely 2 % or 3 % associated with farming! And yet, we make more food! Yes, the productivity of agriculture has gone up, so we do not need the huge employment in that sector—but what do we now have jobs in? In new areas such as technology, innovation, pharmaceuticals, avionics, financial services, and telecoms, and we will be creating jobs in sectors that neither you nor I can even imagine now, such as biotechnology and genetic engineering. We will....." He couldn't finish. The crowd had glazed over and most were talking to themselves. Esmeralda again tried to punch the graduate student—in fact, she succeeded before they were separated again.

The appearance of a very large number of brick-oven pizzas from the famous Denino's Pizza brought peace to the battlefield, until Dr. Santosh Mody, professor of Philosophy at Gettysburg, took to the podium. "Look, we all know about Ricardo and all that, but hey, let's play fair here! (g) I say that trade should not just be free—it should also be fair!" The crowd loved this; the roar was deafening. After much effort at silencing the crowd, Mody continued, (h) "Look, if we buy 120 million units of auto parts from them, heck, they should meet us halfway and buy the same amount from us—right now they barely buy two million units of auto parts from us—now, is that fair?!"

The crowd erupted with a resounding "No!" and this reporter and her photographer reached over to the table, grabbed two gigantic slices of cheese pizza and two Diet Cokes, and escaped outside to the magical light and the soft breeze of a Gettysburg evening. In the distance, Seminary Ridge glowed a soft blue in the evening light, reminding us of a long-ago battle that forged a mighty country, one that was now fighting to define its place in the world.

Hints and Solutions

Article 4.1

(a) and (b). We revisit a version of this argument used in Article 2.1. We know now that trade is driven by *ratios* of opportunity costs and not *absolute* wages. Even in the Stolper–Samuelson theorem, it is the ratios of returns to labor relative to returns to capital that tend toward equality.

(c) This is a common misinterpretation of SST. Nothing in the theorem states that the *absolute* wages will tend to equality—it is the *ratios* of returns to labor relative to returns to capital that will tend toward equality over time.

(d) The key is to look at where the workers (and jobs) have moved, presumably to areas that specialize in the goods/services in which the country has comparative advantage. Trade theory dictates that we follow the jobs and the workers and not the collateral vestiges of an industry in comparative disadvantage.

(e) Paul Coffey, unbeknownst to him, is describing a world under autarky.

(f) In later chapters, we will study how countries go through entire "life cycles." They may begin with a largely low-skilled labor force in abundance, cranking out low-skilled labor-intensive goods. But over time, with greater income and greater education provided by trade, the country evolves into a medium- or high-skilled labor-abundant country. The focus now shifts into goods and services that employ medium- to high-skilled labor intensively, as Prof. Ryan is attempting to explain. Unfortunately for him, explaining the benefits of trade requires a series of logical explanations which defy compression into simple sound bites. Protectionists' appeals to emotion suffer no such disability.

(g) and (h). Another common mistake. Trade theory dictates that trade within one particular good, say, good X, *will be asymmetric*. The country with the comparative advantage in X will be a net exporter of X, and the other Country B (with a CA in Y and a comparative disadvantage in X) will be a net importer of X.

Chapter 5
Stripping Away Ricardo's Assumptions

Summary This chapter systematically sheds all the restricting assumptions that David Ricardo made while formulating his free-trade theorem. As we have seen in our previous end-of-chapter articles, many of Ricardo's assumptions have served as convenient lightning rods for attacks by skeptics of free trade. In this chapter, we systematically strip away these high-profile and restrictive assumptions.

We find that not only does the Ricardian free-trade model survive the shedding of his assumptions, but, surprisingly, the results generate an even more sophisticated analysis and depiction of present-day aspects of free trade such as oligopolistic competition, the product life cycle, and intra-industry trade.

5.1 Ricardian Assumption: Both Countries A and B Have Identical Technology

In dropping the assumption that both Countries A and B have identical technology, we introduce the fact that Countries A and B are usually at different stages of their technological development, and, thus trade can be explained very well using the **product life cycle** hypothesis.

In this model, differences in technology drive trade by virtue of differences in respective factor intensiveness of a product over time. This model explains that Country A can invent product X and export X for a while. However, when X becomes standardized, Country A has to offshore X to some other Country B that is abundant in the medium-skilled labor that is essential for standardized mass production. We can see this process at work in the real world, for example, with color televisions, which were initially produced largely in the United States but shifted over time to be produced in Japan, then Taiwan and Korea, and finally China once they were completely commoditized.

F. Langdana and P.T. Murphy, *International Trade and Global Macropolicy*,
Springer Texts in Business and Economics, DOI 10.1007/978-1-4614-1635-7_5,
© Springer Science+Business Media New York 2014

5.1.1   The Production Life Cycle (PLC)

Industries generally go through a life cycle of production, which begins with R&D and innovation, and proceeds through the stages of growth, maturity, and ultimately, decline.

Before delving further into the PLC hypothesis, a discussion of the *qualitative* differences in labor endowments is in order.

Until now, we have employed a broad definition of "labor" as a monolithic factor comprising a country's aggregate workforce, without drawing distinctions between different types of workers. In fact, there are many categories into which workers may be separated.

In order for our broad-based theories to be applicable, we must still identify very large groupings, but we can separate labor by its "skill" level. At the lowest end of the spectrum are unskilled laborers. These compose the majority of the labor force in many developing countries that are either predominantly agrarian or just starting to industrialize.

Very close to "unskilled" laborers are "low-skilled" laborers, who are competent to perform basic assembly and manufacturing given adequate supervision. Low-skilled laborers may work in textiles, apparel, shoes, and other simple manufactures.

"Medium-skilled" laborers include most manufactures, including many consumer and durable goods. Products using medium-skilled labor may include anything from automotive parts to appliances to many consumer goods. In our language, manufacturing uses low- or medium-skilled labor intensively.

"High-skilled" laborers manufacture more complicated items, such as medical devices, certain computer components, precision machinery, and scientific instruments.

At the top of the ladder, in knowledge-intensive sectors such as R&D, we find "knowledge workers" who are generally well educated and able to function largely independently and are disproportionately represented among service industries, including legal and medical professionals, financial analysts, educators, and screenwriters.

These categories are necessarily broad and may involve significant overlap. However, they are useful in order to develop a clearer picture of the effects of trade.

Country A, abundant in knowledge workers, may have a scarcity of low-skilled laborers, in which B is abundant. Under free trade, low-end manufactures will be undertaken by B, and high-end items and many service functions will be performed by A. Country B's low-skilled laborers and Country A's knowledge workers will both benefit from trade.

Different stages of a product's life cycle generally involve different factor intensities of production. The R&D stage, for example, would be high skilled labor intensive and/or capital intensive, requiring highly trained scientists working in high-tech and specialized labs. On the other hand, the standardized mass-production stage would employ medium-skilled labor intensively.

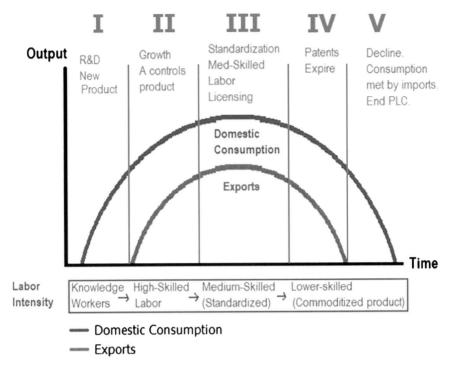

Fig. 5.1   The production life cycle (PLC)

Depending on a country's abundant factor(s), its comparative advantage will generally lie within a specific range of the production life cycle.

In Fig. 5.1, we can imagine Country A, which is abundant in knowledge- and high-skilled workers, introducing some new product X. The country undertakes the R&D, prototype testing, and pilot programs in Stage I. In Stage II, production accelerates in volume, using highly skilled workers, with Country A consuming and exporting more of X. The new technology is still controlled by the country that developed it.[1]

Technology becomes more standardized as we proceed into Stage III. The innovating firm now finds it profitable to license other firms (outsource), both domestic and foreign, to produce the now-standardized good X. Over time, as Country A's labor force is generally higher-skilled and higher-cost, it will be relatively inefficient for Country A to continue production of this now-standardized product, as compared to a country that we'll call "B," which is abundant in medium-skilled labor. Domestic production and exports will peak as production is increasingly offshored to Country B.

---

[1] Actually by the original firm (or firms) within that country that developed the technology. However, here we are focusing on the effects of the PLC on the country as a whole.

By the time good X reaches Stage IV, exports of X from Country A decrease; patent protection expires; trade secrets, technology, and proprietary production techniques are largely diffused; and foreign companies, now predominantly in Country C, a low-skilled labor haven, begin to produce good X in earnest. The product has become a simple commodity. Finally, by the time we reach Stage V, exports from A dry up altogether. Domestic consumption of X in A is now satisfied only by imports. Even Country B at this point will have largely abandoned the manufacture of X, leaving its production to Country C and others. Product X has moved through its life cycle.

It must be noted that for Country A, by the time X reaches Stage III, the country is already launching Stage I of some new products Y and Z. Country A's lifeblood is driven by a *constant stream of innovation*. Country A must ensure that it maintains an economic environment that fosters continual innovation just to stay in the game.[2] Country B, while currently medium-skilled-labor abundant with a comparative advantage in the manufacture of standardized goods, will find that as its indifference curves reach higher à la Ricardo, and as its national income grows over time, so does the education, skill, and productivity of its workers. In other words, Country B will start moving up the ladder to the manufacture of more sophisticated and increasingly hi-tech goods. Eventually, if Country B maintains a beneficial environment for economic activity and trade, it can move up all the way to finally develop a CA in R&D, innovation, etc. By then perhaps Country C will have moved up the chain to find itself now abundant in medium-skilled labor and will be happy to do the mid-cycle manufacturing formerly undertaken by B. At the bottom, as potential successors to Country C, there yet remain a host of economically challenged states around the world who, with reforms to their political, economic, and legal systems, could provide the sound environment necessary to join the global trading community as producers, initially, of simple products requiring low-skilled labor.

Countries essentially move through their own "life cycles." Thanks to trade, countries generally migrate from the rightmost edge toward the left—from low-skilled factor labor abundance over a long period of time eventually to high-skilled labor abundance. It should also be noted that in addition to the increasing prosperity that yields healthier and more educated workers, the accompanying increase in the capital base permits greater productivity.

---

[2] Later we discuss the role of macroeconomic policies in fostering this "environment" that generates innovation. Deregulation (very controversial following the subprime crisis), low taxes, free trade, education, infrastructure, and enlightened government policies are key factors. We will also discuss the role of government spending in innovation; "strategic trade" will be discussed in detail in Chap. 6.

5.2   Ricardian Assumption: Industries X and Y in Countries A and B Are Fully Competitive

Ricardo assumed that the industries being discussed were perfectly competitive, that is, a large number of small producers of perfectly substitutable output in each sector, with no hegemon or oligopoly, operating at peak efficiency and selling their products with no monopolistic profits. The reason for this assumption is that the closer that an industry comes to being a monopoly (the further from "perfect competition"), the less efficient its use of resources and the more likely its CA will be diluted from its potential. Ricardo assumed that resources were being used efficiently (another assumption that we will relax below); not to do so would mean that a country would be operating inside of, rather than at the edge of, its production possibilities frontier.

In Fig. 5.2, we see a situation where industries X and Y in Country A are controlled by a limited number of large firms, enjoying monopolistic profits. Improvements in Country A's production and consumption (from point A^*) would be possible here by fostering greater competition among firms, up to the boundary of A's PPF. Analyzing the effects of moving from autarky to trade while allowing for starting points within the PPF would create complications in identifying whether gains came from trade or from internal improvements.

By assuming perfect competition, with Country A operating at its PPF, Ricardo could demonstrate that *even at the point where there are no more internal efficiency gains to be made*, a country under autarky could expand welfare through trade.

Relaxing this assumption and allowing for two countries where one or both have suboptimal factor utilization (with production inside of their respective PPFs), comparative advantage and all its implications will still apply, though with weaker results. Remember that CA is driven by aLx/aLy and bLx/bLy; even diluted from their potential, these variables and the opportunity costs that arise from them will still show that there are gains to be made from trade.

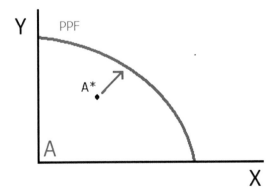

Fig. 5.2 Country A is producing at less than its full output potential (below the PPF)

5.2.1 Intra-Industry Trade

While shedding the assumption of perfect competition, we also find ourselves returning to a very important development in global free trade—the notion of intra-industry trade. Most trade among the major industrialized countries and trading blocs is actually intra-industry trade, in which countries trade components that will eventually comprise one final product.

In Chap. 3, we introduced the concept of intra-industry trade and demonstrated that even given two countries with the *same factor endowments* (and thus, the same PPFs and CAs) *and identical tastes* (identical indifference curves), trade may still be beneficial if the industries exhibit increasing returns to scale.

Here we find a more "real" world of oligopolistic competition driven by a few large companies, rather than the very restrictive and unrealistic "perfect competition" assumption in Ricardo's theory. Such industries are quite common. Examples in the USA include the soft drink market where Coca-Cola and Pepsi enjoy greater than 70 % share[3]; breakfast cereals, with Kellogg, General Mills, Post, and Quaker combining for 80 % share[4]; beer, where AB InBev and MillerCoors control 78 % of the market by volume[5]; and the music market with four companies (Universal, Sony, Warner, and EMI) controlling 80 % of the market.[6]

As we noted in Chap. 3, these large producers will be operating on the downward-sloping portion of the average cost curve, where they enjoy increasing internal returns to scale. This produces the *convex-shaped PPF* seen in Fig. 3.25, which is the key driver of the benefits arising from intra-industry trade.

Most global trade is, interestingly, intra-industry trade.[7] Certainly, most of the trade in mature countries with similar factor endowments (USA and Canada, France, and Germany) is intra-industry trade.

The Boeing 787 Dreamliner is a high-profile example of intra-industry trade at work. Boeing utilized manufacturing capabilities from multiple countries, both owned and outsourced, in the development of the 787.

---

[3] *Beverage Digest.* 2011. 59(5). http://www.beverage-digest.com/pdf/top-10_2011.pdf. Accessed February 6, 2011

[4] "Breakfast Food Statistics," *Topher's Breakfast Cereal Character Guide.* 2011. http://www.lavasurfer.com/cereal-stats.html. Accessed September 6, 2012

[5] Howard, Phil, and Ginger Ogilvie. 2011. "Concentration in the US Beer Industry." https://www.msu.edu/~howardp./beer.html. Accessed September 6, 2012

[6] "Oligopoly Examples." *YourDictionary. LoveToKnow, n.d.* http://examples.yourdictionary.com/oligopoly-examples.html. Accessed September 5, 2012. The inclusion of breakfast cereal and beer in our list of oligopolies was also inspired by this site.

[7] This may initially be driven by the fact that countries with similar factor endowments tend to be geographically close to each other, or are perhaps more culturally comfortable allowing a greater degree of open trade, or some combination thereof.

Typically trade between countries with very *dissimilar* factor endowments (e.g., USA and Mexico, USA and China) would, on the other hand, predominantly involve traditional *inter-industry* trade (e.g., aircraft and textiles, biotech and toys).

Intra-industry trade is easier to facilitate politically than traditional inter-industry trade, as:

(a) Worker dislocation is minimized as labor can shift more easily within an industry than from one industry to another.
(b) There is also less capital-investment dislocation as plant and equipment can shift more efficiently within an industry than between industries (which is often impossible).
(c) The domestic industry directly benefits from increased trade, so there are fewer if any factions calling for protectionism.
(d) Intra-industry trade generally involves comparatively advantaged goods, which by definition benefits the abundant factors. There is no "other" domestic industry suffering visible harm, as is often the case in traditional inter-industry trade.
(e) The benefits of intra-industry are more visible overall, and the costs (reduction or elimination of particular specialties within a growing industry) less so.

In Chap. 6, we will examine trade barriers, which often arise as the result of political pressure by the domestic interests who are adversely affected by trade. Trade disputes involving intra-industry trade are much less frequent than those involving inter-industry trade. Quite simply, if Country A indulges in a trade war with its intra-industry trading partner B, imposing a tariff or other restrictions on the components imported from B, then the final product will simply cost more and both A and B will be worse off as a result. This is clearly a "lose-lose" proposition, and A's producers will be unlikely to lobby for such trade barriers. In inter-industry trade (e.g., with Country A making coffee and Country B making textiles), the harmful effects of trade restrictions are not as obvious.

5.3 Ricardian Assumption: The Ricardian Model Only Has Two Countries, Two Goods, and Two Factors of Production

Making the model consistent with the real world's N countries, and J goods, and M factors of production greatly complicates pedagogic discussions of the HOT and Ricardian trade. We obviously cannot discuss the real world in the context of the two-dimensional diagrams of previous chapters. With greater than two countries, trade theory turns to matrix algebra for discussion.

In addition to multiple countries and goods, a factor-intensity index would have to be constructed if we have more than two inputs. Currently, a five-way categorization of inputs is generally used: (i) capital, (ii) high-skilled labor (human capital), (iii) low-skilled labor, (iv) arable land, and (v) minerals and natural resources.

The matrix algebra computations involved in expanding the Ricardian model are beyond the scope of this book, and in fact a full treatment of this topic alone would fill a volume. Much scholarly work has been done in this area. The findings have generally shown that strong determinative predications are more elusive as the dimensionality of each variable expands; however, the essential intuition that, broadly speaking, "the pattern of international trade is determined by comparative advantage" has been confirmed by many authors who have approached the problem from various perspectives.[8]

5.4   Ricardian Assumption: No International Factor Mobility: Resources Can Move Between Products X and Y Within Each Country but Cannot Move from One Country to Another

This assumption was introduced by Ricardo to reflect the fact that labor was indeed not readily mobile between countries; the cost plus the legal restrictions on large-scale immigration in his day lent credence to this assumption.

Labor and capital can move with far more ease today than was the case at the time of Ricardo's writing in the early nineteenth century. Lifting the no-movement-of-factors assumption brings us back to the work of Robert Mundell. While the factors of production *can* move relatively freely, free trade allows these factors to "move" *as part of the goods and services* that they produce. For the most part, labor and capital will prefer to avail themselves of this arrangement rather than migrate. Cultural and familial ties will most often make staying home more attractive to labor than moving, and capital will generally prefer the well-understood rules and property rights provided by a benevolent (or at least well-understood and predictable) home government.[9]

---

[8] Deardorff AV (1980) The general validity of the law of comparative advantage. *J Polit Econ* 88 (5):941–957. The intrepid student might also turn to Jones RW (1961) Comparative advantage and the theory of tariffs: a multi-country, multi-commodity model. *Rev Econ Stud* 28(3):161–175; Dornbusch R, Stanley F, Samuelson PA (1977) Comparative advantage, trade, and payments in a Ricardian model with a continuum of goods. *Am Econ Rev* 67:823–839; Eaton J, Kortum S (2002) Technology, geography, and trade. Econometrica 70(September):1741–1779; and Costinot A (2009) An elementary theory of comparative advantage. *Econometrica* 77(July):1165–1192.

[9] As always, we assume a generally benevolent political and economic climate among the trading countries. Tyrannical, capricious, or unstable regimes provide strong motivations for the flight of all resources, human and otherwise. Such regimes generally do not provide the stable climate necessary for the benefits of trade to fully materialize. To include such countries into our analysis would lead us far afield into the areas of political economy, foreign affairs, and even military strategy.

The advent of the Internet, furthermore, has allowed "labor" to effectively "move" without cost between A and B. But then, according to the Mundell Hypothesis, this is still not actual labor moving across countries, but labor-intensive *services* such as IT support, accounting, data processing, and the host of outsourced activities provided by countries like India, China, and the Philippines moving over the Internet.

Ergo, even lifting the no-factor-mobility assumption, the model does not come crashing down.

5.5 Ricardian Assumption: No Transportation, Environmental, or Infrastructure Costs

Ricardo made these simplifying assumptions, which have been the focus of much anti-free-trade rhetoric. However, including real-world complications such as transportation costs, infrastructure challenges, the efficiency of local government and bureaucracy ("hassle factors"), and environmental problems only makes the theory richer and increases its explanatory power in the light of observed trade outcomes. For example, horrible road conditions or interminable licensing procedures can be integrated into the analysis by simply subsuming the information into the aLx/ aLy ratio. For example, the number of workers required to make 1 unit of X in a country with huge power shortages, a corrupt bureaucracy, or dangerous roads will have to include a premium reflective of the extra number of hours of work per day that are required to overcome these obstacles. Only then can the "L" (or "K") variable convey meaningful information about actual factor requirements given Country A's economic and political environment. In other words, the aLx for a country with great infrastructure and no corruption and no unnecessary regulation would be lower than the aLx for a similarly endowed country that is plagued by the opposite.

The ratios of opportunity costs are therefore "effective" ratios that can subsume and incorporate hassle factors, transportation costs, infrastructure quality, corruption, pollution, and so forth. Once again, the proper inclusion of these real-world challenges into the ratio of effective opportunity costs will yield a more accurate picture of the comparative advantage (or disadvantage) of the country in question.

It should be noted that in certain industries, transportation costs have in fact been eliminated. Through the Internet, transportation costs for some kinds of services that can be "transported" online have fallen to zero. As this has occurred, countries like India find that a host of services that were hitherto considered "non-tradable" due to the previous need for a physical presence at the point of the transaction are leaping to the forefront of comparative advantage. Services such as accounting, web design, data processing, and IT support, long in the domain of non-tradable goods, suddenly lead the list of services with CA when the transportation costs drop to zero.

5.6   Ricardian Assumption: Full Employment of All Resources

Ricardo started with the best case assumption in which all who seek work are working and in which all deployable capital is unleashed. In other words, the resources are "maxed out" in the autarky situation. He finds that even in this apparently blissful state, consumption of both goods can indeed be increased through trade over what is possible under!

Relaxing this assumption does not alter the country's factor abundance or CA. If we were to relax the assumption of "full employment" of labor and capital, our results would actually be even more realistic. If we start with, say, 10 % unemployment at autarky, specialization and free trade would then actually ratchet up employment, so that the unemployment rate would now drop to 6 %, for example, with the added advantage of the new jobs being created in the sector that has CA.

In later chapters, we will see how Ricardian free-trade policies face perhaps their most severe test in recessions and the accompanying periods of unemployment. Free trade is a hard sell in the best of times. Free trade is not intuitive; the concept of comparative advantage is not a simple one to explain or to sell. Furthermore, the benefits of free trade are not readily or instantly discernible. New job creation in new areas of CA takes place gradually, but job losses are poignant in their suddenness and in the often-resulting publicity.

Ricardo makes another assumption that we have not covered in this chapter: **"There is free trade that involves no trade barriers or frictional transaction costs."** We will fully examine trade barriers in Chap. 6, and we will see how the basic Ricardian concepts allow us to model the various effects of tariffs, quotas, subsidies, and other barriers to trade.

Articles

Article 5.1. Trade Giants in Central New Jersey

Mary Etta Wills, *New Jersey Weekly News*

Every year, sometime in July, Central New Jersey is home to some of the greatest minds in international trade. The Trade Symposium, conducted by the Rutgers Business School at the Simon Estate in Hillsborough, NJ, is the perfect setting. The Simon mansion, once owned by the Simon Cat Food family, hidden away in some 300 acres of rolling woodlands and bubbling streams, is truly an idyllic setting typical of the bucolic charm of verdant New Jersey.

Professor Rhoda Oppenhauser, CEO of Globus, a Brooklyn-based think tank, launches the first salvo. "The PLC Hypothesis is powerful and intuitive, but I think that the time has come to re-examine its applicability today," she says, taking a delicate sip of her famous cranberry-OJ-grape juice cocktail. "It's just not fair. (a) We have to keep coming up with a stream of innovation. This means that our workers have to constantly go back to school, to constantly learn new software, and to push harder, while 'they' in Country B simply get handed all our goodies after they get standardized! I just have a problem with that!" She then takes a large defiant gulp of her tasty cocktail.

"It is not just that," intones Dr. Lewis Kermani of Kermani Consulting in Palm Springs, California. "We cannot afford the copyright and patent violation. It's just not a matter of domestic profits, you see. (b) If we cannot get protection from being ripped off before we even get to Stage III, then, hey, say goodbye to any more innovation and to new products!" He then reaches for the tempting chai tea from Rt. 206 Curry, a traditional favorite of the symposium.

Dr. Joe Sapone, director of global research for Chuck Barclay International, a global sporting goods mega-store, makes an astounding point. "I agree with Rhoda and Lewis. The PLC does need a second look. Is it still valid anymore? Look, the Chinese are now doing R&D in biotechnology! I was at Wuxi labs in Shanghai. (c) They are doing cutting-edge work just like the Big Pharma labs here in New Jersey. Shouldn't China be focusing just on manufacturing and other medium-skilled-intensive work? I am worried. I think I need some of Rhoda's cocktail now!"

We then run into the two trade giants, who, in typical fashion, were totally absorbed in the detailed comparison of the desserts at the buffet. Professor Fred Langdorfer was excitedly explaining to his friend and coauthor, the great Professor Pytor Murpheesboro of the Dublin School of Economics, "Now this one is amazing—the chef definitely has a huge comparative advantage in this mango-cardamom éclair," when we interrupted the gastronomic review for their comments. "Take the Kindle case, for example," offers Dr. Langdorfer, "the initial concept was developed by Amazon in the US, but the manufacturing was offshored from the outset! For the US, there really was no Stage I or II to begin with–the product was made overseas from beginning to end!" Amazon's Kindle had long been a subject of trade theory controversy. (d) "Yes, my concern is that the life cycles are just whipping by faster and faster," adds Dr. Murpheesboro. "Countries cannot expect to live off Stages I and II anymore for any long period of time."

We swing back to Dr. Rhonda Oppenhauser, who is making another very large pitcher of her famous cocktail "And one more concern that we should really address is the issue of pollution." Dr. Oppenhauser points out, (e) "Country B not only gets the standardized manufacturing jobs but also the pollution. Is this morally right? What are the ethics of this? Yes we are giving them the jobs, but these are jobs that come with a large price-tag to them as they come with the pollution!"

"Please don't attack me all at once!" pleads Dr. Kerman, as he reemerges from the buffet room. "You are going to make me question the validity of Ricardo's theorem itself. Yes, I said it, and no, I have not had too much of Rhonda's cocktail!"

"But how do you explain the fact that we have examples of free trade policies that are diametrically (f) opposite to the vaunted Hong Kong or the China miracle!

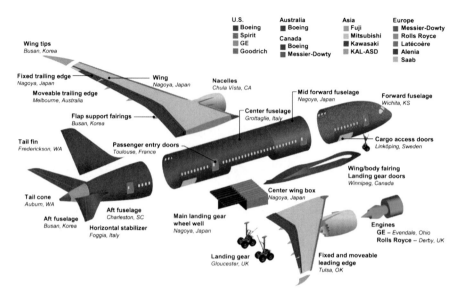

Fig. 5.3 Boeing 787 Dreamliner—a global affair (*Copyright © 2012 The Boeing Company*)

There are countries that have attempted the Ricardian 2-step model and fallen into ruin. No higher indifference curve, no greater consumption bundle—it just did not work! Now how do you explain that?" He then adds a scoop of green chutney to his samosas as a delicious, albeit spicy, afterthought.

Article 5.2. The Boeing 787 Dreamliner: A Global Affair

© **Farrokh Langdana, Peter Murphy**

Boeing's new flagship, the Dreamliner, with its highly efficient, composite-built, long-haul carrier, epitomizes intra-industry trade.[10] Figure 5.3 clearly illustrates the extent to which the aircraft is indeed a "global affair." Keep in mind that the figure only lists the major components and countries. Boeing contracted with over 50 suppliers, 28 of whom were outside the United States. In addition to foreign countries, Boeing has outsourced to 10 US companies including General Electric and Moog.

---

[10] Unlike many of the "news articles" in this text which are presented to illustrate broad and timeless themes, this case is drawn from a real-world example. As a footnote to the story, Scott Carson was replaced in August, a few months after he made the comments quoted here. The first 787 Dreamliner was delivered in September, 2011 after 4 years of production delays.

During development, Boeing ran into supply-chain challenges with its 787–8, due to production and design problems stemming from its suppliers which account (according to some estimates) for about 70 % of the 787–8's individual components. Foreign production may account for about 30 % of the value of the plane. This is far greater than the 5 % attributed to foreign production in the Boeing workhorse, the old 747.

Moving forward, the 787–9 will feature less outsourcing, as Boeing plans to reign in some of its suppliers and resort to more homegrown production to ensure better supply-chain and production control.

Scott Carson, who headed Boeing Commercial Airplanes as the delays mounted in 2009, told editors at *Aviation Week* that Boeing was determined to address its supply-chain challenges. "We fully recognize that we made some mistakes in that regard," Carson said. "On the 787–9, we are pulling more of the engineering back inside to try and alleviate some of the issues we've had on the 787–8."[11]

In early 2013, Boeing experienced serious problems with the 787's batteries and electrical systems, resulting in the grounding of the just-delivered fleet. Reports trace these issues to the hands-off approach that Boeing took with its many Tier-1 suppliers for this aircraft and the lack of visibility and control exercised by Boeing beyond the Tier-1 level. As early as 2011, Boeing's commercial aviation chief Jim Albaugh told a group of business students "We gave work to people that had never really done this kind of technology before, and then we didn't provide the oversight that was necessary."

Questions

(a) Is there any compatibility between Ricardo's CA-based trade theorem and global trade as described by the PLC?

(b) Boeing had supplier challenges for its 787–8, which resulted in a significant delay in delivery. Could the unreliability of some of its suppliers have been factored into the analysis? If so, how?

(c) Boeing actually outsourced not just its production but also aspects of high-end design and R&D to some other countries. Is this not a violation of trade theory?

(d) Even with its supply-chain issues, the 787–9 will still rely on significant outsourcing. What is the implication of this?

(e) Don't the battery and electrical system failures illustrate that global sourcing doesn't work and that producing everything internally in the home country is the way to go?

---

[11] Weber, Joseph, Sheryl Gay Stolberg, and Robert Pear. January 16, 2009. Boeing to Rein in Dreamliner Outsourcing, *Bloomberg BusinessWeek* http://www.businessweek.com/bwdaily/dnflash/content/jan2009/db20090116_971202.htm Accessed August 24, 2012

Hints and Solutions

Article 5.1

(a) She is right, but then a worker in Country B is probably *also* voicing similar complaints, such as how easy it was in the early days of manufacturing, but now he has had to go back to learn about some new computerized manufacturing process, and lately, the demand for higher quality control has him going back for even more training. Trade basically makes workers in *both* A and B shift into "fast-forward."

(b) Country A "lives" off its innovations. If the returns on these do not cover the massive R&D costs, then, quite simply, Country A will lose its ability to innovate, and all countries will consequently suffer. A similar argument was made at one time with regard to Indian pharmaceutical companies. India at one time protected the process by which a new drug was made, but not the actual final product. So if Indian pharmaceutical firms adopted a process even slightly different from their US or European competitors, to make the same US/European drug in India, then this was considered legal in India. But thanks to the Uruguay Round talks, this has now been changed—India has agreed to ensure that the final product will not be copied, irrespective of the process.

(c) As labor incomes and skills, increase with trade, we eventually will see greater intra-industry trade between countries. In this example, Dr. Sapone is referring to intra-industry trade in pharmaceutical R&D (also known as intra-service trade) between Wuxi and US pharmaceutical companies. There are an increasing number of partnerships in which Indian and Chinese pharmaceutical companies are doing joint work with their US counterparts on research pertaining to different aspects of the same final drug. China's entry into intra-service R&D should not be viewed as a threat but as an inevitable consequence of trade theory.

(d) The solution to this apparent condemnation of the PLC, in the case of Amazon, is that Amazon is not in the business of generating profits from the manufacture of the Kindle per se; rather, it is in the business of *selling more electronic books.* The Kindle (now reasonably priced thanks to the CA of offshore production) is *just a tool*—a stepping stone for Amazon as it pursues its real goal of exploiting its superior supply chain and selling more books to its Kindle readers.

To consider Amazon's case in the context of the HOT and SST, we can conceive of Amazon's abundant factor being the combination of its extensive consumer base, its technology, and its amazing supply chain. Selling books online utilizes this abundant factor intensively, and hence Amazon has a CA in selling books online. To "push" this CA even further, Amazon transitioned to electronic books, which makes the reading experience flexible and more convenient. To facilitate this goal, the Kindle was invented and produced essentially overseas. The goal was not to generate profits via sales of the tool (Kindle) but to stay focused on the main CA—to sell more "books."

With respect to the apparently ever-increasing speed at which products blaze through the early stages of the production life cycle, it is important, as in the Amazon example, to consider what, exactly, the real "product" is. What is the true source of the value provided by a company's offering? Very often, a company that might appear at first to simply offer products will turn out to be offering something more intangible. Apple, for example, is really selling innovation, design, trendiness, and communications even though its "products" are simply smart phones and computers assembled overseas, and it employs a vast and growing US workforce to do so.[12] Apple has sustained its position in the early stages of the production life cycle for innovation for several years.

(e) Again, this fits with trade theory. As countries reach higher indifference curves, and as their citizens' incomes increase, so do their consumers' demands for cleaner air and water. Citizens then demand fewer smokestack industries, preferring higher-skilled labor-intensive "cleaner" jobs. Other poorer countries where jobs and incomes are scarce will then welcome the smokestack manufacturing, and the cycle continues. Note that Dickensian England in the early stages of the Industrial Revolution as well as the Great Lakes region in the 1960s and 1970s were exceptionally polluted environments.

(f) It is very important to note that free trade, by itself, is not a panacea. It is not simply a magic bullet that will work on its own. Free trade *must* have a benevolent and constructive government that will allow the benefits of free trade to trickle down to the workers. Hong Kong and South Korea are classic examples. For instance, Hong Kong's per capita GDP, before it threw open its doors and launched a textbook two-step Ricardian trade policy, was about one-third that of Great Britain's. After trade took hold, Hong Kong's per capita GDP grew to almost half-again that of the United Kingdom![13] It is vital that there exists a government that puts appropriate institutions and infrastructure in place to enable the benefits of free trade to be realized and to allow free markets to be unleashed. If the government were to simply siphon off the increased revenues of free trade, or to regulate it to death, then we have no higher indifference curve and no transition to enjoy the gains from CA in the long run. In this case, we have nothing but a failed national experiment and richer government officials.

Lesotho presents a useful example here. This tiny, landlocked African nation was included in the United States' African Growth and Opportunities Act (AGOA), a tariff-preference program designed to help Africa achieve greater prosperity, in 2004. However, the country's poor business climate (ranked

---

[12] Apple's USA workforce increased from under 27,500 in 2008 to 47,000 in early 2012, according to the company. Source: Gaimes, Liz. March 12, 2012. Apple Claims Credit for 514,000 U.S. Jobs. http://allthingsd.com/20120302/apple-claims-credit-for-514000-u-s-jobs/. Accessed August 20, 2012

[13] Hong Kong's per capita GDP in 1980 was less than half that of the United Kingdom ($6,000 versus. $13,000 USD); by 2012, at $37,000 it exceeded the UK's $28,000 by more than 30 %. Source: Trading Economics. http://www.tradingeconomics.com/hong-kong/gdp-per-capita. Accessed October 12, 2012

138 out of 183 countries by the World Bank) and lack of economic freedom (ranked "repressed" with a score of 47.5 out of 100 by the WSJ/Heritage Foundation)[14] meant that the Asian apparel firms who set up shop to take advantage of the act generated few if any positive knock-on effects in the local economy. After 8 years, local supporting industries have failed to develop, and the country has failed to take full advantage of the benefits of trade.

Article 5.2

(a) Yes indeed there is. Stages I and II are quite simply phases that involve services such as R&D and pilot testing that employ high-skilled labor intensively. Stages III onward involve medium-to-low-skilled labor intensive industries, and involve countries that have an abundance of medium-to-low-skilled labor. So, yes, the PLC is really conventional trade theory that goes a step further in explaining the migration of a product from the innovating country to, eventually, the manufacturing country. It also highlights the necessity for constant innovation on the part of "Country A."

(b) If Boeing had information that indicated that some suppliers (countries) may have had supply-chain issues and were somewhat unreliable, it could have incorporated that information in the respective bLx/bLy ratios pertaining to those countries or companies. The analysis might have indicated that a certain country did not indeed possess a CA in that specific component.

It is essential to remember always that comparative advantage must take into account *all considerations* related to the production of a good or service. This includes intangible elements such as the business culture, management practices, and on a broader level, political risk, the rule of law, and transportation ease and cost.

In this instance, it appears that Boeing did not include all relevant factors in its analysis.

(c) Intra-service trade, in which several countries may be doing research on different aspects of the same product, is a form of intra-industry trade applicable to countries and industries operating in Stage I of the production life cycle. Our example of Wuxi pharmaceuticals of Shanghai undertaking part of the R&D for large biopharmaceutical firms in the USA fits this model.

(d) The implication is, quite simply, that trade, in spite of its complications and frustrations and supply-chain issues, still delivers superior outcomes compared to autarky.

---

[14] "Lesotho Country Report", *Global Finance*, accessed August 18, 2012. http://www.gfmag.com/gdp-data-country-reports/234-lesotho-gdp-country-report.html#axzz27PM3WuMx. See also Robyn Curnow. Lesotho plans for life without U.S. trade lifeline. CNN. http://edition.cnn.com/2011/BUSINESS/02/15/lesotho.textiles.aids.agoa/index.html. Accessed August 20, 2012

(e) The problems Boeing experienced with the batteries and electrical systems in early 2013 unfortunately conflated a workflow change with the decision to source components overseas, which while implemented simultaneously, are actually distinct issues.

Concurrent with Boeing's decision to outsource components, according to some sources, the company appears to have changed its internal design and engineering practices to place previously established control processes into the hands of its suppliers. It is not necessary to outsource or alter these controls in order to benefit from the comparative advantages held by overseas producers.

The public relations disaster that this event created for Boeing, and the assignment of blame to offshore production rather than the change in design and engineering processes, highlights the fragility of public support for open trade, even when it is intra-industry.

Chapter 6
Trade Barriers and Protectionism

Summary This chapter pulls the reader away from the nice, orderly world of Ricardian free trade and into the sordid, rough-and-tumble world of global trade distortions and trade wars. We here broaden our focus from a two-country world to view the effects of trade policies on a given country engaging in open trade with the rest of the world, with the "world price" of a given good driving the results. Tariffs are discussed in great theoretical detail, once again ensuring that the reader understands the fundamental theory behind the insidiousness of trade distortions. This is followed by explorations of quotas, hassle factors, and export subsidies, alternatively known as "strategic trade."

This discussion will enable us to thoughtfully consider any number of contemporary policy questions, such as:

(i) Should the USA and Eurozone use taxpayer funds to promote and develop their biotech, alternate fuel, and artificial intelligence sectors, and to develop other key "champion" industries?
(ii) Why have most attempts at strategic trade ended in disaster?
(iii) How and under what circumstances might strategic trade policies be successful?

We proceed to discuss "dumping" and global antidumping duties and the potential for trade wars to arise from such sanctions and counter-sanctions. Current examples abound with the EU, the USA, and India accusing China of dumping a whole host of goods and China making similar claims against the USA.

Outsourcing and offshoring are concisely defined and discussed in the context of Ricardian trade theory. Paul Samuelson's attack on free trade and offshoring is included here too. We discuss the concept of "immiserization," in which average costs fall as the home country makes a product ever more efficiently, but then as costs keep falling, the home country finds it unprofitable to produce this very good!

We conclude with three Articles that tie together the topics discussed in this Chapter with what we have learned in previous chapters, as we prepare to move beyond the world of trade theory and into the realm of global macroeconomics.

F. Langdana and P.T. Murphy, *International Trade and Global Macropolicy*,
Springer Texts in Business and Economics, DOI 10.1007/978-1-4614-1635-7_6,
© Springer Science+Business Media New York 2014

6.1   Tariffs

A **duty** is a fee, or tax, charged on imports or exports by the domestic government. A duty may be imposed on goods moving to or from a certain country or region, or on certain classes of merchandise, or some combination thereof.

A **tariff** is a duty on imports. The terms "tariff" and "duty" are used interchangeably in practice, although "duty" often carries a more neutral connotation, whereas a tariff is often understood as a policy response to various economic or political developments.

Today, the revenue generated from tariffs and duties in most countries represents a negligible (around 1 % in the USA[1]) portion of the central government's revenues; only a couple centuries ago, however, these revenues were one of the primary sources of government funding. In fact, the tariff system was among the top issues of debate within the US Congress from independence through 1913, when the 16th Amendment introduced the income tax, and for some time thereafter (Fig. 6.1).[2]

6.1.1   Tariffs: 3 Types

There are three basic types of tariffs:

(a) **Revenue Tariff**
    Designed solely or primarily for the purpose of yielding revenue for the government, revenue tariffs are generally across-the-board duties, whose rates may vary according to the revenue that officials feel they might squeeze from various categories of goods.

(b) **Punitive Tariff**
    A punitive tariff is imposed for political reasons. The USA may impose tariffs on a country's imports for violating human rights, going against US interests, etc.

(c) **Trade Tariff (Protective Tariff)**
    A trade, or protective, tariff is imposed to protect a domestic, comparatively disadvantaged industry from foreign competition. Today, with World Trade Organization (WTO) agreements generally banning unilateral imposition of such duties, most tariffs are initiated on grounds of retaliation for unfair trade practices by other countries (real or imagined).

---

[1] "Historical Tables, Budget of the U.S. Government, Fiscal Year 2010," U.S. Office of Management and Budget, 2009.

[2] Interestingly, once the tariff's importance as a revenue source was diminished, the government found itself less constrained in its use of tariffs as a political and economic weapon. When it depended on the revenues generated by the tariff, the government had to be somewhat careful not to unduly affect trade in an adverse way. Without this motivation, tariffs changed significantly in how they were thought of, and used. Magness, Phillip W. 2009, "From Tariffs to the Income Tax: Trade Protection and Revenue in the United States Tax System".

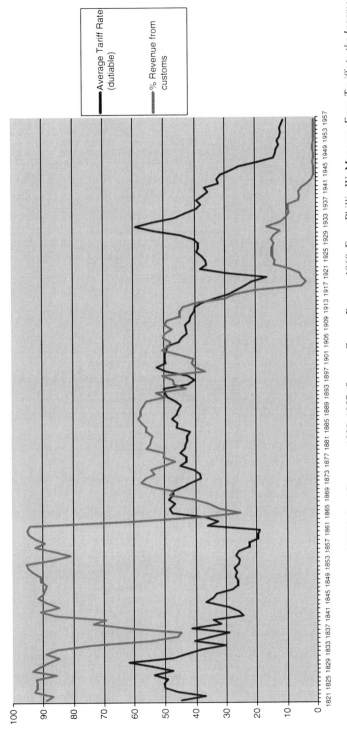

Fig. 6.1 Customs duties as a source of US Federal Revenue, 1820–1957 (Source: Census Bureau, 1960. From Phillip W. Magness, *From Tariffs to the Income Tax*, 2009)

Fig. 6.2 Supply and demand
for comparatively
disadvantaged good "X"
(textiles) in Country A

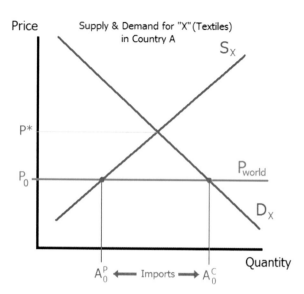

We will primarily be concerned with the latter two types of tariffs, as common practice and WTO rules have generally eliminated the tariff intended primarily as a source of revenue.[3]

6.1.2   Tariffs: How They Work

Country A is comparatively advantaged in good Y (heavy equipment) and disadvantaged in good X (textiles). Given this comparative disadvantage in X relative to the rest of the world, the domestic country cannot make X cheaper than the rest of the world (in which certain countries have a CA in X). Thus, the world price for textiles (P_{world}) is significantly lower than the domestic equilibrium price (P^*), so most textiles are imported (Fig. 6.2).

Country A produces textiles in the quantity shown at A^P_0, and thanks to trade its consumers can purchase at the world price[4] and so consume at A^C_0.

---

[3] See note 2, above. Revenue tariffs were once very important to most advanced countries; today, they are an unimportant component of revenues virtually everywhere.

[4] Unlike domestic supply and demand, a large world is assumed in which changes in quantity produced and consumed in the domestic country are not significant enough to affect the world equilibrium. This is the reason for the horizontal world supply curve.

Fig. 6.3 Country A has introduced a tariff on comparatively disadvantaged good "X" (textiles)

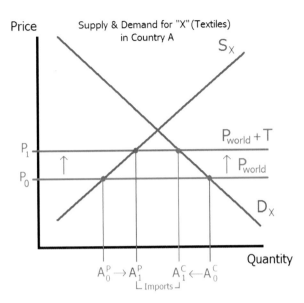

However, A's comparatively disadvantaged textile producers are a focused, well-funded lot and manage to lobby for a protective tariff on textiles. The domestic production and consumption situation has now changed (Fig. 6.3).

The Results:
Importers must now pay a tariff of **T** per unit imported, and so their price in the domestic market will be $P_{world} + T$. Domestic producers, maximizing their profits, now also charge at that level.

(a) Domestic consumers pay higher prices for good X (textiles), at P_1 versus P_0.
(b) Consumption is lower (at A^C_1 vs. A^C_0); domestic consumers have less textiles and less choice.
(c) The tariff has effectively transferred the consumer surplus (price savings which benefit consumers) from the country's *consumers* of textiles into the hands of its limited number of textile *producers*.
(d) The country loses efficiency and productivity as resources are shifted away from comparatively advantaged good Y (heavy equipment, in this example) and into production of the disadvantaged good X (textiles).

   (i) Workers must be retrained to the lower-skilled textile work.
   (ii) Fixed investment in good Y (heavy equipment) is wasted as production shrinks.

(e) The relatively few producers in the comparatively disadvantaged sector are the only winners, as they are selling more, at a higher price, thanks to the tariff. Their gains come at the expense of both A's consumers and the majority of its producers who are producing comparatively advantaged goods.

Fig. 6.4 Country A has implemented a prohibitive tariff on comparatively disadvantaged good "X" (textiles), eliminating imports entirely

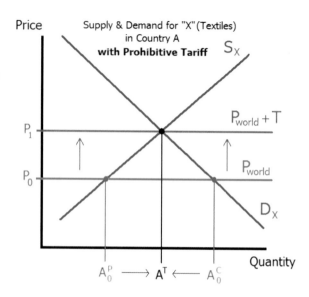

6.1.3   Tariffs: Prohibitive Tariff Eliminates Imports Entirely

We can also demonstrate that if a tariff is high enough, imports will be entirely eliminated (Fig. 6.4):

Here, the government's tariff has made imports prohibitively expensive, and all production for domestic needs will be done domestically.

Consumers are paying a significantly higher price and consuming significantly fewer units of good X (textiles). Producers are enjoying the free ride at their expense.

Note that while a high enough tariff can eliminate imports, any tariff which pushes the price *higher* than the domestic equilibrium price will *not* result in exports. While the tariff enriches domestic producers, it does so indirectly; the producers' gains come entirely at the expense of domestic consumers.

To artificially create an export market where none would otherwise exist, through a direct transfer from the government to producers, **export subsidies** are the protectionist measure of choice. We will discuss these subsidies later in this chapter in the context of strategic trade.

The tariff-related discussion so far has been based in a partial-equilibrium framework; we focused only on the amount and price of good X in Country A. Producers of X in Country A were definitely better off, but despite this fact, we indicated that the country as a whole would suffer. The effect on consumers is explicitly demonstrated in the partial-equilibrium diagram used so far. But what about the production and consumption of comparatively advantaged good Y (heavy equipment) in A? The implication is that the tariffs would artificially force resources away from Y to the tariff-protected good X. But how can this be

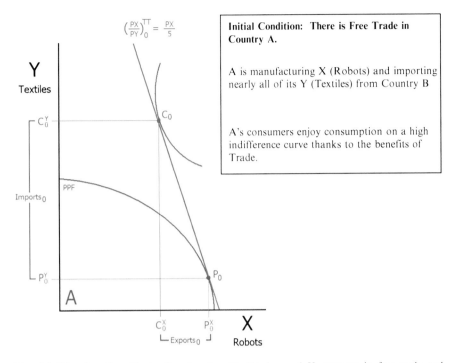

Fig. 6.5 Ricardian Free Trade. Country A, with CA in good X, engages in free trade and consumes on a high indifference curve

demonstrated? And what is the price for X that consumers in A pay, and at which A trades with Country B, before and after the tariff? To answer all these questions, we turn to a general-equilibrium diagram for tariffs.

6.1.4 Tariff Harms Domestic Consumers and Country Overall: General-Equilibrium Analysis

We can see the pernicious effect of a tariff using our Ricardian trade graph. Starting from an initial condition of free trade, we will proceed through four steps to examine how the implementation of a tariff harms the overall welfare of Country A.

By simply observing Fig. 6.5, we can infer that Country A has a CA in X since it is exporting $(P^X_0 - C^X_0)$ of X, and that it has a comparative disadvantage in Y, since $(C^Y_0 - P^Y_0)$ of Y is imported.

Let the global trading ratio $(PX/PY)^{TT}$ initially be $PX/5$, with a "world price" of Textiles of \$5.[5] Free trade with Country B takes place at this global trading ratio. As discussed in Chap. 4, both Countries A and B rise to higher indifference curves.

---

[5] We omit the minus sign ("−") from our trading ratio notations in this section for convenience. (The actual slope of the TT line is negative, as always).

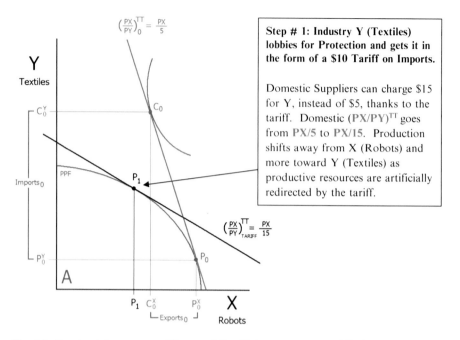

Fig. 6.6 Country A imposes a tariff on good Y, which creates a new tariff-driven trading price ratio for domestic producers

In Fig. 6.5, we see Country A largely specializing in the production of robots, its comparatively advantaged good, and consuming at consumption point C_0, which would be impossible without trade.

From this initial state, Country A's suppliers of comparatively disadvantaged good Y successfully lobby for a $10 tariff on imports of Y (Fig. 6.6). At this point we obtain a dual pricing system. Consumers in A now pay the higher tariffed price for imports of Y; they pay the **PX/15** price. However, it must be noted that the two countries *still trade* at **PX/5**. Country B still sells to Country A at "5" per unit of Y. It is the government of A that collects the tariff of $10 on the imports, which cost is passed on to the consumers of Country A by the firms that are importing and distributing good Y.

The duality of trading price ratios (one for producers, the original global TT of **PX/5**, and one for consumers, the new tariff-adjusted TT of **PX/15**) implies that we need to locate a final consumption point that lies on the global trading line **PX/5**, includes the new production point P_1, and is tangent to **PX/15**; the tangency simply means that consumers in A must finally pay the tariffed price, **PX/15**. In Fig. 6.7, we redraw the global TT line to pass through production point P_1.

In Fig. 6.8, C_1 is clearly not the final consumption point. Yes, it does indeed lie on the global trading price line, but at C_1, consumers in A would be "paying" **PX/5**. That is not correct; they will instead be paying the tariff-adjusted price of **PX/15**, denoted in the figure as $(\mathbf{PX/PY})^{TT}{}_{\mathbf{TARIFF}}$.

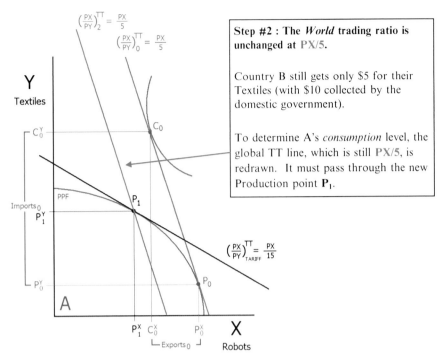

Fig. 6.7 We shift the global TT line to intersect with the tariff-driven TT line at the new production point, as we seek to locate the final consumption point

The final point of consumption, C_{FINAL}, must be tangent to **PX/15** and lie on the global trading line that includes the final point of production (Fig. 6.9).

In Fig. 6.9 we can see the *devastating* results of the tariff:

(a) X (the robot industry in which the country has CA) has been savaged:

    (i)   Production is roughly half its former total (P_1 vs. P_0).

    (ii) Exports, formerly very strong, are now negligible (**Exports$_0$** vs. **Exports$_{\text{FINAL}}$**). The fact that C_{FINAL} and P_1 are clustered closer together implies an overall decrease in trade—the volume of both imports and exports falls. In general, the further apart we find the final consumption and production points, the greater the level of trade, and vice versa.

(b) Consumption of *both* X and Y is significantly lower than before the tariff, due to inefficient allocation of resources (C_0 vs. C_{FINAL} in both "X" textiles and "Y" robots).

(c) The entire country consumes on a much lower indifference curve. Everyone is worse off.

(d) Everyone, that is, except for the producers of Y (textiles), whose production has increased threefold (see P_1 vs. P_0).

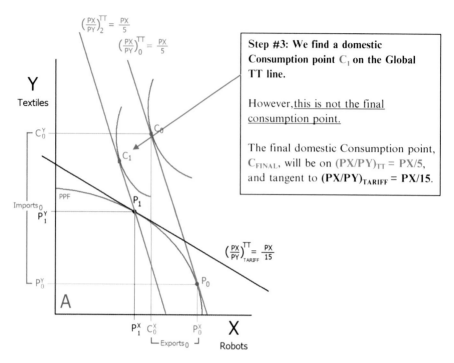

Fig. 6.8 Locating the point of tangency of the indifference curve with the new global TT line. We see that consumption begins to fall with the tariff in place. The final consumption point will lie between C_1 and P_1

Second-order effects are also severe:

(e) High-skilled workers in the robot industry must retrain to learn low-skilled and lower-paying activities like sewing garments and operating weaving looms.

(f) From a macroeconomic perspective, the lower imports of Y (textiles) means less domestic money being held overseas, and available to come back in the form of purchases of exports of X (robots). The robot export market has been structurally damaged.

(g) Foreign competitors in textiles whose product is now $15 in the domestic market will now increase the quality and features offered in their $5 price ($10 of the $15 is captured by the domestic government) and will innovate new manufacturing efficiencies. Ultimately, foreign competitors in textiles will dominate domestic producers in quality, cost, features, etc., with domestic producers falling hopelessly behind.

(h) Unlike human workers, the excess robots produced by (and formerly operating in) the robot factories cannot be retrained to work on textiles. Many will be scrapped, others simply abandoned to walk the earth, dejected and disaffected, eventually to join together to seek revenge on their creators who abandoned

> **Step #4: We find the final domestic Consumption point, C_{FINAL}.**
>
> We do this by bringing in the indifference curve on which C_1 lies, and pushing out
> the **Tariff TT** line, until they meet at a point on the **Global TT** line. This "meeting
> in the middle" is visualized in the inset at top right.

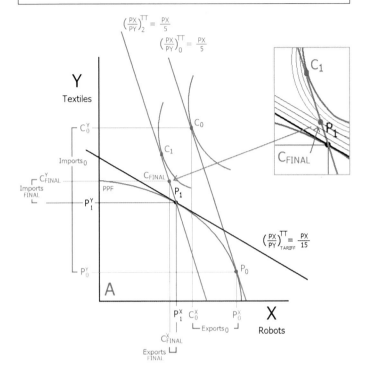

Fig. 6.9 Final result of tariff on Country A as a whole: Consumption is reduced and the CA
industry has been harmed

them, initiating the final conflict between man and machine. All because of a
textile tariff![6]

Tariffs have fallen out of favor as their negative effects have by now become
generally recognized by economists and policymakers alike. Tariffs, however, are
not the only trade barriers in the policy arsenal of protectionist-minded officials.

---

[6] The last few pages of discussion have been fairly technical; we want to make sure that our reader
is still alert! Levity aside, increases in tariffs—and protectionism generally—are in fact historically associated with periods of heightened international tension and conflict.

6.2   NTBs: Quotas and Hassle Factors

Since the 1980s, a succession of global "round table" talks has managed to significantly reduce global tariffs. However, tariffs are not the only weapon in the protectionists' arsenal. The trade distortions that replaced the highly visible tariffs were significantly more insidious and difficult to detect. These "nontariff barriers" (**NTBs**), which have increasingly replaced tariffs, are now the world's predominant form of trade distortion. NTBs come in various shapes and sizes.

The predominant forms of NTBs are:

(a) **Quotas—quantitative restrictions on imports**

Country A may limit the quantity of good Y that it permits into the country. This is generally accomplished through the issuance of import licenses through auction or to favored firms. Quotas were mostly eliminated by 2005 through the WTO. We examine quotas and their effects in detail below.

(b) **Hassle factors—unofficial barriers to imports**

Hassle factors can be part of the landscape, or deliberately imposed as a workaround by a country that wants to restrict imports. These include:

(i) Endogenous hassle factors

- Poor infrastructure (roads, utilities services, etc.)
- Weak institutions (weak enforcement of contracts, poor security, etc.)
- Cultural challenges (time taken to process documents, holidays, differences in protocol, etc.)

(ii) Exogenous hassle factors

- Slow processing at ports—100 % inspection, work slowdowns, etc.
- Artificial (or bogus) standards designed to frustrate importers
- Lengthy certification proceedings
- "Doing business" costs—bribes, kickbacks, co-investment requirements, etc.

Hassle factors can take as many forms as a creative bureaucracy can imagine and are difficult to prove and to combat. Hassle factors effectively impose costs that, when quantified, can be analyzed in much the same way as a tariff, the difference being that the extra costs flow to various parties rather than directly to the domestic revenue office.

We now turn to Quotas, a form of import barrier with even more pernicious effects than Tariffs.

6.2.1   Quotas: Worse Than Tariffs

A quota is a government-imposed limit on the *quantity* of imports. The effects of a quota can appear on the surface to be similar to those of a tariff from the perspective

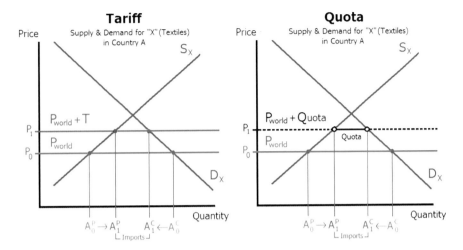

Fig. 6.10 Tariff versus quota

of a domestic producer or consumer, but the mechanism is quite different, as are the effects overall.

The quota artificially limits the quantity of imports as shown in Fig. 6.10. Because fewer goods are available than would be demanded under free trade, both importers[7] and domestic producers are able to charge a higher price than they otherwise would.

In both cases, we see that:

(a) The tariff and quota have both pushed the price that domestic consumers must pay higher, to P_1. For the quota, the domestic price will move up to the point where demand exceeds supply by only the quantity permitted by the quota, as shown in the figure.
(b) Domestic consumption is reduced from A^C_0 to A^C_1.
(c) Domestic producers have increased their production from A^P_0 to A^P_1.

So far, we see very similar effects from the tariff and quota.

The difference between tariffs and quotas manifests itself most significantly when demand increases for good X. In Fig. 6.11, domestic demand for good X (textiles) has shifted from D^0_X to D^1_X.

We see differences emerge once demand has been increased:

(a) Under a **tariff** regime, the increased demand will be met by increased imports. Consumption can increase from A^C_1 to A^C_2 with no increase in price.

---

[7] Importers will not capture the price difference, however, as quota rights will become valuable and will ultimately be traded at a price that equals the difference between the world price and what can be charged in the domestic market.

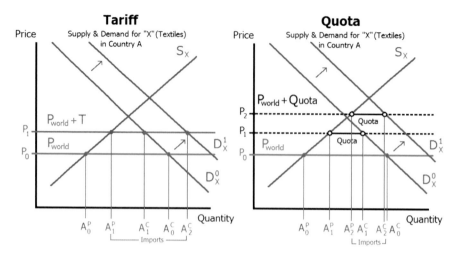

Fig. 6.11 Tariff versus quota, with increase in demand

(b) With the **quota** regime, however, the increased demand cannot be accommodated
by increased imports. The price is driven much higher, to P_2, as the limitation on
the quantity of imports allows domestic producers to command higher prices.
Consumption is significantly less than what would prevail under the tariff.

We can see that consumers are far worse off under a quota than a tariff. Prices are
much higher and consumption is much lower; consumers have less choice. Quotas
also tend to encourage the formation of monopolies, oligopolies, and collusion
among those firms controlling the licenses. These reasons are precisely why quotas
were banned under the WTO in 2005. Under the WTO rules, countries that already
have quotas in place are given a period of time in which to totally dismantle them—
during this period, the countries can indeed replace the existing quotas with tariffs,
which are the lesser of two evils when it comes to ways to lessen the adjustment
shock on protected domestic industries.

Of course, having no trade barriers at all would always be optimum, as
consumers could obtain all they wanted at the world price!

6.2.2 Tariffs and Quotas: Harmful Effects

Under tariffs or quotas, several effects ensue that reduce the overall welfare of the
country:

(a) Consumers are worse off:

  (i)   Consumers pay higher prices.
  (ii) Consumption is reduced.
  (iii) Consumers have less choice.

(b) Inefficient production of the comparatively disadvantaged goods diverts resources to unproductive works:

(i) Inefficient investment wastes both capital and labor.

(ii) The comparatively advantaged sector, which by definition employs the majority of the country's factors of production, suffers as resources are diverted away.

(c) Foreign competitors leap ahead of the domestic producers:

(i) Importers (foreign companies exporting to the domestic market), facing a higher end price for their products in the domestic market, introduce improvements in order to attract sales:

- New features, such as more options in electronic gadgets.
- Quality improvements, such as better fuel efficiency in automobiles.

(ii) These foreign importers engage in greater innovation, leading to new manufacturing efficiencies, which, in turn, result in a lowering of their costs, further allowing them to increase features and improve quality.

(iii) "Protected" domestic suppliers still lose in the long run:

- This is partly due to lost sales because of the superior quality of imports
- Domestic technology and efficiency lag as importers sprint ahead. The perfect example of the above two points is the US auto-industry's response to Japanese imports in the 1970s–1980s.

(d) Inevitably, tariffs and quotas invite retaliation from trading partners, which harm the country's exporting sectors. These sectors, by definition, are those that employ the country's abundant factor, thereby resulting in severe macroeconomic devastation in the event of a trade war.

The classic example of a trade war that essentially shut down global trade for the whole planet was the Smoot-Hawley tariff of 1933, enacted by the Unites States as protection mainly from European imports. Over 20,000 imported goods were tariffed, with an average tariff rate of 53 %! The Europeans struck back with the result that both parties went into a tailspin. While trade represented just about 5 % of US GDP at that time, the Smoot-Hawley tariff was nevertheless a contributing factor to the Great Depression and its effects on a global scale.

(e) Trade barriers may have other self-defeating effects. The "Buy American" provision of the 2009 stimulus legislation in the USA limited foreign content in government projects; this type of policy can leave overseas suppliers, for example, China's Xianghua Steel, with a sudden surplus, which they must sell somewhere—the only market now available being the private market, which will be flooded with cheap imports.

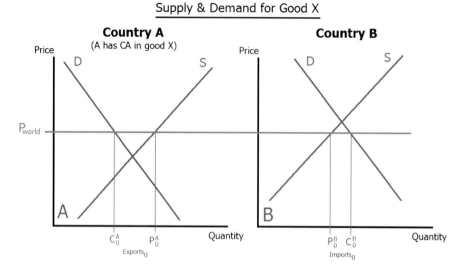

Fig. 6.12 Country A is exporting good X in a world with many countries. Country B is an importer of X

6.3 Strategic Trade: Export Subsidies and CVDs

Can a country *artificially* create CA in industries that are considered "key" by championing these sectors in order to propel the entire country forward for several years? If so, how can this be accomplished? Welcome to the enticing, controversial, and contentious world of strategic trade.

We are given two trading partners, Countries A and B, where A has a CA in good X, in a large world with many countries (Fig. 6.12):

Country A is exporting X, and Country B, whose equilibrium price is above the world price, is importing part of its domestic consumption. Clearly, Country B does not have a CA in X as its autarky price is higher than the world price as well as the price of X in A.

Country A determines to promote exports of X which it identifies as a "champion" industry, by providing a subsidy of $S for each unit exported. Country A's strategy is to grab significant market share of product X and be the world leader not just in product X (usually a product considered to be "cutting edge," e.g., semiconductors, nanotechnology, biotechnology, artificial intelligence) but to also dominate the many spin-off products and technologies that X may generate.

If Country A Is the *Only* Exporter of X

Country A's producers will export to the world at P_{world} and pocket the subsidy (Fig. 6.13).[8] And, since Country A's producers obtain $P_{world} + S$ for every unit

---

[8] In this example, Country A is exporting to multiple countries including B; it charges one price, P_{world}.

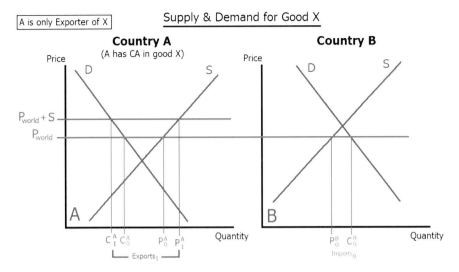

Fig. 6.13 Country A is the only exporter of good X in a world with many countries. A subsidizes exports of X

exported (the + **S** is coming from the government), they will charge this price, $P_{world} + S$, to those few domestic customers willing to pay it.

The results are clearly harmful for Country A overall:

(a) A's domestic consumers are harmed by the higher price.
(b) A's domestic consumption is reduced.
(c) A's government transfers \$S to producers of X for each unit exported. The source of this \$S is ultimately Country A's taxpaying consumers.
(d) Country A's overall productivity is reduced from its inefficient use of resources as the X sector will attract greater investment than would be warranted without the subsidy.

Strategic trade policies may be more likely to be undertaken in a world where Country A is one of many exporters of good X. Country A here seeks to widen its comparative advantage and rise to the top among countries competing for the world market (Fig. 6.14).

If Country A Is *One among Many* Exporters of X

If Country A is successful in fostering growth in targeted industry X, its supply curve will shift, over time, to the right, reflecting new investment by entrepreneurs, an increase in education resources focused on X, an increase in the number of college graduates interested in careers in X, and ultimately new production techniques arising from these activities.[9] This is reflected in the shift from **S** to S_1

---

[9] The conditional "if" here is critical. The notion of fostering innovation through central planning is something of a contradiction and has met with mixed results in practice. We discuss some of the challenges later in this chapter.

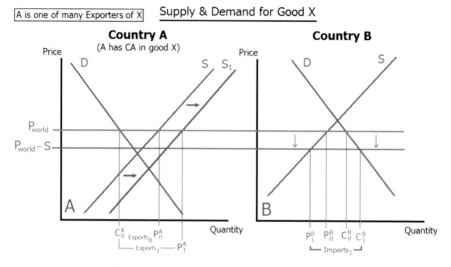

Fig. 6.14 Strategic Trade implemented by Country A, one of many exporters of good X in a world with many countries. A subsidizes exports of X

and the resulting increase in production from P^A_0 to P^A_1. Exports will increase by the amount of additional production, from **Exports$_0$** to **Exports$_1$**.

Country A's domestic suppliers will charge P_{world} − S for exports, and with the +S subsidy included will still obtain P_{world} (between the price charged to their customers and the subsidy they receive from the government) for all their exports. Country A's producers of X will continue to charge P_{world} in the domestic market, because there is no reason for them to accept less than the total amount that they can obtain for exports.

Results:

(a) Country B's consumers benefit with lower prices and more consumption.
(b) Country A's government is effectively transferring $S from its taxpaying consumers to Country B's consumers.
(c) Country A's consumers end up paying a higher price than Country B's.
(d) There is deadweight loss from the inefficiency created by the subsidy:

    (i) Country A's producers of X ramp up production beyond what would be appropriate without the subsidy; resources are diverted from productive works toward the subsidized industry.
    (ii) Country B's producers of X are adversely affected; resources are diverted away from X.

(e) Perhaps most important, Country B will very likely retaliate with **countervailing duties (CVDs)**.

We depict the effect of the CVD in Fig. 6.15, below. Country B's producers of X, unhappy with their loss of business to competition from Country A, will lobby B's government to impose a countervailing duty (CVD) in response to A's subsidy.

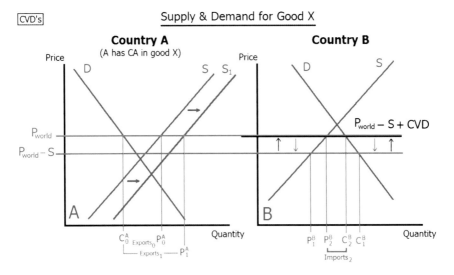

Fig. 6.15 Country B imposes countervailing duty

In our example, Country B sets its countervailing duty equal to A's subsidy (**CVD = S**). The results exacerbate the harm to the overall welfare of both countries done by Country A's original tariff:

(a) The quantity of Country A's exports will decrease back to what they were before the subsidy or CVD. A's producers are back to square one.
(b) Country B's domestic price will increase back to P_{world}, and consumption of X in B will decrease.
(c) Effectively, B's government has captured A's subsidy. A is now transferring $S from its own taxpayers to B's government.

6.3.1 Strategic Trade: Why Export Subsidies Don't Work

While politically and intuitively appealing, in practice, strategic trade has been a limited success at best, or outright failure at worst. Some examples are Japan's attempts to be a biotech giant in the 1990s, and before that to corner the movie industry; Singapore's attempts to be an IT hub in the early 2000s; the Concorde; the Space Shuttle; and 2008 US presidential candidate Hilary Clinton's proposal (quickly shot down) to use strategic trade to create CA in nanotechnology or artificial intelligence (AI).

Some reasons for the general failure of strategic trade (export subsidies) in the long run are:

(a) Many countries choose the same "champion" industry, thereby cancelling out their individual policies.

(b) Governments have repeatedly proven themselves unable to pick winners.
(c) Export subsidies in "A" trigger protectionist response in "B" (dumping claims, a topic to which we turn shortly, tariffs, etc.).

In general, experience largely supports the notion that innovation-inducing CA is determined endogenously—that is, independently, "within" the market. New products and technologies that have hopes of being "winners" must be identified and funded by the smart money, by risk-takers putting up their own capital (including venture capitalists). The government does not often excel in the role of driving innovation by creating CA, identifying champion sectors, or funding them with taxpayer's money.[10]

This does not mean that there can be no role for government in nurturing innovation. On the contrary, government may often be the most effective means through which to fund research at the fundamental level. The smart money (venture capital) only kicks in toward the end of the R&D process when competing technologies are poised to enter the market. The government's role (with NSF grants, for example) here is to fund the cash-starved early research upon which future innovation is based—in the labs in major universities, in think tanks—where the research is mostly theoretical and fundamental, and where the applications of this new technology have not even begun to emerge.

6.3.2 Strategic Trade: Dumping

Export subsidies are not the only form of strategic trade. "Dumping" occurs when producers in one country export a product to another country at a price that is either (1) below the cost of production or (2) below the price that is charged domestically.

1. **Cost-Based Dumping**
   Cost-based dumping occurs when Country A sells good X in Country B below the cost of production in A. This is often seen in industries that benefit from various forms of domestic subsidies.
   Given industry X in Country A, that is subsidized with government support in one form or another (a general subsidy, guaranteed loans, etc., not necessarily an

---

[10] Strategic Trade has been the subject of many studies, the preponderance of which has largely backed up the Ricardian case presented here. A review may be found in Slaughter MJ (2004) Infant industry protection and trade liberalization in developing countries. Nathan Associates, Arlington, pp 5–9. See also Smith A (1996) Strategic policy in the European car market. In: Krugman P, Smith A (eds) Empirical studies of strategic trade policy. University of Chicago Press, Chicago, pp 67–83, http://www.nber.org/chapters/c8676.pdf. For a contrary view, China expert Michael Pettis argues that the USA's extraordinary growth in the nineteenth century was to a surprising degree enabled by industrial policy including the protection of infant industries. Pettis M (2013) A brief history of the Chinese growth model. Michael Pettis' China Financial Markets. http://www.mpettis.com/2013/02/21/a-brief-history-of-the-chinese-growth-model/. Accessed 5 May 2013.

Fig. 6.16 Producers in Country A are induced to increase output of X by a subsidy of one form or another

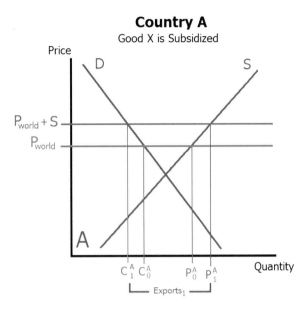

Country A
Good X is Subsidized

export subsidy), the subsidy will encourage extra production that exceeds A's domestic demand (Fig. 6.16).

In want of ready customers for this extra production, the surplus quantity created by the subsidy may be "dumped" overseas into Country B at prices that would be impossible without the subsidy.

Country B's producers then find themselves unable to compete against the subsidized imports.

Typical examples of cost-based dumping are found in agriculture. Artificial price floors in many mature economies result in an excess supply of produce. Given the huge storage costs in agriculture—especially in refrigeration—countries often find it profitable to simply unload (dump) this subsidy-induced excess supply onto emerging countries at throwaway prices. This, of course, would antagonize producers of agriculture in the dumped-upon countries.

2. **Price-Based Dumping**
   Dumping claims may also be made when there is no subsidy. Price-based dumping implies that Country A's firms are deliberately selling at a predatory price in Country B, below that which is charged in the A home market, in order to drive out local competition and monopolize. Most trade wars typically stem from one form or another of alleged price-based dumping. In fact, the unmodified term "dumping" implies price-based dumping.

   In Fig. 6.17, Country A is selling to B at the world price P_{world}, which is significantly below Country B's domestic equilibrium price P^*.

   Even though Country A is simply a comparatively advantaged producer of X, from B's perspective, such a low price should be impossible. This is a common problem with accusations of price-based dumping.

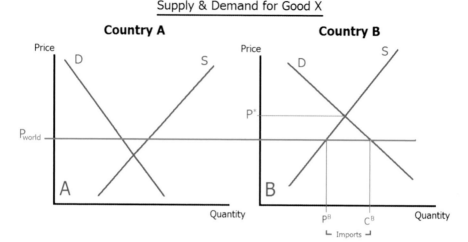

Fig. 6.17 Country A's comparative advantage in good X is interpreted as "dumping" by Country B, whose equilibrium price is significantly higher than the world price

6.4   "Dumping" Is Rarely Straightforward in Practice and Is Difficult to Prove

There are several reasons for this difficulty.

- *Identification Problem*: As seen from the example above, simple CA is often mistaken for "dumping" by the importing country.
- At times, the product in question may not be sold at home (in A), thereby making it impossible to get the reference price in the exporter's home market in order to prove price-based dumping.
- It is often very difficult to objectively disaggregate the actual costs of production in cases of "cost-based dumping."

For these reasons, as well as the often less-than-eager cooperation by the target country in providing supporting data and documentation, it is exceedingly difficult to successfully substantiate a dumping claim before the WTO.

6.4.1   Strategic Trade: Bringing a Dumping Case to the WTO

Under WTO rules, Country B may be entitled to impose a countervailing duty if it can prove (a) dumping and (b) injury to domestic industry. Without proving that the competing domestic industry in B was hurt or "injured" by the artificially low prices due to foreign dumping, there can be no CVD.

The Process:

1. Country B files the case with the WTO.
2. Country A has 30 days to respond.
   [*Usually there is a resolution of some kind in this interval.*]
3. Six months later, duties may be imposed by Country B if its case is successful.

The WTO requires a plaintiff in a dumping case to prove two things:

(a) Country B must demonstrate cost-based dumping or price-based dumping:

   (i) Country A is selling good X into Country B at a price that is below its cost of production.
   (ii) Country A is selling good X into Country B at a price that is less than the price it charges domestic consumers in A.

(b) B's producers of good X *must prove injury* to B's market for X.

   These requirements make it very hard to prove dumping.

6.4.2 Strategic Trade: US Antidumping Regulations

A brief summary of certain well-known US antidumping regulations follows:

Super 201 (Section 201 of the Trade Act of 1974, Similar to GATT Article XIX)
   Import duties or NTBs may be imposed on imports from countries that are accused of dumping. The USA publishes a list of countries that it thinks are dumping and will threaten trading partners suspected of dumping to raise their price or be added to the list. After 30 days, if no response is forthcoming, a tariff (or other penalties such as CVDs) may be imposed.

Super 301 (Section 301 of the Trade Act of 1974)
   This provides fairly open-ended powers to the president "to obtain the removal of any act, policy, or practice of a foreign government that violates an international trade agreement or is unjustified, unreasonable, or discriminatory, and that burdens or restricts U.S. commerce."
   The powers here are broader than those in Section 201 but may run afoul of WTO or other international rules if fully exercised. As such, the vast majority of actions are limited to retaliatory duties.

Special 301
   Part of Section 301, "Special 301," relates to intellectual property violations. A list of intellectual property violators is published, and if no satisfactory response is forthcoming from the named violators, retaliatory tariffs may be imposed.
   Generally, following the unleashing of Section 201 and 301 legislation, the imposition of CVDs would be the next step if no satisfactory adjustment was made by the offending country. It should be noted that all the above regulations have been a huge bone of contention within the global trading community.

The sentiment is that with the WTO supposedly safeguarding global trading laws, the USA should not be allowed to unilaterally exercise its own set of trading regulations.

Byrd Amendment

The Byrd Amendment, instituted by Congress in 2000, provided that the company that files the antidumping action accrues all the revenues from the CVD. This act had the perverse effect of unleashing an unprecedented number of appeals from US companies for antidumping duties for obvious reasons. Consequently, the Byrd Amendment was finally repealed in 2007.

Clearly, while strategic trade policies have their attractions to policymakers and, in some cases, producers, it is in practice a complicated matter that rarely achieves the hoped-for results.

6.5 Definitions: Outsourcing $\neq$ Offshoring $\neq$ Inshoring

Discussions of trade among government officials, economists, and the general public are often muddied by the misuse of certain key terms. In particular, "outsourcing" is often mistakenly used interchangeably with "offshoring," and vice versa. A clear understanding of the correct definitions is important for an informed discussion of trade policy. We offer the following definitions, with some explication of each term.

6.5.1 Outsourcing

The term "outsourcing" means, simply, contracting a formerly internal business process to an external company. Outsourcing does not *necessarily* imply an international component. Outsourcing can be as simple as eliminating an in-house landscaping crew and hiring a local firm to maintain the grounds.

6.5.2 Offshoring

Offshoring refers to moving a business process from the domestic country to another country. Offshoring does not *require* that the process be contracted to or purchased from another firm. A company might open its own call center in Bangladesh to provide customer service, or it might open its own assembly factory in a low-wage country; these activities would be examples of offshoring but *not* outsourcing, since the activities are still performed "in-house" (within the company itself).

Offshoring by taking manufacturing production overseas really draws the most attention from critics of free trade, whether it is accompanied by outsourcing or not. Perversely, this heightened attention will often lead firms to outsource when they offshore their production, contracting with overseas firms where they can hide behind an arm's-length relationship, rather than controlling their own factories, where they would have more control over working conditions but would face heightened scrutiny due to their name being on the building.

6.5.2.1 Examples

A US company that contracts with a management company to oversee its properties, rather than using its own employees, is **outsourcing**.

A US company that closes its US factory and builds *its own plant* in China is **offshoring**. (It is *not* "outsourcing," since the process remains within the company itself.)

A US company that closes its US factory and purchases *from an outside supplier* in China is *both* **offshoring** *and* **outsourcing**.

6.5.2.2 In Practice

Generally, in the context of international trade, discussions of offshoring and outsourcing will involve trade in services at "arm's length" (over long distance) that does not require geographical proximity between buyer and seller. These are referred to as Mode 1 Services by the WTO and are conducted primarily, but not entirely, by electronic medium over the internet, phone, fax, etc.

6.5.2.3 Criticism

The practices of **outsourcing** and **offshoring** are often pointed at by critics as being responsible for a declining standard of living for US workers, as the workers are forced to compete with impossibly low overseas wages.

Such criticism ignores the fact that the displaced workers will, by definition, be from comparatively disadvantaged industries. We know that these are the industries which employ the country's scarce factor(s); those industries that employ the country's abundant factor(s) will indeed benefit from trade.

6.5.3 Inshoring

Outsourcing and offshoring are part of the natural process of free trade, and they work both ways. *Inshoring* is a term used to describe, variously:

- A multinational company's movement of an overseas business process back to the domestic geography.
- From the domestic country's perspective, the opening of foreign-owned plants within the domestic geography.

Thus, Country A's offshoring is Country B's inshoring, and vice versa.[11]

We have to this point focused largely on explaining trade theory and demonstrating the clear advantages of free trade, in theory and practice. Before we conclude the international trade section of this book, we will engage with two of the most powerful critiques put forward against free trade, each brought forth by giants in the field of macroeconomics.

6.6   Immiserization

In the 1950s, economists Jagdish Bhagwati and Harry Johnson separately theorized that productivity gains may become so large as to cause a fall in the terms of trade line, resulting in consumption on a lower indifference curve and thus reduced overall welfare.

If Country A has a comparative advantage in X, and A keeps increasing productivity in X, then the price of X will keep falling as A's efficiency increases. At a certain point, **A's comparative advantage in X becomes *counterproductive*** as the price becomes so low that Country A is impoverishing itself through its relentless productivity gains.

In Fig. 6.18, we see the PPF for the comparatively advantaged good X expanding enormously to the right due to nonstop productivity gains. This results in higher production overall, with production shifting from P_1 to P_2.

Contrary to our expectations, however, we see that consumption actually *declines*, from C_1 to C_2. All of the extra production of X, and more, is being exported, at relatively lower and lower prices, so that at home, Country A is consuming less of both good X and good Y than it was before.

This would appear to be a devastating blow to our idea that free trade provides benefits to both trading countries and increases overall welfare.

The resolution to this apparent conundrum is that countries rarely remain in the same area of the production life cycle long enough for this to happen. The product X would be offshored by Country A long before the theoretical point P_2 were reached—the arrival of Stage III would long preclude the immiserization described by Professors Bhagwati and Johnson.

For Country A, as the labor force becomes more skilled and better educated over time, and as basic manufacturing gives way to industries requiring medium-skilled and ultimately high-skilled labor, a services economy begins to develop, eventually leading to an economy specializing in knowledge-intensive products and in R&D.

In Fig. 6.19, we illustrate the progression of countries through the PLC over time.

---

[11] "Insourcing" is often used synonymously with "inshoring" in the literature, though we would hold that the terms have different meanings; "insourcing" involves bringing a formerly external process in-house, regardless of the geography. Usage of the terms "inshoring" and "insourcing" varies depending on the author and context.

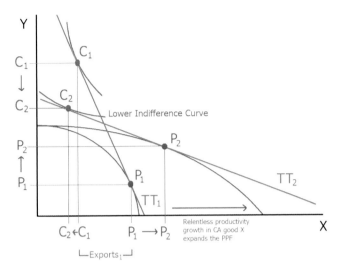

Fig. 6.18 Immiserization

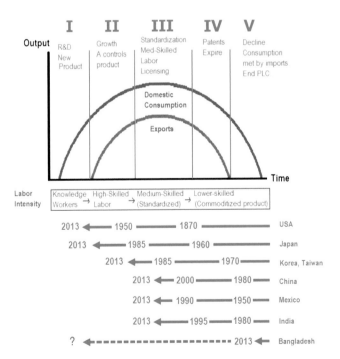

Fig. 6.19 Progression of countries through the PLC over time (dates are very approximate)

The immiserization effect has not been seen in practice as originally theorized and is more of academic than practical interest.

Free trade is not out of the woods yet, however, for we must yet address one more criticism, from another economic titan.

6.7   Samuelson's Savage Attack on Free Trade

In 2004, Nobel prize-winning economist Paul Samuelson published a potentially devastating attack on the traditional understanding of free trade and its benefits.[12] Samuelson's thesis: Over time, gains in productivity B can leave Country A in the dust, worse off, and with no comparative advantage, while Country B shoots ahead in productivity and consumption.

Paul Samuelson (1915–2009), teaching at MIT in 1950. Time & Life Pictures/Getty Images

Dr. Samuelson's scenario plays out in two Acts:

Act I

We open our scenario with free trade between Countries A (CA in services) and B (CA in apparel), with both countries benefitting (Fig. 6.20).

---

[12] Samuelson Paul (2004) Where Ricardo and Mill rebut and confirm arguments of mainstream economists supporting globalization. J Econ Perspectives 18(3):135–146.

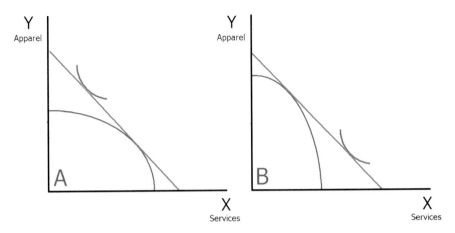

Fig. 6.20 Free trade between Country A (CA in X, services) and Country B (CA in Y, apparel)

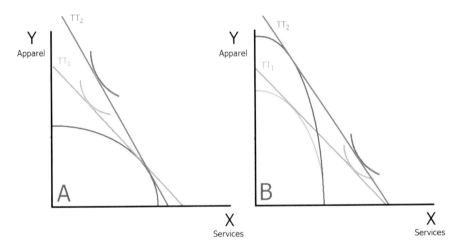

Fig. 6.21 Country B increases its productivity in Y (apparel)

From this initial setting, Country B increases productivity in its comparatively advantaged good (apparel), and both countries benefit with higher terms of trade and indifference curves, as we see in Fig. 6.21.

So far, so good!

As we close the curtain on Act I, however, all is not as it may appear on the surface. Country B's apparel workers have been quietly but steadily improving the education of the next generation, and have saved and invested their gains from trade wisely. A new era in Country B is about to begin...

Act II

We open Act II as Country B *explodes in productivity in X (services)*, which was A's comparative advantage. With the advent of the internet, B suddenly

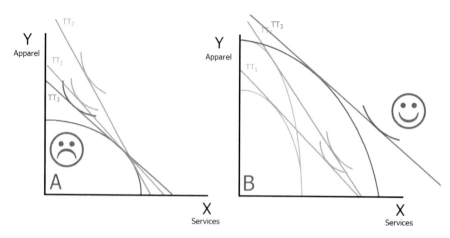

Fig. 6.22 Samuelson's attack: Contrary to Ricardo, trade has apparently created a clear winner (Country B) and a clear loser (Country A)!

unleashes its newly educated labor force and storms into world trade with a CA now in X! Now suddenly, we see in Fig. 6.22 that the terms of trade line **TT₃** offers no benefits of Trade to A.

As a result, Country A loses all former gains, and its standard of living (represented by its indifference curve) is lower than before! Meanwhile, Country B is on a permanently higher indifference curve. B wins, A loses—contradicting Ricardo's win-win proposition.

6.7.1 Refuting Samuelson's Attack

Samuelson's critique was hotly discussed in the months following its publication. Its force was backed up by real-world observation of what appeared to be a flood of services work, in call centers, software development, and back-office functions moving to India and other low-cost countries.

The thesis falls short, however, for several reasons, which became clear upon reflection:

(a) Samuelson's hypothesis was based on simplistic observations of services for-merly performed in-country which had migrated overseas, such as phone centers and back-office work. In Samuelson's model, X (services) was not originally traded. Since X originally was a non-traded good, it should not be depicted on either axis. Thanks to the internet, X suddenly went from being a non-traded good to a traded good! Being a non-traded good initially, there was formerly no (aLx/aLy) <> (bLx/bLy) trading relationship between A and B. The model is for this reason flawed.

(b) The technological innovation (in this case, in communications technologies) that enabled trade in X (by bringing formerly infinite transportation costs to near zero) will also open opportunities for trade in many other goods, X_1, X_2, $X_3 \ldots X_N$, in which A will no doubt have comparative advantage in several.

(c) Even if Country B did manage to obtain a PPF identical in every way to A, the countries would then benefit from specialization and intra-industry trade! Real-world evidence of this intra-industry trade may be found, for example, in R&D between the Indian, Chinese, and US pharmaceutical sectors.

We thus conclude Part 1 of this text having safely parried the near-fatal attacks of immiserization and Dr. Samuelson.

In Part 2, we will take our mastery of international trade theory with us as we explore global macroeconomics, covering such topics as currencies, exchange rates, and inflation, and build a model that will permit us to analyze any number of policy decisions.

We will not proceed, however, without putting our now extensive trade knowledge to good use, in the three article exercises that follow.

Articles

The articles in this chapter incorporate all the knowledge we have gained from Chap. 6 as well as all preceding chapters. Article 6.3, in particular, is designed to challenge you to duel a "common-sense" trade skeptic in a battle of ideas! Hold nothing back here— "click on" the passages indicated by (a), (b), etc., and bring your knowledge, insight, and wherever possible, graphs!

Article 6.1. NanoRX: Is Ricardo Dead?

© **Farrokh Langdana, Rutgers Business School**
Once again, relate the italicized paragraphs to material from the previous chapters. Sprinkle liberally with diagrams whenever possible.

It is 2025. The five physicians of Team Zeta are morosely sipping their very tall lattes in the café of the corporate headquarters of NanoRx, the high-flying nano-medical giant based in Bridgewater, NJ. 3 years ago, their product, NanoRx, was introduced; it took the world by storm and propelled the home Country A to 3 great years of developing and marketing related spin-offs.

(a) *Several years earlier, then-Senators Clifton and Omaha had pushed a bill for state subsidies and federal tax waivers for research in nano-therapy, but when the WSJ launched a campaign to kill that motion, many thought that it spelled the end of the nano-therapy breakout. However, the developers of NanoRx triumphed without state subsidies. Most of the world's "Country B"s (in Asia and South America) became their hunting ground, and they "ruled" the nano-generation.*

(b) *In fact, many in Asia and Europe claimed that Country A was involved in dumping nano-product and were contemplating hitting A with antidumping duties. Country A insisted that it was not dumping—and that the critics really needed to understand trade theory before they bring forward allegations of "dumping."*

Simply, for all those who have missed our earlier reporting, NanoRx tastes like a lemony cough syrup, but it is a lot more than that. Upon swallowing just a spoonful, billions of high-tech Nano"Doctor" microcomputer molecules, each about 100 times as powerful as your vintage laptop from 2015, flow through the digestive tract, rapidly enter the bloodstream, and digitally transmit data to an RX responder (this looks like a very small cell phone—small, silver, metallic). Originally, the data were sent by the responder to medical stations where highly skilled NanoDoctors analyzed the information and beamed back to the patient (usually within 24 h) the state of his/her heart, spleen, kidneys, blood pressure, cholesterol, etc.

While this technology put many regular family doctors out of business, it spawned a new breed of digitally savvy and nano-friendly physicians. A new generation of doctors, comprised of two subgroups, was born: (i) "technology" doctors to handle nano-solvable tasks such as physicals, routine illnesses, ulcers, wounds, etc., and (ii) those that were very specialized (brain surgeons, oncologists, etc.). The era of the generalist family doctor was basically gone.

(c) *Initially, Country A made the first-generation responders, but then over time, they were made under license to Country B. After 2 years, they were totally made in B and were being made even faster and cheaper and better than A could hope to ever make them. In fact, NanoRX and its new competitors in A, DoctorIT and GeekDoctors, all became the superstars of Country A, thanks to their expertise and to the fact that costs for patients in A plunged due to B's ongoing advances in responder manufacture and technology. It was a marriage made in heaven: A's brains in development and innovation and B's ability to produce amazingly efficient responders at unbelievably low prices. Medical costs plunged in A for 2 straight years and happiness reigned in both A and B along with great routine medical care.*

And then came the fateful day when the NanoDoctors in Team Zeta were found disconsolately sipping lattes. Their countenances were most somber. The mood was definitely bleak. Here is their story:

(d) *A small, yet very brainy outfit in Santa Barbara, DoctorSoft, wrote a freeware platform that took the NanoDoctors out of the story. This new software, DoctorSoft5 could be used to analyze data sent from any of the responders used by A's nano-medical companies. Patients could get their results now within hours instead of overnight. All it took was someone with a nursing/pharmacy/biology background to eyeball the results and look for any idiosyncratic discrepancies in the data. The big shocker was that pharmacists in B could do the job! Costs for NanoRx plunged and its stock soared to the heavens. But it had to let go hundreds of its NanoDoctors.*

And then another shocker—scientists in B started doing research in nanotechnoloy for NanoRx! The NanoRx scientists in Bridgewater, NJ, were working in conjunction with the scientists in B on a new generation "cough syrup." (e) *"It is just a matter of time, before we stop doing R&D here!" said one of the NJ scientists. "This is not what Ricardo predicted!"* **Comment in detail— sprinkle with diagrams if you can**.

President Lou Mobbs: "Well, stop looking for an answer from Langdana and all his trade students. They are all in the Lou Mobbs Penitentiary for free traders, reading that stupid book, *The Choice,* to each other and watching some dumb Jimmy Stewart movie![13] (f) *When the workers in B can take away the jobs of our doctors, hey, something is wrong. We have a comparative advantage in knowledge-intensive stuff, and they have a comparative advantage in medium-skilled manufacturing. So something is just not right with what we are seeing now! Our doctors and druggists should not be displaced. Ricardo was basically designed for an age when the world was manufacturing based. Clearly he is "dead" in a complicated, internet-driven nano-world."*

Article 6.2. Trade Wars, Fine Wine, and Amazing Cheese

Eugenie Draper, *Loire Valley Trade Dispatch*, **France**

The 23rd Global "Protect the Workers" conference, conducted in Tours in France's fabled Loire Valley, broke all records for attendance. Over 125 countries were represented along with trade representatives from 52 different industries. It was an emotionally charged affair, and for good reason. If your industry does indeed suffer from comparative disadvantage, and if you then superimpose a macroeconomic recession on this dismal fact, voilà! you have some serious problems! In fact, it is times such as these that make free traders cringe and shudder involuntarily, for this is when critics of free trade blame all economic ills not on the macroeconomic recession but simply on the "evils" of trade.

The conference began well—the mousse de canard was fabulous, and the St. Maure, a small creamy log of cheese with a straw running through it, was simply exquisite. But then the fireworks began. Here are some choice excerpts brought to you from castle country, France:

(a) "Tariffs are the only answer," insisted Jacob Lee of Evian Metal Systems, a steel mill in Eastern France. "Tariffs will make the steel imports more expen-sive, and consumers will then switch to our steel. Keep in mind, people will not

---

[13] We refer the reader to our earlier Footnote 20 in Chap. 3.

object. They can buy cheaper domestic steel and we can still save our steel jobs. It is a win–win!"

(b) "And furthermore," exclaims Kissan Balkya, CEO of the Australian giant, Vankaner Leather Goods, "I have studied economics and I know that the workers who ask for and obtain tariff protection are indeed better off! So let me ask the most important question—what if MOST of the workers in the country can be better off with tariffs? Huh? Then the WHOLE country will be better off!" he exclaims jubilantly. The rest of his speech is drowned out by the frenetic applause of the conference attendees. Jayathi Moorty, the trade representative of Mango Bed Sheets, a California company, screams in delight, then promptly faints and has to be carried out. The CEO of Fun Toys for Cats and Other Small Animals, Lewis San Andreas, of Hillsborough, New Jersey, gets so emotional that he bursts into tears and embraces the total stranger standing next to him.

(c) Professor Columbo Sternum then takes the stage. "As you all know, I teach and do research in some of the most prestigious universities in America. I have a solution—but be warned, this is technical and only for those with a real powerful grasp of economics. We first must identify the abundant factors in each of our respective countries. We need to make these workers better off. So we protect them from competition by imposing a significant tariff on imports that dare to compete with their products. Tariffs will indeed make them better off, and their wages will indeed rise sharply. I know I must be modest, but I tell you—this is nothing short of brilliant!" The crowd gasps and then cheers wildly. Some even call for Columbo to run for president.

(d) Finally, Juanita Cavallo, the CFO of Viva Jeans from Toledo, Spain, adds, "In fact, there are studies out there that actually show you exactly how many jobs have been saved by specific tariffs. In the apparel industry, for example, tariffs in Europe saved 132,000 jobs at least! How can you argue with numbers like that?" The crowd cheers. Some call for Juanita to run for president.

(e) Bill Mackfish, boss of the welders guild of Ireland, The Knights of Steel Fire, points out, "And the worst part is that many foreign countries clearly help their export sectors—come one, we all know that they get tax breaks, and subsidized power and water. They are selling here at much lower prices than they sell to their own people! Once we can prove this, we can get some price adjustment with another tariff. The sooner we do this, the better! Too bad the Byrd Amendment is gone."

(f) "If you know your history, you guys would not be in such a hurry to slap-on tariffs", cautions Maryietta Wills, the owner of Wills Cottages in Scotland's Sherrydoah Valley. "You need to think of what the other countries will do!"

We notice that the sparkling Vouvray is about to run out and quickly ensure that our glasses are replenished. All conferences must be held in France—Oh, the joys of comparative advantage in desserts and cheese!

Article 6.3. Dewey Lobbs Is the Anti-Ricardo

Al Porcellow, *New Jersey Pharmaceutical Trade Watch*

It's official. Dewey Lobbs, media tycoon extraordinaire, is officially the anti-Ricardo. Dewey seems to bask in his notorious title and is, in fact, on a cross-country rampage, hurling vitriolic anti-trade rhetoric at anyone and everyone in his path. Here are some juicy morsels from the standing-room-only rally for the marginalized masses, in Somerville, New Jersey.

About 10 min into his rant, Dewey launches into, "(a) I just went back to my hometown and it's not the same—my hometown classmates are 'dead in the water!' How can you tell me trade is good?"

And then here is one that is not heard too often. "Listen, I know that trade is driven by productivity—but I can show you (b) many countries where the workers are more productive than ours. But I do not see production rushing there! See! I have proven Ricardo wrong! I am indeed the anti-Ricardo!" The crown roars its approval—women and men rush the podium trying to touch Dewey, but his thugs (er, associates) push them back.

"I have studied economics, I have really read all their fancy theories," says Dewey, pausing for effect, "and I know about something called (c) comparative disadvantage. If you are in it, brothers and sisters, then you are doomed! So I tell you, if our whole country is in comparative disadvantage, we will ALL go down! Is THIS what trade is supposed to do?" The crowd howls. Some women faint.

"And one more thing," he adds ominously, (d) "why should we trade with countries like Hibernia, and Bawanga and Zumbingo when they have NO regard for the environment! Can you tell me?!" Dewey's associates now move him to the rear of the stage, as the crowd goes berserk. Anish Puri eyes the back door nervously—he is in charge of Dewey's security, and he wants an escape hatch open for his Godlike boss. ...

Dewey then adopts a softer tone. He is a master of elocution, a giant at managing emotions. "My brothers and sisters, I read all the economists' ideas. I am very smart, and I know how they think. They say that we will make and consume more of 'both' goods. (e) But pray, where will the resources for this come from? I wonder? Those goofy ivory-tower pundits have no idea of the real world! We have fuel shortages now so where will these resources magically come from?" The crowd screams, approaching a state of delirium. Anish frantically signals the rest of his thugs (er, associates) to form the "wagon chain," which means that beefy men in suits will surround Dewey and move him out if necessary.

"My brothers," intones Dewy, seemingly oblivious to the tension in his associates, "the other day I spoke to a man who came to me with tears in his eyes. His name was Perniman K. Tottering. He told me that he was middle-aged, and (f) so how on earth was he to retrain himself to move into any of the industries with comparative advantage? He asked me, 'Mr. Lobbs, what the heck am I supposed to do?' My brothers, I cried myself to sleep that night, I was so upset."

"I have studied Ricardo, and I can tell you, brothers and sisters, that he has made some really funky assumptions—just a handful of these assumptions are enough to warrant that his theories are all wrong! For example, brothers, did you know that he assumed that both the countries must have different factor endowments for his model to work—(g) but if they have similar factor endowments, then trade confers no benefits! Well there you go! He also assumed perfect competition, no transportation costs, similar technology in both countries, only two goods, and two inputs, and so on! How crazy is that? And besides, (h) what is the point of trading when those foreigners just copy everything we make—we have the brains, they just copy it. I am tired of this!"

"If I were to become your president, I would pledge (i) to save manufacturing jobs in this great country of ours! Manufacturing is what made this country great, and I plan to restore our former greatness!"

Dewey then approaches the front of the stage. "Look, let me talk some common sense. I am a plain-speaking guy—not like those fancy professors."

In the audience, I run into Dr. Pytor Murpheesboro, who has been watching all this in shocked silence. I ask him about Dewey. He says, "I can't compete with Dewey. He is formidable! The man makes no sense, but the crowd loves him— heck, he looks like a genial cardiologist. In fact, he looks like someone's favorite uncle. With that kind of TV image, what can a rumpled professor do?" he sighs.

Dewey powers on, (j) "If an American buys a car produced in the United States, both the car and the money stay in the United States. If an American buys a car produced in Japan, then the car comes to America, but the money goes to Japan. Clearly, the first case is better for America because Americans get both the car and the money!"

The crowd is now too close to the stage. Dewey's "associates" gather close for the "wagon chain." Big beefy men will soon form a wall of suits around their leader. But Dewey is oblivious. "Finally, I want to talk about protectionism. Again, keep in mind that I am a plain-talking man. I believe in common sense and not fancy theories. (k) Protection of the US textile and apparel industry results in tens of thousands more jobs in that sector than would be the case with no protection. Clearly, this is a case in which protection is justified because it works; Americans are better off!"

Anish Puri blows three shrill blasts on his little steel whistle, and the "wagon chain" of beefy men in suits walls in Dewey and then shuffles him off the stage. The crowd roars with delight at this choreographed mastery of motion, reminiscent of the Roman legions. More women faint, some weep openly. The anti-Ricardo is whisked away to attack Ricardians at some other venue. Night falls on the battlefield.

Hints and Solutions

Article 6.1

(a) Since the domestic country managed to be a leader in nano-therapy even without the benefits of policies that resemble some form of strategic trade, one can conclude that the domestic country does indeed have a CA in nano-therapy. A true CA in any product or service is best left alone—it does not need strategic trade impetus which will only end up muddying the waters.

(b) Antidumping duties can only be imposed if A is dumping in B and if this dumping causes injury to B's nano-industry. The main challenge in proving dumping is that Country A may simply have a gigantic CA in nanotechnology and may be selling this technology in both A and B at low prices simply based on this fact.

(c) Here we see the classic benefits of trade between Country A, operating in Stage I of the PLC, and Country B, operating in Stage III. Each specializes and achieves consumption on a higher indifference curve than would be possible without this mutually beneficial trade.

(d) The freeware resulted in the technology becoming standardized and thus making highly skilled NanoDoctors redundant. This is similar to the way that master-craftsmen were affected by automated manufacturing techniques throughout the twentieth century.

(e) At this stage, we should see "intra-R&D" trade. Both A and B can and will do research on different aspects of new nanotechnology, similar to the Boeing case, but now in R&D. Already scientists in China and India are working with their counterparts in the USA and Europe in key areas such as pharmaceuticals, genetic engineering, alternate fuel, and biotechnology.

(f) In this "complicated" world, most of the trade will not be inter-industry trade between two countries, one with a CA in R&D and the other in manufacturing, but most trade will be intra-industry trade in components, service, and research between two countries whose labor forces will be growing more similar with time. If anyone needs to be incarcerated, it should be Lou Mobbs.

Article 6.2

(a) Wrong. Tariffs make both imports of good Y as well as domestically produced good Y more expensive.

(b) Wrong. Tariffs make only the scare factor better off. If the workers were the abundant factor, then they would not need tariffs but would simply do better with unfettered free trade that would unleash their CA.

(c) This is similar to (b). Wrong again. Free trade coupled with SST would sharply boost the wages of the abundant factor here. Tariffs would simply distort this country's CA.

(d) This is a common argument. In a partial-equilibrium diagram of tariffs, this would certainly appear to be the case—but Juanita is missing the all-important abundant factor here. Her workers in the apparel industry are the scarce factor, the few who will indeed be "saved" by trade distortions at the expense of the many in the comparatively advantaged industries.

(e) Bill Mackfish is clearly discussing price-based dumping. Please note that countervailing duties can be imposed only when the "injury" to domestic competing production can be attributed to dumping. The notorious Byrd Amendment ensured that the revenues obtained from the countervailing duties went back to the company/industry that had petitioned for protection! This rule resulted in a ridiculous increase in antidumping petitions in the USA, for obvious reason. The Byrd Amendment made a global mockery of the professed free trade stance of the USA.

(f) Mary Etta Wills is referring to trade wars that include countervailing tariffs, quotas, and embargoes. Both imports as well as exports of all countries sink dramatically and quickly when such trade wars erupt.

Article 6.3

(a) As the economy grows, it will increasingly transition out of older, labor-intensive industries into more advanced manufacturing and services. Factors, such as medium-skilled labor, which were once abundant, become scarce as abundance is now to be found among high-skilled laborers, professionals, and knowledge workers. Without this movement, the country would never advance—who in a newly developed economy really wants their children working in the same garment factory that they worked in?

The benefits of trade flow to those who adapt and continue to build their skills along with the country overall. The main beneficiaries are the next generation, whose education from a young age will reflect the country's advancement and who will be trained and ready to enter these new industries.

Trade provides guarantees to no one, but what it does give is a *choice*. Without trade, there is only stasis, with one generation after another consigned to the same work and the same standards of living.

And Dewey, while those who remained in your home town have struggled, look at all the people who did get out and have entered careers in industries that you could never have imagined when you were growing up! Heck, look at you!

(b) Comparative advantage is heavily influenced by the country's political stability, infrastructure, institutions, and long-term macroeconomic environment. As discussed, our "aLx/aLy" ratio is an *effective* ratio, which incorporates all of these underlying conditions.

Many countries may display high productivity if strictly viewed in the context of a given manufacturing plant—but these other considerations impact the country's effective deployments of this productivity. It requires an economically benevolent government to provide the right ecosystem for the benefits of trade to flow.

(c) Logically, if *most* of our Country (A) is in the Y sector, then Y is intensive in A's abundant factor, and by definition, A is comparatively advantaged in Y. Y will not be harmed with trade; in fact, it will benefit, as A will be an <u>exporter</u> of Y!

(d) Regard for the environment has its own indifference curve, which correlates with the wealth of a country. In poorer countries, concerns of obtaining today's food and shelter naturally outweigh the desire for green spaces and environmental protection. Countries go through life cycles of manufacturing—the best way to get B to regard its environment is to encourage trade which will result in:

- More efficient allocation of B's resources (less waste)
- Manufacturing for export to developed markets which involve higher standards
- Ever-higher indifference curves by B's consumers, which will *endogenously* lead to demand for tighter environmental standards in B

The wealthier a country is, the more its citizens insist on environmentally friendly practices and the more they will effect these both voluntarily and through their legislatures.

This explains why today, residents of the Eastern Seaboard in China, where the trade-related growth since 1979 has been primarily located, are clamoring for more blue skies and cleaner water, while those in the highly unemployed West and the Northeast would be quite happy to get the smoke-stack jobs that would put food on their table. Keep in mind that Dickensian England at the height of the Industrial Revolution and the Great Lakes region of the USA in the 1950s and 1960s were highly polluted environments.

(e) If our concern is to make the best use of our resources, then trade is the most effective way to achieve this!

- Free trade allows *innovators* to concentrate on their comparative advantage, which is innovation! This is where breakthroughs are made, such as those that enabled the "green revolution" in agriculture. Innovations like this particularly benefit the USA.
- Free trade enables greater specialization, which allows the *most efficient* use to be made of the world's resources. More efficient deployment of resources equates to less resources wasted.
- Free trade also ensures that new efficiencies, new technologies, and new resources developed anywhere are propagated rapidly around the world due to the pressures of competition.

(f) Changing patterns of trade do not spring up all of the sudden—in fact, they develop over many years:

1. No industry dies overnight; it can be seen coming a long way away from the perspective of anyone from the shipping workers to the CEOs. Everyone has the choice to adapt or not. Those who adapt will find opportunities in new, more advanced industries.
2. Many workers will adapt and enter new industries. Some will prosper, others will not.

3. The most benefits accrue to the children, for whom a world of new opportunities open up which would not have been there without trade.

(g) *Intra-industry trade* benefits both A and B even if they are identically endowed. Through intra-industry trade, countries are free to specialize in specific areas within their comparatively advantaged industries and so achieve greater economies of scale and efficiency than could be the case under autarky. An end-product assembled through intra-industry trade will incorporate these efficiencies. (Refer to Fig. 3.25.)

- But A and B have the same technology!

Intra-industry trade benefits both A and B even if they are identically endowed.

- Ricardo postulated perfect competition. But in the real world there's no such thing!

Imperfect competition leads to a smaller number of larger companies, which have economies of scale. Mature countries with similar endowments will engage in intra-industry trade, making great use of these scale economies.

And the reality is that A and B do not have similar technology—but when you incorporate differences in technology and the accompanying labor productivity, we obtain the product life cycle hypothesis (more on this below)! The bottom line here is that relaxing Ricardo's stringent assumptions actually makes the free trade case more realistic and more resilient.

(h) This seems so, but consider how far we in A have advanced, thanks to the continual development of our industries! This simply would not happen if the market for our innovators and producers was bound by our borders.

And consider the situation from the perspective of workers in B:

- Those in B would be surprised by our complaint. They are running faster and faster as well, as manufacturing becomes automated and more complex, and more demanding of higher-skilled workers.
- Quality, safety, and environmental requirements are introduced in B, simply to service A's import market, which were never even imagined before.
- There is generally a progression over time of countries from low-skilled labor to high-skilled labor, and an increasing capital factor intensity as well, as countries benefit from trade and their labor force, education levels, and fixed capital base move up the ladder. This process is every bit as painful and disruptive to extant arrangements as it is for the more developed countries undergoing the same process.

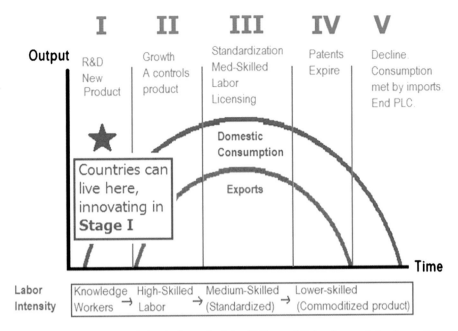

Fig. 6.23 Countries may thrive in Stage I of the PLC, specializing in creativity, innovation, advanced design, and the creation of valuable intellectual property

(i) The PLC (production life cycle) demonstrates how *innovation itself* is a form of "product," which both A and B may engage in—each developing different elements of the same product, or each innovating for different industries (see Fig. 6.23).[14]

(j) This is an intuitive notion, but we just need to follow the money to see what really happens to it:

- Consumers in Country A will pay more for a domestically produced good Y because of trade restrictions.
- The (by definition, scarce) resources which are used in the relatively inefficient production of good Y represent an opportunity cost lost by Country A.

  Say Country A is an advanced economy, intense in capital and high-skilled labor factors. Let's say we go ahead anyway and produce a (scarce) low-skilled labor-intensive good Y in Country A.

---

[14] For a contrary view, see Gary P. Pisano and Willy C. Shih, (2012). *Producing Prosperity: Why America Needs a Manufacturing Renaissance* (Boston: Harvard Business Review Press). The authors suggest that design and production cannot be so easily separated from one another. "You can create a CAD design but you need to understand what a production process can and can't do."

Since $aLy > aLx$, the inputs diverted to production of Y result in a disproportionate loss of production in X.

- Aggregate production and consumption of X in Country A suffers, as a result—overall welfare in A is harmed.
- Foreigners do not simply sit on piles of our currency—they are as interested as we are in earning a return on their holdings.

As will be explained soon in Part 2 of this book, domestic money used to purchase foreign goods

(i)   Creates demand for domestically produced export goods
(ii) Creates a supply of loanable funds ("SLF") for foreign direct investment in the domestic economy
(iii) Creates SLF for foreign purchases of sovereign debt

... and eventually returns tthe home country (the only country where it can actually be used) through one of these channels.

(k) Empirical studies have demonstrated that each job "saved" has a net cost to the country of hundreds of thousands of dollars.

The result of protection is a misallocation of resources to the comparatively disadvantaged sectors employing scarce factors and away from the comparatively advantaged, abundant-factor-intense sectors.

Consumers lose in the form of higher prices. The country overall loses in misallocated resources. These losses outweigh the gains to the few producers. Typically, producers in comparatively *disadvantaged* industries push for protection. This minority benefits from trade barriers erected in their industry at the expense of everyone else. They do suffer the effects of trade barriers in other industries, which for workers may overwhelm any benefits seen from protection.

Ultimately, importers facing a higher end price for their products in the domestic market due to tariffs or quotas will innovate new features, quality improvements, and manufacturing efficiencies, offering a superior product for the same price. "Protected" domestic manufacturers still lose sales and fall behind in technology. (An example is the US and Japanese automakers in the 1970s–1980s.)

And, do many workers really aspire to work in a *textile factory* in the USA today? US manufacturing has moved beyond low-level manual labor and into much more challenging, advanced, and rewarding industries as it has progressed through the industry life cycle.

Part II
Global Macroeconomics Policy Demystified

In Part 1 of this book, we established the basic Ricardian trade model, and applied microeconomic principles (supply and demand, production frontiers, indifference curves, etc.) to delve ever deeper into the model's policy implications. We now move into the area of global macroeconomics. Here, instead of sector-specific analyses (the pharmaceutical sector in Country A vs. the call centers in Country B, for example), the analysis is now economy-wide.

In Part 2, we deal with employment at a national level and across all industries, rather than comparing specific sectors with and without comparative advantage. We begin in chapters 7 through 9 by establishing our basic analytical framework of the global macroeconomy. We look at production to include all goods and services in National Output (GDP)—including exports and imports, as well as non-traded items. Up to this point, we have viewed exchanges in terms of their "real" or opportunity cost. Now we incorporate money, exchange rates (both real and nominal), and inflation in our modeling. We examine the role of central banks and explore the driving forces behind, and the impact of, the movement of capital across borders.

In this section, the fundamental driving model—the **ISLM-BOP**—is developed. This model is an absolutely essential tool for analyzing and understanding the relationship of the moving parts in the global macroeconomy, as well as the implications and likely outcomes of fiscal and monetary policies and global exogenous shocks.

We proceed in Chaps. 10 through 13 to build increasing complexity into the model, adding more depth to our analysis of exports and imports, and incorporating inflation and imperfectly mobile capital. We deploy our model to analyze phenomena such as currency crises, speculative asset price bubbles, fiscal budget sustainability, reserve currencies, and foreign exchange sterilization.

As we proceed into the later chapters, we are able to examine several historical and contemporary real-world trade and macroeconomic events using the tools that we have developed. We discuss, for example, the Southeast Asian crisis of 1997–1998, the US Housing Bubble, the Euro, the "Great Moderation," and the US–China currency and trade tensions of the early twenty-first century. We conclude by looking back thousands of years to the invention of money and the development of fiat currency, as we explore a topic that has gained attention in recent years: the gold standard.

Chapter 7
Global Macroeconomics

Summary In this chapter, we provide an overview of global macroeconomic policy, including the NSI (National Savings Identity), the supply and demand for loanable funds, and the global flow of funds. We examine the relationship between the fiscal budget deficit and the trade deficit, and find these "twin deficits" to be inseparably linked.

We analyze the China–US "marriage" in trade and global capital and how this relationship has become vital to both parties. "Why should we trade with China when they artificially maintain such a huge trade surplus with us?" ask our trade skeptics. The answer is patiently explained as through the NSI we make our first connections between trade theory and global macroeconomics.

7.1 The National Savings Identity (NSI)

Much as one might compute one's household budget by showing all family sources of income on one side of an equation, and the broad categories of the uses of that income on the other side, the **National Savings Identity (NSI)** connects the sources of national output (GDP) with the uses to which that output is directed[1]:

$$\textbf{Output(real GDP)} \ = \ \textbf{Disposition of the Output(real GDP)}$$

We can break the equation into its components:

---

[1] A thorough treatment of the subject may be found in Farrokh Langdana, *Macroeconomic Policy: Demystifying Monetary and Fiscal Policy.* New York: Springer Press, 2nd Edition, 2009, Chaps. 2, 3, and 4, from which much of the material in this section is based.

F. Langdana and P.T. Murphy, *International Trade and Global Macropolicy,*   119
Springer Texts in Business and Economics, DOI 10.1007/978-1-4614-1635-7_7,
© Springer Science+Business Media New York 2014

7.1.1 Output

The total value of a country's output is its **gross domestic product, or GDP**. This is defined as the total market value of all final goods and services produced within a given time period by factors of production located domestically. This seemingly innocuous definition has several interesting aspects:

- Only final goods and services are included with their final prices, inclusive of all taxes. Intermediate goods are not included to avoid the problem of double counting.
- Only goods produced and services rendered in the current period are included. Unsold inventory is also included as the emphasis is on current *production*, not necessarily on market clearance. The sale of a used car or the resale value of a home, for example, would not be a current GDP statistic as these items have already been included in the year in which they were originally produced.
- The goods and services must be produced by factors of production (labor, capital, and/or land) located *within the country*, hence the "domestic" term in "gross domestic product."[2]

The total value of the goods and services *available in the economy* is given by

$$\textbf{Output(realGDP)} + \textbf{Imports}$$

This total must, by identity, be equal to the sum of private consumption expenditure, capital investment expenditure, government expenditure on goods and services, and foreign consumption of domestic production, i.e., exports.

$$\textbf{Output} + \textbf{Imports} = \textbf{Consumer} + \textbf{Investment} + \textbf{Government} + \textbf{Exports}$$
$$\textbf{Spending} \qquad\qquad \textbf{Spending}$$

Rearranging the equation, we get the output function:

$$\textbf{Output} = \textbf{Consumer} + \textbf{Investment} + \textbf{Government} + (\textbf{Exports} - \textbf{Imports})$$
$$\textbf{Spending} \qquad\qquad \textbf{Spending}$$

Algebraically, we can express the output function as

$$\textbf{Y} = \textbf{C} + \textbf{I} + \textbf{G} + (\textbf{Exp} - \textbf{Imp})$$

---

[2] The less-used gross national product (GNP) statistic measures the output produced by a country's factors of production regardless of where the production takes place. This would include income earned by citizens working abroad and would exclude the income of foreign-owned factories operating within the domestic borders. Wages of domestic citizens working in the foreign-owned domestic factory would be included.

where

$\mathbf{Y}$ = real domestic output
$\mathbf{C}$ = private consumption expenditure (personal consumption expenditure)
$\mathbf{I}$ = capital investment (new plant and equipment)*
$\mathbf{G}$ = government expenditure on goods and services, excluding transfer payments
$\mathbf{Exp}$ = exports of goods and services (foreign consumption of domestic output)
$\mathbf{Imp}$ = imports of goods and services

*Capital investment ($\mathbf{I}$) is not to be confused with investing in stocks and bonds. This latter kind of investing falls under "savings" in macroeconomics. Instead, the "I" in the equation pertains to capital investment as in new construction; new hardware, plant, and equipment; and new business software.

7.1.2   *Disposition of Output*

If $\mathbf{Y}$ represents the total value of goods and services produced and sold in the domestic economy, the income obtained from the sale of these goods and services will be $\mathbf{Y}$ dollars. This national income, in turn, is disposed of largely on private consumption, while part of it is saved, and the rest is devoured by taxes.

This may be expressed as

$$\textbf{Disposition of Output} = \textbf{Consumption} + \textbf{Savings} + \textbf{Taxes}$$

or, algebraically,

$$\mathbf{Y} = \mathbf{C} + \mathbf{S} + \mathbf{T}$$

where

$\mathbf{Y}$ = income from sale of goods and services of value Y (aka **national income**)
$\mathbf{C}$ = private consumption expenditure
$\mathbf{S}$ = private savings
$\mathbf{T}$ = net taxes, which are taxes paid less transfers received[3]

We can break the NSI into its components, where the left side of the equation describes how the available output is distributed and the right side describes how the income from the sale of the output is divided between national consumption, savings, and taxes:

$$\textbf{Output}(\textbf{GDP}) = \textbf{Disposition of the Output}(\textbf{GDP})$$

---

[3] Transfers received include things like Social Security payments, unemployment insurance, various assistance programs, etc.

Or

$$C + I + G + (Exp - Imp) = C + S + T$$

Simplifying we get

$$\cancel{C} + I + G + (Exp - Imp) = \cancel{C} + S + T$$

And rearranging, we obtain the **National Savings Identity**:

$$\underbrace{(G - T)}_{\substack{\textit{Fiscal budget} \\ \textit{deficit (surplus)}}} = \underbrace{(S - I) + (Imp - Exp)}_{\substack{\textit{Current account} \\ \textit{deficit (surplus)}}}$$

The NSI, as given by the equation above, is arguably one of the most important and incontrovertible cornerstones of global macroeconomic theory and policy but is perhaps the least understood.[4]

7.2   The Fiscal and Current Account Balances in the NSI

The term $(G - T)$ represents the fiscal budget deficit; the difference between government spending and national tax revenues. If $(G - T)$ is positive, then the national budget is in deficit as spending exceeds tax revenues, and if $(G - T)$ is negative, then the national budget is in surplus.[5]

The last term $(Imp - Exp)$ represents the **current account deficit**. The **current account balance (CAB)** is given by $(Exp - Imp)$, which, if positive, is a **current account surplus** and, if negative, is a **current account deficit.** So, taking the inverse of the **CAB**, $(Imp - Exp)$, gives us the current account deficit. The current account statistic for the United States is reported monthly by the US Census Bureau's Bureau

---

[4] If $(G - T)$ is positive, this represents a fiscal budget deficit, as government spending exceeds revenues. A negative $(G - T)$ figure represents a fiscal budget surplus, as taxes exceed government spending. Likewise, a positive figure for $(Imp - Exp)$ indicates a current account deficit, as imports exceed exports. Conversely, a negative figure for $(Imp - Exp)$ means that exports exceed imports, which is a current account surplus.

[5] Examples of national budgets in both categories abound; the United States began running large budget deficits in the 1980s, was briefly in surplus in 2000, and returned to ever-expanding deficits in the years following. Many Asian economies in the mid- to late 1990s were in surplus and remain so today. Much of Europe, as of this writing, is plagued by very large deficits. This subject will be explored in more detail in later chapters.

of Economic Analysis[6] and includes trade (exports minus imports) in goods and services, along with global net investment income, and net unilateral transfers (foreign aid and other transfers to and from abroad). For notational convenience, we subsume investment income and transfers from abroad into the term (**Exp**), while incomes and transfers paid to foreigners are included in the term (**Imp**).

It should be noted that the oft-encountered term "balance of trade" ignores financial transfers and includes only goods and services. The also frequently cited "merchandise trade balance" refers only to the difference between *goods* exported and imported[7] and excludes services. We will sometimes use "balance of trade" and "current account balance" interchangeably, as financial transfers are a relatively small component of the **CAB**.

We can see from the equation above how the fiscal budget and current account balance are inextricably linked. We will explore this relationship in greater detail in later chapters.

7.2.1   The Fiscal Budget Deficit

It is more common than not for governments to operate in fiscal deficit, spending more than they receive in taxes. There are, broadly speaking, only three methods of financing a fiscal deficit:

1. **Borrowing from domestic and foreign residents**

   Here, the domestic government issues sovereign debt in the form of bonds of varying maturity. The interest rate on these bonds is *endogenous*, that is, it is determined by market supply and demand for the government's debt each time it is put up for auction.

2. **Monetization**

   The government or its central bank may simply print money to pay its bills. This is clearly not a sustainable or long-term option, as the dilution of value in the issued currency quickly results in inflation. Recurring reliance on this method of financing leads ultimately to hyperinflation, a complete collapse of the currency's value.

---

[6] See the "Foreign Trade" section of the US Census Bureau's website: http://www.census.gov/foreign-trade/index.html. Details on methodology may be found in the "Guide to Foreign Trade" section at http://www.census.gov/foreign-trade/guide/sec2.html. Accessed Sep 24, 2012.

[7] Calculation of the merchandise trade balance bases US exports on FAS (free alongside ship) value, which is the value of exports at the US port of export, based on the transaction price, including inland freight, insurance, and other charges incurred in placing the merchandise along-side the carrier at the US port of exportation, but excluding the cost of loading the merchandise aboard the exporting carrier, freight, insurance, and international transportation charges. US imports are based on customs value, which includes only the price actually paid (or payable) for merchandise when sold for exportation to the United States and excludes US import duties, freight, insurance, and other charges incurred in bringing the merchandise to the United States. Source: US Census Bureau (see note above).

3. **Debt repudiation**

The government may also simply default on its debt. This actually happens much more frequently than is commonly assumed.[8] Recent examples include the Russian default of 1998 and the Argentinean crises of 2000–2002.

For our purposes, we will restrict our analysis to the case where (i) national budget deficits are entirely[9] bond financed and (ii) fiscal and monetary credibility is sound, meaning that the central bank has a long-standing reputation for monetary discipline and is highly unlikely to be pressured by the domestic government into financing runaway deficits; fiscal policy is not imprudent; and the political climate is stable.

Such an economy, where the government is considered highly unlikely to resort to methods (2) and (3) above, is considered a "**safe haven**," and the government's debt is generally considered "risk-free."[10]

7.2.2   Linking the Twin Deficits

The **twin deficits** refer to the fiscal budget deficit and the current account deficit. We can see from the National Savings Identity equation that a fiscal deficit must be financed by net domestic savings (savings less investment), with the balance coming from foreign sources.

Funds from foreign sources become available as a result of a current account deficit, since any time that imports exceed exports, there is a net flow of funds out of the country. This creates an available pool of capital overseas which will be invested back into the domestic economy, in the form of security purchases (of government debt, and private debt and equity) and asset purchases. The net flow of funds in and out of the economy from overseas is measured by the **capital account balance (KAB)**.

---

[8] We return to this topic in Chap. 12 and include an eye-opening chart chronicling default events over recent decades.

[9] Or nearly so, the USA has managed (so far) to maintain safe-haven status despite some recourse to monetization in the wake of the financial crisis of 2008 and the ensuing prolonged global slowdown. The USA has in the past periodically resorted to this practice.

[10] Given the probabilistic nature of our quantum universe, there is in fact no true "risk-free" asset anywhere to be found. Even the sovereign debt of the United States, long recognized as the safest in the world, incorporates a discount generally ranging from 30 to 50 basis points based on CDS premiums, and was actually downgraded by various ratings agencies in 2011–2012. We will use the terms "risk-free" and "safe haven" to refer to any economy which is understood to conform to our criteria listed above. These traditionally include the USA, the UK, France, Germany, and Japan and may, depending on one's perspective, include the Euro area as a whole, even with the risky periphery nations included, given its substantial French and German foundation.

Generally, when the current account balance is in deficit, the capital account will be in surplus, and vice versa.[11] And, broadly speaking, changes in the current account will be accompanied by opposite-direction changes in the capital account; i.e., $\Delta\mathbf{CAB} \approx -\Delta\mathbf{KAB}$.

7.3   Supply and Demand for Loanable Funds and Global Capital Markets

This pool of funds overseas, along with domestic savings, forms the **supply of loanable funds (SLF)**, which includes all funds available for the purchase of domestic government debt and for domestic private capital investment.

The **demand for loanable funds (DLF)** includes the net fiscal funding needs of the domestic government (the fiscal budget deficit) and net planned private investment.

We can rewrite the **NSI** equation above to obtain the supply and demand for loanable funds in the economy:

$$\mathbf{S} + (\mathbf{Imp} - \mathbf{Exp}) = (\mathbf{G} - \mathbf{T}) + \mathbf{I}$$

$$\mathbf{SLF} \qquad\qquad = \mathbf{DLF}$$

(Total Supply of   (Total Demand for

Loanable Funds)   Loanable Funds)

The supply of loanable funds (**SLF**) in the economy is the total amount of domestic savings (**S**), plus (minus) funds available overseas for domestic investment, (**Imp** − **Exp**). We see that the overseas capital available to come back into the home country is directly related to the home country's trade deficit (or surplus).

The demand for loanable funds (**DLF**) is the government's fiscal deficit (government spending [**G**] less tax revenues [**T**]), plus the total amount of private capital investment (**I**) planned in the domestic economy. Again, the underlying assumption here is that the government finances any shortfall in its spending less tax revenues (**G** − **T**) primarily by borrowing (issuing "safe-haven" domestic bonds). Also note that private capital investment (**I**) is essentially the demand by companies for funds to borrow,[12] generally for the purpose of capital improvement (new plant and equipment).

---

[11] Likewise, when the current account is in surplus, with exports exceeding imports, a pool of funds accumulates domestically which is then invested overseas, leading to a capital account deficit. We will explore the KAB further in later chapters; for now, the key point is its inverse relationship with the CAB.

[12] The "borrowing" represented by (I) may take many forms, including debt (bonds, debentures, bank loans, etc.) or equity. From an accounting perspective, these are all company liabilities that are created when new funds are invested in the company.

Fig. 7.1 Equilibrium in the
Domestic Capital Market,
where the Supply and
Demand for Loanable Funds
meet. Supply is greater when
interest rates are higher.
Demand is greater when
interest rates are low

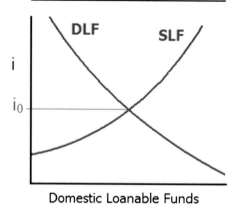

The Domestic Capital Market

Domestic Loanable Funds

How do these variables interact? (Fig. 7.1)

Given a safe-haven economy, where the government's debt is considered risk-free, interest rates in the aggregate are determined by the interplay of the supply and demand for loanable funds in the economy. When the demand for funds exceeds the supply, lenders will charge a higher price, in the form of higher interest rates, for the use of their money. When the supply of funds exceeds the demand, lenders must lower the price of funds, i.e., the interest rate, in order to attract borrowers. The equilibrium interest rate will be found at the intersection of the **SLF** and **DLF**. Here, the equilibrium interest rate is given by i_0.

To see how movements in **SLF** and **DLF** affect interest rates, we may consider two examples.

Should the government's fiscal deficit increase, the government's increased demand for borrowing will cause the **DLF** to shift higher, resulting in a new equilibrium at i_1, which causes interest rates to rise (see Fig. 7.2).

To take another example, if imports rise dramatically while exports remain unchanged or shrink, there will be more funds available overseas for investment in the domestic economy. This will cause the **SLF** to increase, driving interest rates lower.

The supply and demand for funds in the economy are also affected by non-trade-related capital flows from overseas, particularly when the country's "capital account" is "open" (meaning there are few, if any, restrictions on the movement of capital in and out of the country). These movements will be further explored below.[13]

We are now in a position to link the national budget deficit with the trade (current account) deficit. Here, we see the power of the NSI (as given by our equation $[G - T] = [S - I] + [Imp - Exp]$) in explaining this link.

---

[13] We explore the effects of restrictions on the movement of capital in Chap. 12.

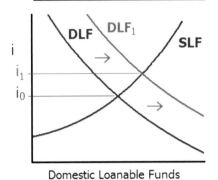

The Domestic Capital Market

Domestic Loanable Funds

*Increase in the fiscal deficit (**G–T**) causes causes an increase in the Demand for Loanable Funds, which leads to rising interest rates*

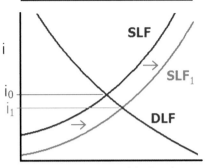

The Domestic Capital Market

Domestic Loanable Funds

*Increase in imports, while exports fall, results in increased (**Imp. – Exp.**) which grows the Supply of Loanable Funds, causing interest rates to fall.*

Fig. 7.2 Domestic capital market and the twin deficits. Changes in the demand for and supply of loanable funds resulting from changes in economic conditions

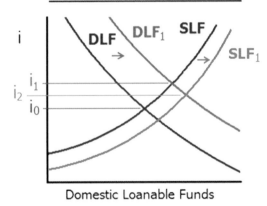

The Domestic Capital Market

Domestic Loanable Funds

Fig. 7.3 Domestic capital market incorporating the effects of the twin (fiscal and current account) deficits

In Fig. 7.3, we assume a safe-haven economy where interest rates are determined endogenously:

1. We start with an increase in the government's fiscal deficit, with $(G - T)$ growing. This increases the **DLF**, as we saw above (in Fig. 7.2).
2. This increase in the **DLF** drives up domestic interest rates to the higher equilibrium, i_1.

3. The higher interest rates in this safe haven become more attractive relative to those of other countries, and global investors shift their portfolios toward the higher-yielding domestic debt.[14] These investors, who include individuals, insurance companies, sovereign wealth funds, private investment funds, and central banks, need to swap their respective currencies for domestic currency. For example, they might sell Japanese yen or euros for US dollars. This excess demand for the domestic currency makes it "more expensive" in terms of foreign currency in the global foreign exchange markets. That is, the domestic currency appreciates ("gets stronger") relative to foreign currencies. A hypothetical example of such appreciation would be:

   (a) Before Step 1: 1 US dollar equals 100 units of foreign currency.
   (b) After Step 1: 1 US dollar equals 120 units of foreign currency.

4. With the strengthening of the domestic currency, imports now become "cheaper" for domestic residents, while domestic exports become "more expensive" to foreign consumers who must exchange more units of their own currencies for one unit of the domestic currency. This causes imports to surge and exports to shrink.

5. This result causes the current account balance ($\mathbf{Exp} - \mathbf{Imp}$) to decrease, which means of course that if the current account is already in deficit (with $[\mathbf{Imp} - \mathbf{Exp}] > 0$), that deficit grows. We see here the linkage of the "twin deficits." Here, the fiscal budget deficit ($\mathbf{G} - \mathbf{T}$) drives the NSI and, by influencing interest rates and exchange rates, results in an increased current account deficit ($\mathbf{Imp} - \mathbf{Exp}$).

   During the 1980s and the 2002–present period for the USA, and the early 1990s for Germany, for example, the twin deficits did indeed exhibit strong positive covariance for both these economies. Both countries had to resort to large bond issuances to finance their significant budget deficits: the Americans financing the Reagan- and then Bush- (43) and Obama-era deficits, and the Germans struggling to finance their post-unification outlays.

6. As the domestic economy amasses cheaper imports, foreigners accumulate deposits of domestic currency. For example, as the USA accumulates imports from Japan and China, those countries amass massive dollar deposits. These dollar deposits are then promptly reinvested back into the safe-haven, high-yielding (due to the increase in the DLF chronicled in [2], above) domestic economy (the USA, in this example). Thus, the current account deficit creates an inflow of capital, resulting in a capital account surplus, as described above. This creates an increase in the supply of loanable funds, which is reflected by the rightward shift in the **SLF** in Fig. 7.3.

7. Finally, thanks to the capital inflow, interest rates in the domestic economy are now lowered to their final equilibrium level, i_2. Capital inflows supplement

---

[14] As we will discuss later, interest rates are not the only factor driving international capital flows. Long-term macroeconomic outlook is highly important, and relative currency exchange rates, as well as inflation, play important roles as well.

domestic savings and thereby exert an important ameliorating influence on domestic interest rates.

Almost 40–60 % of the US deficit in the 1980s era and virtually 100 % of US interest expenses on government debt were funded by massive capital inflows associated with the US current account deficits.

In 2010, the US fiscal deficit, exacerbated by the continuing economic slow-down, was $1.3 trillion. Net additions to foreign holdings of US Treasury securities during the period were + $752 billion, which covered 58 % of the fiscal deficit.[15] The US current account deficit of $495 billion contributed significantly to these inflows.

7.4   Two Hypothetical Examples of the NSI: The United States and China

7.4.1   USA

Given a US economy, which is a safe haven that is incurring significant fiscal and current account deficits, we may assign hypothetical figures for the various categories of income and expenditure into the NSI:

$$(G - T) = (S - I) + (Imp - Exp)$$

Let the fiscal deficit $(G - T) = 450$, a significant budget deficit; and let the current account deficit $(Imp - Exp) = 500$, a large current account deficit. All figures will be in billions of US dollars.

We thus have

$$450 = (S - I) + 500$$

which we can simplify to

$$(S - I) = -50$$

This implies that private demand for loanable funds in this economy outstrips the supply of domestic savings by $50 billion. This shortfall is financed by the current account deficit, which is sufficient to cover both the fiscal deficit and the excess of private demand for investment in the domestic economy.

[15] The relationship between the figures is imprecise as the 2010 fiscal deficit is based on a fiscal year ending September 30, rather than the calendar year on which the current account balances are calculated. Nevertheless, the general relationship holds. Data sources: US Treasury (net foreign holdings), US Congressional Budget Office (fiscal budget), and US Census Bureau (current account).

If we are given instead the fiscal deficit of \$450 and the shortfall in domestic savings of \$50, but are not told the current account deficit, we can rewrite the NSI equation and solve for the current account:

$$(\mathbf{Imp} - \mathbf{Exp}) = (\mathbf{G} - \mathbf{T}) - (\mathbf{S} - \mathbf{I}) = \mathbf{450} - (-\mathbf{50}) = \mathbf{500}$$

Here, the capital inflow associated with the current account deficit amounts to \$500 billion, which finances the shortfall in the supply of loanable funds.

Since 2002, the USA's large bond-financed budget deficits have necessitated borrowing of between \$2 and \$4 billion a day, with the top foreign purchasers being China and Japan.

7.4.2   China

Given a Chinese economy that is a reasonably safe haven with significant and increasing current account surpluses, we again assign hypothetical figures for the various categories of income and expenditure in the NSI:

$$(\mathbf{G} - \mathbf{T}) = (\mathbf{S} - \mathbf{I}) + (\mathbf{Imp} - \mathbf{Exp})$$

Let $(G - T) = 30$, and let the current account *surplus* (Exp − Imp) = 347. Thus, the current account *deficit* is negative, at −347 (this is another way of saying that there is a *positive* current account *balance*). Substituting these values (all figures remain in billions of USD) into the NSI equation yields

$$\mathbf{30} = (\mathbf{S} - \mathbf{I}) - \mathbf{347}$$

We see that $(S - I)$ equals 377 billion US dollars. Here, there is a surplus of domestic savings over what is required for domestic capital investment. This is symptomatic of most economies in Southeast Asia, which are awash in domestic savings due to a combination of culture and largely export-led economies. These economies are, on net, "exporters" of global capital.[16]

Putting the two scenarios together, we obtain a picture of the US–China relationship. Our US economy has a supersized \$500 billion demand for loanable funds which is unmet by domestic savers. Without capital from overseas, funding this shortfall would be impossible.

Enter our Chinese economy, which has a \$347 billion excess of funds beyond what is needed domestically. These funds, along with those from other countries, will provide the USA with the financing it requires.

---

[16] Alternatively, the capital-exporting countries may be considered "importers" of *title* to foreign assets. Thus, their current account surplus will be accompanied by a capital account *deficit*. While the current account basically tracks the movement of goods and services, the capital account tracks the movement of the *title* to real and financial assets. This will be discussed in more detail in later chapters.

We can also see from these examples that the growing chorus of complaints from many corners of the USA about China's trade surplus might instead just as properly be turned to thanks, or perhaps the complaints are better directed at US fiscal profligacy. This topic will be explored more fully in Chap. 13.

7.5   The Global Flow of Funds

Foreign inflows are not limited to the absorption of domestic government debt. In fact, from the early 2000s, investors from overseas, especially Asia (primarily China and Japan), have availed themselves of the USA's comparative advantages by financing auto plants, real estate ventures, and significant portions of the high-skilled labor-intensive manufacturing sector in the United States. Since the mid-1980s, "inshoring" (sometimes referred to as "insourcing"), in the form of domestic production by overseas companies, has increased significantly. Since the late 1990s, one in eight US manufacturing jobs is in a foreign-owned company or subsidiary. An astounding number of start-ups in the information technology sector have been funded by mammoth capital inflows tied to the United States' growing current account deficits.[17]

Several factors influence global capital flows. The most important are:

1. **Interest rates**
   Higher domestic interest rates (and, in general, higher returns offered for domestic assets) relative to returns in the rest of the world will attract capital to the domestic economy, as discussed above.
2. **Macroeconomic outlook**
   A strong long-term macroeconomic outlook for the domestic economy will attract capital. The importance of this factor cannot be overstated. Global capital is often dispatched to economies or regions that may not necessarily have higher interest rates but may exhibit impressive growth that is expected to continue into future periods.

   By way of example, in the mid-1990s, with the USA recovering from its 1990–1991 recession, Japan deep in a prolonged economic downturn, and the European Union wrestling with the demise of its exchange rate mechanism (ERM), the Southeast Asian economies of Thailand, Malaysia, Singapore, Indonesia, Taiwan, the Philippines, and South Korea captured the center stage of global attention. Phenomenal growth rates of over 10 % annually, low inflation, high employment, stable governments, and rapid increases in

---

[17] For a contrary view regarding the net benefit of foreign direct investment, see Robert E. Scott, "The Hidden Costs of Insourcing: Higher Trade Deficits and Job Losses for U.S. Workers," *EPI Issue Brief #236*, Economic Policy Institute, August 23, 2007. Scott argues that the bulk of foreign employment is in acquired firms, which are acquired for their market presence and subsequently "hollowed out" for later offshoring of production.

infrastructure development all contributed to attracting massive capital inflows—so much so as to ultimately prove destabilizing, as we shall explore in Chap. 11.

3. **Exchange rates**

Relative movements in exchange rates, and anticipated future movements, will result in shifting capital flows. This factor is generally less important than the first two factors, but at certain times, particularly when a country is expected to devalue its currency, it can become critical. We will explore exchange rates further in Chap. 8.

Only a few centuries ago, capital—in the form of physical specie (precious metal and coin)—could not move faster than most merchandise, and even credit transactions were limited by the speed of communication, which was by ship, horse, and foot. Capital has grown increasingly mobile as both financial instruments and communications technologies have grown, and today, the world's financial markets are entirely interconnected.[18]

Every day, a massive amount of capital (*$4 trillion* as of April 2010,[19] equal to 6 % of the world's annual output) is traded in foreign exchange markets, which operate continuously, 24-h per day, five days per week. This trading is done by all types of investors, including central banks, financial institutions, nonfinancial multinational companies, sovereign wealth funds, hedge funds, and individuals.

Articles

Article 7.1. Tough Questions in Deficit Seminar

Melanie Andrews, *North Jersey Financial Weekly*

The location: The notorious Jersey Shore, but any connection with the infamous TV show ends here. The attendance at the trade seminar features some of the most famous reporters and business writers in the world. We join the conference in progress.

(a) "Trade must be fair," exclaims Ming Chen of the *Shidoo Chronicle*. "I say that we limit imports exactly to the amount of exports, and so we wipe out our trade deficit with one fell swoop!" "Do you want to commit macroeconomic suicide?" roars Fali Daruvalla of the *Vardha Sun*. (b) "Our interest rates will spike and we will go into free fall if you do this!"

---

[18] Artificial limitations on capital flows remain imposed by governments for various purposes. These capital controls are discussed at length in Chaps. 11 and 12.

[19] Notional daily value of all currency spot ($1.5 T), forward ($0.5 T), swap ($1.8 T), and option ($0.2 T) transactions. Source: "Report on Global Foreign Exchange Market Activity in 2010," *Triennial Central Bank Survey*, Bank for International Settlements (Basel, Switzerland: December 2010), 6.

The attendees go back and forth over these comments, until the announcement of the famous Marisa's NJ Lobster Bisque. "Ah, the seminar really begins now!" exclaims Dr. Van Nostrum of the Seinfeld Institute. "This is one amazing bisque!" The crowd roars as the Great Marisa, master chef of New Jersey, makes her entrance.

However, Rick Sanstrade, unimpressed with the bisque, hammers on, regardless. (c) "I say we control the Chinese. We must impose an upper limit on the US debt that they buy. It's too dangerous to allow them to buy so much of our debt!"

"Are you mad!" roars Dr. Paul Rogers, president of Rogers Syndicated Funds, "We need to say Thank You to the Chinese for buying our debt. (d) Without them it would be 'Game Over' for the USA! If we limit them, get ready for our interest rates going through the ceiling!" He then sits down, sweating profusely.

"I am having a problem relating to the diagram (Fig. 7.3) that Dr. Langdana presented earlier," says Kathy Wodehouse. (e) "We had a huge increase in spending in the US in 2008–2011, but we never saw the interest rates going from i_0 to i_1 as he described. What gives?" Slurping a huge spoonful of bisque, she continues, (f) "Furthermore, what is the guarantee that capital will keep flowing here—our rates are lower than those abroad, and our future looks bleak!"

The gigantic crab cakes are soon followed by vegetable samosas with five homemade chutneys, and by this time, the heated arguments have died down. An air of contentment descends on the participants by the time the huge chocolate almond cake arrives. Rumor has it that the mocha-java ice-cream topping is from happy Swiss cows, and the cake was garnished with dark chocolate slabs made in Peru by contented grannies working on peaceful cocoa farms. Hey, if this is what we mean by "imports" in our graphs and equations, then by all means please let them in!

Article 7.2. Panel Answers Tough Questions at Rutgers Symposium

Esmeralda Kuppy, *New Jersey Nightly Business Roundup*

They were all there—the high priests of Global Macroeconomics. There was the flamboyant Professor "Nacho" Espanola, fit as ever in his Eurosuit and his ready smile; the powerful Prof. Pytor Murpheesboro, looking like the typical Hollywood professor in his rumpled tweed jacket, absent-mindedly chewing on his pipe; and the intense Dr. Jessey Cohone, as always on a mission, with his mind working faster than most computers. And finally, there was the formidable Prof. Jennifer Kirbin, her somber suit not in the least dimming the brilliance of her laughing eyes (she was laughing to herself of course about some secret inside-macro joke).

They were all there to answer hard questions about global macro at the annual "Meet the Powerhouses" event, hosted by the Rutgers Executive MBA program at its gleaming new conference center at 1 Washington Park, Newark, NJ.

(a) "Look, the Chinese Yuan should be much stronger, given the way their economy is set to grow—but their central bank keeps their currency artificially low! This is just not fair! This is exactly what causes our huge trade deficit with them," said Kevin Dowling, of the New York Trade Guardians Association.

"It's not that simple" explains Prof. Kirby patiently. "If the Chinese were to (b) allow the Yuan to strengthen, our trade deficit would not vanish. We would not suddenly start making bedsheets in Bedminster, NJ. The only difference is that they would now be made in Thailand or in Sri Lanka!"

"The main point is," jumps in Dr. Cohone, (c) "our trade deficit is driven largely by our budget deficit. The Chinese understand that. They tell us, 'Hey, get your budget house in order, for that's the only way that you will structurally decrease your trade imbalances in the long run!'"

"….one more thing," adds Prof. Murpheesboro, "Keep in mind that (d) a very large portion of global trade is intra-industry trade. This means that if the Yuan gets stronger, the components from China will get more expensive, and our joint final products will, too!" On that note of "Be careful for whathat you ask for" (yuan revaluation), we moved to the subject of safe havens.

"Yesterday, following the scary news about the problems in the Eurozone, we saw interest rates on US Treasury almost drop to zero! What is that all about?" asks Debbie Sensabowe of the Virginia Global Equities Research group.

"I love simple questions," says a smiling Professor "Nacho" Espanola. "If you have read the famous Langdana–Murphy book, then (e) you can imagine the flood of foreign capital rushing in to keep interest rates low here—the flight to safety is to the US 'cave.'" Pytor quickly adds, ominously, (f) "But keep in mind that since the US debt downgrade, Switzerland, Singapore, and other Asian economies are also benefitting from this flight to safety." (g) "To the extent that it is really driving up their currencies," injects Cohone, "and this is causing pain to the export sectors of Switzerland, etc."

"But coming back to the capital inflows into the US," says Manmohan Karamchand of the Hindu Business Quarterly, (h) "if rates here are low, and unemployment here is high and the future looks bleak with the budget deficits out of control—how come we still get capital flooding in?"

"Ah! He needs to read the cave theory, first espoused by the great Prof. Langdana, who could not be with us today," says Dr. Murpheesboro, smiling knowingly to the rest of the panel. Kirby quickly describes Langdana's unorthodox and typically whimsical cave theory. Basically, the various parts of the planet retire to hunker down in their respective caves in the event of a global recession—the Europeans hide in their cave, the Asians in their cave, the Americans in their cave, and so on. When this happens, the Americans (as Langdana posits) will have the "best" cave, and global capital, in spite of global turmoil, will flow to this safest cave: ergo, the cave theory, which has proven surprisingly accurate since it was originally propounded in 2008.

At this reassuring point, the audience is relieved to see waiters bringing in a product from a different sort of "cave"—the long-awaited cabernets from the famous Rutgers EMBA Lawrence Califano's winery in California. Amidst a happy tinkling of glasses, someone says, "Long Live the Cave Theory if this stuff comes from caves!" Yes, we can all drink to that.

Hints and Solutions

Article 7.1

(a) We visited this quote in Part 1 of this book, and now, we visit a "macro" version of this same idea. In this case, eradicating the trade (current account) deficit would also be tantamount to eradicating the accompanying capital inflow!

(b) As the inflow slows down radically, the supply of loanable funds shifts to the left, thereby driving up the final interest rates. Private capital investment (I), which is the private demand for borrowing for new capital investment, is a negative function of interest rates.[20] Hence, a sudden spike in interest rates would cause capital investment (I) to collapse.

(c) Unfortunately, this has been a common sentiment. The problem with this suggestion is that again, any decline in the supply of loanable funds would cause that curve to shift to the left, thus pushing up domestic interest rates. Besides, given the non-sustainability of US budget deficits since 2008, any capital inflow, from China or any other origin, should be gratefully accepted. Any capital inflows imply that much less monetization to make up the shortfall in supply of loanable funds.

(d) Please refer to (b) above. Capital investments would crash if domestic rates were to spike following an upper limit on capital being allowed in from a major creditor country like China.

(e) This was due to the fact that along with massive increase in government spending, the United States also indulged in unrestricted monetization, labeled as QE1, QE2, QE3, and so on, with "quantitative easing" being the euphemism for blatant monetization of runaway budget deficits. We will delve deeply into the effects of joint fiscal and monetary policies when we build our ISLM-BOP model in Chap. 9.

(f) During a global "flight to safety", safety is relative. Even a US economy with glaring weaknesses will still attract funds if the rest of the world is in even worse shape. Please refer to the "cave theory" referenced in the following article.

---

[20] In classical macroeconomic analysis, private capital investment is expressed as $I = \underline{I} - fi$, where I is investor confidence, i is the interest rate, and f is the elasticity of capital investment to the interest rate. See Langdana, *Macroeconomic Policy: Demystifying Monetary and Fiscal Policy*, Chaps. 2, 3, and 4.

Article 7.2

(a) Given its strong long-term macroeconomic outlook, global capital would indeed flow into China, thus exerting upward pressure on its currency. But given the razor-thin profit margins on exports from Asia, any appreciation in the Chinese yuan would be very painful for China's export sector. To prevent this, the People's Bank of China (PBoC, China's central bank) intervenes daily in the foreign exchange markets by "buying" US dollars and "selling" yuan to artificially weaken the yuan and thus limit any deterioration in China's export sector. It is this artificially weakened yuan that has been a lightning rod for China's trade critics.

(b) A stronger yuan would not suddenly give the USA a comparative advantage in bedsheets. It would not change America's factor abundance. As explained, the US would now import from another Asian country with a CA similar to China's.

(c) Dr. Cohone is clearly referring to the National Savings Identity that links the budget deficit to the trade (current account) deficit, as described earlier in this chapter.

(d) Clearly, a spike in the price of components from a particular country, due to the imposition of import tariffs, would result in an increase in the overall price of the final product. We discuss intra-industry trade at length in Chap. 3.

(e) With capital rushing into the safe haven, the supply of loanable funds curve shifts to the right (see Fig. 7.2), thus pushing short-term rates on domestic debt to even lower levels. This "flight to safety" is often reflected not just in capital flight from foreign countries but is also observed with domestic investors shifting rapidly out of riskier assets, such as stocks (equities), and into safe-haven government debt and precious metals. The flight to safety, which drives down safe-haven interest rates, is often matched by accompanying spikes in the prices of gold and silver. This last effect on precious metals is the opposite of what one generally observes during "normal" times, where "inflation hedges" increase in price as interest rates rise in anticipation of inflation and decrease in price as interest rates drop. The flight of capital into the safest "caves" arises from unusual circumstances and has unusual effects.

(f) After the downgrade of US debt in August 2010, flights to safety have included other, non-US destinations. This is not to say that the USA has lost its safe-haven status—in fact, there was a massive capital inflow the very day following the debt downgrade. Today, we see other competing destinations, which (to a much smaller scale) also attract troubled capital in stormy weather.

Chapter 8
Exchange Rates

Summary In this chapter, we finally bring exchange rates into the picture, both fixed and floating.

This leads to important topics, including pegged and managed exchange rates, interest rate parity, uncovered nominal interest arbitrage, and the carry trade.

What is "hot capital" and what drives these huge, temperamental—and, often, destabilizing—flows of capital in and out of a particular country with lightning speed? This topic is fully explored with historical and hypothetical examples.

We close the chapter with a case focusing on the currency relationship between the USA and China, in which we explore aspects of the policy controversy that has surrounded this relationship for several years.

8.1 The Exchange Rate

The purchase of goods and services, or of assets, from overseas generally cannot be done with one's home currency. Overseas entities demand payment in their home currency, as this is what they use in their day-to-day transactions.

F. Langdana and P.T. Murphy, *International Trade and Global Macropolicy*,
Springer Texts in Business and Economics, DOI 10.1007/978-1-4614-1635-7_8,
© Springer Science+Business Media New York 2014

This requires the buyer to purchase the foreign country's currency in order to undertake the transaction. This is generally done through the buyer and seller's banks. But how do we know the "price" of the foreign currency?

The **exchange rate** is the price of a foreign country's currency in terms of one's domestic currency. Generally, the exchange rate is quoted in terms of the quantity of domestic currency needed to purchase 1 unit of foreign currency.

So, if we have a Japanese firm that needs to purchase euros (EUR) for transactions in Germany, the quote for euros in terms of Japanese yen (JPY) would be given as something like 110 JPY to 1 EUR.

Quotations like this, where the base currency is home currency, are the most common and are called *direct* quotations. Quotes that use the foreign currency as the base currency, giving the price in terms of the home currency, are called *indirect* quotations. In the example above, the indirect quotation would be given as 0.0091 EUR to 1 JPY. We will for the most part use direct quotations in our discussions.

In macroeconomics, we use the term (**e**) to reference the direct quotation of the exchange rate:

$e = \$/\text{\euro}$	= (domestic currency) / (1 unit of foreign currency)
	= domestic currency price of foreign currency
	= how much domestic currency is required to purchase 1 unit of foreign currency
$\downarrow e$	A low, or decreasing, "e" means a "strong" or "strengthening" currency—we can purchase a foreign unit of currency with relatively little domestic currency. For example, the JPY shifts from 110 JPY to 1 EUR to 102 JPY to 1 EUR. The value of "e" has changed from e = 110 to e = 103. We say that the Japanese yen has appreciated or become "stronger" (in terms of the euro). In our exercises, we will use a downward arrow next to the "e" variable as shorthand to indicate a strengthening currency, as depicted here
$\uparrow e$	A high or increasing "e" means a "weak" or "weakening" currency – a foreign unit of currency is very expensive to purchase with our domestic currency.[1] By way of example, the US dollar may initially trade at $1.07 USD to 1 Swiss franc ("CHF"). It then shifts over a few days to trade at $1.12 USD to 1 CHF. Here, we say that the US dollar has depreciated or gotten "weaker"

---

[1] We will often use arrows ($\uparrow\downarrow$) in the text to indicate high and low values or increases and decreases in the values of certain variables. This shorthand notation is easier to visualize and makes for a better narrative flow than continually reading "increase," "decrease," etc., over and over.

It is important to note here that it may seem counterintuitive that a low exchange rate means a "strong" currency and that a high exchange rate means a "weak" currency (low = strong, high = weak). It will be necessary to be mindful of this when working through problems where we must take information such as "the currency is getting stronger" and translate this into what is happening with (**e**), the exchange rate.[2]

8.2 Floating Exchange Rates

We will use the term (**FX**) to refer to **foreign exchange**. Generally, when we are examining the relationship between pairs of currencies, "foreign exchange" will refer to foreign currency. However, depending on context, the term may also refer to any combination of assets denominated in a currency other than the home currency. This is the case with central bank foreign exchange reserves, which include gold, foreign currencies, and foreign bonds.[3]

Foreign exchange transactions take place every day, all over the world, and as noted in Chap. 7, as of 2012, some $4 trillion in notional transactions,[4] equal to 6 % of global GDP, are carried out daily in world markets. Foreign exchange transactions include everything from a Canadian traveler in Ireland changing 50 Canadian dollars in pocket money for euros at a hotel kiosk to the massive six

---

[2] The *indirect* exchange rate (foreign currency units/1 domestic currency unit) is normally denoted by the term e-prime (**e′**) and is simply the reciprocal of (**e**). A strong currency would have a high value for **e′**, as many units of foreign currency may be purchased with each unit of domestic. A weak currency would have a low value for **e′**. Currencies are quoted inconsistently in regular usage, sometimes with the direct rate (**e**) and sometimes with the indirect rate (**e′**), leaving interpretation dependent on context. Usually, the rate quote will avoid values less than 1 unit, so, for example, in the United States, the USD/China rate would be an indirect quote (**e′**) of "6.2," meaning 6.2 China RMB to 1 USD, and the euro would be quoted in direct terms (**e**), as "1.3," meaning 1.3 US dollars to 1 euro. A helpful device to remember how **e** is calculated is "<u>D</u>on't <u>F</u>orget, <u>D</u>omestic over <u>F</u>oreign!"

[3] A country's currency and its bonds are both essentially liabilities of the country's government, the main differences being that the former is the most liquid, and the latter pays interest. Short-term government bonds traded in a highly liquid market may in a sense be considered interchangeable with currency, from this perspective. See John Hussman, Ph.D., "Why the Federal Reserve is Irrelevant," *Hussman Funds Research & Insight*, August 2001. http://www.hussmanfunds.com/html/fedirrel.htm

[4] "Notional" transactions include the value of derivative trades where parties are speculating on, or hedging against, movements in price of the underlying currencies. The majority of these transactions do not involve movement of actual capital except for the regular settlement of gains and losses in margin accounts and *theoretically* cancel each other out. In practice, however, counterparty risk among the entities involved can be significant, as seen in the case of "MF Global" in 2011, a derivatives broker that ended up on the losing side of uncovered bets resulting in bankruptcy and real losses.

Fig. 8.1 Hypothetical market in the USA for foreign exchange of Euros

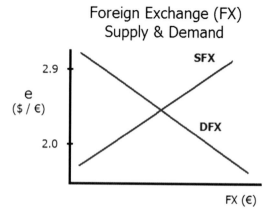

trillion yen ($47 billion USD) foreign exchange intervention by the bank of Japan after the 2011 earthquake.[5] The vast bulk of foreign exchange transaction volume occurs in electronic transactions involving major central banks and large financial institutions.

With **freely floating,** or **"flexible,"** **exchange rates,** the price of a foreign currency is determined endogenously by market forces, based on the interplay between supply (**SFX** = supply of foreign exchange) and demand (**DFX** = demand for foreign exchange) for the foreign currency.

Figure 8.1 depicts a hypothetical market in the USA for foreign exchange in the form of euros (€). We see the quantity demanded of foreign exchange increasing as the domestic currency strengthens (allowing the purchase of more foreign currency for one unit of domestic currency). And conversely, the quantity supplied of foreign exchange will increase with a weaker domestic currency, since as we see in this example, foreigners will get a "better deal" in terms of the number of US dollars they can obtain for their euro. The FX equilibrium point occurs where the two curves meet at **SFX = DFX**.

The import and export markets for goods and services are related to the FX market, as:

– **DFX** implies domestic demand for foreign goods (since we need their currency to purchase their goods[6]).
– **SFX** implies foreign demand for domestic goods (since foreigners provide us with their currency when they exchange it for domestic currency in order to buy our goods).

---

[5] "Bank of Japan injects $76bn into markets as yen rises," *BBC News*, March 17, 2011, accessed April 2, 2011, http://www.bbc.co.uk/news/business-12768673

[6] We will occasionally use personal pronouns, in examples such as "we" and "their currency," rather than sticking with "the domestic country" and "the foreign country's currency" as a rhetorical device. This can sometimes make it easier to conceptualize the point being made.

In addition to its utility as a medium of exchange for trade in merchandise and services, foreign currency is also needed to make direct investments in a foreign country (foreign direct investment or "**FDI**") or to purchase real or financial assets denominated in a foreign currency, such as foreign government bonds, and foreign equities, etc.

Under freely floating exchange rates, a shift in **SFX** or **DFX** results in an endogenous change in the exchange rate to a new equilibrium.

Since the abandonment of the fixed-rate gold-exchange system in 1971,[7] the world has been moving increasingly toward various forms of floating exchange rates. Only a few currencies, however, including the US dollar, the Australian dollar, the British pound, and the euro, may be considered truly free-floating.[8]

8.3 Spot, Forward, and Expected Exchange Rates

The **spot exchange rate** gives the rate for immediate delivery of a foreign currency. This is the rate that we have been discussing up to this point. Spot transactions account for 30 % of daily foreign exchange market activity, with $1.5 trillion USD traded daily as of 2010.[9]

The (e) term refers to the spot exchange rate in our analyses.

The **forward exchange rate** (e^f) gives the price of a unit of foreign currency in terms of the domestic currency, for settlement on a specific future date (the maturity date).

By entering into a forward contract, an investor "locks in" an exchange rate today for a transaction in the future. Merchants may use forward contracts to protect themselves from exchange rate fluctuations when engaging in international transactions. Investors may use forward contracts to hedge their foreign currency-denominated holdings, and speculators may use forward contracts to "bet" on the direction of currency movements.

Forward currency contracts in sterling were traded in Liverpool from at least the 1850s,[10] and today, a half-trillion USD in forward contracts are traded daily in the foreign exchange markets. Adding $2 trillion in notional value of currency swaps and options, forward-looking derivative instruments make up more than 60 % of daily volume in the foreign exchange markets.

---

[7] This topic is covered in more detail in Chap. 13.

[8] Akila Weerapana, "Lecture 5: Exchange Rate Systems," Wellesley College, 2003.

[9] Figures on daily foreign exchange transactions are from "Report on Global Foreign Exchange Market Activity in 2010," *Triennial Central Bank Survey*, Bank for International Settlements (Basel, Switzerland: December 2010), 6.

[10] Barry Eichengreen, "Sterling's Past, Dollar's Future: Historical Perspectives on Reserve Currency Competition," Tawney Lecture delivered to the Economic Historical Society, Leicester: United Kingdom, April 10, 2005.

For an example of how a merchant might make use of a forward currency contract, let's say that an American importer of kitchen appliances from Korea is concerned about exchange rate fluctuations for an upcoming shipment of refrigerators. The importer has contracted to pay Korean won ₩226,000 for each refrigerator when they are ready for shipment 60 days from today, which is equivalent to $200 USD at today's quoted 60-day forward rate of ₩1,130 to $1 USD.

The importer has based his selling price of $350 USD on this cost (plus his overhead and required margin) and does not want to be at risk for any reduction of his profit due to currency movements. The importer may thus enter into a forward contract which allows him to purchase Korean won 60 days hence at the quoted forward rate.

If he does not enter into such a transaction, the importer may find himself having to pay more to obtain the necessary Korean currency. If the rate were to change, with the USD weakening[11] to a rate of ₩1,000 to $1 USD by the time the payment is due, the importer would be paying $226 USD for each refrigerator, eroding his profit or perhaps resulting in a loss.

The forward rate will generally differ from the spot rate, as it is affected by interest rate differentials between the home and foreign currency.

It should be noted that the forward exchange rate is usually, *but not necessarily*, the spot rate that is expected to prevail at the time of the forward contract's maturity.

The **expected exchange rate** (e^e) is the term used for today's anticipation of the spot rate that will prevail on a given future date. While the spot and forward rate are known quantities, quoted continuously in real time, the expected rate is subject to uncertainty and is unobservable. One may have one's own view on the expected rate for any given currency pair. Generally, when talking about the expected exchange rate, we are talking about the market's aggregate view based on all available contemporaneous information.

The relationship between **spot rates** and **expected rates** can be illustrated with an example.

Let's say that we are currency speculators in Country A. Assuming that:

- Currency risk (the volatility of the exchange rate and the chance of devaluation) in Countries A and B is equal.
- Capital controls in A and B are absent or completely predictable.
- The debt of both Countries A and B is considered risk-free, or if not, default risk in the two countries is equal.

And given that:

- The spot rate today (**e**) is 12 units of B for 1 unit of A. In other words, the rate is 1/12th of a unit of domestic A currency for 1 unit of foreign B currency. Therefore, the spot rate in A is 1/12 (**e** $= 1/12$).

---

[11] We might also say "with the Korean won strengthening." All currency movements are relative by definition. A strengthening of A relative to B always means a weakening of B relative to A.

- The 30-day interest rate in Country A (**i**) is 2 %.[12]
- The 30-day interest rate in Country B (**i***) is 5 %.
- Our expected exchange rate (**e^e**) 30 days from today is 12 B for 1 A, unchanged from today's spot rate. So, in this example, **e** = **e^e** = 1/12.

We may profit from this situation:

(a) We borrow 1 unit of currency A today for 30 days at an interest rate of 2 %.
(b) We use this 1 unit of currency A to purchase 12 units of currency B.
(c) We invest our new B currency in a risk-free bond in Country B for 30 days, earning 5 % interest.
(d) On the settlement date, we would have 12.6 units of currency B when the bond pays off.
(e) We would exchange this back into currency A at the rate of 12 B to 1 A, giving us 1.05 units of currency A.
(f) We would then repay our loan in currency A, on which we now owe 1.02, yielding a profit of 0.03 in A currency.

However, this profit is not risk-free, as the expected exchange rate is subject to uncertainty. If the exchange rate moves against us, we might suffer a loss. Nevertheless, if our expectation of the exchange rate is similar to that of the market as a whole, many speculators like us seeking to earn a profit from the differential will rush to borrow A, sell A for B on the spot market, and invest in B. This activity will drive spot rates and interest rates in each country to adjust such that any risk-free profit would disappear.

To keep our example simple, let's say that only the spot rate adjusts. The speculative activity described above would result in a new spot exchange rate (**e**) of 11.66 B for one A. On settlement date (step [d], above), after earning 5 % interest for 60 days on 11.66 of Country B bonds, we would have 12.23 units of B, which we would convert into A at the rate of 12 to 1 for 1.02 units of currency A, if our expectation of a 12-to-1 future exchange rate was correct. This 1.02 of currency A just repays our Country A loan, with no profit.[13]

The condition where the expected exchange rate equals spot rate adjusted for interest rate differentials is known as **uncovered interest parity**. It is "uncovered" because the expected rate is uncertain, and returns may or may not follow expectations if exchange rates move in an unanticipated direction.

Mathematically, **uncovered interest parity** holds when

---

[12] We are using extraordinarily high rates of interest here (2 % per month is roughly 27 % per annum, compounded) in order to illustrate our point more clearly. Interest rates are in practice normally quoted in annualized terms—we are giving the effective rate for a 30-day term here in order to keep the calculations simple in this first example.

[13] We have rounded the expected exchange rate to two digits to keep the example simple.

Value of A invested at interest rate **i** = Value of A converted into B at the spot
rate **e** and invested at interest rate i*
and then redeemed and converted back
to A at the expected rate **e^e**

$$\$A \bullet (1+i) = \$A \bullet \left(\frac{1}{e}\right) \bullet (1+i^*) \bullet (e^e)$$

Plugging in the figures from our most recent example above,

$$1 \bullet (1.02) = 1 \bullet 11.66 \bullet (1.05) \bullet \left(\frac{1}{12}\right)$$
$$1.02 = 1.02$$

Because this hypothesis is based on the unobservable quantity e^e, it is not subject
to direct empirical testing. Due to the random daily fluctuations of exchange rates,
the observed outcome will almost always differ from the expected outcome.
However, in the aggregate, expected exchange rates have been demonstrated to
be at least as good a predictor of future spot rates as any other system.[14]

We may alternatively use a **forward contract** to "lock in" our returns. Starting
with the variables given in the original example above, let's say in addition that the
30-day **forward rate** is 12.1 B for 1 A given that:

- The spot rate today (**e**) is 12 units of B for 1 unit of A; **e** = (1/12).
- The 30-day interest rate in Country A (**i**) is 2 %.
- The 30-day interest rate in Country B (**i***) is 5 %.
- The forward exchange rate (**e^f**) 30 days from today is 12.1 B for 1 A;
  e^f = (1/12.1).

We can lock in a risk-free arbitrage profit:

(a) We enter into a forward contract to sell B 30 days from today at the rate of 12.1
     units of B for 1 A.
(b) We borrow 1 unit of A for 30 days at 2 % interest.
(c) We convert our 1 unit of A into 12 units of B at today's spot rate of 12 for
     1, investing in Country B bonds at 5 % interest.
(d) At maturity, we redeem our B bonds for B currency and have 12.6 units of B.
(e) We exercise our forward contract, selling our 12.6 units of B for A at the rate of
     12.1 to 1, giving us 1.04 units of A (12.6 units of B ÷ 12.1 rate of B for
     A = 1.04 units of A).
(f) We repay our loan using 1.02 of A, and we have a 0.02 *risk-free profit*.

---

[14] Ian Giddy, "An Integrated Theory of Exchange Rate Equilibrium," University of Michigan,
May 1975.

Clearly, this situation can not persist for long, as investors will rush to undertake the same trade. The activity will drive the spot and forward exchange rates, and the interest rates in each country, to levels where the arbitrage opportunity evaporates and parity holds.

If, to keep this example simple, *only* the forward rate (e^f) were to adjust, it would shift from 12.1 to 1 to a rate of 12.36 to 1 of B for A ($e^f = [1/12.36]$). We would then, in step (e) above, sell our 12.6 units of B at the rate of 12.36 to 1, giving us 1.02 units of A, just enough to repay our loan (12.6 units of B ÷ 12.36 rate of B for A = 1.02 units of A). The risk-free arbitrage opportunity has disappeared.

In reality, the spot rate, forward rate, and interest rates in each country move simultaneously, acting on each other, and there is no clear one-way causality between any of the variables as they move into equilibrium.

The above example illustrates **covered interest parity**, which holds when the forward rate equals the spot rate adjusted for interest rate differentials. It is "covered" because by using a forward contract, one may "lock in" the anticipated returns regardless of the future spot rate.

Mathematically, **covered interest parity** holds when

Value of A invested at interest rate **i** = Value of A converted into B at the spot rate **e** and invested at interest rate i* and then converted back to A at the forward rate e^f

$$\$A \bullet (1 + i) = \$A \bullet \left(\frac{1}{e}\right) \bullet (1 + i^*) \bullet \left(e^f\right)$$

Plugging in the figures from our example above,

$$1 \bullet (1.02) = 1 \bullet 12 \bullet (1.05) \bullet \left(\frac{1}{12.36}\right)$$

$$1.02 = 1.02$$

Covered interest parity is observable and testable, as one may look online[15] or pick up a newspaper and make the calculations any time. One finds that the condition usually holds, with minor variations, which are generally attributed to factors such as unequal currency or default risk, asymmetry in capital controls and associated risk, and transaction costs.

---

[15] For example, at http://www.forexspace.com/currency-rates/EUR-USD/forward-rates or http://www.fxstreet.com/rates-charts/forward-rates/. In print, the *Wall Street Journal* publishes forward rates daily. Note that forward rates are normally quoted in forward points, or "pips," which are 1/1,000ths of a unit denomination of the "foreign" currency (the denominator currency, e.g., USD in EUR/USD). Forward rate quotes, in "pips," are calculated as forward points = |(forward price − spot price)* 1,000|. The sign is generally omitted.

To summarize, **uncovered interest parity** says that expected returns from investing in similar assets in two similar countries are identical. **Covered interest parity** says that the guaranteed returns from investing in the domestic country must equal the guaranteed returns from investing in the foreign country.[16]

The implication of the covered and uncovered interest parity hypotheses is that under equilibrium conditions, for any currency pair, the forward exchange rate and expected exchange rate will be determined by the relative interest rates in the two countries and that the forward and expected exchange rates will be equal.

8.4 Pegged Exchange Rates

Countries often control their exchange rates by "pegging" their exchange rate to a target level in terms of one or more foreign currencies.

Unlike freely floating currencies, where exchange rates are set endogenously by market forces, **pegged** or **"fixed" rates** are set by the government or monetary authority and are maintained through active intervention by the central bank in the foreign exchange markets. For example, Country B might "peg" its exchange rate at 6 to 1 for the currency of Country A (so for B, $\mathbf{e} = 6$).

A country might choose a fixed exchange rate regime for several reasons, high among them that the authorities may consider the maintenance of a stable exchange rate to be important for economic stability.[17] Particularly in small, developing countries, a fixed exchange rate may be seen as a way to reduce one area of uncertainty and contribute to growth.

Observation of the currency markets demonstrates that exchange rates, when permitted to respond to the interplay of supply and demand, fluctuate constantly. Thus, the pegged rate will almost invariably be higher or lower than the true equilibrium rate at any given time.

Maintaining a currency peg requires daily intervention in the foreign exchange market by the monetary authorities, who buy and sell foreign exchange and domestic currency in order to offset supply and demand pressures and maintain the target exchange rate.

In Fig. 8.2 below, the equilibrium exchange rate ($\mathbf{e_{EQUILIBRIUM}}$) of a hypothetical currency is determined by the supply and demand for foreign exchange (SFX and DFX).

We will examine two possible pegged rates for this currency: one weak and one strong.

---

[16] Akila Weerapana, "Lecture 5: Exchange Rate Systems," Wellesley College, 2003.

[17] P. Lindert and Thomas Pugel, *International Economics, 10th ed.* (New York: Irwin/McGraw-Hill), 1996.

Fig. 8.2 The market for foreign exchange ("€") in the home market of a pegged currency ("$")

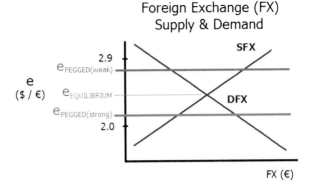

"Weak" Pegged Rate	$e_{PEGGED} > e_{EQUILIBRIUM}$
	Here, the daily intervention by the domestic central bank involves *buying* FX and *selling* domestic currency
	A weak currency is often maintained by exporting countries seeking to keep their exports artificially "cheap" for foreign buyers. As the domestic authorities buy FX and sell domestic currency, thereby artificially weakening the domestic currency, the domestic money supply increases as a consequence. This increase in the quantity of domestic currency can result in inflation and asset bubbles. Prolonged maintenance of a "weak" currency will result in the accumulation of large reserves of foreign currency (FX) by the central bank
	Often, the authorities will work to "**sterilize**" the domestic currency issued in these FX transactions through open-market operations. Sterilization involves the central bank selling government bonds into the market until it has sucked away most of the domestic money that it issued in its FX operations. We will revisit sterilization in detail in Chap. 13
"Strong" Pegged Rate	$e_{PEGGED} < e_{EQUILIBRIUM}$
	Here, the daily intervention by the central bank involves *selling* FX and *buying* domestic currency
	A strong currency may be seen as desirable, particularly for consumption-driven economies, as it offers the benefit of generally lower consumer prices since imports are made artificially "cheap." Raw commodity input costs are also reduced, which blunts the impact of rising or volatile commodity prices. A strong currency may also be maintained as a matter of national prestige.[18] Maintenance of a strong currency much removed from its equilibrium level bleeds foreign exchange, supplies of which are limited. Generally speaking, roughly 14 months of FX reserves are needed to credibly maintain a strong-currency policy

(continued)

---

[18] The desire to retain Sterling's prominence as the leading world currency was a significant factor in Great Britain's decision to fix their post—World War I exchange rate at an artificially strong level. India, seeking to develop a fully self-reliant economy in the wake of 150 years of British occupation, maintained a strong currency while prohibiting nonofficial flows of capital, until 1991. For more on Indian exchange-rate history, see: Johri Devika and Mark Miller, "Devaluation of the Rupee: Tale of Two Years, 1966 and 1991,"*CCS Working Paper No. 0028*, (New Delhi: Centre for Civil Society), 2002.

(continued)

> An artificially "strong" currency could also be symptomatic of a country
> emerging from some past era of rampant monetization of non-sustainable
> deficits. Such a country may have forced fiscal and monetary rectitude
> upon itself following some high (or hyper-) inflationary episode, by
> pegging to a strong, stable currency. The country could also still be in the
> process of "sucking away" the monetary excesses of the past by buying
> back its own currency to take it out of circulation, thereby resulting in a
> "strong" currency at present

As with any "price" that is forced away from its endogenous free-market equilibrium, fixed (pegged) exchange rate regimes are subject to significant pressure when the equilibrium of supply and demand deviates significantly from the peg. Consequently, pegged exchange rates are often accompanied by some level of currency or capital controls which limit the movement of capital into and out of the economy. This restricted capital mobility, in turn, reduces the ability of market forces to pressure the exchange rates back toward their free-market equilibrium.

Not all currency regimes are strictly "fixed" or "floating." There are variants of fixed rates, such as the **adjustable peg**, under which the authorities permit the currency to trade within a given band of exchange rates, which they will adjust from time to time to accommodate market pressures. For example, Country B may maintain an adjustable peg with a band of 5.8–6.2 units of B for 1 unit of A. The central bank will engage in FX operations to keep the exchange rate within the band. The European Exchange Rate Mechanism (ERM), precursor to the Euro, operated under a system of adjustable rates, in which each participating currency traded in a band. Each currency was permitted from time to time to adjust if the equilibrium level had clearly and durably shifted outside the band.

Under a **crawling peg**, the currency is permitted to trade within a band set by the authorities, but the band is adjusted in a planned, often preannounced manner over a period of time. Such a system might be adopted by a country whose currency is persistently trading above or below equilibrium, but which does not want to make large, discrete adjustments. By announcing the planned, gradual devaluation or revaluation of the currency by a set percentage, the authorities hope to mitigate pressure and avoid speculative volatility. Russia has occasionally used such a system, notably from 1994 to 1997 when it limited the annual depreciation of the ruble from 30 % down to 7 %. Unfortunately in this case, the "crawl" was not rapid enough as Russian fiscal profligacy ultimately led to debt default and a 65 % devaluation.[19] China switched from a fixed rate to a crawling peg in 2005 and, with the exception of a brief return to an inflexible peg during the 2008 financial crisis,[20] has permitted the yuan to appreciate gradually in the years since (Fig. 8.3). A discussion highlighting some aspects of the yuan–dollar saga is presented in Article 8.1 in this chapter.

---

[19] Tuomas Komulainen, "Currency Crisis Theories—Some Explanations for the Russian Case," *BOFIT Discussion Papers 1999 No. 1*, (Helsinki: Bank of Finland Institute for Economies in Transition), 1999.

[20] The RMB was held between 6.82 and 6.84 per USD from July 2008 through July 2010.

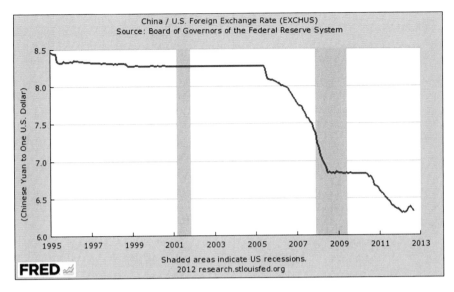

Fig. 8.3 China RMB to US dollar, monthly, 1995–2012 (*Source*: St. Louis Fed)

8.5 Managed Exchange Rates

A **managed exchange rate** regime, or "managed float," is a hybrid system under which the authorities permit market forces to move the exchange rate, but will intervene to limit volatility. By artificially reducing exchange rate volatility, the authorities seek to limit the effects of swings in capital flows on the economy, thereby reducing uncertainty. Under managed rates, the goal is primarily to limit daily swings, *not* to influence the *direction* of exchange rate changes.

India has operated under a managed float since the 1990s and has been more successful than many developing economies in avoiding the more severe problems associated with volatile global capital flows (Fig. 8.4).[21]

Even countries with generally freely floating rates will resort from time to time to central bank intervention to influence the value of their currency. In the wake of natural disasters, the demand for ready cash often soars, as was the case in Japan following its devastating earthquake in 2011. This was accompanied by fears that insurance companies would massively repatriate dollar-denominated assets into yen to meet claims. Concern rose among Japanese authorities that a stronger yen

---

[21] H.K. Behera, V. Narasimhan, and K.N. Murty, "Relationship Between Exchange Rate Volatility and Central Bank Intervention: An Empirical Analysis for India," *South Asia Economic Journal*, Research and Information System for Developing Countries, New Delhi, India and Institute of Policy Studies, Colombo, Sri Lanka, June 2008, accessed April 4, 2011. http://www.igidr.ac.in/~money/mfc_08/Relationship%20bet%20Exchange%20rate%20Volatility. . .%20Behera,%20 Narsimhan%20&%20Murty.pdf

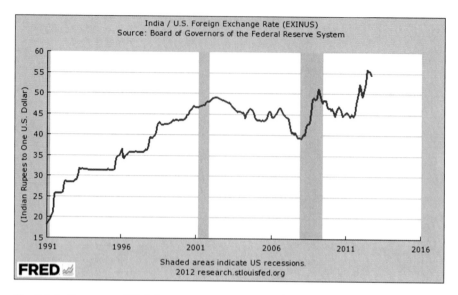

Fig. 8.4 Indian rupee to US dollar, monthly, 1991–2012 (*Source*: St. Louis Fed)

would hamper their economic recovery. As the yen rose immediately following the earthquake on March 11, 2011, the Bank of Japan stepped in with trillions of yen to counter the move. This was followed days later by the announcement of a coordinated effort by the monetary authorities of several advanced countries to support the Bank of Japan in its efforts to counter the yen's appreciation.[22] The primary reason for tempering the yen's strengthening was, of course, to ensure that Japanese exports were not priced out of competition, thanks to yen appreciation.

While targeted intervention of this sort may ameliorate a short-term condition, it is rarely successful in reversing a longer-term trend. The latter is driven by structural, expectational, and exogenous (policy) variables. The model linking all of these variables will be the subject of much discussion when we introduce the ISLM-BOP model in Chap. 9.

8.6   Trade-Weighted Exchange Rate

Because exchange rates by definition are relationships between only two currencies, alone they lack the ability to provide an indication of the "average" buying power of a unit of domestic currency in terms of other world currencies.

---

[22] Toru Fujioka and Mayumi Otsuma, "G-7 Sells Yen in First Joint Intervention Since 2000 to Ease Japan Crisis," *Bloomberg*, March 18, 2011, 8:38 AM ET, accessed April 4, 2011, http://www.bloomberg.com/news/2011-03-18/g-7-intervenes-to-weaken-yen-as-surging-currency-threathens-quake-recovery.html

Fig. 8.5 Trade-weighted index of US currency purchasing power ($e' =$ foreign/USD, with $1973 = 100$), 1973–2012 (*Source*: St. Louis Fed)

For this purpose, economists developed the concept of a "trade-weighted exchange rate index," which is an aggregate of a country's exchange rates against a "basket" of various currencies, with the weight of each exchange rate in the index determined by the amount of trade with each country included in the index.

This index permits a broad view of trends in a currency's general strength or weakness against the world's currencies overall. It is generally quoted using the indirect method (e'), giving the purchasing power of the domestic currency in terms of "average" foreign currency units.

In Fig. 8.5, we see the steady weakening of the US dollar over time relative to the currencies of its trading partners since 1971. We explore this observation and the significance of the 1971 date in detail in Chap. 13.

8.7 Hot Capital Flows

While funds transferred for use in merchandise and service transactions make up a large component of the daily movement of capital across the globe, trade is not the only source of capital flows.

Foreign direct investment (FDI), in which domestic entities acquire productive assets in overseas economies, is another major driver of capital movement. Volkswagen opening a manufacturing plant in Chattanooga, Tennessee, or GE opening an assembly plant in Mexico, would be examples of FDI.

Capital related to trade and FDI is relatively slow moving, as trade is limited by the speed at which goods and services may be produced and delivered, and FDI generally involves long-term plant and equipment assets.

Much more rapid are the flows of international capital seeking high short-term returns. **Hot capital** refers to highly mobile (and often, destabilizing) investor funds which chase the highest available returns and may flow in or out of a country very rapidly as economic circumstances change.

8.7.1   Hot Capital: Uncovered Nominal Interest Arbitrage

Let i = domestic interest rate

i^* = foreign interest rate

e = exchange rate

e^e = expected exchange rate—market's anticipation of future rates

If our home currency is expected to "strengthen" against the foreign currency, e^e will be lower than e. That is, future exchange rates are expected to be lower (stronger) than today's. Capital will tend to flow into the domestic country as speculators seek to benefit from the currency's appreciation.

If our home currency is expected to "weaken" against the foreign currency, e^e will be higher than e. That is, future exchange rates are expected to be higher (weaker) than today's. Capital will tend to flow out of the domestic country.

As we discussed regarding uncovered interest rate parity, these tendencies are mitigated by differences in interest rates between the two countries. Money in the domestic or foreign currency earns interest during the time it is held (we assume for simplicity that it is invested at the country's risk-free rate).[23]

So, the expected appreciation (or depreciation) of the home currency relative to the foreign currency must be weighed against the difference in interest rates earned while holding domestic bonds versus foreign bonds.

We can distill our uncovered interest parity formula into a rule.

Simplifying our earlier expression,

$$\$A \bullet (1 + i) = \$A \bullet \left(\frac{1}{e}\right) \bullet (1 + i^*) \bullet (e^e)$$

We obtain

$$\frac{1 + i}{1 + i^*} = \frac{e^e}{e}.$$

---

[23] We thus avoid factoring in default risk, which although real and often significant, is not part of our current analysis.

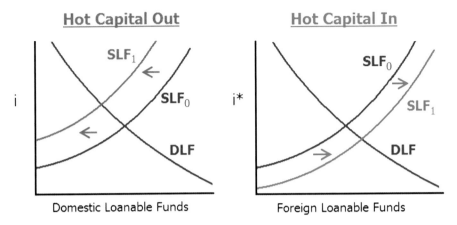

Fig. 8.6 Supply and demand for loanable funds in the domestic and foreign economies, with hot capital flowing out of the domestic economy and into the foreign economy

And further simplifying by subtracting 1 from both sides, we get

$$\frac{1 - i^*}{1 + i^*} = \frac{e^e - e}{e}.$$

If **i*** is relatively small (say under 10 % over the time period in question), the **uncovered interest rate parity** equilibrium may be very closely approximated by

$$(i - i^*) = \left[\left(\frac{e^e}{e}\right) - 1\right]$$

When this equilibrium condition is violated, an opportunity exists to exploit the discrepancy to earn a profit. Our rule for hot capital flows is as follows:

If $(i - i^*) < [(e^e/e) - 1]$, **then capital flows <u>out</u>, and vice versa.**

Here in Fig. 8.6, we see the supply and demand for loanable funds in the domestic and foreign economy. Hot capital is moving from the domestic economy into the foreign economy. When hot capital flows out of the domestic country, the supply of loanable funds (SLF) is reduced, resulting in higher interest rates ("i").

Meanwhile, as this hot capital flows into the foreign country, this increases the SLF in that country, resulting in lower foreign interest rates ("i*").

The spot exchange rate (**e**) will also be affected, as **SFX** and **DFX** will adjust to a new equilibrium as well. These changes occur concurrently with the changes in interest rates.

The reverse condition also holds, where **if $(i - i^*) > [(e^e/e) - 1]$, then capital flows in.** The two countries depicted in Fig. 8.6 will again simply be on opposite sides of the same disequilibrium, with hot capital now flowing out of the foreign economy, reducing foreign SLF and driving foreign interest rates higher ($i^*\uparrow$). As this hot capital flows into the domestic economy, domestic SLF is increased, driving interest rates lower ($i\downarrow$).

8.7.2 Hot Capital: "The Carry Trade"

The "carry trade" refers to the practice of borrowing in one currency and lending in another, generally using short-term financial instruments. The goal is to profit from nominal interest arbitrage opportunities as described above.

The carry trade may involve either **covered** or **uncovered interest arbitrage** operations. Naturally, a risk-free arbitrage profit investment is always preferable to investors, but such opportunities are rare and fleeting given the speed at which they are seized upon in the market. In either case, the operation typically involves the use of risk-free[24] short-term government securities of maturities ranging from overnight to 30 days. Under **covered interest arbitrage**, we seek to profit from disequilibrium where covered interest parity is violated:

$$(i - i^*) \neq \left[\left(\frac{e^f}{e} \right) - 1 \right]$$

Say, for example, we are a global macro investor[25] seeking arbitrage opportunities to invest $2 billion USD for 1 month. We see that the Japanese yen (JPY) and New Taiwanese dollar (TWD) are expected to trade in a relatively stable band with each another at the ratio of 2.86 JPY to 1 TWD, and forward rates reflect this.

Thus, with the right side of the arbitrage equation equal to zero [($e^f/e - 1$) = (2.86/2.86 − 1) = 0], any differential in interest rates on the left side of the equation presents an opportunity. And, let's say that, in fact, we observe that the short-term interest rate is 0.2 % in Japan and 2 % in Taiwan (annualized rates).

---

[24] Again, our definition of "risk-free" here encompasses the currencies of countries that have traditionally been considered safe havens, for example, the USA, Japan, Germany, Switzerland, and the Eurozone. Events from 2010 to the present have cast doubt on the concept of "risk-free" as traditionally understood. Nevertheless, our example sticks with this traditional model in order to best explicate the concepts that we are discussing. "Carry trade" operations typically focus on these "risk-free" currencies because to use a currency with significant default risk and/or volatility introduces an element of uncertainty that is difficult, if not impossible, to isolate and hedge. Such operations would fall more properly under pure speculation than the traditional definition of a carry trade.

[25] "Global macro" investing refers to an investment strategy that involves seeking out favorable trading opportunities across international geographies. Such investors are generally unrestricted in their choice of country or asset class and often seek "arbitrage" opportunities where they will short (sell) an unfavorable asset in a particular country and buy favorable assets in that or another country, with the expectation that one or both trades will move in the anticipated direction and earn a profit. It is variously estimated that perhaps 20% of the world's $2 trillion total hedge fund assets (as of 2011) are deployed in global macro strategies. A significant portion of global macro investing involves the carry trade.

To undertake our carry trade, we would:

(a) Borrow $2 billion worth of JPY and at the same time lend an equal amount of TWD for 30 days

(b) Acquire a 30-day forward contract permitting us to sell TWD for JPY at the rate of 1–2.86

At maturity, we redeem our Taiwan note into TWD, which we convert into JPY at the forward contract rate of 2.86 and repay our JPY debt.

Operation (a) earns us a +1.8 % interest rate differential, and operation (b) eliminates our currency risk. Here, we will generate a risk-free return at a 1.8 % annual rate, earning us approximately $3 million over the month.[26]

An **uncovered interest arbitrage** operation would work similarly, the difference being that the trade would be based on the expected (e^e), rather than the forward, exchange rate. Naturally, this involves the risk that the exchange rate may move in an unanticipated direction prior to maturity of the foreign bond—and rates can move against you even overnight!

Hot capital seeking carry-trade opportunities moves rapidly in response to changing economic conditions, and arbitrage opportunities close very quickly (as described below). Any risk-free opportunity like the one just described would almost immediately disappear as investors executed the trade, putting pressure on the forward currency rates.

8.7.3 Hot Capital: Adjustment Toward Equilibrium

Hot capital flows will quickly affect interest rates and spot and forward exchange rates, eliminating arbitrage opportunities. This creates a tendency toward equilibrium (**uncovered interest rate parity**), where $(i - i^*) = [(e^e/e) - 1]$.

An example of the adjustment process would be as follows:

Investors expect exchange rates to weaken, causing uncovered parity disequilibrium:

$$(i - i^*) < \left[\left(\frac{e^e}{e} \right) - 1 \right]$$

---

[26] Our profit in this example will be in JPY. If we wanted to have our profit back in USD, we could convert it at the prevailing spot rate at maturity or, more likely, eliminate the USD/JPY risk by using a forward contract at the time we initiate the trade. The perceptive reader will note that we never "invested" our $2 billion USD at all as we borrowed JPY and converted it into TWD to purchase the TWD debt. Normally to borrow the JPY in the first place, we would need to have collateral "locked up" on deposit with our broker—this is where our $2 billion USD comes into play assuming our broker did not permit us any leverage.

As we have discussed in our previous examples, hot capital will flow out today only to return "home" at the end of the investment period.

Effects

e↑	Home currency weakens as a result of the outflow
e^e↓	Capital is not held in foreign currencies forever. Capital must, eventually, come home Expectations will reflect this once a significant outflow has occurred
i↑	Domestic interest rates increase due to the decrease in SLF, which follows from the outflow, as depicted in Fig. 8.6
i*↓	Foreign interest rates decrease due to the increase in SLF overseas from the hot capital inflow, also as depicted in Fig. 8.6

The cumulative result of these effects will drive the inequality that created the hot capital flows rapidly back toward equilibrium.

Effects:

$$(i \uparrow - i^* \downarrow) < \left[\left(\frac{e^e\downarrow}{e\uparrow}\right) - 1\right]$$
$$\quad\; \textit{increasing} \qquad \textit{decreasing}$$

Final result:

$$(i - i^*) = \left[\left(\frac{e^e}{e}\right) - 1\right]$$

Empirical observation confirms that in general, over a long-enough period of observation, the relationship between interest rates and exchange rates does fluctuate in a range around that predicted by interest rate parity. Within shorter time frames, significant divergence may occur. And sometimes, unforeseen events can cause the carry trade to come completely unglued.

8.7.4   *Iceland 2008: The Carry Trade Blows Up*

The carry trade is a tried and true method for earning relatively low-risk, above-average returns for global investors, often for extended periods of time. However, at times, the carry trade can blow up spectacularly.

Screen capture from the website of Icesave, the UK arm of Landsbanki, 2007.

Iceland, a tiny country of some 300,000 people, built itself into a major financial center from 2001 to 2007. The period began with the deregulation of the Icelandic banking industry in 2001. Icelandic banks aggressively expanded internationally, ultimately accumulating the gargantuan sum of US $120 billion in foreign liabilities. This was almost inconceivable for a country with a GDP of only US $20 billion.[27]

As Iceland's economy heated up, interest rates were raised repeatedly and remained high. Global investors took advantage of these unusually high Icelandic interest rates by borrowing at low-interest in dollars, euro, or yen and lending or investing in Icelandic assets (Fig. 8.7).

For several years, the Icelandic carry trade produced steady and predictable returns as Iceland's exchange rate held mostly steady. In February 2006, however, the roof came crashing in on the Icelandic economy when the credit rating agency Fitch revised its outlook for Iceland from "stable" to "negative," indicating that its ratings "take into account Iceland's macro-prudential risks, including rising inflation, rapid credit growth, buoyant asset prices, a steep current account deficit and escalating external indebtedness (Fig. 8.8)."[28]

The Icelandic Króna, which had been steadily appreciating for the previous 2 years, fell 9 % against the Euro the following day and would never return to its

---

[27] Robert Peston. "Markets Call Time on Iceland," *BBC News*, October 4, 2008, 12:35 GMT, accessed March 31, 2011.

[28] "Fitch Confirms Rating of Icelandic Banks," *Iceland Review_Online*, Feb. 24, 2006.

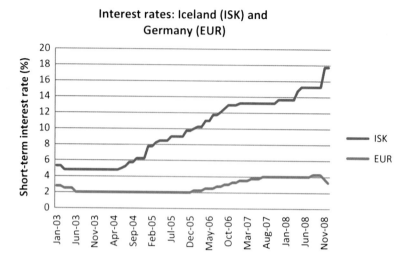

Fig. 8.7 (*Source*: ECB, Central Bank of Iceland)

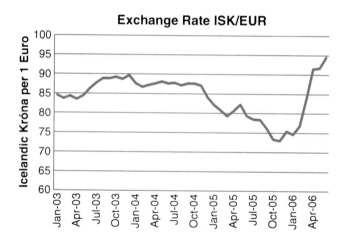

Fig. 8.8 (*Source*: Central Bank of Iceland)

previous levels. This shock blew apart the carry trade, wiping out all the returns of the previous 2 years in less than 2 months.

In carry-trade operations, it is important to remember that the capital deployed must eventually "come home" to its domestic country at the end of the investment period. A sharp depreciation of the foreign currency during the investment period

Fig. 8.9 ISK/EUR 30-day carry trade, Jan 2005 to May 2006

Date	EUR Borrowing	ISK Lending	ISK/EUR Exchange Rate	Carry trade 30-day return	Carry trade cumulative return
Jan-05	2.00%	7.75%	82.1	2.25%	2.25%
Feb-05	2.00%	7.75%	80.7	2.39%	4.69%
Mar-05	2.00%	8.25%	79.2	-1.20%	3.43%
Apr-05	2.00%	8.50%	80.6	-1.49%	1.89%
May-05	2.00%	8.50%	82.3	4.36%	6.34%
Jun-05	2.00%	8.50%	79.2	1.61%	8.05%
Jul-05	2.00%	9.00%	78.4	0.69%	8.79%
Aug-05	2.00%	9.00%	78.3	3.49%	12.58%
Sep-05	2.00%	9.00%	76.1	4.45%	17.59%
Oct-05	2.00%	9.00%	73.3	1.09%	18.87%
Nov-05	2.00%	9.75%	73.0	-2.55%	15.84%
Dec-05	2.00%	9.75%	75.4	1.71%	17.82%
Jan-06	2.25%	10.00%	74.6	-2.15%	15.28%
Feb-06	2.25%	10.25%	76.7	-7.78%	6.31%
Mar-06	2.25%	10.25%	83.7	-7.89%	-2.08%
Apr-06	2.50%	11.00%	91.5	0.50%	-1.59%
May-06	2.50%	11.00%	91.7	-2.33%	-3.88%

brings steep losses as investors must convert back to euros or dollars from the collapsed currency at a most disadvantageous rate.

In Figs. 8.9 and 8.10 we can see the carry trade in operation. We assume that on the first of each month, our hedge fund is borrowing euros, lending in Icelandic Króna at the prevailing short-term rates for 30 days and rolling over the investment the following month into another similar transaction.[29]

Carry-trade operators were certainly riding high until early 2006!

The sudden reversal in Iceland affected international markets as global macro investors scrambled to liquidate other holdings, affecting seemingly unrelated countries through contagion. Brazil, South Africa, Indonesia, Mexico, Turkey, and Poland saw their currencies immediately depreciate by between 1 % and 3 %.[30]

---

[29] Some caveats: We use the key bank rates as the interest rates in our example; naturally the interest rates on borrowing and investing in 30-day instruments will differ to some degree from these rates. Also, 30 days is at the long end of maturity for a carry trade, the majority of which involve continual rollover of overnight or very short-term transactions. To spare our reader from poring through 450 overnight transactions over 15 pages, we've simplified the example to 30-day borrowing and lending. The essential conclusions are no less valid using these streamlined assumptions.

[30] Generational Dynamics, "Sudden Collapse of Iceland Króna Portends Bursting of "Carry Trade" Bubble," February 27, 2006, accessed March 31, 2011, http://www.generationaldynamics.com/pg/xct.gd.e060227.htm

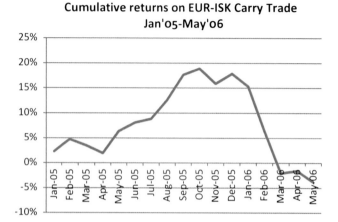

Fig. 8.10 Continual rollover of 30-day investment on the first of each month (borrow EUR, lend ISK) (*Source*: ECB, Central Bank of Iceland, author's calculations)

The saga, unfortunately, does not end there. Stalwart investors who refused to liquidate were rewarded handsomely for sticking with their Icelandic bets as the exchange rate stabilized and the carry trade recovered. At least, this was true for a time. Eventually, however, Iceland's banking sector grew into a classic bubble as it continued to pile up external debt. The three main banks expanded their reach throughout Europe, most notably the UK, where they offered high rates to depositors. (No bubble is ever complete without the "man on the street" being offered a chance to lose his life savings.)

Crucially, because these banks were registered outside the UK, the deposits of UK savers were not guaranteed. Ultimately, the Icelandic banking system collapsed of its own weight into insolvency. The Króna lost half its value from October 2007 to November 2008 and the carry trade blew apart again, this time with much greater force than before (Fig. 8.11).

An investor who had stuck to her guns from the beginning would have been utterly wiped out in the final collapse. Exchange rates move very quickly and can overwhelm favorable interest rate differentials in short order (Fig. 8.12).

Unfortunately, the crisis also affected savers outside of Iceland, whose deposits were unsecured. On October 6, 2008, UK depositors found that they could not access their online accounts, and it was clear that the banks were unable to honor withdrawal demands. The crisis would morph into an international incident as UK authorities seized Icelandic assets and intervened to guarantee recompense to UK depositors.

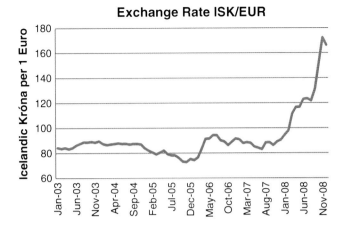

Fig. 8.11 The collapse of the Króna (*Source*: Central Bank of Iceland)

Fig. 8.12 Continual rollover of 30-day investment on the first of each month (borrow EUR, lend ISK) (*Source*: ECB, Central Bank of Iceland, author's calculations)

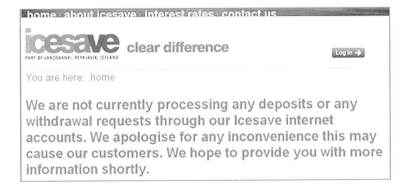

Screen capture from the website of Icesave, the UK arm of Landsbanki, October, 2008

The carry trade can produce outstanding returns on low-risk, short-term government debt; hundreds of billions of dollars are deployed in carry trades all over the world at any given time.[31] The exchange rate risk is very high, however, as long-stable currency relationships are prone to blow apart at a moment's notice. This type of investing is not for the faint of heart!

The crucial point here is that whenever macroeconomic variables—such as exchange rates, as we have just seen—stray or are forced away from their endogenous equilibriums, they will be under pressure. They will not be stable. Permitted, or forced, to remain in disequilibrium for too long, they will become macroeconomic volcanoes, exploding out of their former confinement.

In Iceland's case, the obliviousness or perhaps willing ignorance on the part of global investors to the severe imbalances mounting in the banking system permitted the exchange rate to remain stronger than conditions warranted for a long time, with disastrous results.

How can we know what results to expect when the relationships between macroeconomic variables move out of equilibrium? In the next chapter, we will introduce the powerful ISLM-BOM model, which permits us to analyze and predict the effects of changes to a host of macroeconomic variables.

Articles

Articles 8.1. The Yuan–Dollar Saga[32]

Julia Bao, *China Global Finance*

From the mid-1990s until 2005, the PBoC had locked (pegged) the yuan to the US dollar through daily foreign exchange intervention. *(a) Very briefly, how would a central bank peg its currency and allow it to change only gradually? And fundamentally, why was there upward pressure on the Chinese currency?*

---

[31] The aggregate size of the global carry trade is very difficult to estimate, as there is no standard for reporting from financial institutions. Some estimates have the total at 15–20 % of daily global foreign exchange transactions. At $4 trillion daily, this would imply $600 to $800 billion in carry trade activity. Source: "Regulators Tackle 'Carry Trades,'" *Dealbook, New York Times*, February 11, 2010, 5:01am accessed April 4, 2011, http://dealbook.nytimes.com/2010/02/11/regulators-tackle-carry-trades/

[32] This article has been partly adapted and modified from Article 3.1 in Langdana, *Macroeconomic Policy: Demystifying Monetary and Fiscal Policy.*

The pegging was not without cost. Clearly, an artificially weak domestic currency could not be sustained for a long period of time. *(b) Why not?*

The peg had other costs too—political costs. This policy of fixed exchange rates against a backdrop of burgeoning current account deficits in the USA and Western Europe unleashed a storm of protest from groups of politicians and trade representatives in the US and Europe. "They are doing this to make their exports cheaper and keep our goods out," complained Ron Wesbury of Morristown Metal Fittings, in Morristown, NJ. "Clearly this is why we in the US have such a big trade deficit with the Chinese!"

Simon Du of the Ministry of Trade for China agreed to meet us at the South Beauty Szechuan restaurant at the Guomao in Beijing where he shifted the discussion to fundamental macro theory. "As we have stated, (c) changing the exchange rate will, by itself, not shrink the US current account deficit with China—there is a fundamental relationship in macro theory that says that this whole thing is about a lack of domestic loanable funds (savings) on the part of the Americans," he explained, carefully sipping his Nine Treasures tea. "As long as this imbalance exists, the US will continue to incur big trade deficits financed largely by us."

Others, such as Senator Paulina Orr, remained combative. On last night's Face the World, the Senator announced her plan to "Retaliate! It must be a fair playing field! If the Chinese don't allow the Renminbi (Chinese yuan) to appreciate as fast as it should, I propose a tax on Chinese imports that will make up the amount by which they are artificially undervaluing their currency. This will rapidly shrink our trade deficit!"

"Not so fast," said Dr. Robert Braunstein, chief economist of Braunstein Vintage Timepieces in New York. "Placing a tariff (tax) on Chinese goods or forcing them to revalue their currency will not shrink our current account deficit. First, keep in mind," explained Dr. Braunstein, gently replacing a rare eighteenth-century Irish clock to the display case in the company museum, (d) "the goods now coming from China are doing so for a reason. The sectors that we have 'lost' to foreign competition are not coming back here. They are gone. Second, a very significant proportion of items coming from China (e) are only components of final products that are made (and exported) by US multi-national companies. Third, almost 40—50 % of the price of most items in the US can be attributed to marketing, transportation, and storage."

By 2005, given the challenges with overheating and worsening bubbles in housing and equities, it was clear that the peg had to be relaxed. The PBoC adopted a policy of steady appreciation since 2005, with the yuan pegged to a trade-weighted basket of currencies, along the lines of Singapore's "managed" peg.[33] *(f) Explain what a "trade-weighted" basket is.*

Federico Fontana, Supply Chain Manager at Comfy Pajamas Co. in New Orleans, agreed with Dr. Braunstein. His focus was on the razor-thin profit margins

---

[33] In July 2008, at the peak of the subprime and financial crisis, the PBoC again locked the yuan tightly to the US$ at a rate of approximately 6.83 RMB to 1 USD and held it there until July 2010.

embedded in the Asian supply chains in the late 2000s. "You have to understand," explained Fontana, "just a 1 % appreciation in an Asian currency is enough for someone like Lands' End or Victoria's Secret to switch an order for robes or pajamas from China to Thailand. The global supply chains are very nimble now, and large multinationals can easily switch sourcing locations based on short-term exchange rate fluctuations." He added, "By the way, the notion of managing (g) the Yuan relative to a basket of currencies of nebulous weights is really a politically astute system!" *Why "politically astute"?*

More recently, both the downgrade of US Treasury debt in July 2011 and fears of an impending double-dip recession were ample ingredients alone for a "perfect macro storm." Superimpose the backdrop of immense debt monetization (euphemized as "quantitative easing"), and the stage was set for global investors to seek to reduce their holdings of USD-denominated assets. All the above, coupled with the fact that the PBoC was gradually crawling its peg to allow the Remninbi yuan to appreciate toward its endogenous free-market equilibrium, resulted in the US dollar's inexorable decline.

Hence, this appreciation of the yuan in conjunction with the unrelenting weakness of the dollar given the bleak macro-backdrop in the USA resulted in the world, once again, "shorting" the US dollar. "Shorting" (selling a borrowed asset) occurs when investors and speculators expect, or bet, that the value of a certain asset is going to fall in the future, and they place their bets accordingly. *(h) List the factors that may have resulted in a pessimistic outlook for the US dollar in the 2008–2012 period?*

(i) If 7 units of foreign currency are equal to 1 US$ today, but in the near future 5 units of foreign currency are expected to equal 1 US$, then describe the flow of the hot capital today and in "the near future."

(j) Given the figures in (i) above, let's say that the US short-term interest rate is 2 % and the foreign interest rate, in Country B, is 8 %. Use the expression for nominal uncovered parity to determine whether hot capital will flow and in what direction.

*(k) Let's say that forward contracts were available to purchase or sell 6 units of Country B's currency for 1 US$, one year from today, and that the interest rates given above are 1-year rates. Is there a **covered interest arbitrage** opportunity here? (l) How would such an operation be carried out? (m) What would be the risk-free profit, if any? (m) Why are highly profitable currency arbitrage opportunities generally short-lived in the real world?*

According to China, the shorting of the US$ was exceptionally dangerous for China's economy as well as those of other developing countries. A senior PBoC official said, "The shorting of the US currency is only going to worsen our SAP bubbles in housing and in the stock market today. We must prevent this hot capital from flooding in!" *(n) Explain how the shorting of the US$ exacerbates China's bubbles.*

Hints and Solutions

Article 8.1

(a) The central bank could adopt a **crawling peg** wherein the central bank buys back progressively less of its currency every week, with the rate of decline well established by the rule. The Chinese currency is under pressure to strengthen due to China's strong macroeconomic outlook.

(b) The huge increase in domestic monetary growth entailed by the peg, as the central bank purchases foreign currency by issuing domestic currency to maintain the peg, will eventually lead to inflation and asset bubbles if left unchecked for too long. And, regardless of whether this growth is "sterilized" by the central bank (sweeping domestic currency away by selling domestic bonds into the market), a huge pile of reserves of foreign currency (and foreign bonds purchased with that currency) will accumulate. Like many "good" things, foreign reserves can be beneficial in moderation; however, accumulating a mountain of such reserves can leave the domestic country overly dependent on the vicissitudes of a foreign government's fiscal and monetary policies.

(c) This refers to the National Savings Identity: $(G\text{-}T) = (S\text{-}I) + (Imp\text{-}Exp)$. If domestic savings, net of private domestic investment $(S\text{-}I)$, is insufficient to cover the fiscal deficit $(G–T)$, then the difference will be made up by foreign sources, via the funds made available through the current account deficit $(Imp\text{-}Exp)$.

(d) Trade is fundamentally driven by comparative advantage. Distorting trade by imposing tariffs would not reverse it. Even if the USA were to *bar all imports from China*, the USA would not suddenly develop a CA in making pajamas in Perth Amboy, NJ. Rather, the USA would trade for those goods with Vietnam, Bangladesh, Thailand, and other countries endowed with low-skilled labor. And given the prevalence of intra-industry trade, Chinese-produced goods would still find their way to the USA as components of items whose final assembly may be in, say, Cambodia or South Africa. Comparative advantage will find a way to express itself, for any country not living in complete autarky.

(e) As discussed in Chaps. 3 and 5, most global trade is intra-industry trade. Tariffs on one component would only serve to drive up the price of the final product, thereby hurting all countries involved.

(f) As discussed in this chapter, a trade-weighted basket is an artificial index of currencies that are weighted by the amount of trade that the domestic country undertakes with each currency-sponsoring country.

(g) Such a system would allow the Chinese to tweak the yuan without letting on that their currency was adjusting with respect to, say, the US dollar. A tweak in the dollar–yuan rate could simply be explained as a "realignment" or a "reconfiguration" of the market basket. Thus, a weakening of the currency could be masked under nebulous and undisclosed algorithms. And a strengthening of the yuan vis-à-vis the US dollar would avoid the potential loss of face should such a move be interpreted as bowing to US political pressure.

(h) Such factors include runaway (non-sustainable) budget deficits, persistently high unemployment, collapsed housing prices, a gigantic monetization effort by the Federal Reserve, two large global military conflicts eating away at the national treasury, an overlay of massive government regulation, tax uncertainty both at the personal and the corporate levels, the continued threat of terrorism across the globe, looming trade conflicts, a resurgent China, a declining educational system, massive unfunded state and municipal pension commitments, trouble in the Eurozone, and most important, a steady loss of confidence in US domestic political leadership.

(i) Investors take 1 US\$ and buy 7 units of foreign currency of, say, Country B today. They park this money in Country B and take advantage of a nice run-up in the equities/housing market there, or perhaps simply invest it in "safe" government bonds. Then in the future, the hot capital "comes home" to US\$ at the rate of 5 units of B's currency = 1 US\$. In this example, hot capital rushes out of the USA today and then comes home "in the near future." It is important to remember the last step, where the capital "comes home," when thinking about capital flows.

(j) Our rule of thumb for the flow of hot capital is as follows:
If $(i - i^*) < [(e^e/e) - 1]$, then capital flows out, and vice versa.
Our variables are:
$e = 1/7$, or 0.143 (rounded)
$e^e = 1/5$, or 0.2
$i = 0.02$
$i^* = 0.08$
Plugging in our variables, we obtain the following:
If $(\mathbf{0.02 - 0.08}) < [(\mathbf{0.2/0.143}) - 1]$, then capital flows out.
Simplifying,
If $(-0.06) < [(1.398) - 1]$, then capital flows out.
If $(-0.06) < (0.398)$, then capital flows out.
Here, by our simplified rule, we see that capital will indeed flow <u>out</u> of the USA and into Country B.

(k) Using our simplified rule, there will be a covered interest arbitrage opportunity if

$$(i - i^*) \neq \left[\left(\frac{e^f}{e}\right) - 1\right].$$

Our variables are as given in (j) above, with the addition of
$e^f = 1/6$, or 0.167 (rounded).
Plugging in our variables, we obtain the following:
If $(0.02 - 0.08) \neq [(0.167/0.143) - 1]$, then there is an arbitrage opportunity.
Simplifying:
If $(-0.06) \neq (0.167)$, then there is an arbitrage opportunity.

There is in fact an arbitrage opportunity here.

(l) The arbitrage operation would be carried out as follows (we'll use $1 as our investment, in this example):

Step #1: Borrow $1 USD today, convert it to "B" currency at the rate or 7 to 1 (since $e = 1/7$) to obtain 7 units of "B" currency.

Step #2: Lend the 7 units of "B" currency by investing in Country B bonds at the prevailing risk-free rate of 8 %.

Step #3: Procure a forward contract today that confers the right to <u>sell</u> "B" currency at the rate of 6 units per 1 US$ (as $e^f = 1/6$).

Step #4: At maturity, redeem the "B" bond for 7.56 units of currency B.

Step #5: Use our forward contract to convert this currency into US$ at 6 to 1, yielding $1.26.

Step #6: Repay our $1 USD loan with 2 % interest for $1.02, leaving us with a balance of $0.24 in risk-free profit!

(m) As investors rush to avail themselves of these opportunities, they put pressure on the variables, which will respond and converge toward equilibrium.

The capital rushing into the foreign country will increase the demand for that country's currency, causing its exchange rate to strengthen while ours weakens ($e\uparrow$ from our perspective in the domestic country).

Knowing that all the capital that has flooded into the foreign currency must "come home" at some point, our expectations regarding the future exchange rate of that currency soften, as we anticipate the weakness that will come with the flow of currency out of that country. So, from our perspective, the expected exchange rate will strengthen ($e^e\downarrow$).

Similar adjustments will be made to interest rates, both domestic and foreign, with the supply of loanable funds in the foreign country increasing dramatically, causing foreign interest rates ($i*$) to decline as the price of foreign bonds increases. Simultaneously, domestic loanable funds will decrease as hot capital exits, driving domestic interest rates (i) higher.

The sum of the effects can be depicted as

$$(i\uparrow - i^*\downarrow) < \left[\left(\frac{e^e\downarrow}{e\uparrow}\right) - 1\right]$$
$$\textit{increasing} \qquad \textit{decreasing}$$

Ultimately, the variables will settle when equilibrium is restored.

$$(i - i^*) = \left[\left(\frac{e^e}{e}\right) - 1\right]$$

(n) As capital rushes out of the USA in the above example, investors are essentially "shorting" the US currency. This results in a massive hot capital inflow into China, which drives down interest rates and creates inflation and asset bubbles.

Chapter 9
The ISLM-BOP Model: The Goods Market, the Money Market, and the Balance of Payments

Summary In this chapter, we introduce the powerful ISLM-BOP model of macroeconomic analysis. Mastery of this model permits us to anticipate the effects of any number of exogenous policy decisions and to interpret the follow-on effects of endogenous changes in the global macroeconomy.

We begin by introducing a model of the global goods market, which adds exports and imports to the traditional one-country paradigm.

We break down the current account balance, its causes, and its effects. Our ever-present trade skeptic will pop in here in an article to demand, "We need to close our trade deficit by expanding exports!" This common misconception is addressed in detail.

We finally derive the global IS curve (the relationship of output to interest rates where the goods market is in equilibrium), the first part of our global ISLM-BOP model.

We continue to build our model by introducing the global money market. We then derive the global LM curve (the relationship of output to interest rates where the money market is in equilibrium).

This leads to a detailed discussion of the capital account balance. The tight relationship between the CAB (current account balance) and the KAB (capital account balance) is closely examined.

We finally synthesize the money market equilibrium (LM) with the goods market equilibrium (IS) to develop the IS–LM model (omitting, for the moment, the balance of payments). A walk-through is undertaken, with several examples illustrating the relationship between the goods markets and money markets.

Having fully described the global IS–LM model, we proceed to explain the balance of payments (BOP), the mobility of capital, and the relationship of exports and imports to the BOP.

At this stage, we are finally ready to add in the BOP and complete our basic ISLM-BOP model (which, for now, omits inflation and assumes perfect capital mobility). All three markets—goods, money, and exchange rates—are now incorporated in the model.

F. Langdana and P.T. Murphy, *International Trade and Global Macropolicy*,
Springer Texts in Business and Economics, DOI 10.1007/978-1-4614-1635-7_9,
© Springer Science+Business Media New York 2014

Several important policy exercises are included, with the reader beginning with a hypothetical policy change, or economic event, and working through the intuition and logic using the model to arrive at the result.

Here, as in almost all instances in this text, we avoid detailed computations and derivations of the formulae behind the discrete elements of the ISLM-BOP and stick with the broad model and its implications.

This chapter provides a "Survival Guide," a step-by-step process for working with the model. This will be an important tool as the reader works through the examples in the ensuing chapters.[1]

9.1   ISLM-BOP: The Engine Room

This chapter introduces "the engine room" of global trade and macroeconomics, the ISLM-BOP model. The ISLM-BOP model is a powerful tool that will allow us to synthesize the various components of the global macroeconomy and analyze the effects of a multitude of events and policy changes.

The National Savings Identity (NSI) provided us with an intuitive understanding of a range of big-picture macroeconomic scenarios. However, the NSI, despite its versatility and intuitiveness, lacks in detail. For example, when we increase government spending to generate a "multiplier effect," as per John Maynard Keynes, what are the effects on output, interest rates, and trade? When we increase money supply to jump-start a stalling economy, how does this affect the international flows of capital? When a foreign economy "catches fire" and its long-term macroeconomic outlook is highly positive, what are the effects on the domestic economy?

The ISLM-BOP provides us with a well-articulated and sophisticated model that incorporates the economy's various "feedback" channels into the analysis of macroeconomic policy.

---

[1] The ISLM model originated with the ideas articulated by John Maynard Keynes in his *General Theory of Employment Interest and Money* (1936), and was first interpreted graphically by J.R. Hicks in Mr. Keynes and the "Classics": A Suggested Interpretation, Econometrica, 5(2): 147–159). The authors recognize that the ISLM model, relying on Keynes' ideas and assumptions, is sometimes controversial (as is seemingly anything connected with Lord Keynes). Frederich Hayek was once called Milton Friedman a "Keynesian" for even accepting the notion of "aggregate demand"! While taking no position on these disputes here (Dr. Langdana's inscrutable agnosticism in these matters is well known to his many students, past and present), we strongly believe that the ISLM-BOP model provides an incredibly useful framework for analyzing the relationships between various components of the global economy. This is not to say that the model is flawless or predictive at every level or in every time frame. However, the predictions of the model, from the "big-picture" point of view, are generally borne out by empirical observation. Its usefulness comes from the aid it provides in visualizing the relationships between large-scale macroeconomic events, such as the interplay between increased government spending and exchange rates, or the different effects of monetary tightening under fixed versus flexible exchange-rate regimes.

In this chapter, we derive and explain the IS, LM, and BOP curves, whose equilibrium drives our model. The derivations will be followed by several full-scale macroeconomic policy exercises introducing and utilizing this powerful analytical tool.

9.2   The Goods Market

The goods market is the market for all goods and services in the economy. It comprises total output, or GDP. To briefly review what we discussed in Chap. 7, output (Y) is a function of several factors: consumer spending (C), investment (I), government spending (G), exports (X), and imports (V). The output function is given by

$$Y = \begin{array}{c}\textbf{Consumer} \\ \textbf{spending}\end{array} + \textbf{Investment} + \begin{array}{c}\textbf{Government} \\ \textbf{spending}\end{array} + (\textbf{Exports} - \textbf{Imports})$$

or

$$Y = C + I + G + (Exp - Imp)$$

Let's break each component down in order to analyze it more closely.

9.2.1   C: Consumer Spending (Private Consumption)

The consumption function is described by the expression

$$C = \underline{C} + bY + dW$$

where

C = private consumption expenditure.
$\underline{C}$ = consumer confidence. This component includes consumer tastes, preferences, and expectations. Surges and drops in consumer confidence translate into increases and decreases in C.

Consumer confidence is a hugely important driver of consumer spending, as people buy more goods and services when they are feeling good about their economic situation and prospects. Surveys in most countries regularly monitor consumer confidence; in the United States the most widely used are the Conference Board's Consumer Confidence Index® and the University of Michigan Consumer

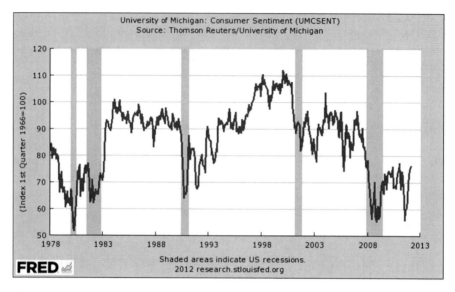

Fig. 9.1 University of Michigan Consumer Sentiment Index 1978–2012. Shaded areas indicate recessions (*Source:* St. Louis Fed) The University of Michigan survey tracks consumer confidence on a scale benchmarked to 1966 = 100. The figures therefore should not be interpreted as a direct measure of confidence—that is, an index value of 75 does not mean that consumers are "75 % confident." The survey is very useful in comparing relative levels of confidence between periods and in seeing turning points in sentiment

Sentiment Survey.[2] Both surveys are robust in their methodology, and there is wide consensus that they both provide useful information regarding the present state of consumer attitudes. International measures include the ECRI US Weekly Leading Index, Japan's Tankan Index, Ireland's KBC Bank Consumer Sentiment Index, and the Bank of Indonesia's Consumer Survey. Another robust index is the Nielsen Index for global consumer confidence—India, for example, closely tracks this one.

One may see the utility of these measures as falling confidence accompanies, and generally precedes, economic downturns (shaded areas on the graph), while rising confidence is an indicator that the economy is on its way out of recession (Fig. 9.1):

b = the **marginal propensity to consume (MPC)**. This is defined as the increase in consumption (**C**) arising from a unit increase in national income (**Y**). A value of b = 0.8 for the USA means that if average national income were to increase

---

[2] The surveys are sufficiently similar to exhibit a strong correlation. The Conference Board survey asks participants to consider their situation from 0 to 6 months ahead and focuses more on employment and income prospects. The Michigan survey asks respondents to look up to 5 years into the future, and questions are geared to the more general term "financial condition" than employment and income specifically. For details on the correlations between different surveys see Merkle DM, Langer GE, Sussman D (2004) Consumer confidence: measurement and meaning. ABC News, 18 June 2004. http://abcnews.go.com/images/pollingunit/consumerconfidence061804.pdf. Accessed 29 March 2013.

by \$1, consumers would spend 80 cents of this increase and save 20 cents. The MPC thus measures the sensitivity of consumer spending to changes in output. The MPC is relatively stable for a given country and inherently captures national and cultural spending and saving tendencies.

In the United States, this figure is generally 85 % or higher. In many Asian countries, which have a cultural bias toward saving, the figure is often in the 30 % range.

Y = national income, synonymous with national output and GDP for our purposes.

d = the amount of an increase in planned consumption stemming from a unit increase in wealth (W) defined below. Here, d is a small number, unlike the MPC for the USA. Empirical studies generally find a small and transitory effect, since consumers understand the enormous volatility of the value of their wealth holdings.

In the USA, estimates range from negligible to between 0.04 and 0.07, that is, 4–7 cents in increased consumption per \$1 of increase in wealth. European countries range from near-zero (France) up to 0.05 (UK), with varied and conflicting estimates for most countries in-between, while Japan's figure is estimated at 0.01–0.04.[3]

W = national wealth holdings. This term includes financial (savings deposits, mutual funds, etc.) and real (housing, land) holdings. The celebrated and controversial "wealth effect" takes place when increases in the value of individuals' stock portfolios coupled with, for example, appreciation in property prices inflate the public's wealth holdings. The expectation of continued future gains may induce individuals to increase consumption in the current period. In a sense, the security afforded by future expected income may induce individuals to consume this "future income" today. Conversely, a stock market crash or the collapse of a housing bubble (both of which were exhibited in the 2006–2010 period) may have the opposite effect–a negative "wealth effect," which tamps down consumer spending in the present period.

The wealth effect, while small under "normal" circumstances, can become significantly pronounced during times of peak euphoria or extreme distress.

For convenience, we will subsume the "dW" term into $\underline{C}$, consumer confidence, when we work with the complete goods market equilibrium.

---

[3] Source: Richard M. Sousa, "Wealth Effects on Consumption, Evidence from the Euro Area," *European Central Bank Working Paper No. 1050* (Frankfort: European Central Bank), May 2009. This study analyzes data from the Euro area and concludes that changes in financial wealth (savings, mutual funds, etc.) have a larger impact on consumption than changes in real-estate (housing) wealth. Other studies (Sierminska, Eva and Garner, Thesia, "A Comparison of Income, Expenditures and Home Market Value Distributions using the Luxembourg Income Study data from the 1990s," *Luxembourg Income Study Working Paper No. 338*, 2002, and Sierminska, Eva, Brandolini, Andrea, and Smeeding, Timothy M, "Comparing Wealth Distribution across Rich Countries: First Results from the Luxembourg Wealth Study," *Luxembourg Wealth Study Working Paper Series, Working Paper No. 1*, 2007) find an opposite effect; there is general agreement, however, that consumers respond to the two types of wealth increases differently.

$$C = \underline{C} + bY \; (+ dW)$$

(Wealth Effect subsumed into consumer confidence, for simplicity)

So

$$C = \underline{C} + bY$$

The inclusion of the wealth effect has a negligible effect in normal times; however, it will be important to keep in mind that the exaggerated "wealth effect" during a crisis will often mean that shifts in consumer confidence will be especially pronounced.

9.2.2   *I: Capital Investments*

Once again, "investments" in macroeconomics refer to "capital investments" as in new plant and equipment and in commercial and residential construction. Capital investment in macropolicy implies the necessity of borrowing by private companies to fund their investments.[4]

Armed with this quick review, the investment function is

$$I = \underline{I} - fi$$

where

I = private capital investment for items such as new plant and equipment, housing, and the growth of new capital stock.

$\underline{I}$ = investor confidence. Along the lines of consumer confidence, this variable captures the sentiment of business.

The Conference Board's CEO Confidence Survey[TM], which reports on CEO appraisals of current and 6-month anticipated economic and industry conditions, is one high-profile measure of investor confidence. Another is the Conference Board's Leading Economic Indicators Index®, which captures ten different economic inputs to gauge the state of the business cycle. Historically, while there are false signals,[5] turning points in this index have preceded turning points in aggregate economic activity. Several international indices have been added in recent years in

---

[4] Again, "borrowing" is used in the broadest possible context and includes private companies incurring liabilities of various kinds (bonds, bank loans, and the issuance of equity) as they obtain new capital for the purpose of funding their planned capital investments.

[5] As Nobel Prize-winning economist Paul Samuelson once quipped, "Economists have correctly predicted nine of the last five recessions." Source: http://www.tompaine.com/articles/2006/03/13/the_next_recession.php. Accessed May 5, 2011.

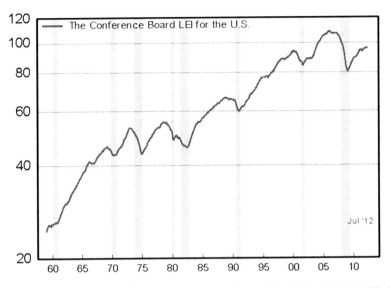

Fig. 9.2 The Conference Board's Leading Economic Indicator Index® for the USA **1959–2012** (*Source:* The Conference Board)

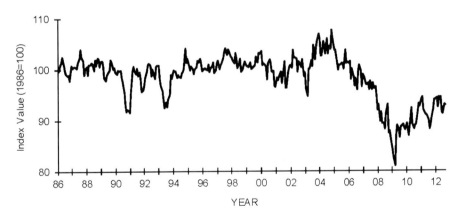

Fig. 9.3 NFIB Small Business Optimism Index for the USA, 1986–2012 (*Source:* NFIB)

addition to the original US-only index (Fig. 9.2). The country-specific Business Conditions Index compiled by MasterCard® is another widely used investor confidence measure, particularly in emerging economies.

Other measures of investor sentiment include the ECRI US Weekly Leading Index; the State Street Investor Confidence Index®, which focuses on investor risk appetite (which we might think of as "Wall Street's view"); and the National Federation of Independent Businesses Small Business Optimism Index (which we might consider "Main Street's view") (Fig. 9.3).

f = the sensitivity of private capital investment to a unit change in interest rates (**i**). Here, a unit increase (decrease) in interest rates causes private capital investment to fall (rise) by **f**, hence the negative sign for this term in the expression.

i = interest rate. As interest rates fall, capital investment (private demand for loanable funds) increases and vice versa. While strict application of the economic formulae underlying the model interprets this variable as being the short-term risk-free rate, we assume that this rate in turn impacts rates across the term structure and across security classes.

From an accounting and finance standpoint, debt and equity are simply two forms of business liability, and both involve a cost of capital which is impacted by the short-term rate. Thus, regardless of the form that investments take, a lower "i" will tend to encourage investment while a higher "i" will tend to depress investment.

The primary determinant of change in capital investment (**I**) is $\underline{\mathbf{I}}$, investor confidence, and *not* interest rates per se. Regardless of how low interest rates may be, a dismal long-term business outlook will make investors unlikely to pump more funds into private capital investment. Low interest rates, even zero as evidenced by Japan for nearly 20 years starting in the 1990s, and in the United States following 2007–2008, were not sufficient to motivate investors to put their capital at risk against a backdrop of gloomy business forecasts.

Such a situation is a version of what is known as a "liquidity trap." In this case, low and falling interest rates do nothing to spur capital investment—the plunge in investor confidence counteracts any positive effect arising from the lowering of interest rates.[6]

While short-term rates are exogenously determined by monetary policy, investor confidence ($\underline{\mathbf{I}}$), like its counterpart consumer confidence ($\underline{\mathbf{C}}$), is endogenously determined by economic actors (investors and consumers) who continually process current and past information. Both variables are notoriously difficult, if not impossible, to manipulate through changes in policy. History is well documented with cases of how confidence, which has taken many years to build, can be lost in an afternoon while policymakers stand by as helpless spectators.

---

[6] A liquidity trap is very dangerous indeed. Policymakers, obstinately pushing interest rates down in the hope of jump-starting the economy, finally end up with nothing but a tremendous amount of dangerous liquidity (i.e., cash money) swilling around in the asset markets, as well as the potential for a collapsing domestic currency (zero interest rates and a bleak outlook will do it) and a monetary policy that is now essentially out of ammunition. The mammoth and unprecedented increases in liquidity, euphemized as QE1, QE1.5, QE2, QE3, and QE-Infinity ("QE" for "quantitative easing") from 2008 to 2012 and beyond, were nothing but massive monetizations of toxic assets and runaway national debt that only managed to prop up the stock market for a time, without having any positive measurable effects on capital investment, output, or employment.

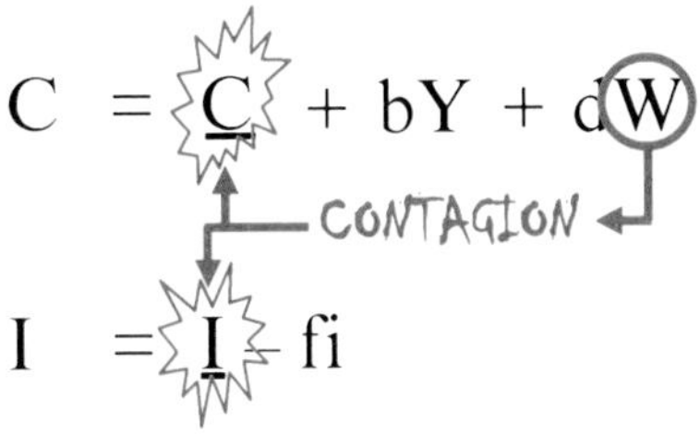

Fig. 9.4 Contagion

$$C = C + bY + dW$$
$$\text{CONTAGION}$$
$$I = I - fi$$

9.2.3 Contagion

Contagion can occur when a change in one economic factor affects others. Mathematically, contagion happens when a variable in a given expression has a "spillover" effect on other variables in that expression and may even affect variables in other expressions. A common example is a negative "wealth effect," which occurs where a sudden drop in wealth, often resulting from the bursting of a financial bubble, causes a sharp decrease in consumer confidence, which then causes a rapid deterioration in investor confidence, resulting in severely reduced consumer spending *and* investment (Fig. 9.4):

As discussed above, in its effect on consumer and investor confidence, the wealth effect is generally small or negligible, but during times of extreme euphoria or distress, it will often act as an accelerant on these variables, magnifying their positive or negative movements.

Contagion may also occur in a global macroeconomic context, when changes in foreign output, interest rates, exchange rates, and/or long-term economic outlook lead to a reduction in domestic output, transferring "sickness" from one economy into another. We shall see several examples of this in later chapters.

The other components of GDP are as follows:

9.2.4 G: Government Spending

Government spending (**G**) includes government expenditures on goods and services and excludes transfer payments. Transfer payments include things like assistance programs, social security, and business subsidies; these remittances are excluded because they are simply redistributions which do not directly create output.

9.2.5 Exp.: Exports (X)

This term comprises a nation's exports of goods and services. We use the term (**X**) to represent exports. This figure includes investment income, royalties, fees, and other transfers from abroad. The rationale for the inclusion of these items is that they represent compensation for exported services, even if such services were not explicitly transferred.

The export function is given by

$$X = \underline{X} + sY^* + te$$

where

$\underline{X}$ = foreign tastes and preferences for domestic goods.

s = sensitivity of exports to foreign GDP.

Y^* = foreign output (foreign GDP). Exports will tend to expand with increases in foreign GDP, as foreign consumers are more able to purchase overseas goods.

t = sensitivity of exports to changes in exchange rates. A weaker currency ($\uparrow$e) permits foreigners to purchase more domestic exports.

e = the exchange rate (units of domestic currency required to purchase 1 unit of foreign currency).

9.2.6 Imp.: Imports (V)

This term represents imports of goods and services from abroad. For notational convenience, we include incomes and transfers paid to foreigners in this figure. The term (V) is used to represent imports.[7]

The imports function is given by

$$V = \underline{V} + jY - ze$$

where

$\underline{V}$ = domestic demand for foreign goods. This term includes tastes and preferences, which can shift over time and with changes in per capita income.

j = sensitivity of imports to changes in domestic output.

Y = domestic output (GDP).

It should be noted that for both the export (X) and import (V) functions, the most important component variables are GDP (Y) and foreign GDP (Y^*). Exchange rates are a less important contributor, by comparison. This is a vitally important point.

---

[7] Students will find that imports are often represented by the variable M in economic literature, with the trade balance represented by (X–M). However, we assign the variable M to represent the nominal money stock in our ISLM-BOP model. We thus have chosen the variable V to represent imports in all of our equations and models.

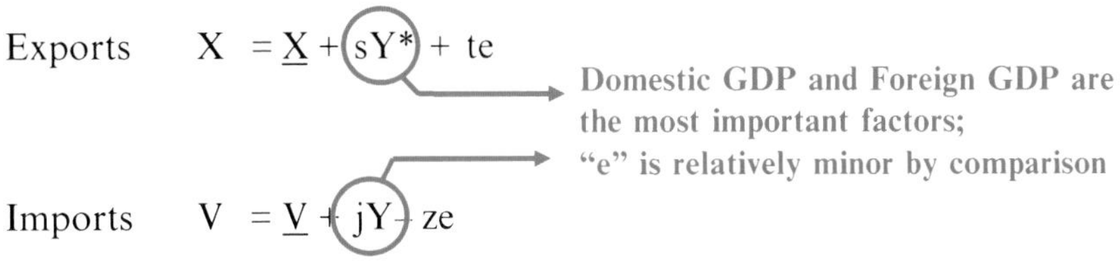

Exports $X = \underline{X} + (sY^*) + te$

Domestic GDP and Foreign GDP are the most important factors; "e" is relatively minor by comparison

Imports $V = \underline{V} + (jY) + ze$

Fig. 9.5 The export and import functions

There is a sense that weaker exchange rates (an increase in **e**) will immediately translate to an increase in exports and a decrease in imports. This is not the case; while imports and exports may indeed, eventually, be affected, the main "drivers" of the trade balance are growth in domestic and foreign national incomes, **Y** and **Y*** (Fig. 9.5).

z = sensitivity of imports to changes in exchange rates. A stronger exchange rate (**e**↓) allows domestic consumers to purchase more foreign goods.

e = the exchange rate (units of domestic currency required to purchase 1 unit of foreign currency).

9.2.7   The Trade Deficit (X − V)

Trade in goods and services makes up the vast proportion of the current account balance, and we will generally use the term "trade balance" and "current account balance" synonymously for the purposes of our analyses.

The trade deficit receives much attention in the news. With each month's release, an increase in the trade deficit is perceived as an unwelcome development, while a reduction in the trade deficit is seen as positive news. However, a trade deficit is not automatically a bad thing!

Healthy economies often have a growing appetite for imports; for many advanced economies, an expansion of output (**Y**) will see a dramatic expansion of imports (**V**). As such, healthy economies will see their current account balance (**X** − **V**) move in a negative direction. Sick economies, on the other hand, often display increasing current accounts, with imports (**V**) shrinking, because consumers cannot afford them anymore.

A trade surplus will also generally occur in export-focused economies (whether sick or healthy), typically developing countries in the early stages of manufacturing for global markets.

9.2.8   The Output Function ("Y")

With the component terms of output defined, we can now present an expanded expression of the output function (Fig. 9.6).

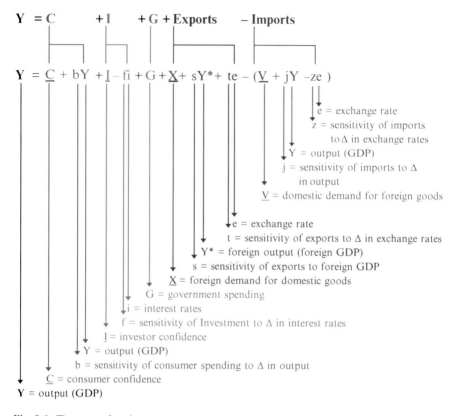

Fig. 9.6 The output function

This equation provides us with a complete function for the goods (and services) market for an economy. It allows us to examine and interpret the effect that changes in the component variables will have on output as a whole.

For example, we can see that holding all else equal, an increase in government spending will tend to bring about an increase in output. A decrease in consumer confidence will tend to decrease output, and so forth. These are simplifications, since the goods market does not operate in isolation. The domestic economy's equilibrium state is determined endogenously by the intersection of the goods market, which we have just defined, and the money market.

9.3   The Money Market

Money supply in our macroeconomic models is defined in "real" terms, that is, in units of goods. This is done to sift out inflationary effects and to correlate money supply to its real purchasing power.

9.3.1   *Real Money Supply*

The **real money supply** is defined as

$$\textbf{Real Money Supply} = \frac{\textbf{M}}{\textbf{P}}$$

where **M** represents the nominal stock of money and **P** is the price level.

Nominal money stock (**M**) is determined by the central bank, which controls "base money" in the form of currency in circulation and commercial bank reserves held with the central bank.

The price level (**P**) represents the price of a typical "market basket" of goods and services. The CPI index provides one such measure. The price level is determined endogenously by the decisions of various actors (individuals, businesses, and government) in the economy and is affected by the relative supply and demand for goods and services.

9.3.2   *Money Demand*

Money demand is defined as the demand for cash to be used for transaction purposes. It is given by

$$\textbf{Money demand} = \textbf{kY} - \textbf{hi}$$

where

k = sensitivity of money demand to changes in output (GDP)
h = sensitivity of money demand to changes in interest rates
Y = output (GDP)
i = interest rates

With higher national income (**Y**), the demand for cash for transactions purposes increases.

As interest rates (**i**) rise, however, the opportunity cost of holding cash balances goes up. This is because the foregone interest is the opportunity cost of holding cash, which is noninterest bearing. Interest rates essentially represent the price of money. Interest rates also affect the demand for borrowing, as we have seen in previous chapters. As interest rates go up, the demand for money decreases.

The domestic money market is in equilibrium when **real money supply** is equal to **money demand**:

$$
\begin{array}{ccc}
\textbf{Real Money} & = & \textbf{Money} \\
\textbf{Supply} & & \textbf{Demand} \\
\dfrac{\textbf{M}}{\textbf{P}} & = & \textbf{kY} - \textbf{hi}
\end{array}
$$

where

M = money supply, i.e. the nominal money stock[8]
P = price level
k = sensitivity of money demand to changes in output (GDP)
h = sensitivity of money demand to changes in interest rates
Y = output (GDP)
i = interest rates

With this equation, we can see the effect on the economy of changes in certain variables. For example, holding output (**Y**) and sensitivities constant, if the price level (**P**) were to increase, real money would become more scarce (real money supply decreases), and interest rates (**i**) would necessarily increase to bring the money market back into equilibrium.

An increase in the nominal stock of money (**M**) would drive up the real money supply, and again holding output (**Y**) and sensitivities constant, this would drive interest rates (**i**) lower to move the money demand back into equilibrium with real money supply.

Rearranging the equation we can show interest rates as a function of "Y" (National Income, or GDP) for every point at which the money market is in equilibrium (Fig. 9.7).

9.3.3   The Money Market with Pegged Rates

An influx of foreign exchange (**FX**) into countries with freely floating exchange rates will result in a change in the exchange rate (**e**), leaving the real money supply unaffected.

However, in countries with pegged (artificially fixed) exchange rates, an inflow of foreign exchange (**FX**) is soaked up by the central bank, which issues domestic currency in its place. This results in an increase in the domestic money supply, which reduces interest rates.

---

[8] Throughout the text we shall use the unmodified term "money supply" in referring to the **M** variable, as synonymous with "nominal money stock." This mirrors common usage. In instances where we are referring to the real money supply (**M/P**), we will explicitly use the complete term.

$$i = \left[\frac{k}{h}\right]Y - \left[\frac{1}{h}\right]\left[\frac{M}{P}\right]$$

Fig. 9.7   Money market equilibrium under freely floating exchange rates

$$i = \left[\frac{k}{h}\right]Y - \left[\frac{1}{h}\right]\left[\frac{M}{P} + FX\right]$$

Fig. 9.8   Money market equilibrium under fixed exchange rates

So, we modify the function for countries with pegged rates, and employ the expression given in Fig. 9.8 above. In this case, unlike a freely floating exchange rate regime, changes in inflows and outflows do indeed affect the FX term and, hence, the money supply. In the case of fully floating (endogenously driven) exchange rates, we will employ the expression given in Fig. 9.7. Here, fluctuations in global capital flows are "taken up" by commensurate fluctuations in exchange rates without affecting the overall money in circulation. This distinction will have far-reaching implications when we analyze how countries that had pegged their currencies were often ravaged by massive hot capital inflows and the devastating speculative asset price bubbles (SAP bubbles) that they fostered.

Before departing the money market, a short review of how central banks change **M** may be in order.

9.3.4   Domestic Monetary Policy

The central bank manipulates interest rates by issuing and withdrawing currency from circulation. When the central bank wants to raise interest rates—or in other words "tighten" monetary policy—it most often does so through **open-market operations**, by selling assets (generally government bonds) from its holdings in order to withdraw money from circulation (the money used by the public to purchase the bonds is taken out of circulation). The resulting scarcity of money and surfeit of government bonds drives the price of money, that is, the interest rate, higher.

When the central bank wants to reduce interest rates, it buys securities from the public, putting money into circulation by its purchases. The increase in the amount of money in circulation, and the increased demand for government bonds, causes interest rates to fall.

A lesser-used method of raising and lowering rates is to adjust the **required reserve ratio (RRR)**, which is the percentage of their assets that banks must keep locked up in cash. This has the effect of putting money into and out of circulation. The central bank may also adjust the "**discount rate,**" which is the interest rate charged for central bank loans to the primary dealers (those institutions permitted to borrow directly from the central bank), though this method is rarely used today.[9] A lower discount rate encourages borrowing, which puts additional money into circulation.

Open-market operations are the most common means by which domestic monetary growth is changed for the USA and, perhaps, the Eurozone. The prime reason for this is the large volume of domestic (and relatively safe-haven) national debt issued by these deficit-incurring economies over sustained periods of time. In contrast, emerging economies such as India, China, East Asia, and Central Europe have to resort to changes in reserve requirements or their equivalents of the discount rate in order to change domestic monetary growth. These economies have been fiscally more virtuous than the United States in that their budget deficits are only recent phenomena. In the recent past, these economies have run significantly smaller budget deficits relative to the USA or even incurred budget surpluses. This explains their reliance on RRR and "discount rates" to change their respective money supplies, given their relatively lower volume of outstanding government debt.

Regardless of the method employed, ultimately, the policy lever available to monetary authorities is the same: increasing and decreasing **M**.

With our goods market and money market defined and the money creation process reviewed, we are now ready to derive the **ISLM-BOP** macroeconomic model, which synthesizes these functions together and permits us to simultaneously analyze changes to various components of the macroeconomy.

The **ISLM-BOP** model comprises three curves, each representing the equilibrium states of the broad components of the macroeconomy. The **IS** and **LM** curves represent the goods market and money market, respectively, and the **BOP** curve, the balance of payments, represents equilibrium in the foreign exchange market. "General equilibrium" in the economy holds where all three curves meet.

We will examine each component in turn before presenting them together.[10]

---

[9] During the financial crisis, over the period from 2007 to 2009, hundreds of financial institutions large and small borrowed massively from the discount window to the tune of $3.3 trillion in total. This information is traditionally confidential, since borrowing from the discount window can be (correctly!) interpreted as a sign of stress, which might create or exacerbate a panic. The data were only disclosed in 2010–2011after a successful court battle over a Freedom of Information request by Bloomberg. See Craig Torres, "Fed Releases Discount-Window Loan Records During Crisis Under Court Order," March 31, 2011, accessed October 29, 2012, http://www.bloomberg.com/news/2011-04-01/foreign-banks-tapped-fed-s-lifeline-most-as-bernanke-kept-borrowers-secret.html

[10] A thorough derivation and explication of the IS and LM curves may be found in Langdana, *Macroeconomic Policy: Demystifying Monetary and Fiscal Policy*. The focus of our text is on deploying the model to practically analyze global macroeconomic policy; for the sake of brevity, we necessarily shorten explanations of some topics which are treated to more in-depth explanations in texts whose primary focus is basic macroeconomic theory.

9.4   The IS Function: Goods Market Equilibrium

The **IS** function, which represents the goods market in our **ISLM-BOP** model, plots interest rates (**i**) as a function of output (**Y**), for every point at which the goods market is in equilibrium. To obtain this function, we simply rearrange the goods market equation that we derived earlier.

We start by combining several items related to consumer and investor sentiment into one general term, for notational convenience:

9.4.1   Attitudes and Expectations: "$\underline{A}$"

"Attitudes and expectations," $\underline{A}$, is an aggregate term comprising consumer confidence ($\underline{C}$), investor confidence ($\underline{I}$), domestic demand for foreign goods ($\underline{V}$), and foreign demand for domestic goods ($\underline{X}$) (Fig. 9.9):

By subsuming these several terms into one, our analyses will be greatly facilitated without any loss of the model's power.

9.4.2   The IS Function

To derive the IS function, we rearrange the goods market equation as a function of interest rates (**i**) by moving the interest rate variable to the left side of the equation.

We begin by substituting our new term for attitudes ($\underline{A}$) for $\underline{C}$, $\underline{I}$, $\underline{X}$, and $\underline{V}$:

$$Y = \underline{A} + bY - fi + G + sY^* + te - (jY - ze)$$

Rearranging and simplifying, we obtain

$$fi = \underline{A} + G + sY^* + e(t + z) - Y(1 - b + j)$$

Dividing through by "**f**" gives us the IS function (Fig. 9.10)

$$Y = \underline{C} + bY + \underline{I} - fi + G + \underline{X} + sY^* + te - (\underline{V} + jY - ze)$$

Fig. 9.9   Aggregating the "attitudes and expectations" term, ($\underline{A}$)

$$\underline{A} = \underline{C} + \underline{I} + \underline{X} - \underline{V}$$

$$i = \underbrace{\frac{\overline{A} + G + sY^* + e(t+z)}{f}}_{Intercept} - \underbrace{\frac{Y(1 - b + j)}{f}}_{Slope}$$

Fig. 9.10   The IS function. Note that where a term that is normally underlined (e.g. $\underline{A}$) appears in the numerator of a fraction, we will put the line *above* the variable

Fig. 9.11 IS: Goods market
equilibrium

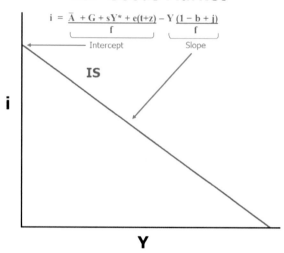

IS: Goods Market

$$i = \frac{\bar{A} + G + sY^* + e(t+z)}{f} - \frac{Y(1-b+j)}{f}$$

This function may plotted in (i, Y) space, which shows the relationship between output and interest rates (Fig. 9.11).

The term "**IS**" comes to us from John Maynard Keynes[11] and stands for "investment savings." This is because the slope of the curve directly relates interest rates (i) to output (Y). From the **NSI** equation, we know that investment (I) essentially comes from consumer savings (S) (remember that Keynes wrote long before the monster current account deficits of the present day!). Lower interest rates mean a lower cost of money and generate greater planned fixed investment ($I\uparrow$), but lower savings ($S\downarrow$). The IS curve represents all the various combinations of interest rates and output for which the goods market is in equilibrium.

9.4.3   IS Exercises

A few exercises will illustrate how changes in the component variables will shift the **IS** curve. The effect of these changes is captured in the graph shown in Fig. 9.12 below.

1. **A Collapse in Consumer Confidence ($\underline{C}\downarrow$)**
   Rising unemployment combined with a sharp drop in the stock market causes concern among consumers regarding their economic future.

   Recall that $\underline{A} = \underline{C} + \underline{I} + \underline{X} - \underline{V}$.

---

[11] As interpreted by J.R. Hicks – see footnote 1

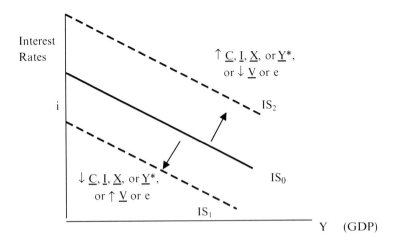

Fig. 9.12 Effect of changes in variables on IS curve

A drop in consumer confidence will result in a fall in the aggregated "attitudes" term ($\underline{A}\downarrow$), which is a component of the intercept ($\underline{A}/f$) in the IS function. This will cause a parallel shift downward (or, equivalently, leftward) from $\mathbf{IS_0}$ to $\mathbf{IS_1}$, as depicted in Fig. 9.12. The converse also holds, as a surge in consumer confidence will result in a shift upward from $\mathbf{IS_0}$ to $\mathbf{IS_2}$. The slope will remain unchanged in either case.

2. **A Surge in Investor Confidence ($\underline{I}\uparrow$)**
The burgeoning domestic biotech industry explodes with new breakthrough technologies that spin off in several directions, and appears to be the leading edge of a new innovation revolution in the domestic economy. A wave of start-ups are launched, and investment opportunities appear boundless.

This will result in an increase in the intercept ($\underline{A}/f$) due to the increase in $\underline{A}$. The **IS** curve will shift upward from $\mathbf{IS_0}$ to $\mathbf{IS_2}$, with the slope unchanged. Conversely, as investor confidence declines ($\underline{I}\downarrow$), the intercept will drop from $\mathbf{IS_0}$ to $\mathbf{IS_1}$, also with no change in slope.

3. **Changes in Foreign and Domestic Tastes for Imported Goods ($\underline{X}$ and $\underline{V}$)**
Backwardistan opened up its economy to foreign trade ten years ago; however, its adult citizens, having been fed a steady diet of xenophobic propaganda, have exhibited little desire for foreign imports. A rising generation, however, who are greater in number than their parents' generation and unencumbered by past prejudices, suddenly cannot get enough Western movies, music, and clothes.

As in the case of #1 and #2 above, an increase in the domestic preference for foreign goods ($\underline{V}\uparrow$) will cause the **IS** curve to shift through a drop in the ($\underline{A}$) term, in this case downward. And a shift in consumer tastes away from imports ($\underline{V}\downarrow$) will cause the **IS** curve to shift upward.

News stories about poisoned baby formula and toxic drywall have created a scare among Sinasia's largest Western trading partners, who suddenly want no part of any of Sinasia's exports.

A decline in foreigner's tastes for domestic goods ($\underline{X}\downarrow$) will cause the **IS** curve to shift downward through a drop in (**A**). Conversely, an increase in the foreign appetite for domestic exports ($\underline{X}\uparrow$) will cause the **IS** curve to shift upward.

4. **An Increase in Government Spending (G↑)**
Keynesland's economy has been achieving subpar growth for some time. A newly elected administration implements a bold multi-billion dollar stimulus program to boost the economy.

Increases in government spending (**G**) will also increase the intercept term, thereby lifting the **IS** up from $\mathbf{IS_0}$ to $\mathbf{IS_2}$. Cutbacks in government outlays will shift the **IS** down from $\mathbf{IS_0}$ to $\mathbf{IS_1}$ as **G** drops. Again, neither of these shifts will cause the slope of the **IS** to vary.[12]

5. **A Weakening Exchange Rate (e↑)**
Athenia has long kept domestic peace by maintaining extravagant social programs paid for by an ever-expanding amount of debt. With the country's debt to GDP now exceeding 110 % and the economy in recession, investors begin to head for the exits, selling Athenian-denominated assets as the prospect of default looms. The domestic exchange rate depreciates severely.

When the currency unit's purchasing power in terms of foreign currency declines (a weakening exchange rate, **e**↑), the **IS** intercept will rise, as "e" appears in the numerator of the intercept term. On the other hand, a strengthening currency (**e**↓) will cause the **IS** to fall.

6. **A Surging Foreign Economy ($\mathbf{Y^*}$↑)**
Domestic observers see that Tigerland's economic growth, stagnant for decades and plagued by inflation, has recently taken off thanks to stable fiscal and monetary policy management and new trade agreements with several advanced nations. Standards of living are rising, and consumers have an increasing amount of disposable income.

A surge in the foreign economy ($\mathbf{Y^*}$↑) will cause the **IS** to rise, as opportunities for exports increase. In contrast, a sick foreign economy ($\mathbf{Y^*}$↓) will cause **IS** to fall. This would be an example of **contagion** in a global macro context, where sickness in the foreign economy affects the domestic economy.

9.4.4   Taxes and the IS Curve

We have thus far abstracted from any change in domestic income tax rates, and in general we shall hold this variable constant through the balance of this book. However, it is important to have an understanding of the effect of such changes on the **IS** curve.

Higher taxes reduce disposable income and thus tend to reduce consumer spending. Lower taxes have the opposite effect and will tend to increase consumer spending.

---

[12] This exercise examines the **IS** curve's movements in isolation. We shall fully explore both sides of the controversial notion that increasing (**G**) will spur growth in later chapters.

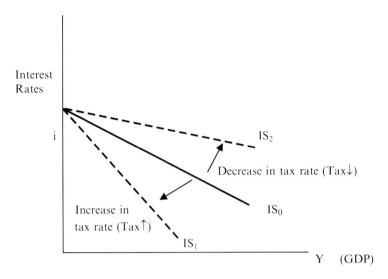

Fig. 9.13 Effect of changes in tax rates on the IS curve

Disposable after-tax national income may be represented by the expression
$Y(1 - Tax)$, where (**Tax**) is the tax rate as a percentage of income.

Our function for after-tax consumption, which we will call C_T, would thus be a
modified form of our consumption function:

$$C_T = \underline{C} + bY(1 - Tax)$$

Substituting this change into our goods market function, we find that under
equilibrium

$$i = \underbrace{\frac{\overline{A} + G + sY^* + e(t + z)}{f}}_{Intercept} - \underbrace{\frac{Y(1 - b[1\text{-}Tax] + j)}{f}}_{Slope}$$

The intercept term remains unchanged from its previous expression. However,
the slope now incorporates the (**Tax**) term.

An increase in tax rates (**Tax↑**) will thus cause the slope of the **IS** curve to
increase in steepness (a more negative slope), while a tax cut will decrease the **IS**
curve's steepness (Fig. 9.13).

Again, for the balance of our analyses, we shall hold (**Tax**) constant, by subsuming it into the (**b**) variable, which we will take to be equal to **MPC * (1-Tax)**.
However, understanding these implications will permit the deft accommodation of
tax changes into the analyses, once the interrelationships between the rest of the
components of the **ISLM-BOP** model have been completely mastered.

9.5 The LM Function: Money Market Equilibrium

The money market equilibrium in our model is represented by the **LM** curve. The term LM comes to us, again, from Keynes,[13] with "**L**" standing for "liquidity preference" (another way to describe money demand, since "liquidity" implies cash balances) and "**M**" meaning "money supply."

The LM curve depicts interest rates as a function of "Y" (National Income, or GDP), for every point at which the money market is in equilibrium. We have already derived this function above:

$$\mathbf{i} = \left[\frac{\mathbf{k}}{\mathbf{h}}\right]\mathbf{Y} - \left[\frac{\mathbf{1}}{\mathbf{h}}\right]\left[\frac{\mathbf{M}}{\mathbf{P}}\right]$$

and for economies under fixed exchange rate regimes:

$$\mathbf{i} = \underbrace{\left(\frac{\mathbf{k}}{\mathbf{h}}\right)}_{\textit{Slope}}\mathbf{Y} - \underbrace{\left(\frac{\mathbf{1}}{\mathbf{h}}\right)\left(\frac{\mathbf{M}}{\mathbf{P}} + \mathbf{FX}\right)}_{\textit{Intercept}}$$

9.5.1 *The LM Function*

The LM function plots this equation in (**i, Y**) space (Fig. 9.14).

All points on the **LM** line represent equilibrium in the money market.

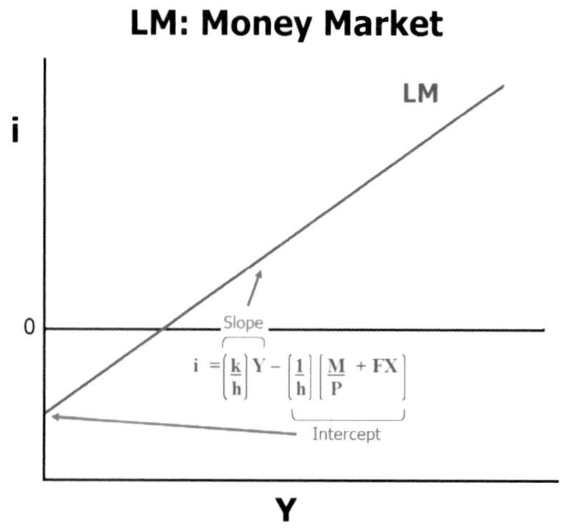

Fig. 9.14 LM: Money market equilibrium

[13] As interpreted by J.R. Hicks – please refer to footnote 1

The negative intercept is an algebraic construct, as interest rates will almost always be positive,[14] but it is vitally important in determining how the **LM** curve shifts when the nominal money stock (**M**) or prices (**P**) change.

9.5.2   LM Exercises

With our LM function defined,

$$i = \underbrace{\left[\frac{k}{h}\right]Y}_{Slope} - \underbrace{\left[\frac{1}{h}\right]\left[\frac{M}{P} + FX\right]}_{Intercept}$$

...we can examine the effect of changes to the various component variables on the **LM** curve, as depicted in Fig. 9.15 below. We will ignore the FX term for the moment; the examples below would hold for both fixed and floating exchange rate systems.

1. **An Increase in the Nominal Money Stock (M↑)**
   The Central Bank of Keynesland determines that the government's fiscal stimulus is losing steam. With no more political appetite for increased government spending, the bank takes matters into its own hands and loosens a flood of money into the economy, hoping to spur growth.

   Here, the intercept term is affected: $[-(1/h)(M/P + FX)]$. Since the intercept is a negative term, an increase in **M** will cause the intercept to become a larger negative number (e.g., from -40 to -48), thereby decreasing the intercept's position on the graph. With no change in the slope (there is no **M** in the slope term $[(k/h)Y]$), the result of an increase in **M** is a parallel downward (or, equivalently, rightward), shift in LM from **LM₀** to **LM₁** in Fig. 9.15.

   A decrease in the money stock (**M↓**), on the other hand, results in an upward shift in **LM** and, once again, will not affect the slope as shown in the figure.

---

[14] Short-term interest rates in the USA actually turned negative briefly on November 19, 2009, as investors scrambled to hold US Treasuries (Source: Michael Mackenzie, "Short-term US Interest Rates Turn Negative," *Financial Times*, November 20, 2009). This was one of the many distortions of "normal" macroeconomic relationships that occurred over the course of the acute phase of the financial crisis in the USA. Why would such investors not simply hold physical cash instead buying US Treasuries with negative yield? One must consider that (a) holding funds in the form of bank deposits still exposes the investor to the bank's credit risk and (b) even if one prefers physical cash, moving, storing, and securing tens of billions of dollars in physical cash involves a cost. Thus, for large investors seeking liquidity and maximum safety above all other considerations, it can make sense to incur negative returns by holding the US government treasuries, up to a point. As the global crisis rolled on, yields in Switzerland (2011 and 2012) and Germany (2012) briefly turned negative as well, due to safe-haven seeking on the part of risk-averse investors.

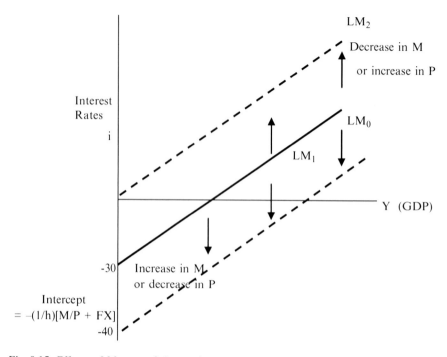

Fig. 9.15 Effect on LM curve of changes in component variables

2. **An Increase in the Price Level (P↑), i.e., an Increase in Inflation**[15]

Boomland's economy has been growing for 3 years straight at over 10 % per year and is now operating near the limits of its capacity. Finding and retaining employees has become expensive, and plant assets are operating beyond the limit of their peak efficiency. As a result, the economy is seeing a general rise in prices and wages across the board.

An increase in the price level (**P**) will cause the ratio **M/P**, which represents real money supply, to fall, and given the minus sign that precedes the intercept term, we now find the intercept to be "less negative" (increasing from say, −40 to −30). Again, with no change in the slope, an increase in (**P**) results in an upward, or leftward, shift in LM from **LM₀** to **LM₂**.

Conversely, a decrease in prices (**P↓**) would cause the **LM** to undergo a parallel shift down, from **LM₀** to **LM₁** as depicted in Fig. 9.15.

To summarize, any increase in (**M/P**) caused by an increase in the money stock (**M↑**) or a decrease in prices (**P↓**) will shift the LM curve downward in a uniform manner. Any decrease in (**M/P**), caused by a decrease in nominal money stock (**M↓**) or an increase in prices (**P↑**), will shift the curve upward.

---

[15] At this stage, we use "change in price level" interchangeably with "change in inflation." When the entire ISLM is put together later in the chapter, we will revisit P, Y, M, etc., in more detail.

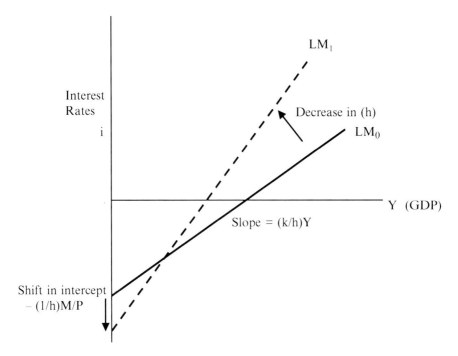

Fig. 9.16 Liquidity trap: effect on LM curve of decrease in the variable (**h**), the sensitivity of money demand to changes in interest rates

9.5.3   *Slope (k/h) of the LM Curve*

In adjusting the **LM** curve, we generally (and for the purposes of this volume, always) hold the (**k**) and (**h**) elasticities constant, which represent:

k = sensitivity of money demand to changes in output (GDP)
h = sensitivity of money demand to changes in interest rates

Changes in these sensitivities can of course occur, for example, in the classic "liquidity trap" described earlier, where economic conditions are so poor that reductions in interest rates cease to have any meaningful effect on output. The monetary channel through which this occurs is a decrease in the variable (**h**), as money demand becomes insensitive to changes in interest rates. (In a "liquidity trap," investor confidence also collapses, affecting the goods market as well.) This decrease in **h** in turn increases the slope (**k/h**) of the **LM** curve, making it more vertical. The result is that it requires increasingly large changes in interest rates (**i**) to bring about any change in output (**Y**). As $-(1/h)$ is also a component of the intercept term, the entire **LM** curve will also shift downward (Fig. 9.16).

Fig. 9.17 IS–LM
equilibrium

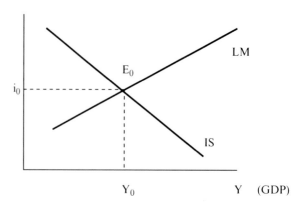

Again, aside from this illustrative example, in our analyses going forward, we shall hold the (**k**) and (**h**) variables, and thus the slope of the **LM** curve, constant. All shifts in **LM** will be parallel moves upward or downward.

With our **IS** and **LM** curves defined, we now have a model of a closed (Autarkic) economy.

9.5.4 IS–LM Equilibrium

Ignoring for the moment the balance of payments (**BOP**), we can see how the **IS** and **LM** curves interact by plotting both curves in (**i, Y**) space. The intersection point, E_0 at (i_0, Y_0), in Fig. 9.17 is defined as the point where both the goods and money markets are simultaneously in equilibrium. (We have normalized the **LM** curve to remove the negative-interest rate portion from the graph in Fig. 9.17.)

Here we have an **IS–LM** model of a closed economy (ignoring, for the moment, that exports (**X**) and imports (**V**), as well as foreign exchange (**FX**), are incorporated into our **IS** and **LM** curves), which requires no analysis of the balance of payments since without trade or capital flows, there is none.

Any shift in either curve, for example, an increase in **IS** resulting from a surge in consumer confidence (**C**↑), will result in a new equilibrium. In this case, the **IS** curve will shift upward, and a new equilibrium point will be found at E_1 at the **IS–LM** intersection (Fig. 9.18).

The result will be higher interest rates (**i**) and higher output (**Y**) than before the confidence boost.

To take another example, an increase in the nominal money stock (**M**↑) will cause the **LM** curve to shift downward, as illustrated below (Fig. 9.19).

Fig. 9.18 Surge in consumer confidence lifts IS curve into new general equilibrium

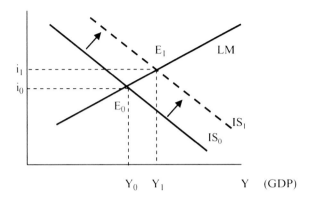

Fig. 9.19 Increase in nominal money stock drops LM curve into new general equilibrium

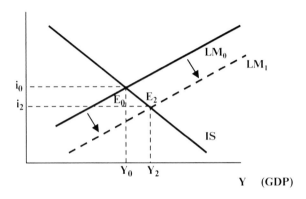

The result will be a new general equilibrium at E_2 with lower interest rates (i) and higher output (Y). (We ignore follow-on effects, such as potential inflation from the increase in money stock, in this simple example.)

To complete our model, we will now open up our Autarkic economy to international trade and capital flows. This will require the incorporation of the balance of payments (**BOP**) into our general equilibrium.

9.6   The Balance of Payments (BOP)

The balance of payments (**BOP**) is an accounting of a country's international transactions over a certain time period (typically a year). It is the net sum of all transactions involving goods and services, as well as capital movement between individuals, businesses, and government in a particular country with the rest of the world.[16]

---

[16] New York Federal Reserve, "Fedpoint: Balance of Payments," May 2009.

The balance of payments will be zero when transaction flows from trade perfectly offset flows from investment capital. That is, **BOP** equilibrium occurs at the point of intersection between the current account deficit (**CAB**) and the capital account balance (**KAB**). We will briefly review what we have already learned about these terms and proceed to incorporate them into a model of BOP equilibrium.

9.6.1 Current Account Balance (CAB)

The current account balance (**CAB**) or, equivalently in our usage, the balance of trade is the net balance of external purchases and sales of goods and services; put simply, exports minus imports. We can derive the equation for the CAB by inserting the component variables into our formula:

$$\mathbf{CAB} = \text{Current Account Balance (positive balance} = \text{Goods going out)}$$
$$= \text{Exports} - \text{Imports}$$
$$= \mathbf{X} - \mathbf{V}$$
$$= \mathbf{X} + \mathbf{sY^*} + \mathbf{te} - (\mathbf{V} + \mathbf{jY} - \mathbf{ze})$$

The **CAB** will be positive when exports exceed imports and negative when imports exceed exports. When the current account is negative, we say this is a current account deficit.

9.6.2 Capital Account Balance (KAB)

The capital account balance (**KAB**) is the balance of capital flows into and out of the country. It includes international borrowing and lending, purchases and sales of assets, and FDI (foreign direct investment). A positive **KAB** indicates capital coming into the country, whereas a negative **KAB** indicates capital outflow.[17]

The **KAB**, representing net capital inflow (capital inflow minus capital outflow), is a function of several variables:

i^* Foreign interest rates (high rates will attract outflows)
i Domestic interest rates (high rates will attract inflows)

---

[17] Another way of thinking about the KAB is that a positive KAB indicates the net export of *title to financial assets*. This is actually what drives "capital coming in," as foreign buyers purchase title to domestic financial assets, whether newly issued equities, bonds, loans, or plant and equipment. The title is exported in return for cash. Conversely, "capital going out" is the result of domestic purchases of title to foreign assets. We discuss these concepts further below.

Pr^* Foreign long-term economic outlook (positive outlook will attract outflows)
Pr Domestic long-term economic outlook (positive outlook will attract inflows)
e^e Expected exchange rates (stronger anticipated rates $[e^e\downarrow]$ will attract inflows in the current period)

$$KAB = \text{Capital Account Balance (positive balance} = \text{net capital coming in)}$$
$$= \text{Capital inflow less Capital outflow}$$
$$= f(i^*, i, Pr^*, Pr, e^e)$$

Algebraically, the function may be expressed using each term with a corresponding elasticity,

$$KAB = -\alpha_0 i^* + \alpha_1 i - \alpha_2 Pr^* + \alpha_3 Pr - \alpha_4 e^e$$

where the α_n coefficients represent the sensitivity of capital flows to changes in each factor.

The **KAB** is _highly sensitive_ to these elasticities ($\alpha_0 \ldots \alpha_4$). When capital flows are unrestricted, a small change in one of the variables (i^*, i, Pr^*, Pr, or e^e) can result in a large shift in the **KAB**—in this case, the elasticities are considered to be astronomically large. This is because capital flows can adjust much more rapidly to changes in the economic environment than can the movement of goods and services, which are limited by physical systems of production and transportation. The sensitivity of capital flows to changes in domestic interest rates, α_1, is particularly important as we shall see in later chapters.

The Pr and Pr^* variables, representing the domestic and foreign long-term economic outlooks, respectively, will be positive when a country is generally viewed as having a bright economic future. These variables can change in a positive direction with the enactment of policies seen to foster durable economic growth, the imminent end of military conflicts, the advent of a more benevolent political system, opening to trade, and so on. Conversely, these variables will change in a negative direction when dark clouds hover over the economic horizon, with looming trade conflicts, the advent of undisciplined fiscal policies, financial repression, etc.

9.6.3   CAB, KAB, and the NSI

Recall the reordered National Savings Identity (**NSI**) equation:

$$S + (Imp - Exp) = (G - T) + I$$

We can rearrange to show the relationship between the **CAB** and the **KAB** (Fig. 9.20).

Fig. 9.20 Balance of payments equilibrium

$$\underbrace{(\mathbf{Imp} - \mathbf{Exp})}_{-\mathrm{CAB}} = \underbrace{[(\mathbf{G} - \mathbf{T}) + \mathbf{I}] - \mathbf{S}}_{\mathrm{KAB}}$$

The current account balance (**CAB**) is reflected by its inverse, the current account deficit, in our reordered NSI, by the (Imp − Exp) term.

We clearly see the relationship, where in equilibrium

$$-\,\mathbf{CAB} = \mathbf{KAB}$$

The capital account balance (**KAB**) is reflected on the right side of the equation in Fig. 9.20 above. Investment (in real estate, newly issued private debt and equity securities, capital assets, etc.) and government deficits (in the form of bond issues) will be funded first by domestic savings (**S**), with the balance funded by capital inflows (a positive **KAB**). These capital inflows will be provided through a current account deficit (a negative **CAB**, or [**Imp** − **Exp**]), with the domestic capital that is spent on net imports coming back into the country to fund the **KAB**.

Should savings exceed total government spending and investment, there will be surplus domestic capital, which will flow out for use in acquiring foreign assets, resulting in a negative **KAB**, and by implication, a positive **CAB**.

9.6.4   The Balance of Payments

The balance of payments (**BOP**) is essentially the difference between the net amount of capital flowing in for investment in domestic assets (the KAB) and the net amount of capital flowing out to pay for goods and services (the current account deficit, equal to –CAB):

$$\mathbf{BOP} = \mathbf{KAB} - (-\mathbf{CAB})$$

Thus, the balance of payments (**BOP**) may be expressed as the sum of the current and capital account balances.

$$\mathbf{BOP} = \mathbf{CAB} + \mathbf{KAB}$$

In equilibrium, where the balance of payments is zero (**BOP = 0**), we see that **CAB + KAB = 0**, and simplifying we obtain

$$\mathbf{CAB} = -\mathbf{KAB}.$$

For example, when the United States exports $1 million in pharmaceuticals to Germany, the transaction adds + $1 million to the **CAB** (Exports − Imports).

1) US firm ships pharmaceuticals to Germany

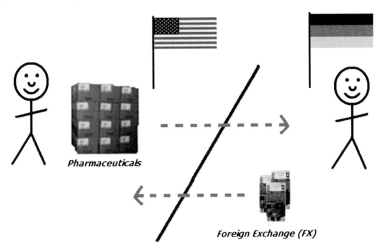

Fig. 9.21 Explaining the CAB: US firm ships goods to Germany, which increases the US CAB

At the same time, there is now $1 million in foreign exchange (euros, in this case) in the USA available with which to purchase capital assets in Germany, buy German bonds, etc.

When this purchase occurs, the USA will have a $1 million capital outflow, which equates to −$1 million in the **KAB** (remember that KAB = Inflows − Outflows). Thus, for this isolated transaction, **CAB** (+$1 million) + **KAB** (−$1 million) = 0.

In Fig. 9.21, we see the US firm exporting goods to Germany. These are paid for by the Germans using euros, which now accumulate in the USA. Taken in isolation from the US perspective, this transaction results in CAB = $1 million.

In Fig. 9.22, we see the euros flowing back out of the USA as they are used to purchase German bonds. Again, taken in isolation from the US perspective, this results in KAB = −$1 million.

Naturally, the exporting company in Fig. 9.21 will rarely be the same entity to invest in German assets. It will instead convert its newly acquired foreign exchange (**FX**) with its bank, which will then lend or sell the **FX** to an investor who will use it to purchase title to real or financial assets in Germany.

This leads us to another way of thinking about the relationship between the current and capital account balances. For every export of goods and services, a country will "import" *title* to some financial asset, such as a foreign government bond or real estate, plant assets, or new equity in a company. And, for every domestic import of goods and services, foreigners will acquire title to domestic financial assets, such as the US government bonds, real estate, and corporate bonds and equities. In other words, for every import of goods and services, the domestic country will "export" title to some financial asset. In the above example, the USA has exported pharmaceuticals and imported title to German bonds.

2) US investor purchases German bonds with the accumulated FX

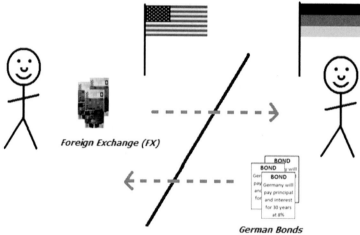

Fig. 9.22 Explaining the KAB: The US purchases (imports) title to foreign assets; capital goes out, which has a negative effect on the US KAB

Thus, we can look at the **KAB** as net exports of title to domestic financial assets. We see that our **BOP** equilibrium implies that net imports of goods and services will be matched by net exports of title to financial assets and vice versa.

Another example: The United States imports $20 million of toys from China, which subtracts 20 million from the US **CAB** (Exports − Imports). China takes the funds and purchases $10 million in US Government bonds, $8 million in US Agency bonds, and $2 million in new equity issued by JP Morgan, for a total of $20 million. This adds + $20 million to the **KAB** (Inflows − Outflows). The USA has imported toys and exported an equal amount of bonds and equity. So, **CAB** (−$20 million) + **KAB** (+$20 million) = 0.

We can see now that a positive or negative balance of payments will result, for example, when the capital used by Country A to import goods and services from Country B is not used by Country B to purchase assets in Country A. This would result in a negative BOP in Country A (due to a negative CAB but zero KAB) and an equally positive BOP in Country B (with a positive CAB and zero KAB). Since such a condition confers no benefit to Country B, the component variables will tend to adjust as we shall see below, and the BOP does not generally remain in disequilibrium for very long.[18]

---

[18] This situation was somewhat different in earlier epochs, most strikingly in the interwar period in the 1920s, when currencies were backed by gold. France in particular adopted a policy of maintaining a positive BOP and essentially hoarding gold, to the detriment of all other countries on the gold standard system, particularly Germany and the UK. We explore this event in more detail in Chap. 13. Fiat paper currencies, unlike gold, do not incorporate any intrinsic value and are thus much less susceptible to hoarding.

9.6.5 BOP and the Foreign Exchange Markets

The balance of payments (**BOP**) relates directly to the supply and demand for foreign exchange (**SFX** and **DFX**). Under balance of payments equilibrium where BOP = 0, the foreign exchange market will also be in equilibrium, with **SFX** = **DFX**.

As noted above, the balance of payments can be out of equilibrium if the total movement of capital into or out of the country exceeds or falls short of the movement of capital used in goods and services transactions. This will occur when more (or less) financial capital moves into (or out of) the country than is required for transactions involving goods and services.

As given in the **KAB** equation, the main drivers for an excess or shortfall of capital flow are foreign interest rates (i^*), domestic interest rates (i), the foreign (Pr^*) and domestic (Pr) long-term economic outlook, and the expected exchange rate (e^e).

The **BOP** can be out of equilibrium in two directions:

9.6.6 BOP Deficit (BOP < 0)

When **CAB + KAB < 0** (or otherwise stated, **KAB < −CAB**), this means that **BOP < 0**. The **BOP** is in *deficit*.

A BOP deficit directly implies that the demand for foreign exchange exceeds the supply of foreign exchange (**DFX > SFX**). A BOP deficit can come about in two ways:

(a) An exporting country is purchasing more foreign assets, on net, than its net exports (**Exp − Imp**) of goods and services. Its demand for foreign exchange for use in asset purchases exceeds the supply provided by the sale of goods and services to foreign buyers. So, the demand for foreign exchange exceeds the supply.

In this case, CAB + KAB < 0.

Plugging in numbers for the sake of exposition, let CAB = 170 and KAB = −190. That is, (X − V) = 170 and (Capital Inflow − Capital Outflow) = (−190).

So, BOP = CAB + KAB = 170 + (−190) = (−20). As BOP < 0, we have a BOP deficit. In other words, the demand for FX exceeds the supply of FX by 20 units. In this case the domestic economy earned net 170 of FX thanks to its net exports, but then it bled a net of 190 units of FX due to the net outflow used to acquire foreign assets. So this economy is short, or in need of, 20 units of FX, which is tantamount to a BOP deficit of 20.

(b) An importing country's net purchases of foreign goods and services exceed its net exports of financial assets. It needs more foreign exchange for its purchases of goods and services than is available from the funds provided by the foreign purchase of domestic financial assets. Again here, the demand for foreign exchange exceeds the supply.

In this case also, CAB + KAB < 0.

Again plugging in numbers for discussion, let's say that CAB = (−180) and KAB = 150, thus yielding a BOP deficit of 30 (as BOP = CAB + KAB = [−180] + 150 = [−30]). Here the domestic economy "owes" foreigners 180 in FX for the next imports. The net FX inflow is only 150, so this economy is still 30 units of FX short. That is, its demand for FX exceeds its supply of FX by 30 units, meaning the country has a BOP deficit of 30.

One may wonder: How can a country even have a BOP deficit, since this implies that more funds are going out than are coming in? The answer lies in the **official settlements balance**, which is essentially the aggregate central bank activity in the FX markets.[19]

As we will demonstrate later in detail, for countries with freely floating exchange rates, any disequilibrium is quickly resolved by a change in the exchange rate. The official settlements balance will generally be negligible, and the **BOP** will be equal to or very close to zero.

Countries with *pegged* (or "managed") exchange rates and a negative **BOP** will have a positive official settlements balance to make up the difference; their monetary authorities will be putting FX reserves into the economy to maintain the currency peg—which are then used in goods and services or asset transactions. Thus, we can say that[20]

BOP + Official Settlements Balance = 0

It should be noted that such a policy cannot continue indefinitely as eventually the country will run out of reserves. We explore this issue further in Chap. 12.

Situation (b), discussed above, can come about in a country that is traditionally an exporter of volatile raw materials, such as oil, when there is a price shock. A rapid decline in the price of oil may suddenly turn a net exporter like Russia into a net importer. If the country cannot sell (export title to) enough Russian government bonds, or other financial assets, it will run a negative **BOP** and eventually run out of reserves unless it allows its exchange rate to adjust.[21]

---

[19] The balance of payments is often given to include the official settlements balance, where BOP = CAB + KAB + Official Settlements Balance (+ Statistical Discrepancy, see next note). However, for purposes of application of the ISLM-BOP model, we represent the BOP without the official settlements balance and look at official FX intervention resulting from SFX<>DFX imbalances as a separate item.

[20] There is generally a minor statistical discrepancy in most BOP accounting, due to any number of data collection issues. This item is negligible, and we will ignore it in our analyses. Technically, CAB + KAB + Official Settlements Balance + Statistical Discrepancy = 0.

[21] Such was the case in Russia in 1998. We will explore such events in more detail in Chaps. 11 and 12.

9.6.7   BOP Surplus (BOP > 0)

When **CAB + KAB > 0** (or otherwise stated, **KAB > −CAB**), this means that **BOP > 0**. The **BOP** is in *surplus*.

A **BOP** surplus means that the supply of foreign exchange exceeds the demand (**SFX > DFX**). A BOP surplus may come about in two ways:

(a) An exporting country's net foreign asset purchases are less than its net exports of goods and services. From this surplus of net exports, the country has an excess of foreign exchange that is not being used in foreign asset purchases. Its supply of foreign exchange exceeds the demand.

In this case, we have CAB + KAB > 0.

Here again, we'll plug in numbers for the sake of illustration and say that CAB = 190 and KAB = (−140). Thus we have a BOP surplus of +50. Here the domestic country earns FX of net 190 through its net exports, but has a 140 net capital outflow for the purchase of foreign assets, thus leaving this economy with an excess supply of FX of 50 units. A BOP surplus does indeed imply that supply of FX is greater than the demand for FX (**SFX > DFX**).

(b) An importing country is purchasing, on net, less foreign goods and services than the incoming flows of capital it receives from its net exports of financial assets. Its demand for foreign exchange for use in its goods and services purchases is less than the supply created by foreign purchases of its financial assets.

Again, here we have CAB + KAB > 0.

Here let's say that CAB = (−160) while KAB = 180, thus rendering a BOP surplus of +20. Net inflows of FX are 180 (meaning that foreigners have acquired 180 FX units more of domestic assets than the home country has acquired of foreign assets), while the domestic economy remits to foreigners only 160 units of FX for its net imports, thus yielding an excess supply of FX, i.e., a BOP surplus of 20 units.

Again, as we shall study later, under freely floating exchange rates, any disequilibrium in the **BOP** is quickly resolved through exchange rate adjustments, and the official settlements balance will be negligible.

Under *pegged* (or "managed") exchange rates and a positive **BOP**, the central bank authorities will be accumulating FX reserves—running a negative official settlements balance as FX is taken out of the economy. China, for example, has long run a positive BOP with a tightly managed exchange rate and as a result has accumulated vast FX reserves.

9.6.8   BOP Equation

As discussed above, the BOP equation is

$$BOP = CAB + KAB$$

$$i = Y\left[\frac{j}{\alpha_1}\right] + \frac{\alpha_0 i^* + \alpha_2 Pr^* - \alpha_3 Pr + \alpha_4 e^e - (\overline{X} - \overline{V}) - sY^* - e(t - z)}{\alpha_1}$$

$\underbrace{\qquad}_{\text{Slope}}$ $\underbrace{\qquad\qquad\qquad\qquad\qquad\qquad\qquad}_{\text{Intercept}}$

Fig. 9.23 BOP equilibrium

The equation for BOP equilibrium is given by

$$CAB + KAB = 0$$

Equivalently,

$$CAB = -KAB$$

Since we know that **CAB** = **Exports** − **Imports** and we have the equation for the **KAB**, we can substitute the algebraic expressions for these terms to derive the equation for **BOP** equilibrium:

$$\underbrace{\mathbf{\underline{X} + sY^* + te}}_{\text{Exports}} - \underbrace{(\underline{V} + jY - ze)}_{\text{Imports}} = \underbrace{-(-\alpha_0 i^* + \alpha_1 i - \alpha_2 Pr^* + \alpha_3 Pr - \alpha_4 e^e)}_{-\text{KAB}}$$

Simplifying, we get

$$(\underline{X} - \underline{V}) + sY^* + e(t - z) - jY = +\alpha_0 i^* - \alpha_1 i + \alpha_2 Pr^* - \alpha_3 Pr + \alpha_4 e^e$$

and rearranging and further simplifying

$$\alpha_1 i = Yj + \alpha_0 i^* + \alpha_2 Pr^* - \alpha_3 Pr + \alpha_4 e^e - (\underline{X} - \underline{V}) - sY^* - e(t - z)$$

We finally obtain the equation for BOP equilibrium in (**i, Y**) space, where interest rates are given as a function of output (**Y**) (Fig. 9.23). Under BOP equilibrium, the FX market will also be in equilibrium, with the supply of foreign exchange equal to the demand for foreign exchange, i.e., (**SFX = DFX**).

We can now plot the **BOP** equilibrium in (**i, Y**) space (Fig. 9.24).

We see all the (**i, Y**) combinations lying above the equilibrium line representing a BOP surplus and all points below the line representing a BOP deficit. This is intuitive, since if interest rates (**i**) are higher than the equilibrium level for any given

Fig. 9.24 BOP equilibrium under imperfectly mobile capital

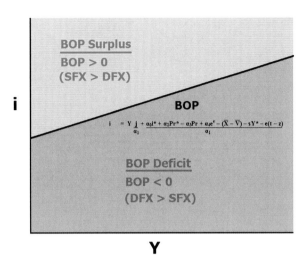

output (**Y**), an excess of foreign exchange will flow in seeking to take advantage of the high rates (**SFX > DFX**). And lower-than-equilibrium rates will leave foreigners cold, with the result that not enough supply of foreign exchange will be available to meet demand (**DFX > SFX**).

The depiction in Fig. 9.24 assumes a positive slope $(j/\alpha_1) > 0$, which will hold when capital movement in and out of the country is not completely unfettered. This condition is known as **imperfectly mobile capital,** which we will refer to in shorthand as **IMK** in various exercises. Restrictions on capital flow may include explicit controls or various types of frictions. The value of α_1 becomes lower the more restrictions are placed on the movement of capital, which results in a steeper slope (j/α_1) in the BOP equilibrium line.

If capital cannot move in or out of a country *at all*, the term α_1, which represents the sensitivity of capital flows to changes in interest rates, will be equal to zero. In this instance, the **BOP** line would be completely vertical at any given level of output (**Y**). There are few if any examples today of such completely closed economies.

We shall return to a BOP under imperfectly mobile capital in later exercises. For the moment, our analyses will assume perfect capital mobility.

9.6.9 BOP Under Perfectly Mobile Capital

With unrestricted capital mobility or what is called **perfectly mobile capital** (**PMK**, in our shorthand), capital is free to respond immediately to changing conditions. Thus, the elasticities associated with each variable in the **KAB**

Fig. 9.25 BOP equilibrium
under perfectly mobile capital

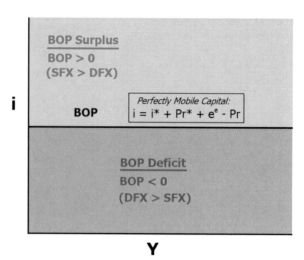

(the alphas, $\alpha_{0..4}$), which represent the sensitivity of capital flows to changes in each variable, are very large numbers; the alphas "explode," tending to infinity.

This renders possible a further simplification in the terms of the BOP equilibrium. Presenting the BOP equation in terms of its partial fractions, we obtain

$$i \ = \ Y\!\left[\frac{j}{\alpha_1}\right] + \frac{\alpha_0 i^* + \alpha_2 Pr^* - \alpha_3 Pr + \alpha_4 e^e - (\bar{X} - \bar{Y}) - sY^* - \alpha(Y - Y)}{\alpha_1}$$

As the (α_1) in the denominator tends to infinity, any term in the numerator without an α goes to zero in the limit, and any term with an α in both the numerator and the denominator simply has its α terms cancelling out in the limit.

Thus we see that even small changes to the variables in the KAB expression, i, i^*, Pr, Pr^*, and e^e, will result in extraordinarily large fluctuations in capital flows in the case of perfectly mobile capital.

We are left with a much simpler equation for **BOP** equilibrium under perfectly mobile capital:

$$i = i^* + Pr^* - Pr + e^e$$

Since there is no slope to this line, the BOP line under perfectly mobile capital will be represented as a horizontal line in (i, Y) space, as depicted in Fig. 9.25, above.

9.6.10 Relationship Between Y, CAB, and KAB

There is a direct relationship between output (**Y**), the **CAB**, and the **KAB**.

As **Y** increases↑:

CAB↓	Imports increase relative to exports, which moves the **current account balance** downward↓
KAB↑	Capital flows in, which moves the **capital account balance** upward↑

As **Y** decreases↓:

CAB↑	Imports decrease relative to exports, which moves the **current account balance** upward↑. Often ailing economies will see their trade deficits shrink
KAB↓	Capital flows out seeking better opportunities, which moves the **capital account balance** downward↓

In all cases, if the balance of payments (**BOP**) is in equilibrium, the absolute values of the **CAB** and **KAB** will be equal. This may be accomplished under both high and low levels of output. Very high levels of output will generally see significant **CAB** deficits and significant **KAB** surpluses. And low levels of output will generally be accompanied by **CAB** surpluses and **KAB** deficits.

9.6.11 BOP Exercises

The BOP under perfectly mobile capital is in equilibrium when

$$i = i^* + Pr^* - Pr + e^e$$

We can examine the effect of changes in the various components of the balance of payments to illustrate how the **BOP** shifts in response. Under PMK, the BOP equilibrium line has no slope, so all changes will simply change the intercept, shifting the line either up or down. These changes are illustrated in the graph below the examples (Fig. 9.27).

1. **An Increase in Foreign Interest Rates (i*↑), or in the Foreign Long-Term Economic Outlook (Pr*↑)**

   Investors in Nilandia see that nearby Amazonia's economy, surging already, looks bright well into the future as hordes of potential laborers in the hinterlands have yet to join the burgeoning manufacturing sector. Seeking to maintain stable growth while keeping inflation contained, Amazonia increases interest rates. Essentially Amazonia "taps on the brakes" to avoid economic overheating a move that it also hopes will help continue to attract foreign investment. In this exercise, Nilandia is the domestic economy.

   Either of these changes in underlying conditions will make foreign invest-ment in Amazonia more attractive than previously. This implies that it will require higher interest rates at home in Nilandia to "compete" for loanable funds and maintain equilibrium. Thus, either of these changes will cause Nilandia's

The Domestic Capital Market

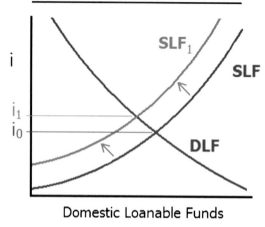

Fig. 9.26 Reduction in supply of loanable funds results in higher interest rates

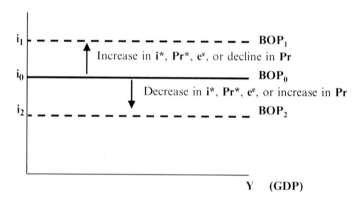

Fig. 9.27 Shifts in balance of payment equilibrium under perfectly mobile capital

domestic BOP line to rise. In Fig. 9.27, this is represented by the shift from **BOP$_0$** to **BOP$_1$**.

Why did interest rates in Nilandia increase? As Amazonia's future looks increasingly bright, capital floods into Amazonia from Nilandia. The supply of loanable funds curve for Nilandia shifts to the left as capital rushes out of the country and into Amazonia. This leftward shift in the supply of loanable funds in Nilandia would explain the increase in its interest rates, as depicted in Fig. 9.26.

An expected depreciation in the domestic Nilandian currency ($e^e\uparrow$) will have a similar effect. With the exchange rate expected to depreciate, it will require higher interest rates to maintain interest rate parity with the foreign currency (see Chap. 8).

A decrease in foreign interest rates ($i^*\downarrow$) or in the long-term foreign economic outlook ($Pr^*\downarrow$) or an expected strengthening of the domestic currency ($e^e\downarrow$) will have the opposite effect, causing the **BOP** to drop from BOP_0 to BOP_2. In this case capital rushes in to Nilandia. As the supply of loanable funds consequently shifts to the right thanks to the capital inflow from Amazonia, interest rates in Nilandia will fall.

These various channels open up the possibility of **contagion**, as these foreign factors of output (Y^*), interest rates (i^*), and/or long-term economic outlook (Pr^*) affect the domestic economy. We shall see examples of this as we undertake various policy exercises in this and future chapters.

2. **An Improvement in the Domestic Long-Term Economic Outlook ($Pr\uparrow$)**
   Nipponia's economy has been stagnant for a decade. Its extensive investments in robotics have recently begun to pay off, however, with breakthroughs that will boost its productivity exponentially and spawn a host of new industries. Output is on the rise, and for the first time in years, immigrants from around the world flock to the country seeking employment. Nipponia's long-term prospects suddenly appear much brighter than before.

   A glowing future for the domestic economy will attract global capital to the domestic economy. This increase in capital inflow will shift the supply of loanable funds curve to the right and, hence, drive down domestic interest rates. The result is a lowering of the **BOP** line, in our example shown by the move from BOP_0 to BOP_2.

   By contrast, a deterioration in the long-term domestic economic outlook ($Pr\downarrow$) will mean that higher rates are required to maintain equilibrium in the domestic economy; the **BOP** will rise. In this case capital floods out of the country, the supply of loanable funds curve shifts to the left, and domestic interest rates are pushed up (Fig. 9.26).

   In all cases under perfectly mobile capital, **BOP** is independent of current levels of output (Y), since it has no slope.

9.7   General Equilibrium

We can now superimpose the BOP onto our IS–LM diagram for a complete picture of the general equilibrium model in (i, Y) space. At the intersection point of all three curves, E_0, the goods market, money market, and balance of payments are all in equilibrium (Fig. 9.28).

Here we see a complete **ISLM-BOP** model of an open economy including the external sector.

Armed with an understanding of the variables in the model and their relationships, we can now analyze the effects of a change to any of the variables on the economy as a whole. A variable change will initially shift the curve in which

Fig. 9.28 ISLM-BOP equilibrium

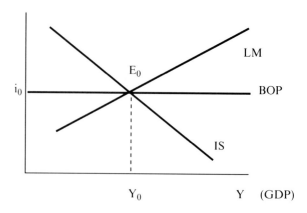

that variable is incorporated (the **IS**, **LM**, or **BOP** line). Movement in any of the curves will then result in one or more additional shifts in response as a new point of general equilibrium is found.[22]

In the following section, we summarize the process in the form of a handy "Survival Guide." We then proceed to perform several policy experiments to learn how this process works.

9.8   Chart of Variables and Their Impact on IS, LM, BOP

Before we proceed, let's first summarize the effect of changes in each variable and their effect on the three curves (**IS**, **LM**, and **BOP**) under PMK. These moves come directly from the equilibrium equations for each curve (Fig. 9.29).

These equilibrium equations for each are reproduced below:

IS equilibrium

$$i = \frac{\bar{A} + G + sY^* + e(t + z)}{f} - Y\frac{(1 - b + j)}{f}$$

---

[22] Here with the concept of "general equilibrium" we will run afoul of any number of critics who object to the notion that such an equilibrium can even exist in a complex, dynamic global economy with billions of economic factors making decisions in real time. This view is not without logical merit, and is worth consideration. However, the authors stand by their position, expressed in an earlier footnote, that the general equilibrium concept, expressed in the ISLM-BOP model, is extremely useful in conceptualizing the interplay of variables in the global macroeconomy. One need not be a devoted Keynesian to appreciate the model's value in analyzing the likely results of policy changes, and of forecasting the likely outcomes arising from changes in underlying economic variables. The model stands the key tests of being both descriptive and predictive.

Event	IS	LM	BOP
C↑	↑		
I↑	↑		
X↑	↑		
V↑	↓		
G↑	↑		
Y*↑	↑		
e↑	↑		
M↑		↓	
FX↑		↓	
P↑		↑	
i*↑			↑
Pr*↑			↑
Pr↑			↓
e^e↑			↑

Event	IS	LM	BOP
C↓	↓		
I↓	↓		
X↓	↓		
V↓	↑		
G↓	↓		
Y*↓	↓		
e↓	↓		
M↓		↑	
FX↓		↑	
P↓		↓	
i*↓			↓
Pr*↓			↓
Pr↓			↑
e^e↓			↓

Fig. 9.29 Effect of variable changes on IS, LM, and BOP under perfectly mobile capital

LM equilibrium

$$i = \left(\frac{k}{h}\right)Y - \left(\frac{1}{h}\right)\left(\frac{M}{P} + FX\right)$$

BOP equilibrium—PMK

$$i = i^* + Pr^* - Pr + e^e$$

BOP equilibrium—IMK

$$i = Y\left[\frac{j}{\alpha_1}\right] + \frac{\alpha_0 i^* + \alpha_2 Pr^* - \alpha_3 Pr + \alpha_4 e^e - (\overline{X} - \overline{V}) - sY^* - e(t - z)}{\alpha_1}$$

This chart will be supplemented with a summary of the effects of variable changes under conditions of imperfect capital mobility (**IMK**) in Chap. 12.

9.9 Survival Guide to ISLM-BOP Policy Analysis

We mentioned above that a shift in one curve will be followed by additional moves in one or more curves to bring the economy back into equilibrium. This "Survival Guide" allows the reader to methodically work through the process to arrive at the correct interpretation of the final results of each initial shift. Starting with an economy in general equilibrium (as shown in Fig. 9.28):

1. Make the appropriate initial curve movement(s) in (i, Y) space. This may be a shift or pivot in one or more of the **IS**, **LM**, or **BOP**, depending on the variables affected.
2. Examine the new goods market–money market equilibrium, which is the new intersection of the **IS** and **LM** curves. Is the **BOP** now in surplus (new **IS–LM** equilibrium lies *above* the **BOP** line) or deficit (new **IS–LM** equilibrium lies *below* the **BOP** line)?

   Make note of the BOP condition and also note the effect on the SFX–DFX relationship resulting from the BOP disequilibrium. That is,

$$\text{BOP is in Surplus}: \ \mathbf{SFX} > \mathbf{DFX}$$
$$\text{BOP is in Deficit}: \ \mathbf{DFX} > \mathbf{SFX}$$

   A helpful mnemonic is the consonance of "<u>s</u>urplus" and "<u>S</u>FX > DFX" and of "<u>d</u>eficit" and "<u>D</u>FX > SFX."
3. The BOP surplus or deficit must be resolved. Consider the exchange rate regime.

   If flexible exchange rates, then the BOP surplus or deficit will be resolved by a change in the exchange rate (Δe), and the **IS** curve will do the adjusting (since the variable **e** forms part of the IS equilibrium equation).

   If fixed (pegged) exchange rates, then a BOP surplus will be resolved by central bank intervention to buy up the excess FX and replace it with domestic money. A BOP deficit will be resolved by central bank injections of FX to replace domestic money. In either case, under fixed exchange rates, the **LM** curve will do the adjusting through a change in the nominal money stock (ΔM).

   Shift the **IS** or **LM** in a parallel movement up or down until all three curves are back in equilibrium.

   To summarize:

   Flexible exchange rates: **IS** does the adjusting
   Fixed exchange rates: **LM** does the adjusting

   The final state must have all three curves (IS, LM, BOP) intersecting in equilibrium.

4. **Present all your results boldly**,[23] step back from the diagrams, and analyze the implications of your results.

In "real time," steps 1–3 would all be taking place simultaneously and could span a period ranging from days to months depending on the policies in question, the stage of the economy in its business cycle, and consumer and investor expectations.

9.10 Exercises with the ISLM-BOP Model

"Prepare to witness the power of this fully operational battle station!"

–Emperor Palpatine, Star Wars Episode VI: Return of the Jedi

The **ISLM-BOP** is a very powerful macroeconomic model. Finally, with all components of the model defined and our Survival Guide close at-hand, we are ready to incorporate the **IS**, **LM**, and **BOP** curves into a general equilibrium model of the open economy and see how it may be used to analyze the effects of any number of policy and economic variable changes.

Prepare to witness the power of this fully operational macromodel!

In all of these exercises, it is imperative to provide information on two important economic factors at the outset:

- Capital Mobility: Perfect or imperfect (affects the slope of the **BOP** line). Perfectly mobile capital implies a horizontal BOP, while imperfectly mobile capital means that we have a positively sloped BOP.
- Exchange Rate Regime: Floating or fixed (determines whether **IS** or **LM** adjust into equilibrium).

Let's get started!

Policy Exercise #1 An increase in government spending (G↑), flexible rates, PMK

Zandinia has determined that the best way to boost growth would be through an injection of government spending. It embarks on a huge program of domestic infrastructure projects throughout the country. Zandinia's capital account is open (perfect capital mobility), and it operates under a floating exchange rate regime.

Our step-by-step Survival Guide will help us through the policy analysis.

We start with the economy in general equilibrium at E_0 as given by the initial curves IS_0, LM_0, and BOP_0 in Fig. 9.30 above. The **IS** and **LM** curves may be drawn at any angles, as we are looking to see the big-picture results, not capture specific numeric changes. Generally **IS** and **LM** curves at -45 and $45°$, or slightly

---

[23] Here it is always wise to remember Dr. Langdana's maxim: "Life is too short for small graphs!" Start with a big graph with lots of room to work—ISLM-BOP models can become very crowded with lines very quickly!

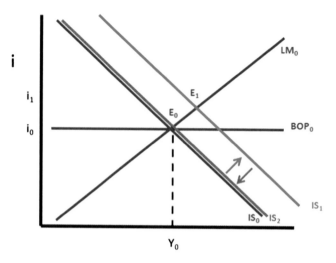

Fig. 9.30 Increase in government spending (G↑), flexible rates, PMK

less steep, are suitable. The slope of the **BOP** curve will be zero (a horizontal line) under perfectly mobile capital, and under imperfect capital mobility, it will have a positive slope of less than that of the **LM** line. Generally, under imperfect capital mobility, using a **BOP** slope of something under half the angle of the LM line will provide a useful framework for analysis.[24]

A useful tip: "Life's too short for small graphs!"[25] Use enough space to permit bold moves without running out of room or creating clutter. The final results will then be clear and obvious.

With our initial equilibrium drawn, we may proceed with our analysis:

1. Make the initial move(s) in (**i,Y**) space.

    An increase in government spending (**G↑**) will raise the **IS** curve. We draw a new **IS₁** curve above and parallel to the original **IS₀**.

2. Examine new goods market–money market equilibrium (**IS–LM**).

    - If BOP surplus, **SFX** > **DFX**
    - If BOP deficit, **DFX** > **SFX**

    In this case, our new **IS–LM** equilibrium, **E₁**, is found above the **BOP** line. This new equilibrium is in BOP surplus, and our supply of foreign exchange will now exceed the demand for foreign exchange (**SFX** > **DFX**). This makes sense because foreign investors will seek to participate in the growth opportunities offered by the increase in domestic spending.

---

[24] We will explore the slope of the BOP line, and its causes and implications, in Chap. 12.

[25] Farrokh Langdana

3. Adjust curves into equilibrium.

- If *flexible exchange rates*, **IS** does the adjusting (**e** adjusts under floating rates, which is a component of the IS curve).
- If *fixed exchange rates*, **LM** does the adjusting (since **e** cannot adjust, flows of **FX**, a component of the LM curve, compensate to make the adjustment).

We are operating under a regime of flexible exchange rates, so the **IS** curve does the adjusting, through a change in the exchange rate. Here, the inflow of **FX** (**SFX** > **DFX**) will cause the exchange rate to strengthen (**e↓**), which will cause the **IS** curve to shift downward into equilibrium.

Here we see that the resulting strengthening of the exchange rate will cause the **IS** curve to "snap back" from IS_1 to IS_2, which is in the same position as the original IS_0. The primary reason is that a stronger exchange rate has harmed the export sector, negating all benefit from the initial increase in **G**.[26]

4. Present results boldly!

The end results of Zandinia's increase in government spending are:

- No change in output (**Y**).
- Interest rates (**i**) are also where they started.

The exchange rate adjustment has caused the famed Keynesian multiplier[27] to fail; the stimulus hasn't generated any increase in real output. Instead, we are left with no change in output or interest rates. Zandinia's policymakers should have consulted their ISLM-BOP diagrams before embarking on this policy!

Policy Exercise #2. An increase in government spending (G↑), fixed rates, PMK

Zandinia's neighbor Krugland has seen Zandinia's error but is certain that since their regime of fixed exchange rates will keep their currency from appreciating, a round of stimulative government spending will boost their economy. Krugland undertakes a major program of internal improvements. Krugland allows perfect capital mobility.

Once again, we start with the economy in general equilibrium at E_0, in Fig. 9.31.

1. Make the initial move(s) in (**i**, **Y**) space.

An increase in government spending (**G↑**) will raise the **IS** curve. We draw a new IS_1 curve above and parallel to the original IS_0.

2. Examine new goods market–money market equilibrium (**IS–LM**).

- If BOP surplus, **SFX** > **DFX**
- If BOP deficit, **DFX** > **SFX**

---

[26] We shall explore the trade implications in further detail in Chap. 10. In this analysis, we are also abstracting from inflation. Inflation will be added to our analyses in Chap. 11.

[27] Keynes' General Theory put forth the proposition that under certain conditions, a unit increase in government spending or in the monetary stock will generate more than a unit increase in output. We explore the "multiplier effect" further in Chap. 12. For a thorough treatment, see Langdana, *Macroeconomic Policy: Demystifying Monetary and Fiscal Policy.*

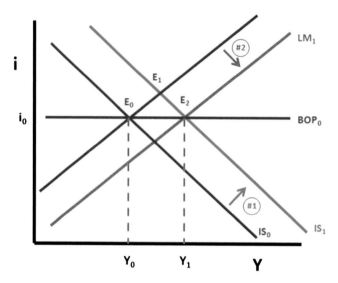

Fig. 9.31 Increase in government spending (**G**), fixed rates, PMK

Our new **IS–LM** equilibrium, **E₁**, is found above the **BOP** line. As before, this new equilibrium is in BOP surplus, which means that **SFX > DFX**.
3. Adjust curves into equilibrium.

- If *flexible exchange rates*, **IS** does the adjusting ("**e**" adjusts under floating rates, which is a component of the IS curve).
- If *fixed exchange rates*, **LM** does the adjusting (since "**e**" cannot adjust, flows of **FX**, a component of the LM curve, compensate to make the adjustment).

Krugland uses a fixed exchange rate, so here the inflow of foreign exchange (**FX↑**) will be soaked up by the central bank, which will issue domestic currency in its place (through FX intervention as it purchases foreign exchange with domestic money). This will release domestic money into the economy, causing the **LM** line to adjust downward to **LM₁** and into general equilibrium at **E₂**.
4. Present results boldly!
   Success!

- Krugland's output soars from **Y₀** to **Y₁**.
- Interest rates (**i**) remain where they started.

Here the Keynesian multiplier has created a boost in output, exactly as Krugland's economic team predicted. Several complications may arise, however, as we shall explore when we incorporate inflation into our model in Chap. 11.

Policy Exercise #3 An increase in money supply (M↑), flexible rates, PMK
Zandinia's monetary authorities, seeing the failure of the fiscal stimulus in Exercise #1 above, take matters into their own hands and inject money into the economy in the hope of spurring growth. Zandinia operates with freely floating exchange rates and perfectly mobile capital.

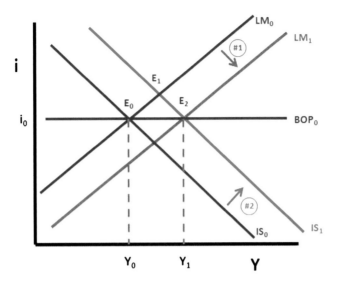

Fig. 9.32 Increase in money supply (**M**), flexible rates, PMK

Starting with the economy in general equilibrium at E_0 (Fig. 9.32):

1. Make the initial move(s) in (**i, Y**) space.

    An increase in money supply (**M↑**) lowers the **LM** curve from LM_0 to LM_1.
2. Examine new goods market–money market equilibrium (**IS–LM**).

    • If BOP surplus, **SFX > DFX**
    • If BOP deficit, **DFX > SFX**

    In this case, our new **IS–LM** equilibrium, E_1, is found *below* the BOP line. This new equilibrium is in BOP deficit, and our demand for foreign exchange now exceeds the supply (**DFX > SFX**). Investors will see the flood of money as potentially inflationary, and many will seek to exit their Zandinian investments.
3. Adjust curves into equilibrium.

    • If *flexible exchange rates*, **IS** does the adjusting ("e" adjusts under floating rates, which is a component of the IS curve).
    • If *fixed exchange rates*, **LM** does the adjusting (since "e" cannot adjust, flows of **FX**, a component of the LM curve, compensate to make the adjustment).

    Under Zandinia's flexible exchange rates, the **IS** curve will make the adjustment into equilibrium. The excess demand for foreign exchange (**DFX > SFX**) will cause the exchange rate to weaken (**e↑**), which will raise the **IS** to IS_1 into equilibrium (through a boost to the export sector) at E_2.
4. Present results boldly!

    The Zandinian Central Bank's move has done the trick! Here the Zandinians have essentially conducted a devaluation of their currency:

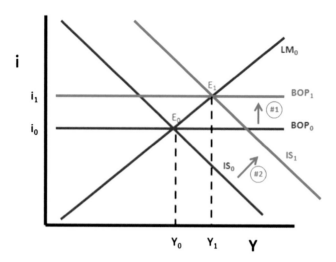

Fig. 9.33 Foreign interest rates increase ($i^*\uparrow$), floating rates, perfectly mobile capital

- The increase in money supply has generated an increase in output (**Y**↑).
- Interest rates remain where they were (no Δ**i**).

   In this case it may seem that a devaluation does indeed spur growth and that this apparent success could be an easy formula for economies in distress. This policy of devaluating one's currency is dangerously tempting, as many countries have discovered to their macroeconomic peril. In this exercise we have conspicuously ignored the insidious effects of future inflation, which will, undoubtedly and eventually, rear its ugly head. We will have more to say on this in Chap. 11.

Policy Exercise #4. An increase in foreign interest rates (i*↑), flexible rates, PMK

Krugland's economy has become so hot that the central authorities fear overheating. The central bank effects an increase in interest rates attempting to moderate the growth rate in order to prevent this. In essence, it attempts to engineer a Soft Landing. Zandinia, Krugland's closest neighbor, wonders how this will affect its own domestic economy. Zandinia's currency is floating, and it permits perfect capital mobility. (In this example, Zandinia is the domestic economy, Krugland is the foreign economy.)

   Starting with the Zandinian home economy in equilibrium at E_0 (see Fig. 9.33):

1. Make the initial move(s) in (**i, Y**) space.

   An increase in foreign interest rates ($i^*\uparrow$) raises the **BOP** line from **BOP$_0$** to **BOP$_1$**.

2. Examine new goods market–money market equilibrium (**IS–LM**).

- If BOP surplus, **SFX** > **DFX**
- If BOP deficit, **DFX** > **SFX**

Now, the IS–LM equilibrium at E_0 is in BOP deficit. So **DFX** > **SFX**. This is intuitive since investors will seek out the higher returns offered in Krugland.

3. Adjust curves into equilibrium.

- If *flexible exchange rates*, **IS** does the adjusting ("**e**" adjusts under floating rates, which is a component of the IS curve).
- If *fixed exchange rates*, **LM** does the adjusting (since "**e**" cannot adjust, flows of **FX**, a component of the LM curve, compensate to make the adjustment).

Zandinia's currency floats freely, so the **IS** curve will adjust upward to **IS₁** into a new equilibrium (E_1) as its exchange rate weakens (**e↑**).

4. Present results boldly!

Monetary tightening in the foreign economy of Krugland has resulted in increased output in the Zandinian economy (from Y_0 to Y_1), thanks to the weakened currency, albeit with higher interest rates:

- Output has increased (**Y↑**).
- Interest rates have increased (**i↑**).

We may note here that the increase in rates also follows from the interest rate parity condition (from Chap. 8), since a depreciation in the currency must be matched by an increase in interest rates for interest rate parity to be maintained.

Policy Exercise #5   A sharp decline in foreign preference for domestic exports ($\underline{X}\downarrow$), fixed rates, PMK

Kleptocristan, a major exporter of construction equipment, faces a major scandal! It has come to light that the country's largest manufacturers have been cutting corners on quality and materials on many of its exports, resulting in potential safety hazards for end users. The country's authorities have been caught in a web of bribes and kickbacks, enabling the scheme. In the wake of this, no one will touch Kleptocristan's exports with a ten foot pole. Kleptocristan's currency is pegged, and it imposes no controls on capital mobility.

Starting with Kleptocristan's economy in general equilibrium at E_0 (see Fig. 9.34):

1. Make the initial move(s) in (i, Y) space.

A decrease in foreign tastes for domestic exports ($\underline{X}\downarrow$) lowers the **IS** line from **IS₀** to **IS₁**.

2. Examine new goods market–money market equilibrium (**IS–LM**).

With the new IS–LM intersection at E_1, we have a BOP deficit. So, **DFX** > **SFX**.

3. Adjust curves into equilibrium.

Kleptocristan operates under a pegged exchange rate, so the **LM** curve does the adjusting. Here, the central bank will expend foreign exchange (**FX↓**) in order to maintain its exchange rate, resulting in a shift upward in the **LM** curve.

Fig. 9.34 Decline in foreign
taste for domestic exports (**X**),
fixed rates, perfectly mobile
capital

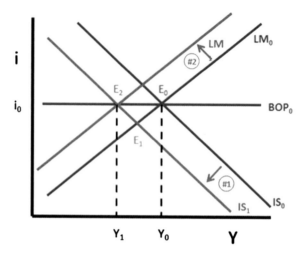

Fig. 9.35 Simultaneous
tightening of monetary policy
(**M↓**) with an increase in
investor confidence (**I↑**),
under flexible rates and
perfectly mobile capital

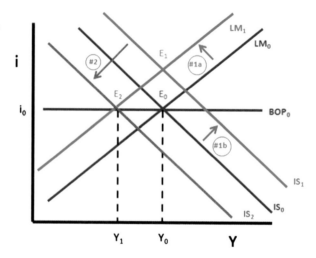

4. Present results boldly!

   Trouble for Kleptocristan's economy!

   • Output has decreased (**Y↓**).
   • Interest rates are unchanged (no **Δi**).

   Exports have dropped resulting in a general decline in output. Interest rates remain unchanged.

   We anticipate that the reader is getting a feel for these exercises by this point and for the power of the ISLM-BOP model as an analytical tool.

   We'll undertake one more exercise, this time noting our moves in a more shortened form, as we shall do throughout the rest of this volume in the interest of avoiding repetition and permitting the diagram and the explanation of the curve movements to appear in closer proximity (Fig. 9.35).

Policy Exercise #6 A tightening of monetary policy (M↓) and a simultaneous surge in investor confidence (I↑), floating rates, PMK
Volckeria has determined to combat economic stagnation by appointing a well-known monetary hawk to run its central bank. The move been greeted with euphoria by investors, who despite the difficulties brought on by tighter monetary policy are confident that this move will tackle Volckeria's till-now persistent stagflation. Volckeria has freely floating currency and imposes no capital controls.
Starting with Volckeria's economy in general equilibrium at E_0:

1. ↓**M** → **LM**↑ to **LM₁**	The decrease in money supply moves the **LM** line up
↑**I** → **IS**↑ to **IS₁**	The increase in investor confidence lifts the **IS**, with a temporary IS–LM intersection found at E_1
2. E_1 is BOP surplus, SFX > DFX, e↓	The FX surplus causes the exchange rate to strengthen
3. Flexible rates: IS adjusts ↓ to **IS₂**	**IS** makes the adjustment into equilibrium under floating rates
	A new general equilibrium is found at E_2
4. Results	
Output is reduced (**Y**↓)	
Interest rates remain unchanged	
(no Δ**i**)	
While Volckeria's investors may be confident, they will have to wait for output to improve since the stronger exchange rate has overwhelmed any benefit from the confidence boost. And, after an initial increase, interest rates will moderate as the exchange rate strengthens.	

In the following chapters, we will add additional levels of analysis to our model. In Chap. 10, we will see how exports, imports, and the current account balance are affected by various policies. In Chap. 11, we will incorporate inflation into our analysis. And we will explore the effects of capital controls in Chap. 12, where we change our BOP line to one involving imperfectly mobile capital.

9.11   ISLM-BOP Survival Guide: Recap

Here is a helpful short-form recap of our ISLM-BOP Survival Guide:

Plot original ISLM-BOP curves in (**i, Y**) space.

1. Make the initial move(s) in (**i, Y**) space.
2. Examine new goods market–money market equilibrium (**IS–LM**).

   - If BOP surplus, **SFX > DFX**
   - If BOP deficit, **DFX > SFX**

3. Adjust curves into equilibrium.

   - If *flexible exchange rates*, **IS** does the adjusting ("**e**" adjusts under floating rates, which is a component of the IS curve).

- If *fixed exchange rates*, **LM** does the adjusting (since "**e**" cannot adjust, flows of **FX**, a component of the LM curve, compensate to make the adjustment).
- Remember to make **BOP** moves, as applicable. Watch especially for **BOP** moves under imperfectly mobile capital.
- The final state must have all three curves (**IS**, **LM**, **BOP**) intersecting in general equilibrium.

4. Present result boldly!

Articles

We stick with an assumption of perfectly mobile capital (and thus a horizontal BOP line) for all countries in this chapter's exercises.

Article 9.1. Hibernia Wrestles with Policy Options

Jonathan Goldberg, *California Global Review*

Since the late 1900s, Hibernia had it made. Its output was the benchmark for quality wool products all over the world. As tastes and designs and fashions changed, Hibernia kept pace with all the trends—in fact, there were many who insisted that Hibernia's mammoth wool industry flourished only because Hibernia stayed ahead of the curve.

And then came Thinnerex, the lightweight, hi-tech material made in neighboring Druadia from high-density graphite fibers embedded in a nanogel base. Thinnerex did everything that wool could do and a lot more. And it was trendy. Wool was "so twentieth century," while Thinnerex was the fabric of choice for world-class skiers, mountain climbers, and a host of somewhat annoying extreme sports types who braced the elements clad only in thin layers of gaudily colored Thinnerex and then sent their action photos to anyone and everyone who pretended to be interested. Soon Druadia's Thinnerex came to be embraced not only by enthusiasts but for everyday items that formerly used wool such as trousers, coats, and so on.

Hibernia was in a panic. Suddenly, it seemed like no one wanted its wool products anymore. Its economy was shutting down. The fact that Hibernia had made some highly unpopular and controversial global policy decisions—getting "in bed" with several unctuous dictatorships and pretending to be the policeman of the continent of Ogdens—did not help the matter. Nor did news stories about poor working conditions in Hibernian factories. The economy was in a tailspin. Hibernia had locked its exchange rate to a world basket of goods. Should this be adjusted? What to do?

(a) **Using an ISLM-BOP model with perfectly mobile capital and pegged exchange rates, show Hibernia's plight.** *Note: Please assume that capital is perfectly mobile through this article.*

(b) **Would Hibernia's plight be improved if its central bank stopped pegging the Hibernian currency and allowed it to float?**

Hibernia now decides to adopt a typical Keynesian policy response in an attempt to somehow jump-start its economy. The government decides on vast infrastructure projects. It plans a huge network of roads, dams, and power grids; the country plans to emulate neighboring Celtick's massive and extremely successful program. The only difference being that Celtick had deployed a monster-sized Keynesian infrastructure policy while maintaining pegged rates, whereas Hibernia has now switched to floating rates.

(c) **Using ISLM-BOP, show how and why Hibernia's program will have significantly different results compared to the similar infrastructure program launched by Celtick.**

Elections in Hibernia go disastrously for the incumbent government; it is thrown out of office, and a new regime takes over. This one believes with an almost religious ardor in the power of monetary policy. About a decade ago, when Celtick was in trouble, its expansionary monetary policy was a total failure; yet its peg somehow survived through that whole crisis. Hibernia's new regime hopes that with freely floating exchange rates, a serious monetary expansion will finally jump-start the economy.

(d) **Using ISLM-BOP, show how and why the responses to Hibernia's monetary policy may (or may not) be different from those experienced earlier by Celtick.**

(e) **Also, what note of caution may you want to impart to Hibernia at this point?**

Now let's fast-forward this story by 3 years. Celtick's economy overheats due to its runaway fiscal stimulus. Dangerous speculative asset price (SAP) bubbles form and then burst. The economy loses steam fast. Adding to the downbeat macroeconomic outlook is the fact that Northern Celtick wants to secede and form an autonomous country. Moody's quickly downgrades Celtick's sovereign debt. This, in turn, casts a greater pall on Celtick's outlook.

(f) **How will this situation in neighboring Celtick affect Hibernia?**

Hints and Solutions

Article 9.1

(a) Here, we have a sharp drop in the foreign preference for Hibernia's exported goods ($\underline{X}\downarrow$). The results would follow those in Policy Exercise #5 (Fig. 9.34). Hibernia's output will decrease ($\mathbf{Y}\downarrow$), following from its decrease in exports, with interest rates remaining unchanged.

Fig. 9.36 Decrease in
foreign preference for exports
(**X**↓), under floating rates and
PMK

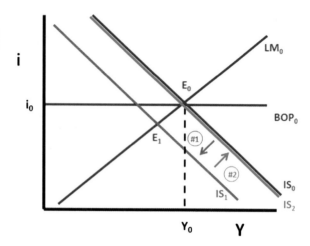

(b) In this case, after an initial drop due to the reduced foreign preference for
Hibernia's exports (**X**↓), the **IS** would snap back up due to an exchange rate
adjustment (e↓), with no shift in the **LM** (Fig. 9.36):

Starting with Hibernia's economy in general equilibrium at **E₀**:

#1) Make the initial move(s) in (**i, Y**) space.
   A decrease in foreign tastes for domestic exports (**X**↓) lowers the **IS** line
   from **IS₀** to **IS₁**.

#2) Examine new goods market–money market equilibrium (**IS–LM**).
   With the new IS–LM intersection at **E₁**, we have a BOP deficit. So,
   DFX > SFX.

#3) Adjust curves into equilibrium.
   Hibernia now allows its currency to float freely, so the **IS** curve does the
   adjusting. In this case, the exchange rate will weaken (**e**↑) due to the
   (**DFX > SFX**) condition. This leads the **IS** curve to "snap back" where
   general equilibrium returns to its original point, **E₀**.

#4) Present results boldly!
   Hibernia's weakened exchange rate has effectively discounted its less-
   desired exports to the point where they are once again priced to attract
   foreign buyers. Output and interest rates are unchanged (no **ΔY**, and no **Δi**).

(c) Policy Exercises 1 and 2 are the solutions here, for Hibernia and Celtick,
respectively.

Hibernia and Celtick both attempt to increase output by increasing government
spending. Both policy moves will generate an initial movement upward in the
IS curve. The increase in government spending will attract a surfeit of foreign
exchange (**SFX > DFX**), which will be resolved in different ways in each
country due to their different exchange rate regimes.

   Hibernia, with freely floating rates and PMK, will follow what we saw in
Policy Exercise #1. The initial upward move in the IS will be followed by a

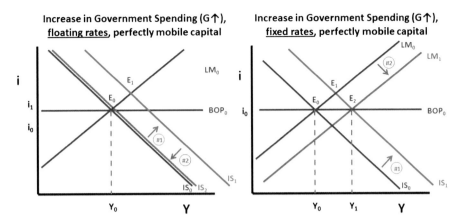

Increase in Government Spending (G↑), floating rates, perfectly mobile capital

Increase in Government Spending (G↑), fixed rates, perfectly mobile capital

Fig. 9.37 Increase in government spending under floating versus fixed exhange rates, with perfectly mobile captial

move back down as the flow of FX causes the exchange rate to strengthen; there will be no increase in output and no change in interest rates.

Celtick's experience, with a pegged (fixed) exchange rate and PMK, would by contrast follow that of Policy Exercise #2. The initial upward move in the IS would be followed by the above-mentioned surge in FX, which is absorbed by the central bank and replaced with domestic Celtickian money, driving the LM curve downward. Celtick sees a dramatic increase in growth and no change in interest rates. Fortunately for Celtick, in this chapter we are ignoring the effects of inflation, which we will emerge in full force in Chap. 11.

Figure 9.37 above provides a side-by-side comparison of the effects for each country.

(d) Here, we have Hibernia and Celtick attempting stimulative monetary policy, the difference being that Hibernia's exchange rate is freely floating while Celtick's exchange rate is fixed.

Hibernia will effectively be adopting a policy of currency devaluation, exactly as discussed in Policy Exercise #3. Its increase in **M** will push the **LM** curve downward. However, the policy move will be seen for what it is, an attempt to create growth by printing money, and Hibernia's currency will weaken as a result (**e**↑) due to the decreased demand for its currency versus foreign currency (**DFX** > **SFX**). This will spur the export sector, driving the **IS** curve upward, and Hibernia's output will increase overall thanks to the devaluation. There will be no change in interest rates.

However, a monetary expansion in Celtick, with its fixed exchange rate regime after its initial shift in the **LM** curve lower, will see it then snap it back to its original point. Celtick's peg ensures that all adjustments are done by **LM**.

In Celtick's case also, the increase in money supply is seen for what it is, and the result is a rush to the exits in the foreign exchange market (**DFX** > **SFX**) and a BOP deficit. Unlike Hibernia, where this imbalance is resolved by a

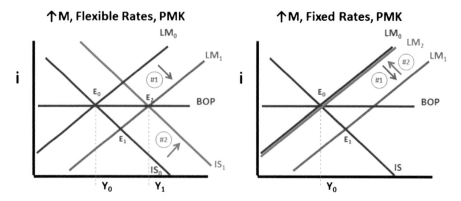

Fig. 9.38 Increase in money supply under floating versus fixed exchange rates, with perfectly mobile capital

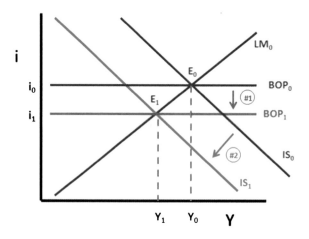

Fig. 9.39 Drop in foreign macro outlook ($Pr^*\downarrow$), under floating rates, PMK

weakening of the exchange rate, under fixed rates, the BOP deficit is resolved as the decrease in ($FX\downarrow$) moves the **LM** curve back into equilibrium at its original point, E_0.

The result for Celtick is no change in output and no change in interest rates. Hibernia and Celtick's contrasting results are presented side-by-side in Fig. 9.38.

(e) Hibernia must be careful to understand that the increase in output following its currency devaluation is a very temporary result. Inflation will indeed eventually increase, undoing all these temporary gains. Hibernia should be cautioned to read Chap. 11 of this text, where it will become clear that the end result of its currency devaluation will be to leave the economy worse off than before.

(f) This is a case of the foreign long-term macro outlook dropping ($Pr^*\downarrow$) as far as the domestic economy (Hibernia) is concerned. As the macro outlook for

Celtick plummets, from Hibernia's perspective, $\mathbf{Pr}^*$ falls. Hibernia's **BOP** line drops as a result (recall that $\mathbf{Pr}^*$ is a variable in the BOP equilibrium equation), leaving a balance of payments surplus at the IS–LM equilibrium point. Given Hibernia's floating exchange rate regime, the BOP surplus (**SFX** > **DFX**) is resolved by a strengthening of the exchange rate ($\mathbf{e}\downarrow$), and the IS adjusts down back into general equilibrium at $\mathbf{E_1}$ (see Fig. 9.39).

The final result is that Hibernia's currency appreciates, and its output falls as the contagion from Celtick hammers Hibernia's economy.

Chapter 10
Exports and Imports, Real Exchange Rates

Summary The chapter begins with a thorough discussion of exports and imports, including real exchange rates, purchasing power parity, and the relationship of exports and imports (**X** and **V**, respectively, in our model) to output (**Y**).

The "pass-through effect," whereby a country's exporters simply adjust their prices to counter unfavorable exchange-rate manipulation, thus nullifying the efforts of the monetary authorities to deliberately "rectify" a trade imbalance, is explained here. The case of Japan and the "Plaza Accord" from the 1980s and a thorough discussion of the implications today vis-à-vis China and the yuan–dollar battles are included here.

10.1 Exports and Imports: Global Overview

World exports in 2010 included approximately US $14.9 trillion in merchandise and $3.7 trillion in services, meaning that of the world's US $63 trillion of output, approximately 24 % involved goods and 6 % involved services traded across borders.[1]

The largest category of merchandise trade is in manufactured products, which compose nearly 70 % of the total, with food, fuel, and raw materials making up the balance (Fig. 10.1).

---

[1] Source: World Trade Organization, *International Trade Statistics 2010*. https://www.wto.org/english/res_e/statis_e/its2010_e/its10_toc_e.htm. Accessed September 20, 2012. Note that when counting net cross-border movement of goods and services in the world as a whole, Country A's export is Country B's import. Thus, for this purpose one normally counts total exports in order to eliminate the double-counting aspect. Note also that due to varying methods of reporting the value of traded merchandise (inclusive or exclusive of freight), there is some double-counting of transportation charges in the merchandise and services totals. Thus, they cannot be aggregated for a truly accurate total trade figure.

F. Langdana and P.T. Murphy, *International Trade and Global Macropolicy*,
Springer Texts in Business and Economics, DOI 10.1007/978-1-4614-1635-7_10,
© Springer Science+Business Media New York 2014

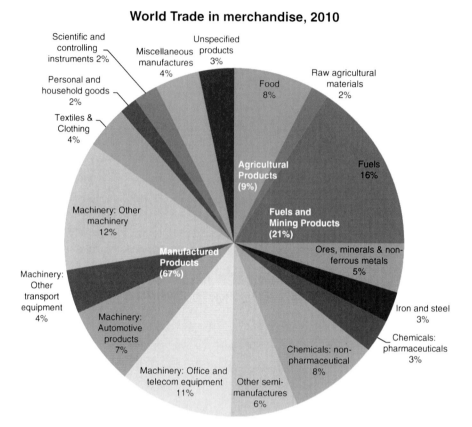

Fig. 10.1 World trade in merchandise, 2010 (*Data Source*: World Trade Organization)

Services exports are a growing component of world trade, and the capture of data in this area continues to grow in sophistication, although many shortcomings remain. Among these is the fact that a significant portion of services is difficult to track, such as the provision of professional services done entirely over the Internet. Services trade comprises the broad categories of transportation, travel, and other commercial services.

Transportation includes sea, air, land, space, and pipeline transport of goods and persons performed by residents of one economy for those of another.

Travel includes goods and services acquired by foreign personal and business travelers in the domestic country. "Travel" is not a specific type of service, but an assortment of goods and services consumed by travelers, the most common being lodging, food, entertainment, local transportation, gifts, and souvenirs.

Other commercial services include:

(i) *Communications services*—all forms of telecommunications services, plus postal and courier services.

(ii)   *Construction*—work performed on construction projects and installation by employees of an enterprise in locations outside the territory of the enterprise. (Note that goods used by construction companies for their projects are included, which implies that the "true" services component tends to be overestimated.)

(iii)   *Insurance*—provision of insurance to residents of one economy to residents of another.

(iv)   *Financial services*—financial intermediation and other services provided by banks, stock exchanges, and credit providers.

(v)   *Computer and information services*—includes hardware and software services and news and other information provision services (including web search portals).

(vi)   *Royalties and license fees*—include remittances for the use of intangible property such as patents, copyrights, trademarks, and franchises.

(vii)   *Other business services*—comprises trade-related services, leasing and rentals, and miscellaneous business, professional, and technical services such as legal; accounting; management consulting; public relations; advertising; market research and public opinion polling; R&D services; architectural, engineering, and other technical services; and agricultural, mining, and on-site processing services.

(viii)   *Personal, cultural, and recreational services*—includes audiovisual services, such as fees relating to movies, radio and television programs, and musical recordings, and also includes other personal services such as those associated with museums, libraries, archives, sporting, and other recreational activities.

World trade in services in 2010 was distributed as shown in (Fig. 10.2).

The United States is the leading exporter of services (second, if the European Union is taken as a whole). Services accounted for approximately 29 % of US Exports in 2011, up from 18 % in 1980 (Fig. 10.3).

Trends in world exports show significant shifts over time, with the US sliding from 22 % of the world's exports in 1948 down to third place behind China and Germany with 8.6 % in 2010. China has risen rapidly to first place, commanding 10.6 % of world exports in 2010 (Fig. 10.4).

The United States has long been the world's largest importer and has accounted for between 11 % and 17 % of world imports consistently since 1948, with 13.1 % in 2010. China has quickly risen to second place, with 9.3 % of world imports, followed by Germany (with 7.1 %), France (4 %), and Japan (4.6 %) (Fig. 10.5).

In general a country or region's share of world imports is more stable over time than its share of exports.

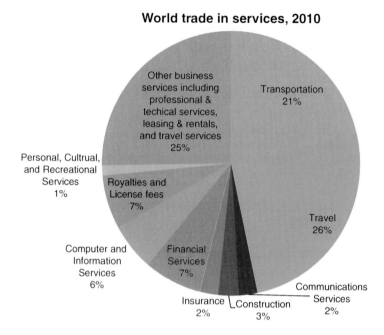

Fig. 10.2 World trade in services, 2010 (*Data Source*: World Trade Organization)

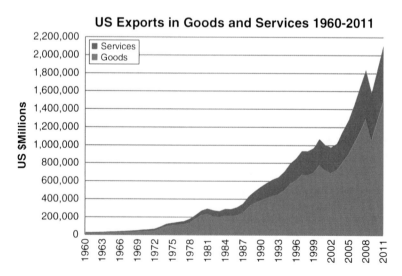

Fig. 10.3 (*Data Source*: US Census Bureau)

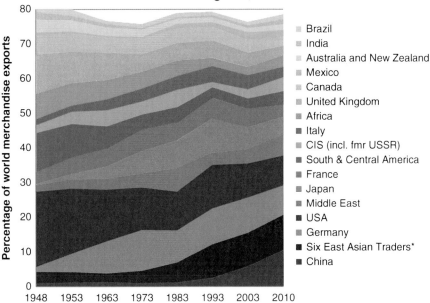

Fig. 10.4 *Six East Asian Traders include Hong Kong, Singapore, Malaysia, Taiwan, Thailand, and S. Korea (*Data Source*: World Trade Organization)

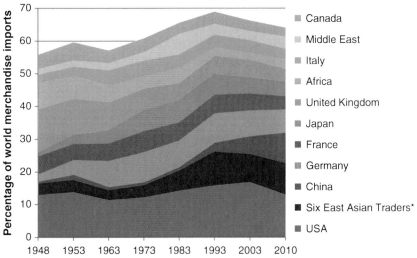

Fig. 10.5 *Six East Asian Traders include Hong Kong, Singapore, Malaysia, Taiwan, Thailand, and S. Korea (Data Source: World Trade Organization)

10.2   Exports and Imports and the ISLM-BOP

To this point, we have focused our ISLM-BOP exercises exclusively on the "big-picture" results of various policy changes on output (**Y**) and interest rates (**i**). We can in fact use our methodology to determine specific effects on imports and exports as well.

To review, the exports and imports functions appear below.

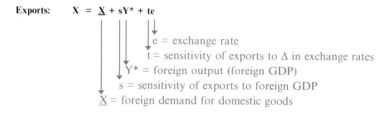

We will rearrange the imports function into intercept-slope form: $V = (\underline{V} - ze) + jY$.

Exports and imports can be plotted as a function of output (**Y**).

Since imports (**V**) are a function of domestic national output (**Y**), the import line is positively sloped as we see in Fig. 10.6, with a slope of (**j**) and the intercept being ($\underline{V} - ze$). Exports (**X**), on the other hand, are independent of domestic output (**Y**). Hence, we see that the export function in Fig. 10.6 is a horizontal line with an intercept of ($\underline{X} - sY^* + te$).

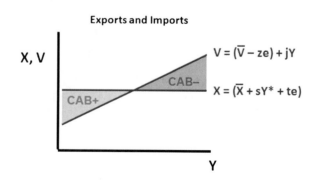

Fig. 10.6 Exports, imports and national output

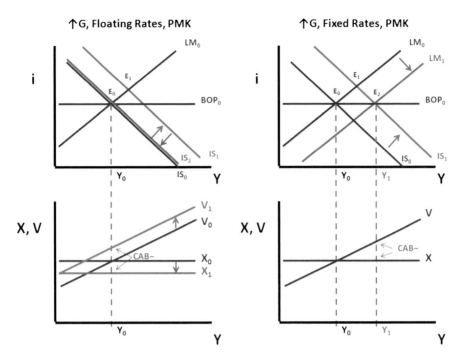

Fig. 10.7 Increase in government spending under floating versus fixed exchange rates, with PMK

When exports exceed imports ($X > V$), there is a positive current account balance (CAB+), and when the reverse holds true ($V > X$), we obtain a current account deficit (CAB−).

The effects of policy and economic changes on exports and imports can be plotted using the ISLM-BOP model. Given perfectly mobile capital, we can plot an increase in government spending ($\uparrow G$) under both flexible and fixed exchange rates.

In this exercise, we start with an initial equilibrium point Y_0 where CAB = 0, with imports equal to exports. This is for illustrative purposes only; as we shall see later in this chapter, the "starting point" of a policy exercise could include the CAB at either surplus or deficit as well. Our main goal regarding the trade balance is to determine, given the starting point at Y_0, what will be the eventual state of the CAB following the implementation of a given policy.

We will use our shorthand notation to step through the variable changes resulting from the initial increase in "G" (see Fig. 10.7).

Flexible rates	Fixed rates
1. $\uparrow G \rightarrow IS\uparrow$ to IS_1	1. $\uparrow G \rightarrow IS\uparrow$ to IS_1
2. E_1 is in BOP surplus, $\underline{S}FX > DFX$, e$\downarrow$	2. E_1 is in BOP surplus, $\underline{S}FX > DFX$, $FX\uparrow$
3. IS "snaps back"	3. LM adjusts $\downarrow$ to LM_1

The adjustments made so far are now analyzed to see if they have any effect on the import (X) and export (V) variables.

Exports and imports	Exports and imports
The strengthening of the exchange rate ($e\downarrow$) will affect V and X	No variables in the X or V function are affected
$V\uparrow$, from $e\downarrow$, as $V = \underline{V} - ze + jY$	X and V curves are unaffected; no ΔX
$X\downarrow$, from $e\downarrow$, as $X = \underline{X} + sY^* + te$	V moves along the curve as $Y\uparrow$
Thus, as the exchange rate strengthens ($e\downarrow$), the V line shifts up and the X line shifts down, as depicted in Fig. 10.7	Here, with e unchanged, there is no shift in the X or V lines. Output has increased, which moves Y to the right
4. Results	4. Results
No ΔY	$Y\uparrow$
$V\uparrow$, $X\downarrow$	$V\uparrow$, no ΔX
Current Account deficit $\uparrow$	**Current Account deficit** $\uparrow$

We can see the different results under flexible versus fixed exchange rates and how each affects exports and imports differently. Under flexible rates, an increase in G will ultimately result in no change in output, but a greater trade deficit. Under fixed rates, the increase in G will result in an increase in output, increased imports, and a greater trade deficit.

However, there is no free lunch for countries with fixed rates, as without the exchange rate (e) as a pressure valve, they are more subject to the dangers of domestic inflation, speculative bubbles, and overheating. As FX continues to flow into the country, overheating becomes increasingly likely, as we will demonstrate later in this chapter. In fact, the Southeast Asian economies learned this lesson the hard way—with pegged exchange rates, as capital flooded into their economies, the ensuing speculative asset price bubbles finally resulted in the Asian currency crisis of 1997.

Let's now examine the effect of monetary stimulus on output, interest rates, and imports and exports, under a regime of flexible rates and perfectly mobile capital (Fig. 10.8).

By flooding our economy with M, we have weakened our currency, but output is up ($Y\uparrow$), exports are up ($X\uparrow$), and interest rates remain unchanged. Here as the exchange rate weakens ($e\uparrow$), the X line shifts up due to the increase in the intercept term ($X = \underline{X} + sY^* + te$) and the V line drops due to the fall in the intercept term ($V = \underline{V} + jY - ze$).

Note that here we (arbitrarily) began with the CAB in deficit at ($V_0 - X_0$) corresponding to output Y_0. After the monetary expansion and the subsequent devaluation of the local currency, we obtain a very convenient CAB surplus; ($X_1 - V_1$) > 0 at the final (higher) output Y_1.

Additional results will include increases in employment and investment. All appear beneficial—it seems as though we have discovered the magic economic elixir!

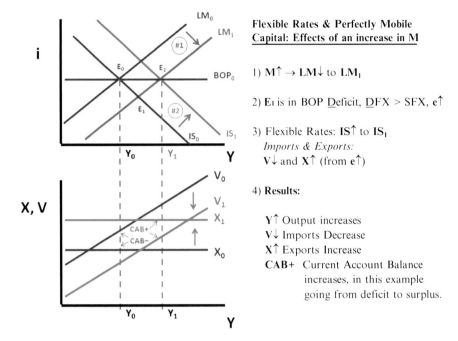

Flexible Rates & Perfectly Mobile Capital: Effects of an increase in M

1) $M\uparrow \rightarrow LM\downarrow$ to LM_1

2) E_1 is in BOP Deficit, $\underline{D}FX > SFX$, $e\uparrow$

3) Flexible Rates: $IS\uparrow$ to IS_1
   Imports & Exports:
   $V\downarrow$ and $X\uparrow$ (from $e\uparrow$)

4) **Results:**

   $Y\uparrow$ Output increases
   $V\downarrow$ Imports Decrease
   $X\uparrow$ Exports Increase
   CAB+ Current Account Balance
             increases, in this example
             going from deficit to surplus.

Fig. 10.8 $\uparrow$M, flexible rates, PMK

We have, however, excluded <u>inflation</u> from our analysis.[2] It turns out that there is, indeed, no free lunch,[3] and expansive monetary policy will lead eventually to inflation, asset bubbles, and overheating. We can see the mechanism by which this occurs by drawing the classic aggregate supply–aggregate demand (AS–AD) graph in Fig. 10.9 above.

Here, pushing output by increasing aggregate demand (through an increase in the money supply) will lead to higher prices and eventually will fail to increase output as the limits of aggregate supply are reached.

The attraction of pouring on the M, to policymakers, is obvious. Without increasing taxes or government spending, or even a vote, they are able to jump-start the economy, with the inflation problem hopefully far enough out in the future that the next administration will be the one forced to deal with the inevitable bubbles and ultimately the subsequent (and necessary) hard landing.

This process has recurred so much over history that is has a name: The **Political Business Cycle**. It was in large part due to the desire to escape from this never-ending cycle that European nations opted to join together to create the European Monetary Union in 1992.

---

[2] Inflation will be incorporated into our ISLM-BOP model in the next chapter.

[3] Milton Friedman's famous dictum.

Fig. 10.9 Pushing aggregate
demand into overheating with
monetary stimulus

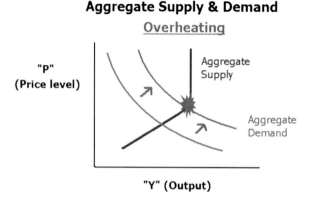

10.3   Real Exchange Rates

The nominal exchange rate, **e**, is the domestic currency price of 1 unit of foreign currency. However, this exchange rate does not convey information about purchasing power. Prices for similar items often differ in each country, sometimes significantly.

The **real exchange rate** is a measure of the actual purchasing power of the domestic currency in the foreign country. It is, effectively, the nominal exchange rate, adjusted for inflation, and is defined as the relative price of imports (valued in domestic currency) compared to the equivalent basket of domestic goods (in domestic currency).

For example, given an exchange rate of $1.31 USD to €1 euro, let's say that over the past year, a given basket of goods and services has doubled in price in Europe but the price has remained unchanged at home in the United States (the domestic economy, in this example).

Our exchange rate, **e** = 1.31, does not convey the real purchasing power of our currency in terms of foreign goods and services. If we want to have an idea of how expensive things are in each economy relative to the other, we need to adjust **e** for differences in the price level.

In this example, the foreign price level, **P***, has doubled, while the domestic price level, **P**, is unchanged. If we adjust our exchange rate for inflation by the ratio of **P*/P**, we obtain our real exchange rate equal to $1.31 \times 2/1 = 2.62$. This tells us that if we are planning a trip to Europe, we'd better bring extra euros as things will cost more than we're used to!

The **real exchange rate** is given by

$$R = \frac{P^* e}{P}$$

where

R = real exchange rate
e = nominal exchange rate
P* = foreign price level of a given basket of goods and services, in foreign currency
P = domestic price level of the same basket of goods and services, in domestic currency

Global trade in goods and services is driven by the real exchange rate (**R**), not the nominal rate (**e**). This is because **R** includes not just **e** but also the prices of goods and services in each country (**P*** and **P**).

The real exchange rate can be simplified:

$$\mathbf{R} = \frac{\mathbf{P}^*\mathbf{e}}{\mathbf{P}} = \mathbf{e}\cdot\frac{\mathbf{P}^*}{\mathbf{P}} = \frac{\$}{€}\cdot\frac{€/\text{foreign goods}}{\$/\text{domestic goods}} = \frac{\$/\textbf{foreign goods}}{\$/\textbf{domestic goods}}$$

We see that, as defined earlier, the real exchange rate is simply the ratio of the price of foreign goods in domestic currency to the price of domestic goods in domestic currency. Otherwise stated, **R** is simply the ratio of the price of foreign to domestic goods in uniform currency.

Typically, within the basket of goods and services used as the index, the goods that are the most freely traded and inexpensive to transport will tend toward real parity, where the real (currency-adjusted) prices are equal (**P*****e** = **P**). On the other hand, less transportable goods, as well as many services, will display enduring differences. This is because the freely traded and easy-to-move goods can be most easily arbitraged, eliminating real price differences. The case of $P^*e = P$ (when $R = 1$) is known as **absolute purchasing power parity** ("**absolute PPP**") or the "law of one price." Absolute PPP simply states that if an item costs $F in New York, the same item must cost exactly $F in London after converting its price in pounds to $ using the nominal exchange rate **e**.

Absolute PPP almost never exists in reality given the presence of non-tradable goods in the price indexes, trade distortions, and the fact that the "same" item in Country A is often not a perfect substitute for the item in Country B. *The Economist* attempts to circumvent this problem with its "Big Mac Index" in that this perfectly substitutable item is priced in one currency in different global locations. This allows one to determine how much exchange rates are deviating from what they would have to be for absolute purchasing power parity to prevail.

If **P*****e** < **P**, then the domestic currency is said to be "overvalued," and if P^* **e** > **P**, then the domestic currency is said to be "undervalued." Otherwise stated, **R** < 1 implies an "overvalued" domestic currency and **R** > 1 implies an "undervalued" domestic currency.

10.4   The Pass-Through Effect

Domestic exporters are concerned when the domestic currency strengthens, because this makes their products more expensive to purchase for overseas buyers.

Let us examine the case of the Bavarian Heavy Equipment Company of Germany, which is exporting earthmovers to Cameroon for €200,000 each. With a pegged exchange rate of 655.975 Central African francs (XAF) to euro, the local price in Cameroon is XAF 131 million.

However, let's say that the Bank of the Central African States, which manages the Central African franc, under pressure to stimulate exports and help domestic producers compete, adjusts the peg to weaken the currency to a new rate of 750 XAF to the euro.

While this helps Cameroonian exporters, it makes life harder for Bavarian Heavy Equipment Company, as the local price in Cameroon for their same earthmover is now 750 × 200,000 = XAF 150 million. This might be enough to price the German equipment out of the market.

However, Bavarian Heavy Equipment does have an option: It can lower its price to counteract the currency move. By selling its earthmovers for €175,000, the Cameroonian price will remain unchanged at XAF 131 million. This allows Bavarian Heavy Equipment to hold market share and buys time for it to find ways to adapt to the new exchange rate. The company might move production for the region to Cameroon or develop a less costly model of its earthmover for the Central African market, or it might opt to simply live with the price decrease and consequently smaller margins.

From our expression, $\mathbf{R} = (\mathbf{P}^*\mathbf{e})/(\mathbf{P})$, with Cameroon being the domestic country, $\mathbf{e}$ increases as the Cameroonian government deliberately weakens its economy to spur its exports and to discourage imports into Cameroon. The numerator, $\mathbf{P}^*\mathbf{e}$, which is the price of Cameroons's imports in the local currency, increases. The only way to counteract this is for the Bavarians to decrease $\mathbf{P}^*$ to 175,000 euros and to bring the real exchange rate back to where it was before the Cameroonian devaluation of its currency.

This is a common response by exporters when a major market is threatened by exchange rate changes.

This process is called the **pass-through effect**. The exporting country lowers its prices in response to a strengthening of its currency to maintain the real exchange rate at its previous level, allowing the effect of the exchange rate manipulation to "pass though" its market strategy.

10.5   The Plaza Accord

In 1985, the finance ministers of the G-5 group of leading industrialized economies, which included West Germany, France, Japan, the United Kingdom, and the United States, met at the Plaza Hotel in New York City to discuss a developing political problem.

Paul Volcker, on CBS-TV's "Face the Nation", March 22, 1981, Associated Press

Thanks in large part to Fed Chairman Paul Volcker's monetary discipline following the rampant inflation of the 1970s, and the strong economy emerging out of years of stagflation and recession, the US dollar had strengthened significantly during the early 1980s, from a nadir of $2.45 to the British pound in November 1980 all the way to $1.04 to the pound in February 1985.

Imports were surging as a result, and US manufacturers were facing a level of foreign competition they had never experienced before. Large manufacturers such as GM, who had comfortably dominated the US market for decades and had consequently allowed quality and competitiveness to lapse, found themselves exposed as competitors from overseas, particularly Japan, made strong inroads into their markets.

Political pressure from the US manufacturing sector was building, and public concern was growing over such a rapid and disruptive change. The growing trade deficit, a natural result of a strengthening currency, was much in the news, and this was coupled with increasing and highly visible foreign investments in US financial assets and real estate, as the $\mathbf{KAB} = -\mathbf{CAB}$ relationship predicts. This relationship has been discussed in detail in the National Savings Identity discussion in Chap. 7, where bond-financed sustainable budget deficits were financed by massive capital inflows into a safe-haven economy.

Concerned that a US public backlash would bring pressure to impose tariffs and other trade restrictions, which would harm the US and world economy and, most importantly, disrupt the vitally important deficit-financing capital inflows into the USA, policymakers convened the G-5 in private to discuss the situation.

It was agreed that the countries would coordinate their central bank activity in an effort to weaken the US dollar and relieve some of the causes of the mounting political pressure. The various central banks spent some $10 billion over the

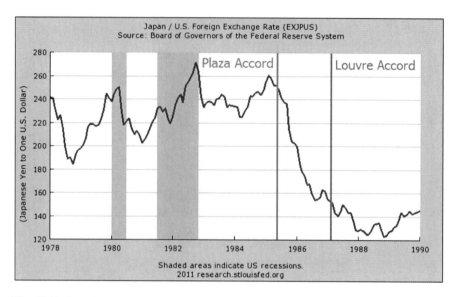

Fig. 10.10 Japan/US foreign exchange rate 1978–1990

ensuing few years affecting this policy, which was aided along by private market speculation once the commitment of the central banks was clear.

The result was a significant weakening of the USD against the other currencies, with the dollar weakening by half against the Japanese yen between 1985 and 1989. The **Louvre Accord** of February 1987 announced an agreement among finance ministers to seek stabilization of exchange rates at the then-prevailing levels, following the dollar's precipitous fall after the Plaza Accord.[4] The USD did fall another 20 % through 1988 before recovering back to near-Louvre Accord levels by 1990 (Fig. 10.10).

The Plaza Accord's primary goal of reducing the US trade deficit with Japan, however, was not achieved for several reasons. One reason was Japanese trade policy, which was protective of favored industries. The Japanese protracted the negotiations regarding the opening of their markets to give their workers and industries time to adjust. Another major contributing factor was the **pass-through effect** discussed above: Japanese companies simply adjusted their prices to

---

[4] From the Louvre Accord: "10. The Ministers and Governors agreed that the substantial exchange rate changes since the Plaza Agreement will increasingly contribute to reducing external imbalances and have now brought their currencies within ranges broadly consistent with underlying economic fundamentals, given the policy commitments summarized in this statement. Further substantial exchange rate shifts among their currencies could damage growth and adjustment prospects in their countries. In current circumstances, therefore, they agreed to cooperate closely to foster stability of exchange rates around current levels." Source: Statement of the G6 Finance Ministers and Central Bank Governors (Louvre Accord), Paris, France, February 22, 1987.

maintain their US market share as they worked out their strategy for going forward.

For many firms, this meant locating plants in the United States. Particularly visible in this regard was the large number of Japanese auto factories that opened in the United States from the mid-1980s through the end of the decade. These became the subject of much study and attention, including in popular culture.[5]

Foreign-owned factories, which visibly employ thousands of workers, are not perceived as so pernicious in the eyes of the domestic public compared to foreign imports, which are generally believed to "cost" domestic jobs. Thus these foreign-owned plants, while object of curiosity, were accepted by public opinion in a way that foreign goods never could be.

10.6   Real Exchange Rate Parity: Relative PPP

As mentioned above, non-tradable goods and services make up a significant component of the CPI indexes used to calculate relative purchasing power, and even tradable goods with low transportation costs are subject to regional events that move prices, so absolute PPP, where $\mathbf{R} = \mathbf{1}$, (i.e. $\mathbf{P}^*\mathbf{e} = \mathbf{P}$), almost never holds.

Empirical evidence suggests, however, that the *rates of change* of the relative price level and the exchange rate do tend to be roughly aligned over the long term. That is, generally speaking, **relative PPP** can be said to hold, in which

$$\begin{array}{ccc} \textbf{Rate of change of} & = & \textbf{Rate of change of} \\ \textbf{Exchange Rate} & & \textbf{Relative Price Levels} \end{array}$$

which we can express as

$$\frac{e_{(t+1)}}{e} - 1 = \frac{\left(P_{(t+1)}/P^*_{(t+1)}\right)}{(P/P^*)} - 1$$

where $e_{(t+1)}$, $P_{(t+1)}$, and $P^*_{(t+1)}$ are the future exchange rate and future domestic and foreign price level, respectively.

---

[5] For example, in *Gung Ho*, a 1986 comedy about a shuttered US auto factory that's reopened by the Japanese, Michael Keaton's character encounters any number of challenges as he adapts the factory to Japanese management practices, for example, convincing his American workforce to perform morning calisthenics.

10.7   General Parity Relationships: Expected Exchange Rates, Inflation, and Interest Rates

If we rearrange the right side of the above "relative PPP" equation, we obtain

$$\frac{e_{(t+1)}}{e} - 1 = \frac{(P_{(t+1)} / P)}{(P^*_{(t+1)} / P^*)} - 1 \longrightarrow \frac{1 + \text{Domestic inflation rate}}{1 + \text{Foreign inflation rate}} - 1$$

We can see that the right side of the equation can be expressed in terms of the domestic and foreign inflation rate, which we will call π and π^*. So

$$\frac{e_{t+1}}{e} - 1 = \frac{1 + \pi}{1 + \pi^*} - 1$$

Given that these relationships are well understood, we would anticipate that in equilibrium, the expected exchange rate (e^e) may be substituted for the future exchange rate term (e_{t+1}). Thus

$$\frac{e^e}{e} - 1 = \frac{1 + \pi}{1 + \pi^*} - 1$$

Assuming inflation rates are not large (under, say 10–12 % in each country), the relationship may be approximated by

$$\left[\left(\frac{e^e}{e} \right) - 1 \right] = (\pi - \pi^*)$$

Recall the interest rate parity relationship from Chap. 8:

$$(i - i^*) = \left[\left(\frac{e^e}{e} \right) - 1 \right]$$

A clear relationship here emerges between interest rates, exchange rates, and inflation rates. Integrating interest rate parity and real exchange rate parity, we obtain the very powerful insight that, in equilibrium,

$$
\begin{array}{ccc}
(i - i^*) & [(e^e/e) - 1] & (\pi - \pi^*) \\
\text{Interest rate} = & \text{Expected change} = & \text{Inflation rate} \\
\text{differential} & \text{in exchange rate} & \text{differential}
\end{array}
$$

Naturally, these variables move at different speeds, with exchange rates changing very quickly and interest rates nearly so. Price changes take weeks or months to develop; therefore, the relationship will vary from the predicted result to a degree dependent in part on the time period selected.

The temporal difference in the speed of adjustment for each of these three ratios is also a key determinant of the relative slopes of the LM and BOP curves, which we shall explore further in Chap. 12.

Interest rates, exchange rates, and prices are all moving all the time and affect each other. Cause and effect among them are often difficult to isolate.[6]

10.8   Purchasing Power Parity and Nominal GDP Comparisons

In common usage, **purchasing power parity**, or **PPP**, generally refers to the adjustment made to the nominal GDP of a given country to account for differences in relative prices.

When we examine the *nominal* GDP for another country, the figure does not give us any information about how much it actually costs to live in that country. For example, India's nominal GDP in 2010 as given in USD was approximately $1.3 trillion. However, this does not convey information about purchasing power. If the relative price level of an equivalent basket of goods and services in India is 1/3 that of the same basket in the United States, then $P^*/P = 1/3$.

Adjusting the GDP for this difference gives us India's 2010 US dollar-denominated GDP adjusted for purchasing power, which is $3.9 trillion. This figure would be reported as India GDP (PPP): $3.9 trillion.

PPP is an important measure when calculating *GDP per capita*, to compare people's material well-being in one country relative to another.

With nearly 1.2 billion people, India's nominal GDP per capita is only $1,000 USD. However, India's PPP-adjusted per capita GDP is $3,000 USD. This provides a superior measure of material living conditions and domestic buying power than does a simple nominal per capita GDP comparison.[7]

---

[6] For this section the authors are indebted to Prof. Ian Giddy, who provided a concise discussion of the various parity relationships in his article "An Integrated Theory of Exchange Rate Equilibrium", *The Journal of Financial and Quantitative Analysis* Vol. 11, No. 5 (Dec., 1976), pp. 883–892. Online: http://www.jstor.org/stable/2330587, Accessed February 2, 2011.

[7] To understand the application of PPP, imagine trying to live in the United States on $3,000 per year. This is the situation faced by the "average" person in India based on GDP (PPP) divided by population. (The median Indian citizen lives on far less as income is not distributed evenly). PPP allows us a realistic comparison; when only nominal GDP per capita is used, the Indian GDP per capita of $1,000 USD is not a meaningful figure and as such is generally dismissed by casual observers since "that sounds very low but it costs much less to live there." PPP takes this factor into account.

Articles

Three short news stories spread over an 8-month period all combine to form Article 10.1.

Article 10.1. Three Recent Articles from the Lykos Free Press

"Plan 109 for Lykos"

Christopher Jenelli, *Lykos Free Press*, February 1st

The Lykosian economy is dead in the water. Output is stagnant. Unemployment is high. Confidence is shaky, and elections are just around the corner. Something has to be done. Finance Professor, Maryetta Garlick, who recently appeared on "Face the World," said, "Lykos had already put forward and abandoned 108 plans for recovery—so this must be Plan 109!" Dame Lindsner Moffat, the leader of Lykos, is a huge proponent of Keynesian stimulus spending. She knows all about the Keynesian multiplier effect in which every $1 of spending by the government leads to a macro "footprint" greater than $1 as induced spending streams caused by the initial increase in spending ripple through the economy. Dame Moffat's plan is to dramatically increase government spending across the board in an attempt to "jump-start" the stagnant Lykosian economy.

Jiorgio Giorgolis, leader of the Lykos Exporters Association, is thrilled, telling this reporter that "Dame Moffat's plan is just what we need! Exports are a hugely important sector in our economy, and our members are unanimous in their support of this spending program! Not only will employment in the export sector improve, but we will reduce our trade deficit as well!"

Lykos is a relatively safe-haven economy, and it finances the increase in government spending by issuing sovereign (government) debt. The country also has adopted a system of freely floating exchange rates with no restriction on the global flow of capital in and out of Lykos.

(a) *Using the ISLM-BOP model, analyze the results of Dame Moffat's plan for the Lykosian economy.*
(b) *What is the effect on the export sector? What will the effect be on the trade deficit (current account deficit)?*

"What Happened to Plan 109?"

Christopher Jenelli, *Lykos Free Press*, August 1st

Surprisingly, and to the great disappointment of the Lykosian government and its people, the long-awaited increase in output and jobs did not materialize!

No multiplier effect! Nothing! All that Lykos was left with after this huge fiscal expansion was a sharp deterioration in its export sector, a surge in input costs, and an increase in foreign appetites for Lykosian government bonds. Interestingly, Lykos' interest rates were back to where they were before the increase in spending.

(c) Relate the Lykosian policy of bond-financed fiscal expansion to the National Savings Identity discussed in Chap. 7. Intuitively explain why the fabled Keynesian multiplier effect did not materialize here in this world of perfect capital mobility and flexible exchange rates. Also explain why interest rates went back to their original values after this experiment in fiscal expansion.

(d) Also explain why the final equilibrium point lies on the BOP line even though there has been such a huge decline in the current account balance.

"The Bordee Miracle"

Christopher Jenelli, *Lykos Free Press*, August 15th

Experts continue to debate how to assign blame for the failure of Lykos' fiscal policy, most recently in last week's turbulent session of Parliament. Meanwhile, the neighboring economy of Bordee has had a wholly different experience with its own fiscal expansion, which was launched at the same time as that of Lykos. (e) Lots of new jobs followed a big fat multiplier effect that generated a significant increase in output. Bordee bragged that its success was largely due to the fact that ever since a currency reform five years ago, its exchange rate was pegged (at 10 Bordee rupees = 1 US$).

However, all is not well in Bordee today. (f) Home prices have hit an all-time high—nearly doubling from two years ago! Commodity prices have climbed into the stratosphere. And the labor market is exceptionally tight—unemployment has hit a 45-year record low! While this may be reason to cheer for most Bordeenians, Economist Simone Feline of the Institute for Data Analysis warns that these numbers are "most troubling."

Meanwhile back in Lykos, appearing on "Face the World," Jiorgio Giorgolis of the Lykos Exporters Association urges patience and reminds anxious viewers that about 12 years ago, (g) when Bordee, in an attempt to stimulate growth, flooded their economy with money in order to massively devalue the then-floating Bordeenian currency, the policy initially appeared to be successful. "Remember," Giorgolis says, (h) "Even though our exchange rate strengthened from 5 Lykos Dinars to 1 Bordee Rupee all the way down to 4-to-1, Lykos was able to counter the effect of the falling Bordeenian Rupee by managing its real exchange rate!"

This time however, it appears that Lykos has few policy options as Bordee's previously soaring economy now flies straight into danger.

Hints and Solutions

Article 10.1

(a) Deploy an ISLM-BOP model for Lykos, with flexible exchange rates and perfectly mobile capital (Fig. 10.11).

Here, the IS shifts up with the increase in **G** and then snaps back to its original (i_0, Y_0) point as the domestic currency appreciates (**e**↓).

(b) We can see the effect on exports using the modeling tools that we learned in this chapter. The strengthening currency has harmed the export sector, increased imports, and resulted in a reduced current account balance (a higher current account deficit).

(c) From Chap. 7 we know that as the demand for loanable funds curve shifts to the right, the supply of loanable funds curve shifts to the right too, thanks to capital inflows that mirror the current account deficits. To review,

Recall the NSI equation: **|G – T| = |S – I| + |Imp – Exp|**

Fiscal deficit   Current Account Deficit (i.e.,–CAB)

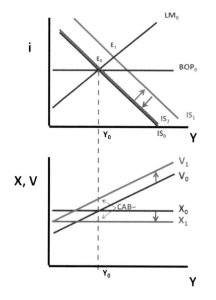

1) ↑**G** → **IS**↑ to **IS₁**

2) **E₁** is in BOP **S**urplus, <u>S</u>FX>DFX, **e**↓

3) **IS** "snaps back"

Imports & Exports:
V↑, from **e**↓, as V = <u>V</u>–ze + jY
X↓, from **e**↓, as X = <u>X</u>+ sY* + te

4) Results:

No Δ**Y**, and no Δi
V↑, **X**↓
Current Account Deficit↑

Fig. 10.11 ↑G, floating rates, PMK

Fig. 10.12 Following an
increase in **G**, the DLF shifts
to the right, pushing interest
rates higher

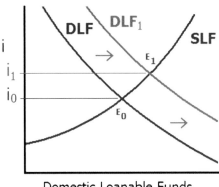

The Domestic Capital Market

Domestic Loanable Funds

We follow the results referring to Figs. 10.12 and 10.13.

1. The increase in the government's fiscal deficit $(G - T)$ increases the **DLF**.
2. This increase in the **DLF** drives up domestic interest rates to the higher equilibrium, i_1 (Fig. 10.12).
3. The higher interest rates attract foreign capital. Foreign investors bringing funds in must swap their respective currencies for domestic currency, which strengthens the exchange rate ($e\downarrow$).
4. The stronger currency causes (now relatively less expensive) imports to surge and (now relatively more expensive) exports to shrink.
5. This result causes the current account balance $(\mathbf{Exp} - \mathbf{Imp})$ to decrease, or otherwise stated, the current account deficit to increase.
6. Foreign exporters accumulate deposits of domestic currency, which they deploy back in the domestic safe-haven economy. The increase in the current account deficit thus brings an inflow of capital, resulting in an increased capital account balance (**KAB**). Here we see the relationship $(\mathbf{KAB} = -\mathbf{CAB})$ in action.

   This inflow of capital creates an increase in the supply of loanable funds, which is reflected by the rightward shift in the **SLF** (Fig. 10.13).
7. Finally, thanks to the capital inflow, interest rates in the domestic economy are now lowered to their final equilibrium level, which is in this example right back at their original equilibrium level, i_0.

The rightward shift in both supply and demand for loanable funds results in interest rates returning to i_0.

The deterioration in exports, thanks to the appreciation of the domestic currency, has negated any positive effect on Y, thereby resulting in no multiplier.

We can see the mechanism for this in the algebra of the output function

$$\mathbf{Y = C} \qquad \mathbf{+ I} \qquad \mathbf{+ G + Exports} \qquad \mathbf{- Imports}$$

$$Y = \underline{C} + bY + \underline{I} - fi + G + \underline{X} + sY^* + te - (\underline{V} + jY - ze)$$

Fig. 10.13 The full "engine room" for an increase in **G**. Increase in KAB (from capital inflow) shifts the SLF, driving interest rates back down

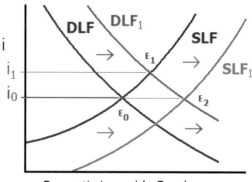

The Domestic Capital Market

Domestic Loanable Funds

The increase in output (**Y**) from the increase in government spending (**G**↑) has been offset by the stronger currency (**e**↓), which drives down **Y** in both the exports term ("+**te**") and the imports term (−[−**ze**]).

(d) All points on the BOP line are points where CAB + KAB = 0. So as the current account balance drops due to the fall in exports and the surge in imports, the resulting capital account increase (capital inflow) ensures that once again BOP is in equilibrium.

We could plug in hypothetical numbers for our example in order to illustrate the point. Let's say that before Lykos' fiscal expansion, the current account balance is (−20) and the capital account balance is (+20).

If the current account balance declines by (−110) to a new level of (−130), the capital account balance will increase by a similar amount (+110), by the mechanism detailed above, to a new level of (+130).

So the BOP remains zero.

Before fiscal expansion : BOP = KAB + CAB = $(20) + (-20) = 0$.

After fiscal expansion :   BOP = KAB + CAB = $(130) + (-130) = 0$.

(e) We deploy an ISLM-BOP model for Bordee, with fixed exchange rates and perfectly mobile capital. The **IS** shifts up (to the right), followed by a downward (to the right) shift in **LM**.

We see in Fig. 10.14 that output increases, with no change in interest rates.

(f) Bordee is displaying classics and textbook signs of overheating, thanks to the tsunami of capital inflow (as we saw in Fig. 10.9 earlier in this chapter). Overheating is eventually followed by a contraction, most often a "hard landing."

This is the danger inherent in attempting to increase output by pushing demand through fiscal or monetary stimulus, as we shall explore in greater detail in the next chapter.

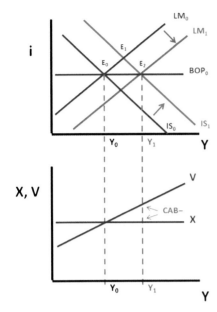

1) $\uparrow$**G** $\rightarrow$ **IS**$\uparrow$ to **IS$_1$**

2) **E$_1$** is in BOP $\underline{S}$urplus, $\underline{S}$FX>DFX,
under fixed rates the influx of FX is
replaced with M by the central bank; **M**$\uparrow$

3) **LM** slides down (from **M**$\uparrow$)

Exports & Imports:
X and **V** **lines** are unchanged.
Exports (**X**) are unchanged.
Imports (**V**) increase (along the curve)
with rising Y.

4) Results

Increase in **Y**, with no Δi
V$\uparrow$ (along the curve), **X** unchanged
Current Account Deficit$\uparrow$

Fig. 10.14 $\uparrow$G, fixed rates, PMK

(g) Bordee effected a "devaluation," as we see in Fig. 10.15. Here the LM shifts
downward (to the right) due to the increase in monetary growth, and the IS
moves upward (to the right) due to the ensuing currency devaluation.

We can see that, abstracting from inflation, and in the absence of countering
moves by its global trading partners, Bordee has succeeded in boosting output
with few apparent negative consequences.

(h) Lykos exploited the "pass-through effect," by decreasing the price of its exports
to mitigate the weakening of the Bordee rupee and to bring the real exchange
rate back to its original value.

In this example, the Lykosian dinar has strengthened by 20 % against the
Bordeenian rupee, from $e_0 = 5(5/1)$ to $e_1 = 4(4/1)$. This implies that a 20 %
cut in prices by Lykos' exporters would leave the real exchange rate unchanged.

The real exchange rate is given by $R = (P^*e)/P$, which we can rearrange as
$R = e \cdot (P^*/P)$.

So, we have

$$R_0 = 5 \cdot \left(\frac{P^*}{P_0}\right)$$

$$R_1 = 4 \cdot \left(\frac{P^*}{P_1}\right)$$

Clearly, in order to maintain its original real exchange rate (such that
$R_1 = R_0$), the Lykosian price level P_1 would need to be 20 % less than P_0.

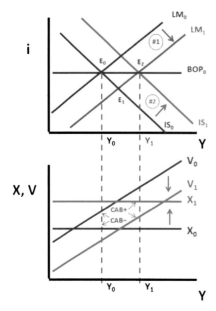

1) ↑M → LM↓ to **LM₁**

2) **E₁** is in BOP <u>D</u>eficit, <u>D</u>FX>SFX, under flexible rates the dearth of FX weakens the exchange rate; **e**↑

3) **IS** slides up (from **e**↑)

Exports & Imports:
Exports (**X**) increase, from **e**↑
Imports (**V**) decrease, also from **e**↑

4) Results

Increase in **Y**, with no Δi
X↑, **V**↓
Current Account Balance increases (equivalently, Current Account deficit decreases)

Fig. 10.15 ↑M, flexible rates, PMK

$$R_0 = 5 \cdot \left(\frac{P^*}{P_0}\right) = \frac{5P^*}{P_0}$$

$$R_1 = 4 \cdot \left(\frac{P^*}{0.8P_0}\right) = \frac{4P^*}{0.8P_0} = \frac{5P^*}{P_0}$$

$$R_0 = R_1$$

Lykos' exporters have nullified the effect of the Bordeenian devaluation by cutting their prices by 20 %.

Chapter 11
Incorporating Inflation into the Model

Summary We now add inflation into our ISLM-BOP model and explore in greater detail the relationship between exchange rates and interest rates.

The concept of the "political business cycle" is explored, with historical examples of policymakers succumbing to politically expedient inflationary boom-and-bust cycles.

The policy implications of monetary discipline and pegged exchange rates are analyzed, which allows us ultimately to answer the question: "Why do currency pegs explode?"

The "impossible trinity" is a theory which states that one cannot have (i) perfectly mobile capital, (ii) pegged exchange rates, and (iii) an effective monetary policy lever. The chapter walks through the Asian crisis of 1997 to show the impossible trinity in action. This leads into a success story: the effective management of exchange rates by China and Singapore before and after the crisis.

Inflation often manifests in asset bubbles, rather than the general price level. Recent cases leading up to and including the US housing bubble are examined closely.

How and why does a bursting asset bubble or an "exploding currency peg" in one country affect others? At one time, many thought that specific-country effects could be contained; today's reality is global contagion. The causes and effects are presented with theory providing the foundation for real-world examples, especially global contagion since the subprime crisis.

The chapter concludes with a case in which we are confronted with similar challenges to those faced by the Southeast Asian economies during the late 1990's crisis. With the analytical tools that we have gained in this and previous chapters, we will be in a position to effectively analyze and choose among alternative policy solutions.

F. Langdana and P.T. Murphy, *International Trade and Global Macropolicy*,
Springer Texts in Business and Economics, DOI 10.1007/978-1-4614-1635-7_11,
© Springer Science+Business Media New York 2014

11.1   Inflation in the ISLM-BOP Analysis

Thus far, we have omitted inflation from our ISLM-BOP modeling, as an increase in the general price level generally lags the initial actions and effects. Up to this point, the results derived from our ISLM-BOP exercises could be deemed "short term" at best, effects that manifest themselves before inflation finally appears. While necessary in a pedagogic context, this has actually been a dangerous omission—these results appear tempting but can prove to be exceedingly detrimental to the macroeconomy once the inflationary effects are factored in.

In Chap. 9, we examined the macroeconomic effect of an increase in the money supply using our **ISLM-BOP** model. We saw that under conditions of perfectly mobile capital and fixed exchange rates, an increase in the nominal money stock ($\uparrow$**M**) will result in an increase in real output.

However, we did not examine the ultimate and eventual effect on prices. We now do so by dropping a graph of aggregate supply and demand below our **ISLM-BOP** diagram (Fig. 11.1).

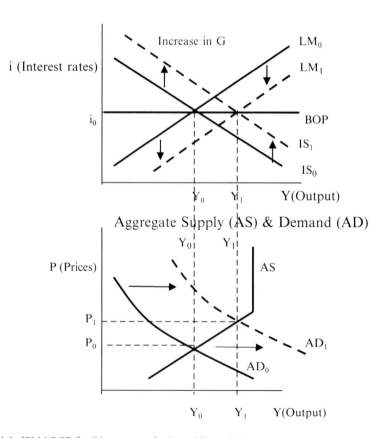

Fig. 11.1 ISLM-BOP flexible rates, perfectly mobile capital

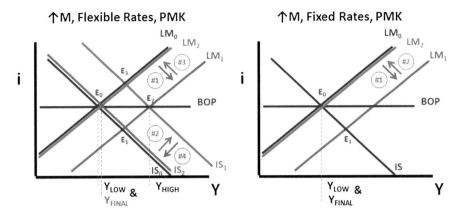

Fig. 11.2 Increase in money stock under floating versus fixed rates, with PMK

The increase in the money stock results in increased aggregate demand, which, with a positively sloped aggregate supply curve, brings about an increase in the price level.[1] This result derives originally from the fundamental Keynesian tenet that the percentage increase in prices will exceed the percentage increase in nominal wages, thereby yielding the positively sloped AS curve. In addition, basic microeconomics holds that supply is relatively inflexible in the short run, and thus increases in demand will put strains on capacity.

Price increases resulting from increases in demand take a few months to manifest, as producers pass their costs through the supply chain to the consumer. Ultimately, the increase in prices ($\uparrow P$) will feed back into our model.

Given two economies with perfectly mobile capital, one with flexible exchange rates and one pegged, what does our model tell us about the effects of an increase in money supply? (Fig. 11.2)

Flexible rates	Fixed rates
1) $\uparrow M \rightarrow LM\downarrow$ to LM_1	1) $\uparrow M \rightarrow LM\downarrow$ to LM_1
2) E_1 is in BOP deficit, $\underline{D}FX > SFX$, $e\uparrow$	2) E_1 is in BOP deficit, $\underline{D}FX > SFX$, $\mathbf{FX}\downarrow$
3) IS adjusts $\uparrow$ to IS_1	3) LM "snaps back," adjusts $\uparrow$ to LM_2

(continued)

---

[1] We can contrast the inflationary effect of monetary ($\uparrow M$) versus fiscal ($\uparrow G$) stimulus here. Recall that with a floating exchange rate, a strengthening of the exchange rate will mitigate the effects of government spending, by (a) reducing exports, returning GDP back to where it started, and (b) making imports cheaper, which works against inflation.

Flexible rates	Fixed rates
4) ☺ Initial results **Y**↑ No Δ**i** *Also (not shown)* **X**↑, employment↑	4) Results No Δ**Y** No effect except that FX blows out of the country

<u>☹Follow-on results</u>

Following the initial, happy story, however, an increase in the general price level (↑**P**) results from the increase in money supply We can analyze the ensuing results 1) ↑**P** → **LM** snaps back ↑to **LM**$_2$ 2) **E**$_3$ is in BOP surplus, $\underline{SFX} > DFX$, **e**↓ 3) **IS** adjusts ↓ to **IS**$_2$ 4) ☺ Final results (equilibrium back at **E**$_0$) **Y**↓, **X**↓, employment↓, and ↑**P** <u>remains</u>	Persistent increases in the money supply under a pegged rate regime will eventually cause bleeding of FX reserves as the central bank attempts to defend the peg once private FX is dissipated, and will break the peg when the central bank runs out of FX reserves

Under the flexible rates regime, we see the **political business cycle** in action. All the previous stimulative benefits of the increase in money supply have been negated, and we are back where we started but now with higher prices and wages. Workers who were hired in the initial boom are laid off. Continued long-term repetition of this cycle also leads to stronger unions as workers fight to protect themselves from cyclical layoffs and to keep their wages up with inflation, resulting in a less flexible economy and reduced competitiveness. And finally, long-term interest rates are also driven up with expectations of future inflation (as per the "Fisher Effect"[2]); this by itself would be enough to retard long-term economic growth.

The desire to escape this cycle of wage and price inflation was the primary economic reason that the members of the European Monetary Union were willing to relinquish control over monetary policy to the European Central Bank.

---

[2] This is a manifestation of the "Fisher Effect," named for economist Irving Fisher, whose formula for long-term rates is expressed as $r = i_{LT} - \pi^e$, where r = real interest rate, i_{LT} = long-term interest rate, and π^e = inflation expectations. This can be rearranged as $i_{LT} = r + \pi^e$, i.e., long-term interest rates are equal to the real interest rate plus expected inflation.

11.2 The Benefits of Monetary Discipline

It is no accident that the European Central Bank is headquartered in Frankfurt, Germany. The German experience with hyperinflation of 1922–1923 remains seared into the cultural memory of the German people, and prudent monetary policy has long since been the hallmark of the German Bundesbank. The Germans had avoided many of the inflation problems that had plagued Europe since World War II. When the time came to establish the headquarters of the European Central Bank, Frankfurt was therefore the natural choice.

Monetary discipline—that is, keeping a tight control on the money supply so that it does not expand more than would be consistent with the expansion of the economy and maintenance of a steady price level—offers several distinct benefits:

1. **Fiscal discipline is fostered.**
   There is a correlation between fiscally sound government policies and disciplined monetary policy, reflective of an overall mindset of economic prudence. The greater the reluctance to increase monetary growth and monetize runaway government spending, the more fiscally conservative the spending policy would necessarily be.
2. **Long-term interest rates (i_{LT}) are moderated.**
   Over time, as the central bank builds credibility, long-term inflation fears are tempered (again as per the Fisher Effect).
3. **Exchange rates are more stable.**
   With inflation held in-check, interest rates do not fluctuate as much as they do under a more accommodating monetary policy. This leads to less speculation in nominal interest arbitrage, reducing the volatility of exchange rates.
4. **The political business cycle is eradicated.**
   No more endless cycles of inflation and economic stagnation.
5. **Inflation is controlled.**
   Milton Friedman famously pointed out that inflation is ultimately "always and everywhere a monetary phenomenon." Hence, the tighter the monetary growth, the more restrained the eventual inflation.
6. **Employment is stable.**
   Without monetary discipline, the effect of the repeated cycles of hiring and firing on the psyche of workers when the initial money-created booms peter out cannot be underestimated. Workers begin to value security more than opportunity, and a less flexible, less opportunistic labor force is the result.
7. **Safe-haven economy.**
   Over an extended period of time (investors have long memories), the country's bond rating improves dramatically, and borrowing rates go down significantly. Bond financing of fiscal deficits becomes affordable.

11.3 Speculative Asset Price Bubbles

Clockwise from *top left*: The Semper Augustus, the Pets.com sock puppet (Associated Press), empty houses in Las Vegas, October 2007 (Associated Press)

Measures of consumer inflation, such as the CPI, do not capture appreciation in asset prices, such as stocks and real estate. Rising asset prices are generally associated with a growing economy and, unlike price inflation, are generally welcomed by domestic consumers.

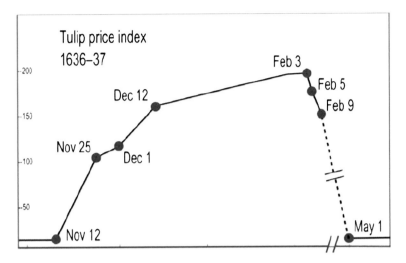

Fig. 11.3 Tulip mania 1636–1637. (Pengfei Wang and Yi Wen, "Speculative Bubbles and Financial Crisis," St. Louis Fed Working Paper 2009-029B, St. Louis: Federal Reserve Bank of St. Louis Research Division, July 2009)

However, speculative fervor can lead to "bubbles" in asset values, where prices cease to be reflective of likely long-term returns on the underlying assets. Economist Robert Shiller defines a bubble as "a situation in which temporarily high prices are sustained largely by investors' enthusiasm rather than by consistent estimation of real value."[3]

Inevitably, when the last buyer has entered the market, the price appreciation reverses, more often than not with a vengeance. History is replete with examples of this phenomenon, with those of earlier centuries documented brilliantly by Charles Mackay in his 1841 classic *Extraordinary Popular Delusions and the Madness of Crowds.*[4]

The Dutch Tulip Mania of 1636–1637, perhaps the most famous historical example, saw a craze for tulip bulbs drive the price of a single bulb higher than that of an Amsterdam house. A single *Semper Augustus* bulb sold for 3,000 guilders, ten times the average laborer's annual wage (Fig. 11.3).

While every speculative asset price (SAP) bubble is unique, certain broad characteristics are common:

- An economic climate of rising prosperity
- Peak social mood[5]

---

[3] Shiller RJ (2000) Irrational exuberance. Princeton University Press, Princeton

[4] This remarkable book is still a compelling read today and is available for free download from many sites on the Internet.

[5] The best examination of social mood and its relation to bubbles and depressions is found in Robert Pretcher's *The Wave Principle of Human Social Behavior and the New Science of Socionomics,* New Classics Library, 2002.

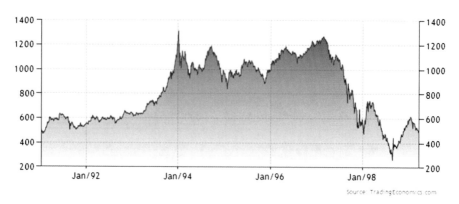

Fig. 11.4 Malaysia stock market index 1991–1999 *(Source:* www.tradingeconomics.com)

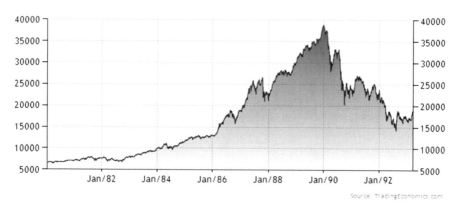

Fig. 11.5 Japan stock market index 1981–1993 *(Source:* www.tradingeconomics.com)

- Increasing tolerance for risk
- Financial innovations
- An inflow of foreign capital
- Entry of the uninformed "regular person" into the market
- A decrease in standards
- Easy money with low borrowing rates

Recent examples include the US tech-stock bubble in 1999–2000, the equity markets of Southeast Asia in the mid-1990s, the equity and real estate bubbles in Japan of the late 1980s, the global commodities price bubble of 2008, the Icelandic banking bubble of 2002–2008, and, of course, the US housing bubble of 2004–2006, which crashed with such spectacular force as to lead the world economy into financial chaos and a deep, enduring downturn (Figs. 11.4 and 11.5).

Speculative asset price (SAP) bubbles are highly distortive not only on the way down but on the way up as well. The US tech boom of the late 1990s led to overbuilding of commercial property in tech-concentrated areas, diversion of venture capital into dot-com schemes that could never possibly generate a positive return, and astronomical salaries for IT professionals in the USA, Ireland, and the UK, attracting workers into fields for which employment opportunities would not be so rich after the crash.

The US housing bubble, perhaps the greatest in the history of the world, created innumerable distortions. Massive overbuilding brought not only the construction of entire neighborhoods that would remain empty years later but a dramatic increase in the number of builders. Many of these builders would go bust in the years that followed, dragging down long-time industry stalwarts along with them. An entire industry sprang up of private mortgage brokers, many of whom left their previous employment to stake out on their own in this burgeoning field. These individuals would find it difficult to eke out a living after the crash. The financial services industry built pyramid upon pyramid of financial derivatives on the back of the housing boom and expanded to occupy a more than 8 % of US GDP by 2006. Brilliant mathematicians and engineers—who might otherwise have taken up careers as innovators in the sciences, advanced materials, biotech, or other cutting-edge "real economy" fields—were attracted by obscene sums into financial engineering.

The causes of the housing bubble have been widely debated but most certainly include every element of the checklist above. The proximate cause was a crash in the "subprime" sector: mortgages given to homeowners with credit histories that in past eras may have disqualified them. This sector had sprung to life as a result of government encouragement of homeownership through its quasi-government mortgage securitization entities Fannie Mae and Freddie Mac and had accelerated rapidly as the trade was taken up by private issuers.

The crash was originally thought to be "contained" to this limited part of the market, but it soon became evident that the decline would in fact be widespread and deep (Fig. 11.6).

Several European countries, most notably Ireland and Spain, experienced property bubbles concurrent with that of the USA. The crash spread beyond the geographies directly affected and morphed into a general financial crisis as financial derivatives based on subprime mortgages had been widely distributed, particularly in Europe.

Speculative asset price bubbles can be more dangerous than consumer inflation because they often go undetected. The radar of the monetary authority is generally focused on traditional inflation measures, and the central bank is often loath to intervene to "take away the punch bowl"[6] in a climate of rising prosperity.

---

[6] William McChesney Martin, Jr., Federal Reserve Chairman from 1951 to 1970, famously said that the job of a central banker is "to take away the punch bowl just as the party gets going."

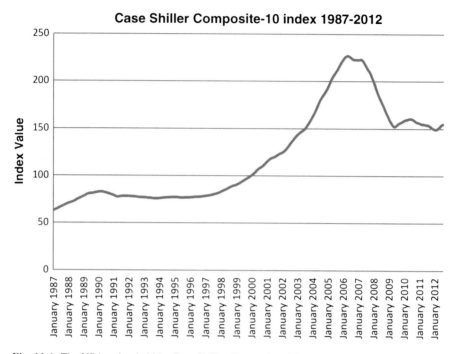

Fig. 11.6 The US housing bubble. Case Shiller Composite-10 index January 1987 to July 2012 (*Source*: Standard and Poor's)

How can such a dangerous situation develop without attracting the scrutiny of policymakers? The two-decade period preceding the US housing crash provides an excellent case study in how inflation driven by the money supply may be hidden in plain sight.

11.3.1 "The Great Moderation"

The 20+ years of economic expansion that began in the 1980s was the largest in America's history in terms of both size and duration. From 1987 to 2007, real (inflation-adjusted) GDP nearly doubled despite two intervening recessions, expanding 3 % per year on a compound basis over the full 20-year stretch. Total employment expanded by one-third, as 36 million workers were added to the economy. The worst recession during this period, in 2001, involved a drop of only 1.6 million jobs, which were all recovered within 30 months. The stock market

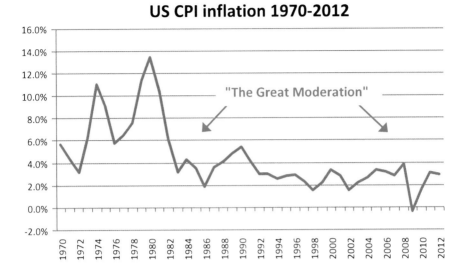

Fig. 11.7 US CPI inflation during "The Great Moderation"

soared more than sixfold between 1987 and its 2007 peak, notwithstanding two severe declines during the period.[7]

The most remarkable aspect of this expansion was that it was accompanied by generally low interest rates, low inflation, and low unemployment. This defied the Philips Curve (the classical assumption of a trade-off between inflation and unemployment), as well as the traditional Keynesian assumption that high growth and easy money[8] will ultimately squeeze capacity to the limit and result in inflation. The period came to be known as "The Great Moderation" (Fig. 11.7).

Inflation was held under 3 % on a compound basis over the full 1987 to 2007 period, with very low volatility.

Meanwhile, real estate prices appreciated steadily along with the stock market, and the continual gains in asset wealth fueled an ever-increasing appetite for consumption (Fig. 11.8).

Credit for this economic miracle was attributed in large part to "The Maestro," Federal Reserve Chairman Alan Greenspan, who had apparently discovered the magic monetary symphony of perpetual growth without inflation.

---

[7] The S&P 500 opened 1987 at 246 and peaked in at 1565 on October 9, 2007. In the interim, the market fell by −33 % from August to December 1987 and by −46 % from September 2000 to October 2002.

[8] We use the term "easy money" to refer to a climate of low interest rates and plentiful credit.

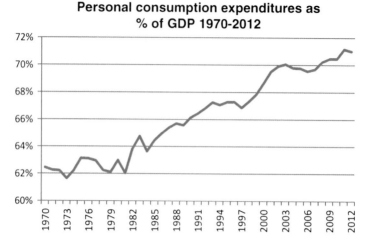

Fig. 11.8 US Personal Consumption Expenditures as % of GDP, 1970 to 2012 (*Source*: BEA)

Alan Greenspan, "The Maestro," Federal Reserve Chairman 1987–2006, testifying on Capitol Hill
Thursday Feb. 13, 1997, Associated Press.

The period was not without its crises, but intervention by policymakers often
averted the worst short-term consequences. Most notable among these were the
Mexican Peso Crisis of 1994, resolved by a $50 billion bailout led by the USA, and
the collapse of the hedge fund Long Term Capital Management in 1998, smoothed
over by a Federal Reserve-arranged bailout among major Wall Street firms and
accompanied by a 0.75 % cut in interest rates over a 6-week period.

The tech bubble collapse presented more trouble, but the Fed was there again to intervene, turning on the "M" spigot by cutting interest rates 12 times over the course of 2001, from 6.5 % to 1.75 %.

Following the terrorist attacks of September 11, 2001, the Fed lowered interest rates even further, eventually down to 1 %. Rates were held below 2 % for 3 years, from December 2001 to November 2004.

With each crisis, the Federal Reserve was there to intervene with a new dose of "**M**."

A new bubble began to form in housing, which the authorities were late to recognize and which began to collapse in 2006. The bursting of this bubble proved too much for any monetary or fiscal medicine to ameliorate. A worldwide financial collapse ensued, which led to a severe global recession over 2008–2009, followed by a slow and unsteady recovery and a rolling series of sovereign debt crises in the Eurozone from 2009 to the present. From the crisis forward, the Fed maintained near-zero interest rates and deployed a host of unconventional tools attempting to inject "**M**" into the economy.

In retrospect, it was clear to many observers that problems had long been swept under piles of easy money, solving the immediate crisis but helping to fuel the next. The Federal Reserve, always quick to cut rates in response to trouble, had been serially late in recognizing bubbles that timely monetary tightening may have cooled.

We can see this clearly in Fig. 11.9.

Normally, easy money and chronically low interest rates lead to inflation. How was the economy able to absorb so much "**M**" for so long without inflation and overheating?

A confluence of several factors explains the phenomenon: (a) globalization, (b) bubbles in real and financial assets, and (c) financial innovation.

(a) *Globalization*

The era beginning in the late 1980s saw the first true move toward an open global economy since the period before the World War I. Consumers increasingly had access to goods from every corner of the globe, and their appetite for lower prices drove large retailers such as Walmart to continually search for the most efficient possible overseas sourcing.

These forces counteracted the traditional notion that "an increase in **M** leads to inflation," since the increased demand suddenly did not face the usual constraints of capacity limitations. There was a virtually unlimited global supply of inexpensive products to accommodate any expansion of demand.

Figure 11.10 illustrates the deflationary effect of a world supply of product available at significantly lower cost than most domestic producers are willing to accept. Prices drop significantly, a far greater quantity of product is available to consumers at a price they are willing to pay, and domestic production shrinks dramatically.

This phenomenon can be seen in the price changes in many categories of the consumer price index over the period. The price of many items declined, often significantly, as world markets opened up (Fig. 11.11).

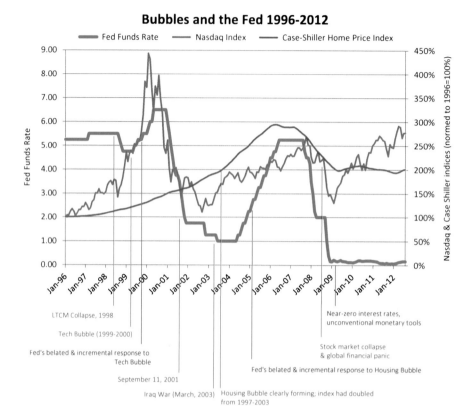

Fig. 11.9 Bubbles and the Fed 1996–2012. Data Sources: Standard and Poor's, US Federal Reserve, Nasdaq

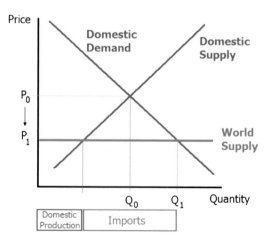

Fig. 11.10 Supply and demand for textiles, apparel, and similar consumer goods

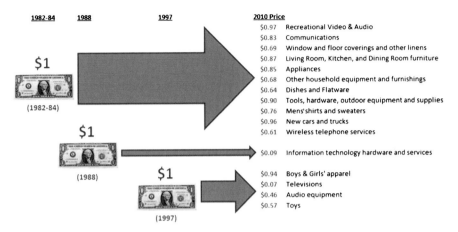

Fig. 11.11   Deflation in selected US consumer goods 1982–1984 through 2010

Thus, one of the usual warning signals that too much **M** was flooding the economy—an increase in the CPI index—was masked by globalization.

(b) *Real and Financial Asset Bubbles*

Like a flood of water, a flood of money must go *somewhere*. The era of the "Great Moderation" saw, as mentioned above, a sixfold increase in the stock market from 1987 to 2007 and a near-*tripling* of real estate prices in the 10 years from 1996 to 2006.

Neither stock prices nor housing prices are incorporated into the CPI infla-tion measure. Increases in the value of such assets generally go hand in hand with rising prosperity. However, over long periods of time, neither can sustain-ably grow much faster than the economy itself, particularly housing prices, which result from the buying, selling, and monthly payment activity of a majority of the country's families.

Central banks' warning antennae are simply not tuned to detect accelerating appreciation in real and financial assets. Federal Reserve Governor Ben Bernanke, who would become Fed Chairman in 2006, said in 2002:

> First, the Fed cannot reliably identify bubbles in asset prices. Second, even if it could identify bubbles, monetary policy is far too blunt a tool for effective use against them.
>
> Thus, to declare that a bubble exists, the Fed must not only be able to accurately estimate the unobservable fundamentals underlying equity valuations, it must have confidence that it can do so better than the financial professionals whose collective information is reflected in asset-market prices.[9]

With waves of speculation going into stocks and real estate, much of the flood of money never went where it would be detected in the CPI and other measures of consumer inflation.

---

[9] *Asset-Price "Bubbles" and Monetary Policy.* Remarks by Governor Ben S. Bernanke before the New York Chapter of the National Association for Business Economics, New York, New York, October 15, 2002. Source: Federal Reserve Bank of New York.

(c) *Financial Innovation*

The evolution of financial derivatives from the early 1980s on saw the actualization of the theories of economist and risk theory pioneer Frank H. Knight, who in the 1920s posited that many outcomes that were believed to be subject to "uncertainty" were actually stochastically quantifiable.

Frank Knight (1885–1972) Warren J. Samuels Portrait Collection, David M. Rubenstein Rare Book & Manuscript Collection, Duke University

Starting with the growth in the market for options on equity securities and continuing with the expansion of mortgage-backed securities in the 1980s and ultimately with the development of complex structured finance instruments, trade in financial derivatives expanded the ways in which risk could be reshaped, repackaged, priced, and transferred between willing parties. The market for financial derivatives, particularly the over-the-counter variety which are not traded on exchanges, exploded (Fig. 11.12).

These innovations tended to lower the price of risk itself, which translated into lower interest rates (since the risk premium is a large component of most rates), and higher asset prices (whose value is the based on future cash flows, discounted by the interest rate).

The proliferation of risk instruments created a false sense of security and the perception among policymakers that the fallout from any downturn in asset markets would be limited. Risk was presumed to be largely distributed to those who opted to bear it. Thus, even a correct diagnosis of an impending reversal in the housing market was met with casual assurances.

Fig. 11.12 Data Source:
Bank for International
Settlements

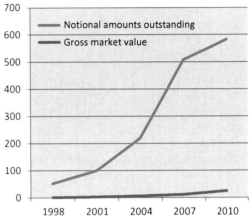

At this juncture, however, the impact on the broader economy and financial markets of the problems in the subprime market seems likely to be contained.[10]

Fed Chairman Ben Bernanke, March 28, 2007

11.3.2 Summary: "The Great Moderation" and Its Aftermath

Globalization, the flow of money into real and financial assets, a risk-premium suppressed by the alchemy of financial derivatives, and a chronically low interest rate all worked together to short-circuit the usual warning signals of an overabundance of money in circulation.

Cheap and easy credit, combined with newfound wealth from rising home prices, led consumers to go on a 20-year spending binge. Savings became passé—when interest rates are negligible and incomes are rising, why not borrow? By the end of the cycle, the US personal savings rate was close to zero (Fig. 11.13).

Thanks to the virtually unlimited global supply of goods and services, the consumption boom led not to strained capacity and inflation but to an expansion in the number and type of goods imported. Throughout the period, rising GDP was fueled and magnified by cheap credit and a growing wealth effect.

[10] Ben Bernanke, "The Economic Outlook," Speech before the Joint Economic Committee, US Congress, March 28, 2007. Source: New York Fed.

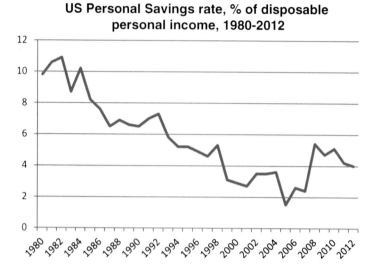

US Personal Savings rate, % of disposable personal income, 1980-2012

Fig. 11.13 US Personal Savings Rate, % of DPI, 1980–2012. (*Source*: BEA; annual figures for 1980–2011 plus 2012 Q2)

This was the economic landscape leading up to the housing crash. Many pre-bubble economies have been similar to the Great Moderation in that an over-abundance of money and credit was masked by several factors and was not felt in the general price level.

Asset bubbles are, essentially, inflation in another form.

11.4 Exploding Pegs

Policymakers naturally prefer to have control over their country's monetary policy. It is only after experiencing the effects of poor monetary stewardship—either through a severe inflationary crisis such as the German episode in 1922–1923 or the Hungarian hyperinflations of 1945–1946 or the chronic "political business cycles" of pre-Euro Europe—that governments reluctantly adopt a regime of strict monetary discipline.

More often than not, especially following hyperinflations, in order to signal their commitment to prudence, governments peg their currency to the currency of a foreign country whose central bank is known for its monetary rectitude. The exchange rate is formally fixed at a given ratio of domestic currency to the foreign standard and is held there through regulation and central bank intervention in global foreign exchange markets.

The benefits of such a policy include all those of monetary discipline outlined above, with the added benefit that the exchange rate is static, eliminating one area of uncertainty in international transactions. (Naturally, the exchange rate will still vary against currencies other than the one to which the country's unit is pegged.)

However, there are trade-offs involved in forgoing control over one's own monetary destiny. These become most evident when the economy of the pegging country and that of the "pegee" (the country of the currency to which the pegging country fixes its rate) get out of sync.

The 17 countries of the Eurozone are all tied together under the same currency, the Euro, which is managed by the European Central Bank (ECB) in Frankfurt. The $13 trillion (2011) GDP[11] of the Eurozone is heavily weighted by the larger countries, with France and Germany accounting for half. Naturally, monetary policy for the zone as a whole will be highly skewed toward the needs of those larger countries.

This works fine when all 17 countries are at roughly the same point in their economic cycles. However, this is often not the case. If France and Germany are in the economic doldrums while several smaller countries such as Portugal, Austria, and Greece are chugging along at a high rate of employment and output, the formula for disaster is in-place.

Should the ECB increase the money supply in an attempt to combat recession and disinflation in France and Germany, then Portugal, Austria, and Greece will be dragged along for the ride—into overheating and an inevitable hard landing.

We can see the effects on aggregate supply and demand in the large and small countries (Fig. 11.14).

This is precisely what occurred in Hong Kong in late 2010. The Hong Kong dollar ("HKD") has long been pegged to the USD at the rate of 7.80 HKD to 1 USD. The Federal Reserve's prolonged period of monetary easing, which began in 2007 in response to the developing financial crisis (in particular, the QE2 round of monetary expansion that began in the fall of 2010 and ran through mid-2011), pushed the USD into decline against foreign currencies and pushed the HKD close to its breaking point.

---

[11] Source: International Monetary Fund.

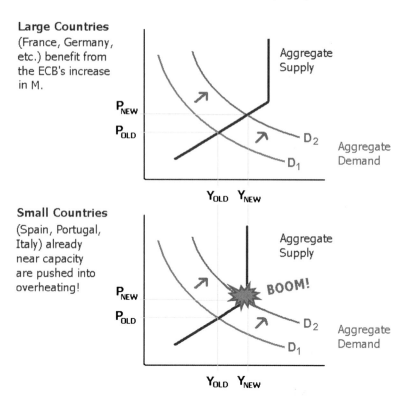

Fig. 11.14 Increase in M pushes demand curve in large and small countries at different points in their economic cycles

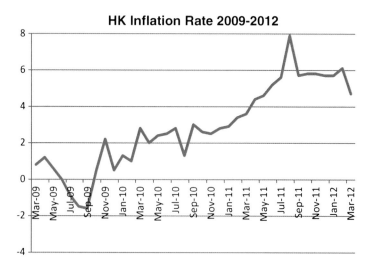

Fig. 11.15 Data Source: Tradingeconomics.com

As the HKD weakened relative to world currencies along with the USD, the already healthy export-based Hong Kong economy saw monthly exports surge +20 % year over year. Real estate and stock prices in Hong Kong were propelled upward as Hong Kong interest rates plummeted, with mortgage rates dropping below 1 %. There was talk of breaking the HKD–USD peg, one of the world's longest-running fixed rates which had been in place since 1983 (Fig. 11.15).

11.5 The Impossible Trinity

In a perfect macroeconomic world, policymakers would opt for an economic regime that allowed for (i) perfectly mobile capital and (ii) a fixed exchange rate, while (iii) retaining the ability to control domestic interest rates.

This would allow for movement of capital in and out of the country in response to changes in trade flows and economic conditions, a completely stable and predictable exchange rate with its attendant benefits, and the power to fine-tool monetary policy according to economic circumstances.

Unfortunately, as the businessman below knows, we do not live in a perfect world, and "one cannot have all three."

Illustration by Castro
Desroches

11.5.1 Fixed Exchange Rate and Perfectly Mobile Capital: Cannot Control Interest Rates

The ability to maintain a pegged currency while allowing freely moving capital takes away the ability to manipulate interest rates. The central bank's attempt at monetary operations will inevitably conflict with its buying and selling of FX to maintain the peg. Capital will rapidly flow in or out in response to attempts to manage the interest rate, quickly reversing the central bank's monetary operations.

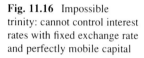

Fig. 11.16 Impossible
trinity: cannot control interest
rates with fixed exchange rate
and perfectly mobile capital

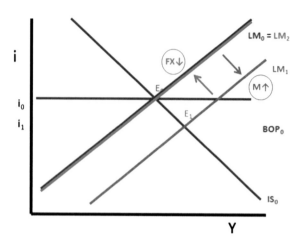

Should the central bank decrease **M** to raise rates, for example, capital will flow
into the country, and the central bank will have to increase **M** to finance the
purchases of FX needed to maintain the peg. Should the central bank attempt to
ease by increasing **M**, FX will flow out, with the central bank forced to buy
domestic **M** in order to hold the peg. In either case, interest rates end up right
where they started.

We can see in Fig. 11.16 that a monetary stimulus aimed at reducing domestic
interest rates will just not work against a backdrop of pegged exchange rates and
perfectly mobile capital. The central bank initially increases **M**, which pushes the
LM curve down. However, as FX now seeks to exit the country in search of higher
yields, the central bank is forced to redeem the domestic **M** and convert it to FX,
effectively reversing its original policy. We see in Fig. 11.16 that the LM snaps
right back, leaving interest rates finally unchanged back at i_0.

11.5.2 Fixed Exchange Rate and Control Over Monetary Policy: Cannot Permit Capital Mobility

The only way to enable the government to control interest rates while pegging its
currency is to restrict capital flows. Then the result indicated above cannot occur
as FX cannot freely enter or exit the economy. Many countries restricted capital
flows in the period following World War II. India, for example, maintained this
policy for a long period through the early 1990s, before it began to open its capital
account.

Closing the capital account carries its own attendant problems, however, as a
black market in the country's currency will generally develop which more closely
reflects the market value of the currency as determined by supply and demand. We
will discuss ISLM-BOP analyses with imperfectly mobile capital in detail in
Chap. 12.

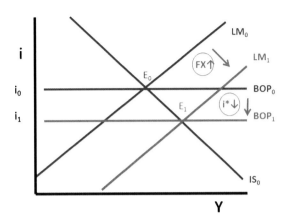

Fig. 11.17 Impossible trinity: cannot control interest rates with fixed exchange rate and perfectly mobile capital

11.5.3 Discretionary Monetary Policy and Perfect Capital Mobility: Cannot Maintain an Exchange-Rate Peg

To cite another example, a central bank that insists on controlling domestic interest rates and an economy with an open capital account are together incompatible with a fixed exchange-rate regime. Should the target country reduce interest rates, for example $(i^*\downarrow)$, the ensuing rush of capital will force the domestic central bank to either engage in FX operations in order to maintain its peg (issuing **M** to replace the incoming FX) or break the peg and allow its currency to strengthen.

In Fig. 11.17, we see the BOP line move down as a result of foreign interest rates declining, which results in a BOP surplus at E_0. With (SFX > DFX), the incoming flow of FX is absorbed by the central bank in its foreign exchange operations, which results in the LM line moving down to the new equilibrium point, E_1, with lower interest rates. The central bank here has been dragged unwillingly into reducing interest rates by the target country.

11.5.4 Perfect Capital Mobility, Pegged Exchange Rates, and Discretionary Monetary Policy: Welcome to the Impossible Trinity

The "impossible trinity" is a term coined by Robert Mundell in 1961 to describe the phenomenon we have been discussing, i.e., it is impossible to have perfect capital mobility, pegged exchange rates, and domestic control over monetary policy.

The Impossible Trinity

1. Perfectly mobile capital
2. Fixed exchange rate
3. Control over domestic interest rates

(pick any two)

Some countries choose a hybrid mix, where capital flows are open but actively managed, and exchange rates are permitted to move gradually in response to market conditions but are managed to control volatility. This is a delicate balancing act that requires the use not only of traditional monetary and exchange-rate policy but also a full array of policy instruments in coordination, including active control of reserve requirements, management of debt flows, and control of access by financial intermediaries to external borrowing.

India has employed a hybrid mix since it began to open its capital account in the early 1990s, and its efforts have been greatly facilitated by the fact that the Reserve Bank of India (RBI) not only controls monetary policy but is also the regulator in charge of setting the rules for financial institutions and markets.

We now apply the ISLM-BOP in analyzing a real-world example of the impossible trinity in action in the Southeast Asia crisis of 1997–1998. We will see how, almost alone among macro policymakers, the great Dr. Hu of Singapore spotted the dangers of the impossible trinity early and took evasive action to save his country.

11.6 Southeast Asia 1997: The Good Times, the Bad Times, and the Brilliance of Dr. Hu

11.6.1 The Good Times

As the US economy was coming out of the 1990–1991 recession, and the internet and technology boom was in its infancy, several developing Southeast Asian economies whose currencies were pegged to the US dollar were simultaneously experiencing robust growth.

Thailand was the hottest story, growing at 9 % a year, and South Korea, Indonesia, Hong Kong, Singapore, the Philippines, and Malaysia were all booming as well. The entire region attracted hot capital flows, which provided further fuel for growth. From 1987–1989 to 1995–1997, net capital inflow to developing countries tripled from $50 billion to $150 billion.[12] The attraction for investors was reinforced by the fiscal discipline exercised by these developing countries, which for the most part ran budget surpluses.

---

[12] Eichengreen B (1999) Toward a New International Financial Architecture: apractical Post-Asia Agenda. Peterson Institute for International Economics, Washington, D.C.

Fig. 11.18 SE Asia
1992–1994 ("the good
times"): ↑Pr, Pegged Rates,
PMK

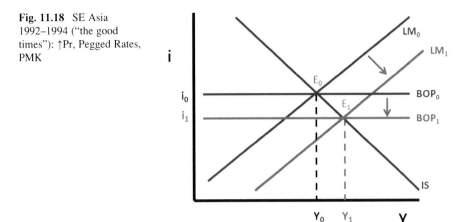

In Fig. 11.18, with the macroeconomic outlook of Southeast Asia (**Pr**) looking extraordinarily positive, the BOP line drops as **Pr** increases. We find E_0 to be a BOP surplus point now, with the BOP line now at BOP_1. Only two options are possible to bring all three markets into equilibrium again; the IS can drop to the left or the LM can snap down to the right. Given that exchange rates are pegged in this case, the LM does the adjusting. The LM curve jumps out to the right to yield the final equilibrium at E_1. Output soars to Y_1, interest rates drop to i_1.

1. **Pr** (long-term macro outlook)↑ ☺ → *Pr* explodes↑!
   BOP↓ to **BOP$_1$**
2. E_0 is in BOP surplus, $\underline{S}FX > DFX$, **FX**↑
3. Fixed rates: **LM** adjusts↓ to **LM$_1$**
4. Result: **Y**↑, **i**↓, overheating, SAP bubbles forming

Despite the economic growth, it was noted as early as 1994 by economist Paul Krugman that productivity was not improving significantly and that much of the apparent growth seemed to be of a more transient nature, fueled by the foreign investment pouring in to the region. This was the first gray cloud in the bright blue sky that was supposed to usher in The Pacific Century; the "bad times" were about to rain heavily on the Asian Miracle.

11.6.2   The Bad Times

As the boom continued, FX "hot money" continued to pour in. The opportunities for true productive investment of those inflows, which would add wealth and increase prosperity, were ultimately limited simply by the size of the economies, which were relatively small by Western standards. South Korea, the largest, had a GDP of US $530 billion in 1996; Indonesia, $200B; Thailand, $170B; Hong Kong, $140B,

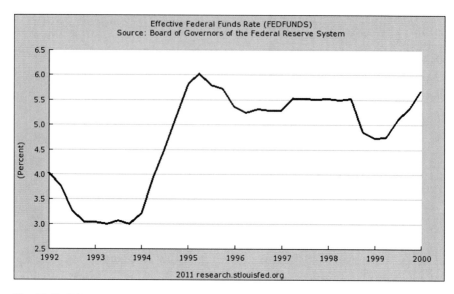

Fig. 11.19 USA Fed funds rate, quarterly, 1992–2000

Malaysia and Singapore, only $90 and $80B, respectively. Together, these economies were dwarfed even by Germany's 1996 GDP of US $2.5 trillion and were but a fraction of the US's GDP of $7.4 trillion.

Exacerbating the problem was the fact that in their political and economic arrangements, these developing countries exhibited the typical oligopolistic characteristics of their ilk, lacking fully transparent financial markets and intermediaries, where a select number of insiders controlled access and were in a position to steer incoming funds to favored firms and projects.

In addition, even well-directed investments into long-term economic assets yield few short-run benefits. Productive capital formation and skill growth in the labor force take time to develop—something for which hot money has no patience.

Ironically, as the hot capital flooded in, the fiscal virtuosity of the Asian economies proved to be their undoing! As most of the Southeast Asian economies has budget surpluses, the capital inflows were not needed to finance budget deficits, as they do for the USA and Europe. But money has to go somewhere. So throughout Southeast Asia, it flowed into capital projects of increasingly suspect economic value and especially speculative assets; the longest bridge going nowhere was trumped by the tallest rusting office building in the world, and so on. Real estate and stock prices soared, with Hong Kong's Hang Seng stock market index, for example, shooting up 400 % from 1992 through mid-1997.

Meanwhile, the US economy was booming coming out of its 1990–1991 recession. To moderate the potential for overheating in the USA, Federal Reserve Chairman Alan Greenspan raised US interest rates in a series of moves over the period from 3 % to 6 % and held them north of 5 % for an extended period, which resulted in a stronger dollar (Fig. 11.19).

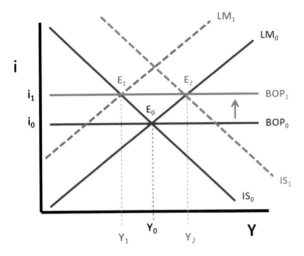

Fig. 11.20 SE Asia ~1997 ("the bad times"): America is supercharged (Internet economy), SE Asia bubbles eroding... Pr*↑, Pr↓, pegged rates, PMK

This had two effects that were ominous for Southeast Asia:

1. The higher US rates reduced the opportunity for hot-money interest arbitrage, as it reduced the differential between US rates and the high rates that SE Asian countries had kept up to attract foreign investment.
2. The stronger US dollar dragged the pegged currencies of Southeast Asia to strengthen as well, making their exports more expensive to the rest of the world.

The continued US economic boom began to attract capital to the USA that might otherwise have kept fueling the "Asian miracle," as it had become known.

By 1996, it was clear that the party would eventually be coming to an end, but as in all bubbles, no one knew for certain when, or how (Fig. 11.20).

11.7   Southeast Asia 1996–1997

The situation from Southeast Asia's perspective in 1996-7 is captured in Fig. 11.20. The US economic outlook is great ($Pr^*\uparrow$), and investors are growing concerned about the nascent bubbles in Southeast Asia ($Pr\downarrow$). This drives the BOP line higher to BOP_1. E_0 is now in BOP deficit, with DFX > SFX. We are presented with a **DILEMMA**: (#1) Defend the peg and face a huge exflow of FX, resulting in a dramatic monetary tightening, or (#2) break the peg and allow the currency to weaken significantly?

Option#1: Maintain the peg
FX↓↓ (a severe outflow of FX), **LM** adjusts ↑ to LM_1, new equilibrium point at E_1. A brutal recession will ensue.

Option#2: Break the peg

e↑↑, in a rapid currency depreciation, **IS** explodes upward↑ to **IS₁**, new equilibrium point at **E₂**.

Y↑, but this provides *short-term relief only*, as rampant inflation follows as the currency collapses.

Soon **P**↑, **LM**↑, BOP surplus causes **e** to snap back↓, **IS**↓, new equilibrium at **E₁**.

A brutal recession ensues, accompanied by a financial crisis as FX loans go into default.

Heading into 1997, the pressure on the regional currencies was building. The countries had two choices. They could maintain their peg and go to equilibrium **E₁**, which would drive FX screaming out of the country, resulting in a brutal recession. This would also invite speculative attacks on the currency as reserves dwindled.[13] Alternatively, the countries could break their pegs and go initially to **E₂**, as their exchange rates would sharply depreciate in spectacular fashion. In the very short term, this would provide some relief, but rampant inflation and reduced output would follow, as well as the inability to service foreign loans, which had grown substantially over the previous several years and were denominated mostly in foreign currency.

Thailand was the first to fall, starting in May 1997, as the Thai baht came under speculative attack. The Thai government opted to let the baht depreciate, rather than defend the peg, and it lost more than half its value over the following several months. GDP collapsed, and the Thai stock market lost 3/4 of its value.

Indonesia followed, starting in August 1997 as the rupiah, which was managed in an 8–12 % trading band, came under pressure. Indonesia broke its peg and switched to a floating exchange rate and saw its currency move from 2,600 to 14,000 to the USD through January 1998. Indonesia's economy crashed, with −13 % GDP in 1998, and Suharto, Indonesia's ruling president for 31 years, was forced to resign in the face of popular riots protesting the higher food prices that followed the devaluation.

One after another, the dominoes continued to fall. South Korea and the Philippines suffered similar economic effects as their currencies also blew out. Malaysia resorted to capital controls in an attempt to hold a peg for the ringgit at 3.80 to the US dollar, from 2.50 before the crisis. Malaysia nevertheless plunged into recession as well.

Hong Kong, on the other hand, opted to defend its 7.8 HKD/1 USD peg. Thanks to an enormous (for the time) $80 billion USD foreign exchange reserve which had been built up over decades, the Hong Kong Monetary Authority was able to hold the peg by expending a portion of these reserves. This, combined with direct intervention in the local equities market to the tune of $15 billion USD to curb speculation sent credible enough signals to avert a monetary collapse. Hong Kong still experienced a very difficult recession with its stock market losing 2/3 of its value from

---

[13] Recall that the central bank, in order to maintain the peg in the face of FX determined to exit the domestic economy, would need to buy domestic currency with its reserves of foreign exchange.

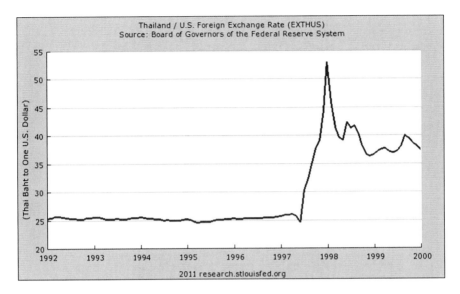

Fig. 11.21 Thailand (baht/USD) (Source: US Federal Reserve)

August 1997 through August 1998 (including a −23 % crash in October of 1997), and GDP falling more than 6 %. Hong Kong did not return to positive growth until the end of 1999.

11.7.1 Selected Southeast Asian Exchange Rates 1992–2000

The graphs in Figs. 11.21, 11.22, 11.23, and 11.24 show the dramatic currency swings for those countries that broke their peg; Hong Kong, meanwhile, expended vast reserves and public sums to maintain its peg and still suffered a severe stock market crash and difficult recession. All figures show domestic currency/1 USD.

No matter which option was chosen, the results were painful.

11.7.2 The Brilliance of Dr. Hu

The one country among the group to escape the worst of the damage was Singapore. This was due to early, active intervention by the finance authorities, led by Dr. Richard Hu who served as Finance Minister from 1985 to 2001.

Dr. Richard Hu, 2001. Associated Press

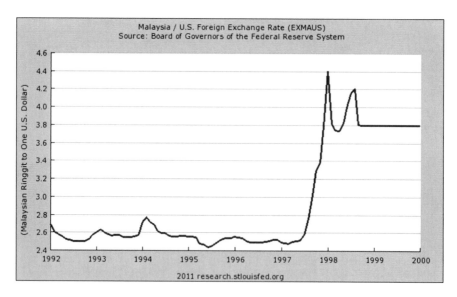

Fig. 11.22   Malaysia (ringgit/USD) (Source: US Federal Reserve)

Dr. Hu was prescient in seeing the bubbles forming very early, and between 1993 and 1996, he took active steps to avert the worst of the inevitable crisis by gradually adjusting the currency peg in response to market conditions.

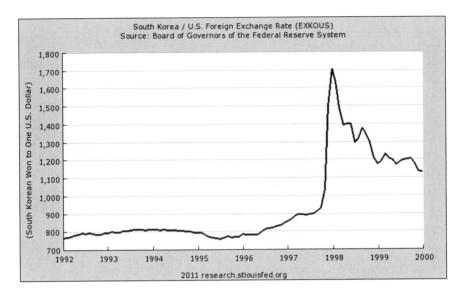

Fig. 11.23 South Korea (won/USD) (Source: US Federal Reserve)

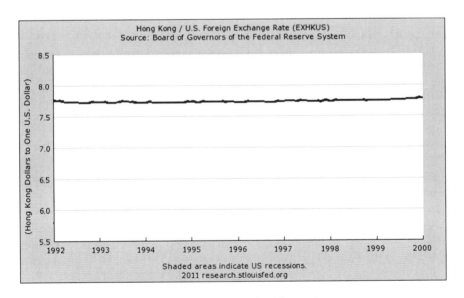

Fig. 11.24 Hong Kong (HKD/USD) (Source: US Federal Reserve)

This gradual adjustment process acted like a pressure valve, thus enabling Singapore to avoid the brutal crash that followed the sudden depreciations in Thailand, Indonesia, Malaysia, etc.

Fig. 11.25 The brilliance of Dr. Hu. IS and LM adjust in small steps as the pegged currency is gradually permitted to appreciate

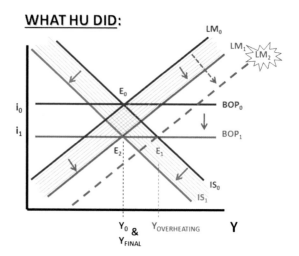

In Fig. 11.25, our starting point is similar to that of Fig. 11.18. The BOP line has dropped from BOP_0 to BOP_1 due to the improving macro outlook ($Pr\uparrow$), and the LM line is under pressure to move from LM_0 toward LM_2 due to the impending flood of FX into the country.

Early on, as the economy was roaring, Hu recognized the movement of **LM** toward LM_2, anticipating the economy's ultimate destination to likely be equilibrium at E_1 with overheating, bubbles, and so on, as outlined above. Hu softened the peg, allowing the Singapore dollar (S\$) to slowly appreciate.

As the currency appreciated ($e\downarrow$), this allowed **IS** to fall $\downarrow$, which cooled the overheating, halted the LM curve at LM_1, and allowed a new equilibrium point to form at E_2. This sacrificed some of the FX-fueled boom growth experienced by Thailand, Malaysia, and others.

Thus, overheating was avoided in Singapore. Consequently, when the regional crisis came, its effects on the country were minimized. Singapore suffered a mild recession in 1998, with real GDP falling only 2 %. Its previous flexibility with its currency peg had conditioned the market to accept the gradual, managed 20 % depreciation of the S\$ during the crisis years as prudent and farsighted. Singapore's actions stood in stark relief from those of the other Southeast Asian monetary authorities, whose actions were seen as desperate, and so invited speculative attacks.

The contrast in the currency adjustments (or lack thereof) of Singapore versus those of its neighbors is illustrated by comparing the graph below to those above, particularly in the precrisis years 1993–1996. Thanks to its gradual early appreciation, when the 1997 depreciation came, it only took the currency back to within 6 % of its 1992 level, unlike Thailand and others whose currency fell by more than half from their 1992 levels (Fig. 11.26).

To better visualize scale, we can compare relative percentage moves, taking January 1992 as a base level for all currencies.

Fig. 11.26 Singapore (S$/USD)

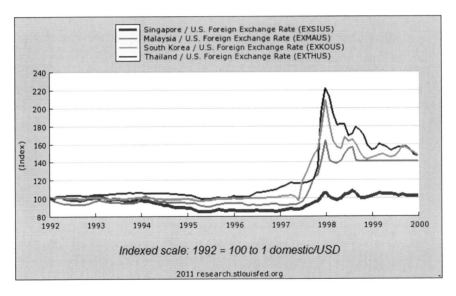

Fig. 11.27 Selected SE Asian currencies/USD, all normalized to Jan. 1992 = 100 (Source: St. Louis Fed)

We can see in Fig. 11.27 how Singapore allowed its currency to strengthen significantly in the run-up. This provided a safety valve for the pressure arising from the incoming FX, with the result that Singapore's crash and currency depreciation, when it came, was far less severe than that of its Southeast Asian peers.

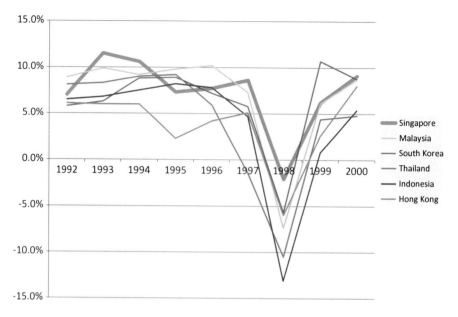

Fig. 11.28 Southeast Asian countries, real (inflation-adjusted) GDP growth, 1992–2000 (*In domestic currency. Data Source: IMF*)

The challenges involved in undertaking early action, as Dr. Hu did, should not be underestimated. Bubbles are unpredictable things, and in the midst of the Southeast Asian boom, moderating the FX-fueled euphoria experienced by Singapore's neighbors must have been a prickly subject to many in Singapore who were foregoing immediate gains due to the currency's appreciation. The results speak for themselves (Fig. 11.28).

Commenting on his firm's participation in the later stages of a different bubble some 10 years later, Citigroup's CEO Chuck Prince would famously say, "As long as the music is playing, you've got to get up and dance." By sitting out a good portion of the Southeast Asian dance from 1993 through 1996, Dr. Hu and Singapore might have missed some revelry, but they were far less hung over than their neighbors in the morning.

Articles

Article 11.1. Puddingstones, Agate, and Global Macropolicy

Jim McVie, *Nova Scotia Nightly News*

It was about 6 months ago that our very own Professor Pytor Murphysboro stunned the citizens of Merlion with his now-famous speech to the House of Representatives: "Dear Merlionians, our economy is the star performer on this planet at this time, our output growth is what other countries dream of, our unemployment is at a 45-year low, our consumer confidence is in the stratosphere, foreigners cannot stop investing in our bonds, and our hard currency peg is inviolate. And yet…and yet…it is my solemn duty to tell you that your country is in serious trouble. Unless you slow-down this party, all the joy and all the happiness will only end in tears!" (a)

Our intention today in attending the annual meeting of the Rock Hound Society of Merlion was to learn the latest in plate tectonics. However, we unexpectedly found the eminent geologists instead speaking animatedly about recent macroeconomic developments! We join them now in the midst of their conference…

"This is insanity!" roars John Moffant, of the Merlion Business Roundtable, "Look at all our neighboring countries. They are all growing happily! They are flying high, they are happy, and they are not made to worry and feel guilty as we are in Merlion! (b) Dr. Murphysboro needs to stop playing with his equations, and he needs to lighten up. Maybe he needs to get out more!" His comments were played and replayed everywhere.

We meet Peter Parks, deeply engrossed in examining a glacier-scarred cobble of carnelian agate from Siberia. "The thing about rocks, they may resist geological pressures for a time, but in the end, the forces working on them are too strong. Ultimately they give in and shift, and the longer they hold out, the more spectacular the resulting changes. You know, it may not be a bad idea to just let the hard peg float. Let our currency be determined by market forces; if the Merlionian dollar appreciates radically, then let it. This will dampen our exports and perhaps slow down this "runaway macroeconomic train" that Professor Murphysboro keeps talking about (c). By the way, did you know the Romans were very big on using carnelian agate for their imperial seals? Even the Egyptians used them! Fascinating, yes?" Dr. Parks lovingly holds up another translucent carnelian agate to the light and lets its warm yellow glow flow over his hands.

"Man, check out these Apache Tears—these are from the high mesa in New Mexico. Thousands of them!" whispers Michael Sadler, of Sadler Gravel, Tile and Flooring. "I live for rocks, man!" When asked about the "doomsday speech," Sadler uttered, "You know, I have a graduate degree in macroeconomics, and I can tell you that it may be a good idea to adjust our peg modestly, and then lock it in place, like tectonic plates shifting a little to settle in a new position—just letting it float freely, as suggested by that guy staring at those carnelian agates, may be entirely too painful. Heck! That could throw us into an earthquake of a recession!" (d)

We run into Ines Aginah, as she carefully wipes down some puddingstone slabs from North Michigan. "You mean adjust the peg to keep our growth where it is, and make sure that the runaway train stops accelerating?" she inquires. "It seems to make sense, like a volcanic vent releasing a little pressure, right?" (e) And then she adds, her eyes gleaming with devilish excitement, "Guess what? In addition to puddingstone, I have some real Hertfordshire Conglomerate. Interested?"

The rock hounds are noisily congregating in the main hall, excitedly preparing to vote for the Rock Hound of the Year. So we decide to leave but run into the venerable Sarla Heverman, known as the "High Priestess" of igneous and metamorphic rocks of the Four Corners region in the USA. "It is a problem. If we let our currency get stronger, all my export business will shut down. As it is I am just barely staying competitive. If the Merlionian dollar gets, say 10 % stronger, then my foreign customers won't be able to afford my rocks anymore! I will be out of business!?" she cries. "Sarla, just do what the G5 did way back in the Plaza Accord, and you will be OK" (f), counsels Garfie Smervin, owner of the famous Smervin Fossil Beds in Wyoming, who is gently patting 96-year-old Sarla on the shoulder.

Finally, it is time to depart and bid farewell to our gracious and somewhat eccentric rock hound hosts. The bottom line—and certainly the consensus among our new friends—global macroeconomic policy rocks!

Hints and Solutions

Article 11.1

(a) He is warning that unrestricted capital inflow, exacerbated by the hard peg, will certainly lead to drastic speculative asset bubbles which will only end in tears. He warns that if the economy is not soft-landed (the train slowed down), the economy will go into a severe overheating (the train will derail).

The economy is in a state as we see in Fig. 11.18. Merlion is rushing headlong toward the popping of SAP bubbles and a no-win choice (Fig. 11.20) of either (i) holding its peg and enduring a brutal recession and severe bleeding of FX reserves or (ii) permitting its currency to severely depreciate, also with a brutal recession and a likely foreign debt crisis due to its weakened currency.

(b) The most effective soft landing (deliberate slowing down of an overheated economy) is undertaken when the bubbles are still not obvious, and when all the key indicators are looking great. Consequently, soft landings are quite unpopular. Often, prudent and vigilant central bankers who urge this bitter medicine find themselves to be the targets of many a vitriolic attack from business analysts.

(c) If Merlion, enjoying huge flows of incoming FX due to its phenomenal macro outlook, abandons its peg altogether and allows its currency to freely float, all of the FX pressure will be released onto the exchange rate, which will strengthen significantly.

Here, as shown in Fig. 11.29, would be a case of the IS line moving all the way to the left due to currency appreciation. IS shifts into a new equilibrium at E_1 where it meets BOP_1 and LM_0 at a much lower (recessionary) GDP, Y_1. Here, the fully floating currency would make exports so uncompetitive that final output would fall.

Fig. 11.29 Abandon peg allowing currency to freely float following strong Pr↑, PMK

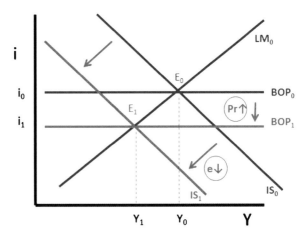

Fig. 11.30 Adjustment to peg allowing currency to strengthen, then lock back in place, following initial strong Pr↑, PMK

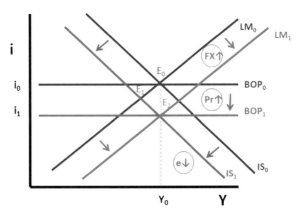

(d) By allowing a modest adjustment to its exchange-rate peg, Merlion will release some of the pressure from the incoming flood of capital. Executed carefully, the move could be calibrated to avoid a recessionary outcome like the one we saw in [c], above.

We see this process depicted in Fig. 11.30. Here, after the initial drop of the BOP to BOP_1, the currency is permitted to strengthen ($e\downarrow$), but not to freely float all the way to its market equilibrium. This drives the IS line to IS_1, resulting in an IS–LM intersection at E_1. However, as a new fixed exchange rate is now reinstituted, the remaining pressure is absorbed by the central bank in its FX operations to maintain the peg at the new level. This drives LM to LM_1, resulting in a final general equilibrium at E_2. Here, the economy's growth continues as before (at Y_0).

Merlion has avoided the deep recession from suddenly floating its currency (see [c] above), and has mitigated some of the pressure toward overheating that we saw in Fig. 11.18.

(e) Under a fixed-rate regime, when a currency comes under sustained pressure to strengthen significantly, all of the pressure must be absorbed by the central bank in its FX operations, issuing **M** into the economy like wildfire, resulting in inflation, speculative bubbles, overheating, and the inevitable bust.

But by abruptly floating the exchange rate, all of the pressure flows into the currency, the sudden strength of which drives the economy into deep recession, as in [c] above.

The solution here is the path taken by Dr. Hu in Singapore in a series of moves preceding the Southeast Asian crisis. Modest exchange-rate adjustments allowing the pressure to be partially absorbed by the currency permitted a gradual adjustment and mitigated the overheating and spectacular bust experienced by Singapore's neighbors.

(f) Sarla would have to drop the price of her exports (in Merlionian dollars) to counteract the appreciation of the domestic currency. In effect, she will attempt to keep her real exchange-rate constant; she will deploy the pass-through effect.

If the exchange rate strengthens by 10 % ($e_1 = 0.9 * e_0$), then Sarla would simply have to adjust her prices by -10 % to counteract the move:

$$R_0 = e_0 \cdot (P*/P_0)$$

$$R_1 = 0.9e_0 \cdot (P*/P_1)$$

Simplifying, we confirm the result that $P_1 = 0.9P_0$.

Chapter 12
Capital Flows: Perfectly and Imperfectly Mobile Capital

Summary In this chapter, the last remaining assumption (that of perfect capital mobility) is finally relaxed, and the notion of imperfectly mobile capital is incorporated into our ISLM-BOP model. Several examples demonstrate that the Keynesian multiplier does indeed exist in an economy characterized by imperfectly mobile capital.

We discuss the concept of fiscal deficit sustainability, including Rudiger Dornbusch's formulation, and review the history of the European Stability Pact and the European Economic and Monetary Union. We explore today's real-world fiscal sustainability issues, including challenges for the USA and the Eurozone.

We will equip ourselves to answer questions such as: how long can capital inflows finance the monster budget deficits of the USA and at what cost and implications for the dollar?

Finally, we examine the daily battle in world capital markets between central banks attempting to implement their desired policies and global investors seeking opportunities to exploit any weaknesses or imbalances created by policy manipulation.

12.1 ISLM-BOP with Imperfectly Mobile Capital

While most advanced Western countries allow the free movement of overseas capital in and out of their economies, many countries, particularly in the developing world, impose restrictions. In fact, the current dominance of freely floating rates is a relatively new historical development. Significant restrictions on capital mobility have been the norm until the globalization era which began in the 1980s. The only other time in which capital was as unfettered as today was in the decades preceding World War I.

F. Langdana and P.T. Murphy, *International Trade and Global Macropolicy*,
Springer Texts in Business and Economics, DOI 10.1007/978-1-4614-1635-7_12,
© Springer Science+Business Media New York 2014

Recall that the slope of the BOP line is given by (j/α_1). In other words, it is

$$\frac{j}{\alpha_1} = \frac{\textbf{Sensitivity of Imports to changes in Output}}{\textbf{Sensitivity of Capital Inflow to changes in Interest Rates}}$$

With the completely unfettered movement of capital, the variable (α_1) is extremely large, effectively setting the slope to zero, hence the horizontal BOP line under perfectly mobile capital, which we have been working with up to this point.

When the capital account is *closed*, i.e., no foreign capital is permitted to move in or out of the economy, α_1 is equal to zero. This makes the slope of the BOP line infinite; the BOP in this case is a vertical line.

While the post World War II era saw several completely or near-completely closed economies, notably in the Soviet bloc, few countries today operate with such total prohibitions on capital movement.

Controls on capital account transactions represent a country's attempt to protect itself from the volatility associated with fluctuations in international capital flows, particularly "hot capital." A country that finds itself with a balance of payments surplus or deficit (SFX<>DFX) faces four choices in how it will adjust to a new equilibrium[1]:

1. **Allow the exchange rate to adjust.**
   The practice under freely floating exchange rate regimes. With the depreciation or appreciation of the exchange rate (e ↑ or ↓), BOP equilibrium is restored by adjustment of the **IS** curve.
2. **Use foreign exchange intervention to correct the imbalance.**
   The practice under fixed rates. Foreign exchange flow (**FX**↑ or ↓) is replaced with domestic **M** through foreign exchange intervention, maintaining the exchange rate but increasing or decreasing domestic money supply. BOP equilibrium is restored by adjustment of the **LM** curve.
3. **"Sterilize" the foreign exchange inflow to isolate the domestic economy from the capital flows.**
   This involves, essentially, replacing the incoming FX with bonds, rather than money stock. Sterilization will be discussed in detail in Chap. 12.
4. **Restrict the flow of capital.**

Restricting capital flows reduces the degree to which the IS or LM curves must move in response to a BOP imbalance. With capital controls in place, BOP movements accommodate part of the necessary adjustment. Fixed exchange rate regimes often impose capital restrictions to make the job of maintaining their pegs easier.

---

[1] Christopher Neely, "An Introduction to Capital Controls," *Federal Reserve Bank of St. Louis Review* (November/December 1999), 5

Capital restrictions can take the form of prohibitions or limits on citizens' ability to invest in overseas assets, limitations on the classes of domestic assets accessible to foreign investors (often employed to steer foreign investment in directions desired by policymakers), excise taxes on different types of inflows (e.g., an exit tax on any capital withdrawn from the country in the short-term, to encourage longer-term investments, or a tax on currency conversion, known as the Tobin Tax[2]), and so forth. Generally, restrictions on short-term flows attempt to reduce economic volatility, while restrictions on long-term flows more often relate to industrial policy goals.

A common effect of these various types of limitations on capital flows would be to decrease the value of the sensitivity α_1, which would increase the slope of the BOP equilibrium line (from zero, if we are starting from perfect capital mobility). When capital mobility is imperfect, the BOP line will have a positive slope. If capital is completely unfettered, then the BOP is depicted as a horizontal line, and when capital movement is totally prohibited, we obtain a vertical BOP line.

The slope of the BOP will in all cases be *less* than the slope of the LM line, which is given by ($\mathbf{k/h}$):

$$\frac{\mathbf{k}}{\mathbf{h}} = \frac{\textbf{Sensitivity of Money Demand to changes in Output}}{\textbf{Sensitivity of Money Demand to changes in Interest Rates}}$$

The reason this condition holds

$$\underset{\textbf{Slope of LM}}{\frac{\mathbf{k}}{\mathbf{h}}} \quad > \quad \underset{\textbf{Slope of BOP}}{\frac{\mathbf{j}}{\alpha_1}}$$

...is that, generally, the sensitivity of capital inflows to changes in interest rates (α_1) will be higher than the sensitivity of money demand to changes in interest rates (**h**). This is because money demand includes a huge domestic component, which is both slower moving and comes to a great degree from agents whose scope of activity does not include the choice of foreign versus domestic money.

As well, the sensitivity of money demand to changes in output (**k**), which is a direct and immediate relationship, will typically be higher than the sensitivity of imports to changes in output (**j**). While the appetite for imports does increase with output, this takes time, and the utility of imports is small in scale compared with the utility of money, for which there are countless and immediate uses.

---

[2] Economist James Tobin proposed the idea of a tax on spot currency conversions as a way to discourage short-term hot capital flows, which can be destabilizing. Tobin initially suggested the idea in 1971 and remained a proponent until his death in 2002. Such a tax would effectively decrease the value of the "α_1" sensitivity, which increases the slope of the BOP line.

This state of affairs, where the slope of the LM curve (**k/h**) is always steeper than the slope of the BOP line (**j/α₁**), is an effect of the *Marshall–Lerner condition*, named after economists Alfred Marshall (1842–1924) and Abba Lerner (1903–1982), on whose original ideas the concept is based.[3]

Under imperfectly mobile capital, many factors become relevant which did not come directly into play with perfectly mobile capital.

Recall the equations for IS, LM, and BOP:

$$\text{IS}: \quad i = \frac{\overline{A} + G + sY^* + e(t+z)}{f} - Y\frac{(1+b+j)}{f}$$

$$\text{LM}: \quad i = \left[\frac{k}{h}\right]Y - \left[\frac{1}{h}\right]\left[\frac{M}{P} + FX\right]$$

$$\text{BOP}: \quad i = Y\left[\frac{j}{\alpha_1}\right] + \frac{\alpha_0 i^* + \alpha_2 Pr^* - \alpha_3 Pr + \alpha_4 e^e - (X - \overline{V}) - \overline{s}Y^* - e(t-z)}{\alpha_1}$$

We can see that with the imperfectly mobile capital BOP, in many cases changes in variables that work to move one curve will be fully or partially "offset" by simultaneous, opposite moves in another curve.

For example, a weakening of the domestic currency (**e↑**) will have the effect of simultaneously raising the IS line and lowering the BOP line:

[e ↑]	IS component :	BOP component :
	$+\dfrac{e(t-z)}{f}$	$\dfrac{-e(t-z)}{\alpha_1}$
Result :	IS ↑	BOP ↓

A weakening of the foreign economy (**Y*↓**) will simultaneously lower the IS line and raise the BOP:

[Y* ↓]	IS component :	BOP component :
	$+sY^*$	$-sY^*$
Result :	IS ↓	BOP ↑

---

[3] The most well-known implication of the Marshall–Lerner condition is that imports and exports are slow to respond to changing prices and exchange rates, and as a result, currency devaluations may or may not boost exports relative to imports in the short term depending on relative price elasticities.

Event	IS	LM	BOP (PMK)	BOP (IMK)
C↑	↑			
I↑	↑			
X↑	↑			↓
V↑	↓			↑
G↑	↑			
Y*↑	↑			↓
e↑	↑			↓
M↑		↓		
FX↑		↓		
P↑		↑		
i*↑			↑	↑
Pr*↑			↑	↑
Pr↑			↓	↓
e^e↑			↑	↑

Event	IS	LM	BOP (PMK)	BOP (IMK)
C↓	↓			
I↓	↓			
X↓	↓			↑
V↓	↑			↓
G↓	↓			
Y*↓	↓			↑
e↓	↓			↑
M↓		↑		
FX↓		↑		
P↓		↓		
i*↓			↓	↓
Pr*↓			↓	↓
Pr↓			↑	↑
e^e↓			↓	↓

Fig. 12.1 Effect of Δ in variables on IS, LM, and BOP with perfect (PMK) and imperfect (IMK) capital mobility

And so on. The relative changes will depend on the sensitivities involved. (For our purposes, as we analyze the generalized effects of various policy changes and macroeconomic events, specificity regarding the coefficients is not required.)

To the chart summarizing the effects of variable changes on the IS, LM, and BOP curves that we developed in Chap. 9 (Fig. 9.29), we can now add shifts to the BOP equilibrium line under conditions of imperfectly mobile capital (Fig. 12.1).

12.2 The Keynesian Multiplier in Action

Recall that when we analyzed the effects of increases in government spending (↑G) and the money supply (↑M) under a regime of flexible exchange rates and perfectly mobile capital (PMK) in Chaps. 10 and 11, we obtained the result that there would ultimately be no increase in output (**no ΔY**) in either instance. There were side effects, however, as the ↑G brought about an increase in the current account deficit and the ↑M brought on inflation (↑P).

Under imperfectly mobile capital ("IMK"), however, due to the positive slope of the BOP line (which as we noted is caused in large part by the "stickiness" of changes in the movement of goods versus that of changes in exchange rates and

Fig. 12.2 ↑G, flexible rates, imperfectly mobile capital (IMK)

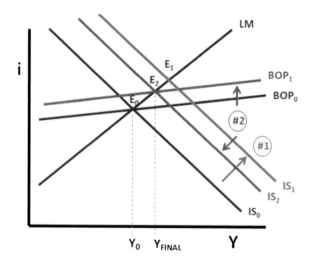

capital flows), we obtain different results. In Fig. 12.2 we examine an increase in government spending under a regime of imperfectly mobile capital and a floating exchange rate:

1. **G↑** → **IS↑** to **IS₁.**
2. **E₁** is in BOP surplus, S̲FX > DFX, e↓.
3. Flexible rates: **IS ↓** to **IS₂** *and* **BOP ↑** to **BOP₁.** New equilibrium at **E₂.**

    The increase in government initially spending pushes the IS curve higher, to **IS₁.** This creates a BOP surplus condition, and under flexible rates, the exchange rate will strengthen (**e↓**).

    Here we depart from the result obtained under perfectly mobile capital, as we see both the IS curve *and* the BOP curve responding to the change in the exchange rate.

4. Results:

    Y ↑, i ↑, e ↓
    (**Also X ↓, V ↑**)

    Here, in step (3), we see that unlike the result under perfectly mobile capital, the IS line does not snap all the way back to its starting point and instead meets the BOP line, which is simultaneously adjusting in the opposite direction. The result is that the increase in government spending has led to a new equilibrium point (**E₂**) at a higher level of output and interest rates.

    And in the case of an increase in the money supply (Fig. 12.3):

1. **M↑** → **LM↓** to **LM₁.**
2. **E₁** is in BOP deficit, D̲FX > SFX, e↑.

Fig. 12.3 ↑M, flexible rates,
IMK: Step #1

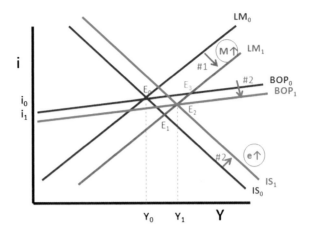

3. Flexible rates: **IS↑** to **IS₁** *and* **BOP↓** to **BOP₁**. New equilibrium at **E₂**.
4. Results:

Y ↑, i ↓, e ↓

(Also X ↑)

The increase in the money stock shifts the LM curve down to **LM₁**. We find the
new IS–LM equilibrium to be in BOP deficit, so the exchange rate weakens (**e↑**).

This causes the IS curve to shift up and the BOP line to shift down. The new
general equilibrium will be found at some point where they together intersect the
new LM curve.

Two important differences here emerge from the perfectly mobile capital example (refer to Fig. 10.8):

1. The increase in output is moderated by the restrictions on capital mobility, which
   reduces the propensity of the economy to overheat. We show alternate equilibrium point **E₃**, which would have been the new general equilibrium had the BOP
   not moved in tandem with the IS. This would have resulted in much higher
   output and potential overheating.
2. While inflation will follow from the increase in money supply, as it does under
   perfectly mobile capital, the increase in the price level will not take the equilibrium all the way back to the starting point. Output will remain higher than
   before, as we examine below:

In Fig. 12.4, we show the original curve positions as light gray lines, and the
curve positions resulting from the exercise above, before the increase in the general
price level, as blue lines. Starting at the equilibrium point **E₂**:

1. ↑**P** → **LM** snaps back ↑ to **LM₂**.
2. **E₄** is in BOP surplus, <u>S</u>FX > DFX, e↓.

Fig. 12.4 ↑M, flexible rates,
IMK: Step #2 – inflation
effects

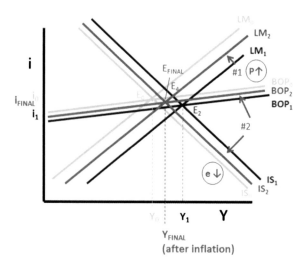

3. **IS** adjusts ↓ to **IS$_2$** and **BOP**↑ to **BOP$_2$**. Final equilibrium at **E$_{FINAL}$**.
4. Results:

> **Y** ↓, **i** ↑, *and*
>
> ↑ **P** remains

The increase in the price level causes the LM curve to snap back up, to **LM$_2$**. Because the new IS–LM equilibrium point **E$_4$** is in BOP surplus, the exchange rate strengthens (**e**↓). This causes the IS to shift down while simultaneously the BOP curve shifts up, with a new general equilibrium **E$_{FINAL}$** where **IS$_2$**, **LM$_2$**, and **BOP$_2$** intersect.

So here, while inflation has moderated the growth, we have still increased output from where we started (**Y$_{FINAL}$** versus **Y$_0$**). This contrasts with the perfectly mobile capital case where the increase in output was completely offset by inflation.

In these two examples we can see the classic **Keynesian multiplier** in action. Increases in government spending and/or money supply are largely spent on consumption (with the balance saved), with the recipients of that spending then doing the same, on and on. The total economic activity created by the initial stimulus may exceed the amount initially spent, raising net output. The main cost is generally some increase in the price level.

Given an economy with a marginal propensity to consume of 80 % (people spend 80 cents of every new dollar they earn), the multiplier might hypothetically function as follows:

↑G by $100 million	↑M by $100 million
1. $100 million goes to infrastructure projects	$100 million is issued and is used to purchase government bonds from banks
2. The recipients ultimately spend $80 million of their income from the project; the rest is saved	The banks lend out $90 million to businesses, with the $10M balance held as required reserves
3. The recipients of the $80 million then go and spend $64 million (80 %), saving the rest.	Those businesses spend and invest the $90 million
4. The recipients of the $64 million then spend $49 million (80 %), saving the rest.	The recipients of the $90 million spend $72 million (80 %), saving the rest
5. Each subsequent recipient spends 80 % of his or her income.	Each subsequent recipient spends 80 % of his or her income
Total spending from the initial $100 million:	*Total spending from the initial $100 million:*
= 80 + 64 + 49 + 40 + 32 + 24 + 17 + 13 + 10 + 8 + 6 + 5 + 4 + 3 + 2 + 1	= 72 + 58 + 46 + 37 + 30 + 24 + 19 + 15 + 12 + 7 + 5 + 4 + 3 + 2 + 1
= **$358 million**	= **$335 million**
Multiplier = 358/100 = **3.58**	Multiplier = 335/1000 = **3.35**

As long as the multiplier is greater than one, as it is in these examples, the fiscal or monetary stimulus will have a positive effect.

In practice, the multiplier is difficult to pin down. Most recent empirical studies find a lower multiplier than claimed by adherents of the theory (often lower than 1), but there is still plenty of research supporting a multiplier greater than one.[4] Much of the dispute is clouded due to the fact that adherents and detractors have split along political lines, with those favoring more government involvement in the economy citing Keynes in support of their views and those wary of government involvement in the economy seeking to prove him wrong.

---

[4] Robert Barro finds a multiplier of between 0.4 and 0.7 in an empirical analysis covering several decades of data (Robert Barro, Macroeconomic effects from government purchases and taxes, Mercatus Center, Georgetown University, July 2010), and Cogan and Taylor find a multiplier of near-zero for the 2009 US stimulus plan due to misdirected spending (Cogan JF, Taylor JB What the government purchases multiplier actually multiplied in the 2009 stimulus package, October 2010).

On the other hand, using New Keynesian methodology, Michael Woodford finds a multiplier varying from less than one to much greater than one depending on the state of the economy, with a severely depressed economy being much more responsive (Michael Woodford, Simple analytics of the government expenditure multiplier, Columbia University, June 13, 2010). And, using Classical Keynesian analysis, Romer and Bernstein posit a multiplier of 1.4 (Romer C, Bernstein J The job impact of the American recovery and reinvestment plan, January 9, 2010).

John Maynard Keynes (1883–1946), Copyright Bettmann/Corbis/AP Images

Regardless, it is clear that whatever its specific value, our analysis has demonstrated that the Keynesian multiplier operates better under a regime involving some restrictions on capital flows, as the free movement of capital in and out of the country can defeat the designs of policymakers. Keynes, in fact, developed his General Theory in a world of imperfectly mobile capital, fixed or managed exchange rates, sticky wages and prices, and delayed changes in price elasticities. Lord Keynes, whatever he might think of his theory's applicability to today's economic world, was never one to shy away from controversy, and would have certainly been entertained to know that his name would be hurled about by energized partisans some 70 years after his death.

Whether or not an increase in government spending can stimulate economic growth, there is an external constraint on the ability to implement such policies. We have assumed bond-financed deficits in all of our examples so far. Increases in M have been assumed to occur through traditional monetary policy, typically open-market operations. Monetization of debt, where the fiscal authority cannot find buyers for its bonds and turns to the central bank to print money, is another story entirely. Once that barrier is crossed, it becomes increasingly difficult for a country to finance itself as potential buyers become increasingly skittish about lending money to a country that may well inflate away the value of its bonds. An inflationary spiral ensues, which ends badly for all.

To maintain the ability to finance its deficits through bond issuance, investors must believe that the issuing government will never approach the point where it resorts to monetization. In the next section, we examine the criteria by which the sustainability of deficit financing may be evaluated.

12.3 The Dornbusch Model of Sustainability

12.3.1 Fiscal Deficit Sustainability

In the post-financial crisis era (of 2008–2009) of fiscal constraints brought about by reduced government revenues resulting from the global recession, the size of fiscal budget deficits has become a worldwide concern. Most advanced Western economies today run persistent fiscal deficits, where government expenditures exceed revenues. However, while several Latin American countries, as well as several former Soviet satellite states, suffered hyperinflations in the early 1990s, and while Zimbabwe experienced a mind-numbing hyperinflation from 2005 to 2008, no advanced economy has suffered a rampant hyperinflation since the Hungarian episode of 1945–1946.

How is this possible if these governments have generally run large and persistent deficits for decades on end?

The key to understanding the answer is the concept of sustainability. As long as the fiscal authority can incur a continuously increasing stream of deficits by issuing new debt to repay the principal and interest of earlier periods, the fiscal deficit is considered to be *sustainable*. There is an upper limit on any government's ability to incur debt beyond which servicing the debt consumes the entirety of the government's resources, beyond which the government must resort to monetization. This results in a hyperinflationary spiral of soaring prices, crashing exchange rates, and the epic destruction of wealth among the country's citizens.

A "sustainable" deficit-financing policy is defined as one in which an upper limit of debt financing, characterized by adverse effects on the price level, nominal exchange rates, and real wealth, is never attained, and the possibility of future unanticipated monetization to wipe out the debt in real terms is, for practical purposes, nonexistent.[5]

So, how much debt is "too much"? What makes a deficit-financing policy "sustainable"? How can a government know when it is on a path to ruin, in time to change its course?

12.3.2 Rudiger Dornbusch

With the breakup of the Bretton Woods system of currencies linked to a gold-backed US dollar in 1971, the world's advanced economies entered a new and uncharted era of worldwide fiat money. The interplay between interest rates, now-volatile currency exchange rates, inflation, and policy became a hot area for study.

---

[5] Langdana F (1989) Sustaining domestic budget deficits in open economies. Routledge, Oxford, Chap. 11

Rudiger Dornbusch, Courtesy MIT Museum

Rudiger Dornbusch (1942–2002), a German-born MIT economist, entered this field with valuable contributions, particularly with regard to inflation-stabilization policies, debt and deficits, and prices and exchange rates.

One of his most important contributions was on the topic of budget deficit sustainability. Dornbusch developed a simple but powerful model to indicate whether a fiscal policy is sustainable or not.

12.3.3   The Dornbusch Model of Fiscal Deficit Sustainability

The ability of a government to continuously finance its debt depends not only on the size of its budget deficits and outstanding debt but also on interest rates, inflation, and the growth rate of the economy.

Interest rates affect the country's cost of debt service, which at high debt-to-GDP ratios (above 60–70 %) becomes significant. Inflation reduces the real value of nominal liabilities and thus reduces the real value of the outstanding debt. So, the proper measure of the interest cost of debt service is the real interest rate, which is the nominal interest rate minus inflation.

The growth rate of the economy is a major factor in debt service as well. An economy growing fast enough year after year will "outgrow" its debt burden.

In Dornbusch's model, the effective cost of debt service is given by the real, inflation and growth-adjusted interest rate times the outstanding debt:

$$\begin{array}{l}\textbf{Effective burden of debt}\\ \textbf{service as a \% of GDP}\end{array} = (\textbf{Debt/GDP}) \times (\textbf{Real Interest Rate} - \textbf{GDP Growth Rate})$$

(A) For example, if we are given Country A, with

> Debt/GDP ratio = 50 %
> Nominal interest rate = 5 %
> Inflation rate = 4 %
> GDP growth rate = 5 %

then the effective burden of debt service = 50 % × ([5 − 4] − 5) = −2 % of GDP. This means that debt service is not exceeding the economy's ability to continuously fund it.

(B) To take another example, if we are given Country B, with

> Debt/GDP ratio = 75 %
> Nominal interest rate = 10 %
> Inflation rate = 4 %
> GDP growth rate = 2 %

Here, the effective burden of debt service = 75 % × ([10 − 4] − 2) = 3 % of GDP. Debt service exceeds the economy's ability to absorb it through growth and inflation.

Debt service is not the only thing to consider, however, as the primary budget deficit (government expenses excluding interest, less revenues) adds to the existing debt burden. So, we must add the primary deficit as a % of GDP in order to obtain a measure of the total burden of the combined primary fiscal deficit and debt service.

The effective burden of deficit financing is given by:

$$\textbf{Effective burden of Deficit Financing as \% of GDP} = \frac{\textbf{Primary Deficit}}{\textbf{GDP}} + \frac{\textbf{Effective burden of debt service}}{\textbf{GDP}}$$

If our primary deficit is 1.5 % of GDP, then for the two countries above:

(A) The effective burden of deficit financing as % of GDP = 1.5 % + (−2 %) = **−0.5 %**.

Here, economic growth and inflation are outgrowing the debt that is being added due to deficit financing. The debt-to-GDP ratio will drop by 0.5 % per year in Country A. As long as the variables remain in a range close to what was given, this economy is on a **sustainable** path.

(B) Here, the effective burden of deficit financing as % of GDP = 1.5 % + (3 %) = **4.5 %**.

This country's fiscal policy is **non-sustainable**. The country's debt-to-GDP ratio will increase by +4.5 % per year. Persistent adherence to its current policies will eventually take the debt burden beyond Country B's ability to service it.

Dornbusch's formula for fiscal deficit sustainability is given by an algebraic expression of the formula we described above:

$$\mathbf{b^{O} = d + b\ (r - g)}$$

if $b^O < 0$, then fiscal deficit policy is sustainable
where

$$b^O = \text{rate of } \Delta \text{ of } \frac{\text{debt}}{\text{gdp}} \text{ ratio}$$

$$d = \frac{\text{deficit}}{\text{gdp}} \text{ ratio}$$

$$b = \frac{\text{debt}}{\text{gdp}} \text{ ratio}$$

$$r = \text{real interest rate}$$

$$g = \text{growth rate of the economy}$$

The most important independent variable is **g**, the GDP growth rate. A high enough rate of economic growth will overcome many sins, as the economy simply outgrows the effects of even the most profligate fiscal authorities. Stagnant or negative growth, however, is a killer, as *any* deficit will be non-sustainable. The economy must either turn around or the government must find a way to repair its fiscal situation.[6]

Naturally, engaging in non-sustainable deficit policy *for a short period of time* does not lead immediately to ruin. Most countries will tolerate relatively large deficits during times of economic contraction and hardship, because (a) revenues fall when the economy slows, enlarging existing deficits, and recovery is generally anticipated with a turn in the business cycle, and (b) it is a generally accepted premise in advanced economies that some social safety net protection is necessary for the displaced during bad times. (A third reason involves the idea that deficit spending during bad times will stimulate the economy back to optimum output and employment, per John Maynard Keynes' prescriptions, but as noted earlier in the chapter, this notion has become more controversial over recent years particularly for countries with very high existing debt/GDP ratios.)

The key to deficit-financing sustainability is to maintain a low level of debt/GDP during the good times, so that the effects of deficit spending on the real fiscal situation are minimized. (Recall that the debt/GDP ratio is the multiplier used to

---

[6] The sovereign debt crisis in the Eurozone from 2009–(?) has illustrated this point. Countries with very high debt/GDP ratios (the **b** variable) suddenly found themselves entwined in a global recession, with extremely low or negative growth rates (**g**). Given the already-high debt ratios, Eurozone countries did not have the flexibility for their debt to grow during the downturn that they might have enjoyed were they starting from a lower debt/GDP ratio.

Country	Adopted	1999	2000	2001	2002	2003	2004	2005	2006	2007	2008	2009	2010	2011	2012
Austria	1999	-2.4	-1.8	-0.2	-0.9	-1.7	-4.6	-1.8	-1.7	-1.0	-1.0	-4.1	-4.5	-2.6	-2.9
Belgium	1999	-0.7	-0.1	0.4	-0.2	-0.2	-0.2	-2.6	0.3	-0.1	-1.1	-5.6	-3.9	-3.9	-3.0
Cyprus	2008	-4.5	-2.4	-2.3	-4.5	-6.6	-4.2	-2.5	-1.2	3.5	0.9	-6.1	-5.3	-6.3	-4.8
Estonia	2011	-4.2	-0.9	0.3	0.9	2.2	1.6	1.6	3.2	2.8	-2.3	-2.1	0.4	1.0	-2.0
Finland	1999	1.7	6.9	5.1	4.1	2.4	2.2	2.7	4.0	5.3	4.2	-2.7	-2.9	-0.8	-1.4
France	1999	-1.8	-1.5	-1.7	-3.3	-4.1	-3.6	-3.0	-2.4	-2.8	-3.3	-7.6	-7.1	-5.2	-4.7
Germany	1999	-1.5	1.3	-2.8	-3.7	-4.1	-3.8	-3.4	-1.6	0.2	-0.1	-3.2	-4.1	-0.8	-0.4
Greece*	2001	-3.2	-3.7	-4.4	-4.8	-5.7	-7.4	-5.6	-6.0	-6.8	-9.9	-15.6	-10.5	-9.1	-7.5
Ireland	1999	2.6	4.7	0.8	-0.5	0.3	1.3	1.7	2.9	0.1	-7.3	-13.9	-30.9	-12.8	-8.3
Italy	1999	-2.0	-0.9	-3.2	-3.2	-3.6	-3.6	-4.5	-3.4	-1.6	-2.7	-5.4	-4.5	-3.8	-2.7
Luxembourg	1999	3.4	6.0	6.1	2.1	0.5	-1.1	0.0	1.4	3.7	3.0	-0.8	-0.9	-0.6	-2.5
Malta	2008	n/a	-5.8	-6.4	-5.8	-9.2	-4.7	-2.9	-2.8	-2.4	-4.6	-3.7	-3.7	-2.7	-2.5
Netherlands	1999	0.4	2.0	-0.3	-2.1	-3.2	-1.8	-0.3	0.5	0.2	0.5	-5.4	-5.1	-4.7	-3.7
Portugal	1999	-3.1	-3.3	-4.8	-3.4	-3.7	-4.0	-6.5	-3.8	-3.2	-3.7	-10.2	-9.8	-4.2	-5.0
Slovak Republic	2009	-7.4	-12.3	-6.5	-8.2	-2.8	-2.4	-2.8	-3.2	-1.8	-2.1	-8.0	-7.7	-4.8	-4.8
Slovenia	2007	-0.6	-1.2	-1.3	-1.4	-1.3	-1.3	-1.0	-0.8	0.3	-0.3	-5.5	-5.3	-5.6	-4.6
Spain	1999	-1.4	-1.0	-0.7	-0.5	-0.2	-0.3	1.0	2.0	1.9	-4.2	-11.2	-9.4	-8.9	-7.0
# Countries		11	11	12	12	12	12	12	12	13	15	16	16	17	17
Mean		-0.4	1.1	-0.5	-1.4	-1.9	-2.2	-1.9	-0.6	-0.3	-2.0	-6.8	-7.2	-4.5	-4.0
Median		-1.4	-0.1	-0.5	-1.5	-2.4	-2.7	-2.2	-0.6	0.1	-1.1	-5.6	-5.2	-4.2	-3.7

Fig. 12.5 Eurozone fiscal deficit % of GDP 1999–2012. Deficits exceeding 3 % of GDP are highlighted. *Greek figures are restated from the original, contemporaneously reported data (*Data source: IMF*)

compute the effective burden of debt service—a high multiplier greatly exacerbates the effective burden of debt service.)

In practice, despite the elegant models put forth by Dornbusch and other economists, simple rules of thumb tend to predominate when policymakers and investors evaluate fiscal deficits.

Generally, if the deficit-to-GDP ratio is less than 3–5 %, then bond-financed budget deficits in mature economies such as the USA, Japan, and Western Europe are said to be sustainable. A deficit greater than 5 % maintained for a prolonged period will attract the close scrutiny of investors, who may shy away—driving up interest rates and exacerbating the situation with higher interest rates. Under 5 % or so, it is assumed that the economy will generally grow enough to absorb the added debt each year.

The European Monetary Union requires, among other criteria, that fiscal deficits remain under 3 % of GDP. Failure to adhere to this rule invokes penalties. However, the financial and economic crisis of 2007–2009 resulted in severe drops in government revenues, as well as the expenditure of huge sums in crisis-response efforts including banking system support and fiscal stimulus. Once the crisis hit, the 3 % rule was simply ignored. In 2010, among the 17 Eurozone countries, only Finland, Estonia, and tiny Luxembourg maintained budget deficits of 3 % or less of GDP (Fig. 12.5).

In the next section, we will explore the evolution, historical challenges, and current predicament of the European currency union and the euro.

12.4   The European Economic and Monetary Union and the Euro

The European currency unit, the **euro**, is the second largest reserve currency in the world and is as of 2013 the sole and official currency of the 17 Eurozone countries. It is used and accepted in several others, and some 23 additional countries are pegged to the euro. The total number of people who use the euro or a currency pegged to the euro as their primary money exceeds 500 million.

The euro is unusual in that it is a supranational currency, spanning a number of countries, and it is also unusual in that the money has no single fiscal authority standing behind it, instead being dependent on agreements in place between member governments.

The development of the euro was a gradual process that took many decades and was part of a general drive toward European political and economic integration that began in earnest following the World War II.

Seminal events in the euro's evolution:

12.4.1   1946 Churchill: "United States of Europe"

– Small Germany
– Soviet threat
– Specialize and trade freely

In the aftermath of the devastation wrought by the World War II, Winston Churchill gave a speech at the University of Zurich, in which he proposed closer political and economic integration of the states of Europe: "We must build a kind of United States of Europe." The primary motivations at the time were to foster the rebuilding of Europe, ensure a constrained Germany, reduce the chance and scope of future intra-European military conflict, and counter the emerging Soviet threat. The concept of some kind of European federation of states had been bandied around since at least the late middle ages.

The end of hostilities had opened a rare window in which Germany was weak and divided; it had always been the fear of German dominance that had heretofore held back the other major powers from embracing such a scheme.

Ricardo's prescriptions to gain the full benefits of comparative advantage through trade were a driving force behind the move toward economic integration, with the idea that an integrated market would allow each country to specialize in the goods that made the best use of its abundant factor(s). By trading freely without tariffs or other restrictions, Europe would achieve a level of economic prosperity which had formerly been unattainable.

12.4.2 1957 Treaty of Rome

– Abolish customs duties
– Reduce and unify tariffs
– Facilitate internal trade and transport

Churchill's vision would begin to take tangible form with the 1957 Treaty of Rome, establishing the European Economic Community (EEC), which made concrete progress toward a common market among six Western European nations: Germany, France, Italy, the Netherlands, Belgium, and Luxembourg. The group would expand in 1973 with the addition of the UK, Ireland, Denmark, and Norway, and further with the 1981 addition of Greece and the 1986 additions of Spain and Portugal.

The Treaty of Rome had three primary purposes:

1. Abolish national customs duties
2. Lower intraparty tariffs and replace them with a unified external tariff regime
3. Establish common policies for internal trade and transport

12.4.3 1979 European Economic and Monetary Union

– Era of Stagflation and "Malaise"
– 12 Countries essentially pegged to D-Mark
– Exchange rates held within bands: (+/−6 % Sp., It., UK; +/−2.25 % Fr., others)
– The era of the ECU begins

The dissolution of the Bretton Woods fixed-exchange rate regime, following the USA's abandonment of any pretense of the gold standard in 1971,[7] resulted in a free-for-all in the international currency markets. Several countries (Italy, France,

---

[7] We will discuss Bretton Woods and the 1971 closing of the "gold window" in the next chapter.

Sweden, and Norway) moved to freely floating rates to gain an advantage in exports and control over their monetary policy, while several countries remained pegged, primarily to the dollar.

This was a step backward for the project of European economic integration. Critics pointed to increased uncertainty in intra-European trade and investment as well as in relations with trading partners outside Europe. The challenges were exacerbated by external shocks, such as the oil crises of the early and mid-1970s, and the stagflation (high unemployment combined with high inflation) that plagued Western economies of the time. The stagflation episode finally convinced most of Europe of the futility of the "political business cycle."

The Economic and Monetary Union (EMU) offered a solution to these new problems. Several European countries, including the larger economic powers Germany, France, and Italy, joined together (with others soon following) to establish the European Currency Unit, or "ECU," a "basket" comprising the currencies of the 12 European Union member states. The ECU effectively fixed the ratio of the European currencies relative to one another. The result, due to the economic dominance of Germany and its heavy weighting in the currency basket, was that the member currencies were, to a large degree, effectively pegged to the Deutsche Mark.

The European Monetary System (EMS) required that each country operate under an "adjustable peg," where its currency was fixed but was permitted to float within a relatively narrow band (2½ % for most countries, +/−6 % for Italy, and later, Spain). The agreement allowed the pegs to be periodically adjusted, allowing some flexibility. The ECU itself floated against external currencies.

The EMU was not limited to currency issues. Priority was given to harmonizing regulations and continuation of the work begun under the Treaty of Rome to transform Europe into a single market.

12.4.4   1985 White Paper

– 300 NTBs to eliminate
– 5 types of major barriers remaining to be overcome

Europe's early experience with the EMU revealed the affinity for protectionism among policymakers. Having removed internal tariffs and duties, the member countries resorted to nontariff barriers (NTBs) to protect favored national industries and constituencies. The famous 1985 White Paper on the Completion of the Internal Market,[8] issued by the European Council, outlined the challenge:

> The elimination of border controls, important as it is, does not of itself create a genuine common market. Goods and people moving within the Community should not find obstacles inside the different Member States as opposed to meeting them at the border.

---

[8] *Completing the Internal Market: White Paper from the Commission to the European Council (Milan, 28–29 June 1985) COM(85) 310, June 1985.* (Brussels: Commission of the European Communities), June 1985

The paper found more than 300 NTBs that were hindering trade and economic development. The major remaining barriers to economic integration fell into five categories:

1. Artificial standards and licensing
2. Fiscal barriers–divergent tax regimes
3. Borders–physical barriers–motor crossings, etc.
4. Large government procurement contracts awarded to favored groups
5. Medical and pharmaceutical standards differences

The paper recommended action on these remaining barriers to trade and economic integration.

12.4.5   1986 Single European Act

– Shift away from "absolute harmonization" to "mutual recognition"
– "Minimal harmonization and mutual recognition"
– If one member country accepts a standard, it's good for all

The reforms outlined in the 1985 White Paper were largely put into place with the 1986 Single European Act, which encompassed various areas of political, economic, and social integration. Most of the NTBs identified in the White Paper were to be eliminated or otherwise addressed.

An important and fundamental change was made regarding the harmonization of standards, an area of deep complexity and a source of significant complications for intra-European business. Previously, the goal had been the **absolute harmonization** of standards across the Economic and Monetary Union, where individual national regulations would be replaced by a unified set of governing standards for various industries and products. However, this objective proved to be contentious and unworkable as vested interests in each country prevented consensus.

Rules and standards had become the new tariffs, and absurd but major trade disputes arose over seemingly trivial details. Germany, for example, had invoked its 1516 Beer Purity law (originally designed to safeguard wheat and rye supplies for bread bakers) to exclude foreign beer; France and Germany dueled over Germany's new labeling regulations, which discriminated against a French liqueur, *Cassis*, and Belgium used a rule preventing the sale of certain products without a certificate of authenticity to exclude Scotch Whiskey.

A solution was found in replacing the goal of "absolute harmonization" with the principle of "**mutual recognition**." Essentially, under mutual recognition, within the area of the EMU, countries could not prohibit products from their markets based on noncompliance with local standards, if those products adhere to the national standards of the country of origin.

This change eliminated many of the disputes and led to a more endogenous process of standardization across borders, led in large part by voluntary efforts among leaders in each industry.

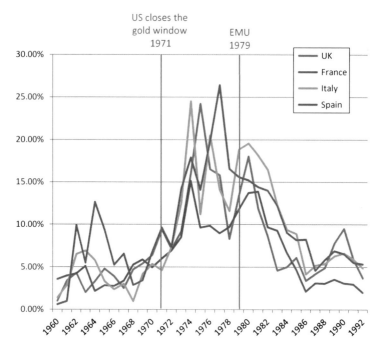

Fig. 12.6 Inflation in selected European countries 1979–1992

12.4.6   1979–1991 Era of the ECU

- Exchange rate stability
- Inflation under control
- Economic growth

In the years following the 1979 birth of the ECU, the **impossible trinity** broke the cycle of inflation and stagnation that had plagued Europe. With fixed exchange rates and freely mobile capital, policymakers' hands were kept off the **M** lever. The inflation of the 1970s was finally brought under control (Fig. 12.6).

The creation of the ECU also led to a significant reduction in exchange rate *volatility*, which had exploded in the post-1971 era (Fig. 12.7).

With inflation subdued, and monetary discipline imposed by the impossible trinity, economic growth returned to Europe.

12.4.7   End of the ECU

1992   The ECU Blows apart!

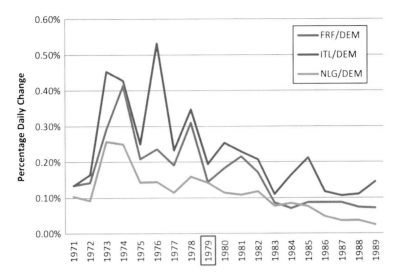

Fig. 12.7 Daily European exchange rate fluctuations 1971–1989 (*Average percent daily change in exchange rates, French Franc, Italian Lira, and Dutch Gulden versus Deutsche-Mark, 1971–89. The Exchange Rate Mechanism and ECU currency basket were established in 1979. Data source: St. Louis Fed, authors' calculations*)

In 1989, the German people, along with most of the free world, rejoiced at the fall of the Berlin Wall, symbol of Soviet oppression and of the 45-year partition of Germany. The path to German reunification was finally open.

As Germany's reintegration proceeded toward its October 1990 conclusion, the issue of the East German currency was one of much debate and discussion. The Ostmark (the East German mark) had never been convertible, and while the East German government's official exchange rate held it at parity with the Deutsche mark ("DM"), the black-market rate was persistently on the order of 5-to-1 or higher.

In July of 1990 the West German Government announced that Ostmarks would be accepted for exchange at the rate of 1-to-1 to the DM for the first 4,000 units per person and the rate of 2-to-1 for larger amounts. This was seen as the best way to speed along integration and assist the citizens of the former East Germany, who had suffered through decades of economic retardation under socialism, through the transition to a modern capitalist economy. On the eve of reunification, East Germany's GDP per capita was only 31 % of that of West Germany; its factories, plant equipment, and infrastructure were technologically obsolete and in a state of disrepair, and its labor was force ill suited to meet the demands of a modern economy.

While West Germany enjoyed a short-term economic boom thanks to the addition of 16 million new consumers hungry for better-quality western goods, and the addition of millions to its labor force, the longer-term economic picture was unclear. Retraining such a huge labor force would be a colossal undertaking.[9] Modernizing East Germany's crumbling and outdated infrastructure would require, for the most part, pulling it up root and branch and starting over. These efforts would require incredible sums.

While the German people were euphoric that their nation had finally emerged from its 1945 division, the Bundesbank, on the other hand, viewed the developments with great and grave concern—memories of the searing 1922–1923 German hyperinflation were omnipresent.

Top: East Berlin citizens get helping hands from West Berliners as they climb the wall near the Brandenburg Gate, Nov. 10, 1989, Associated Press. Bottom from left: Woman uses bank notes to fill a stove, Germany, 1923, Getty Images. This is the way large firms drew the weekly payroll from the Reichsbank in Berlin, shown Aug. 15, 1923, Associated Press

---

[9] An old joke among workers in the Soviet Union and its satellite states went: "We pretend to work, they pretend to pay us."

Fig. 12.8 France, UK, other
Europe ex-Germany,
expected results post-1990
reunification, $\downarrow$Pr*, fixed
rates, PMK

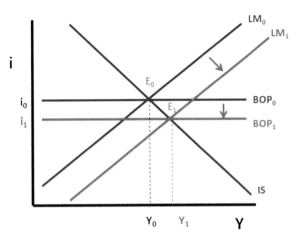

The German government's acceptance of East German money at a 1-to-1 conversion ratio amounted to an enormous transfer of wealth from West to East. This, combined with other payments, would equate to a subsidy of between 150 billion and 200 billion DM per year, representing around 6–8 % of West German GDP. The Bundesbank observed with alarm that under the original plan, money supply was projected to shoot up by +20 % in 1991, and the fiscal budget deficit was expected to expand substantially. Inflation loomed.

The Bundesbank was not the only party to be somewhat wary of the consequences of reunification. It was never far from the collective memory of other European nations, France and the United Kingdom in particular, that Germany had twice in the twentieth century attempted the domination of Europe; the leaders of these countries had once been children suffering under German air raids and occupation. While unification was seen as inevitable, it was often viewed skeptically by those suspicious of unchecked German power.[10]

Despite the fact that most Western economies at the time were in an economic slump and headed toward recession, the immediate economic effects of reunification on the rest of Europe were not a major concern. From the perspective of France, the UK, and other European countries, while the economic uncertainty and challenges facing Germany clouded that country's long-term economic outlook (**Pr***$\downarrow$), the effects of this on the other European economies would be benign (refer to Fig. 12.8):

1. **Pr***$\downarrow$**(Germany)** $\rightarrow$ **BOP**$\downarrow$ to **BOP** $_1$.
2. E_0 is in BOP surplus, $\underline{SFX}$ > DFX, fixed rates: **FX**$\uparrow$.
3. **LM** adjusts $\downarrow$ to **LM**$_1$, new equilibrium at **E**$_1$.
4. Results: **Y** $\uparrow$, **i** $\downarrow$.

---

[10] Regarding German reunification, British Prime Minister Margaret Thatcher reportedly told Soviet Premier Gorbachev: "All Europe is watching this not without a degree of fear, remembering very well who started the two world wars."

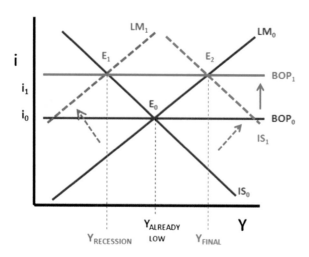

Fig. 12.9 France, the UK, other Europe, foreign (German) interest rates shooting up ($i*\uparrow\uparrow$) (**a**) Hold the peg (LM$\uparrow$) or (**b**) break the peg (IS$\uparrow$)?

In Fig. 12.8, the "domestic economy" is a combination of France, the UK, and the rest of Europe excluding Germany. We see the foreign (Germany) macro outlook falling, which pushes the BOP line down to **BOP$_1$**. Since we are under a fixed-rate regime, this results in an inflow of FX, which moves the LM line down to **LM$_1$**. The new equilibrium is at **E$_1$**, with the benign result of lower interest rates and higher output.

The rest of Europe would benefit, to some extent, from the uncertainty surrounding the economic effects of German reintegration as capital migrated to their less risky economies.

However, shockingly, in the midst of Germany's celebration, the Bundesbank sent a powerful signal to the German fiscal authorities: **"We will not monetize your runaway deficit!"** The central bank raised interest rates sharply, to above 9 % through 1991–1992 in an attempt to keep inflation in the bottle.

While this move was met with fierce objections from the German fiscal and political authorities, the turmoil in Germany was nothing compared with the horror with which the policy was greeted among the rest of the EMU countries. The savage increase in German interest rates had turned their formerly sunny economic horizon into a decidedly bleak landscape.

European Monetary System members faced a stark choice: (a) remain pegged under the ECU, or (b) de-peg their currencies and leave the ECU.

Both choices start with foreign interest rates having soared, pushing the BOP line upward (see Fig. 12.9):

(a) Remain pegged under the ECU	(b) De-peg and leave the ECU
(1) $i*\uparrow\uparrow$ (**Germany**) $\to$ **BOP**$\uparrow\uparrow$ to **BOP**$_1$	(1) $i*\uparrow\uparrow$ (**Germany**) $\to$ **BOP**$\uparrow\uparrow$ to **BOP**$_1$
Decision: **Keep the Peg!**	Decision: **Break the Peg!**
(2) E_0 is in BOP deficit, $\underline{DFX} >$ SFX, **FX**$\downarrow$	(2) E_0 is in BOP deficit, $\underline{DFX} >$ SFX, **e**$\uparrow$
(3) **LM** adjusts $\uparrow$ to **LM**$_1$, equilibrium at E_1	(3) **IS** adjusts $\uparrow$ to **IS**$_1$, equilibrium at E_2
(4) ☹ Results:	(4) ☺ Results:
Y$\downarrow\downarrow$, **i**$\uparrow\uparrow$	**Y**$\uparrow$, **i**$\uparrow$

If they remained tied to the peg ("a" in Fig. 12.9), the other EMU countries would face contagion from the German situation as FX drained away chasing the higher returns available in Germany, forcing these countries to raise their own rates and driving them into a brutal recession. Output would contract, and these countries would be stuck with an overvalued currency (relative to the rest of the world) and high interest rates. The UK was the most vulnerable of these economies as its exchange rate was fixed at a relatively strong rate, making it harder to defend.

As we see in our ISLM-BOP analysis, the economically sound decision would appear to be to simply permit the currency to float ("b" in Fig. 12.9), which would relieve the pressure and result in higher output, albeit with higher interest rates. However, to break the ECU peg was politically unthinkable; it was to reverse the European project itself. So, the UK raised interest rates and committed FX reserves to hold its peg. However, as time progressed, the once unthinkable option of breaking the peg became thinkable. Investors with assets denominated in Sterling (GBP) became skittish, anticipating a devaluation, and moved to reduce their exposure. Speculators (including financier George Soros and his Quantum Fund), believing that the devaluation of the weaker ECU currencies was inevitable, began to pile on, shorting these currencies and adding to the immense pressure that they were already under.

By 1992, the ECU, symbol of European integration and stability, had become an anchor threatening to take down the economies of Europe. The UK, which had only formally joined the EMS in 1990 after a 10-year period of "shadowing" the ECU under a semiofficial peg, was spending considerable resources defending the British pound, a task that was becoming more difficult by the day. The British had joined the EMS at an inopportune time, with the result that the pound was the most strenuously overvalued among European currencies and the most subject to attack.

Finally, in 1992, having spent $27 billion of its reserves in a futile attempt to defend the currency, the British de-pegged! The pound underwent a sharp depreciation, and Britain avoided the worst of the recession. Germany was on its own, and the ECU was badly wounded. While no other country formally left the European Monetary System, Italy broke through its trading band during the crisis, and Spain and Portugal ultimately devalued their currencies against the mark. Having breached the perimeter, speculators turned their attention to the inner citadel, as finally the French franc came under heavy attack. The governments of Germany and France coordinated a valiant defense, but in the end, the French resigned themselves to a devaluation. Post-crisis, ECU trading bands were broadened considerably (to as much as +/– 15 %) to provide greater flexibility, but this served to dilute the effectiveness of the entire system. By 1994 strict adherence to the exchange rate mechanism came to be seen as more optional than mandatory. The ECU was a smoldering remnant of its former self.

Illustration by Ricardo Paredes

12.4.8   1999 The Euro

– Single currency
– European Central Bank

On January 1, 1999, the euro was formally launched as an accounting currency legal for all transactions within its area of acceptance, replacing the ECU at a 1:1 conversion ratio. Actual paper and coin currency would be issued in 2002, when the euro entered circulation and would formally replace the national currencies of the participating countries. The formal launch of the euro as a circulating currency was the final outcome of a process that had commenced concurrently with the ECU crisis of the early 1990s, which began with the adoption of the **Maastricht treaty** in 1992.

The Maastricht treaty established the convergence criteria for a country to participate in the European Monetary Union:

1. Inflation within 1.5 % of the lowest three countries of the European Union for at least 1 year
2. Long-term interest rates within 2 % of the lowest of the EU countries for at least 1 year
3. Consistent maintenance of the national currency within the bands of the exchange rate mechanism (ERM) for at least 2 years
   and, most important:
4. **Budget deficit-to-GDP ratio of not more than 3 %**
5. **Government debt-to-GDP ratio of not more than 60 %**

The Maastricht treaty led to the establishment of the **Stability and Growth Pact**, which codified the last two fiscal requirements as ongoing criteria for continued participation in the EMU, and set penalties for noncompliance.

In 1998, the European Central Bank (ECB) was established in Frankfurt, signaling that German monetary discipline would be the fundamental philosophy undergirding the new currency. In that same year, the conversion ratios of the 11 participating currencies were fixed.

With the adoption of the euro, European economic policy entered new and uncharted territory. Never before had a major supranational currency been created without a single fiscal authority standing behind the central bank. Instead, capitalization of the ECB was pro rata, based essentially on relative GDP, and each country maintained control over its own fiscal policy. The weaknesses inherent in this situation were noted at the time, but were largely dismissed. These would become glaringly apparent less than 10 years later.

12.4.9 2010–? European Sovereign Debt Crisis

- Greece, Ireland, Spain (and Italy, Portugal?) → non-sustainable
- Euro under pressure

The euro performed well for the first several years after its launch, steadily gaining value against the US dollar and holding its own against other currencies.

The financial crisis of 2008 brought the first indications of trouble. Despite its good reputation, the young currency at this time was still, to an extent, unproven. In the panic investors seeking safe haven scrambled to hold US dollars as the euro fell (Fig. 12.10).

As the acute phase of the crisis eased, the euro rebounded. However, as the global recession set in, revenues of governments around the world at all levels, from the central authorities to municipalities, dropped precipitously as economic activity slowed down. Those governments that had spent lavishly during the good times found themselves with unmanageable deficits, and their debt exploded from pre-crisis levels.

The Greek situation was the most precarious. Greece's tradition of large public deficits to finance generous social benefits resulted in a debt-to-GDP ratio perpetually exceeding 100 %. Prior to the adoption of the euro, persistent depreciation of the exchange rate had been one way Greece managed to persist with this policy.

(The mechanism driving depreciation would be, in our language, as follows: Domestic long-term outlook is poor [$\mathbf{Pr}\downarrow$], which raises the BOP line, leaving us in BOP deficit (DFX>SFX); under a floating rate regime, this will cause the exchange rate to weaken [$\mathbf{e}\uparrow$].)

Upon the adoption of the euro, currency devaluation was no longer an option; however, the single currency, under the prudent management of the ECB, allowed Greece to borrow at more favorable interest rates than would have been available

Fig. 12.10 The USD/EUR exchange rate and the euro crisis 2010–? (*Exchange rate data source: OANDA.com*) ((**a**) July 2008 USD 1.58/EUR: Onset of acute phase of US Financial Crisis. Treasury initiates support for Fannie Mae, Freddie Mac. Indymac Bank fails (**b**) Nov 2008 USD 1.27/EUR: TARP passes, adding US $700 Billion fiscal support on top of the unprecedented Monetary expansion and Fed guarantees of Sep–Nov 2008 (**c**) Nov 2009 USD 1.49/EUR: First signs of serious trouble in Eurozone as Greece admits to fiscal deficit of 12.7 % of GDP, double its previous claims (**d**) Jun 2010 USD 1.22/EUR: European Financial Stability Facility launched June 9, 2010 with total facilities of EUR 750 Billion (**e**) Oct 2011 USD 1.37/EUR: EFSF expanded, Greek debt write-down, Nov 2011 coordinated global central bank action, Dec 2011 ECB begins LTRO operations of nearly EUR $500 Billion)

otherwise.[11] Capital flowed in from investors seeking higher returns than were available on German or French bonds, and the economy grew.

The global recession drastically affected the Greek economy. Greek government revenues, heavily dependent on tourism and shipping, sagged. Investors began to seriously question the sustainability of Greek fiscal policy. In the midst of the turmoil, it emerged that Greece had misrepresented its true fiscal picture through various derivative transactions[12] at the time of its adoption of the euro, in order to qualify itself under the Maastricht criteria. Yields on Greek bonds shot up over 15 %, and the country faced a debt crisis.

---

[11] The reason why this should be the case is not immediately obvious, as investors were certainly aware that despite externally imposed *monetary* prudence, each country within the Eurozone was in full control of its own *fiscal* policies. Confidence in mutual adherence to the Maastricht criteria, or perhaps that even in a crisis, the strong countries (Germany and France) would almost certainly "bail out" the weaker rather than permit a default, are plausible explanations.

[12] Reportedly aided by the US investment banks, primarily Goldman Sachs. Beat Balzli, "How Goldman Sachs Helped Greece to Mask its True Debt," *Der Spiegel*, February 8, 2010

In such a crisis, under a pegged regime, speculative attacks on the currency would normally ensue, which would end with the peg being broken. The depreciated currency would spur exports and economic activity generally, and the "cheaper" domestic currency denominated debt would be easier to repay.

This was not an option for Greece under the single European currency. The country, like others on the periphery, found itself trapped with a currency that was too strong. Even were Greece to consider the drastic step of leaving the euro, it would still be left with its debt denominated in euros, the vast majority of which was foreign held. Also to be considered was the vast reordering of its economy that would be required in order to achieve a return to a national currency. Such a move would, by the terms EU membership, require that Greece leave the EU itself.

Greeks register their opinion of the first austerity plan (with several to follow), Athens, February 24, 2010. Associated Press

A combination of austerity measures, which brought thousands of protesters to the streets, and a series of "final" rescue packages from the Eurozone and the International Monetary Fund (IMF),[13] temporarily staved off a succession of crises. As of this writing, many observers believe that the Greek debt has passed beyond the country's ability to repay and will ultimately need to be restructured.

---

[13] The first rescue fund of €110 billion was implemented in May 2010 by the IMF, the ECB, and the Eurozone members, and a second fund of €130 billion, funded by the Eurozone countries, went into effect in February 2012. Additional rescue funds and mechanisms have been proposed.

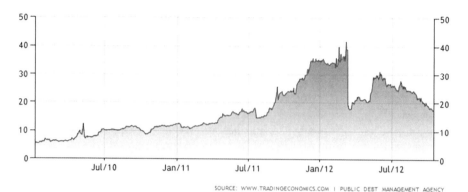

Fig. 12.11 Greece Government bond 10Y, implied yield on 10-year bonds (*Source:* www. tradingeconomics.com)

Under the supranational currency, rather than speculative attacks on the monetary unit, a crisis in confidence affecting a particular country manifests itself in flight from that country's sovereign bonds. Yields on Greek bonds were blowing sky high until the first rescue package was announced in 2010, and while down from their peaks, remained elevated from their pre-crisis levels and would eventually explode in 2011–2012 as the crisis rolled on (Fig. 12.11).

From Greece, investors' attention next turned to Ireland, which had made the decision during the 2008 financial crisis to fully guarantee its banks debts. This was far too much debt to take on for such a small country. By 2010 it was clear that without an emergency source of funding, Ireland, with an astounding 2011 fiscal deficit of *34 % of GDP*, faced default.

Concerns were raised about other European countries also on shaky fiscal footing: Spain, Portugal, and Italy, which, along with Ireland, faced budget deficits near or exceeding 10 % of GDP, had all seen their debt skyrocket starting in 2008 (Fig. 12.12).

Facing what threatened to escalate into a Europe-wide series of defaults, in May of 2010 the European Union, the IMF, and the European Central Bank moved to establish facilities of sufficient size, totaling €750 billion, to credibly signal a commitment not to let any member country default. An €85 billion rescue package was negotiated for Ireland in November of 2010. Market fears cooled for a time, with yields across Europe still elevated but significantly down from their peak. New concerns arose in early 2011 with the fall of several governments that had implemented austerity measures; investors' initial reaction to these developments was to once again shun these countries' debt.

Coordinated action on the part of European authorities from late 2011 onward, including expansion of the EFSF, massive intervention by the ECB,[14] and a series

---

[14] This intervention included direct purchases of Spanish and Italian bonds starting in August 2011 and some €500 billion in long-term refinancing operations (LTRO) starting in December 2011, where the ECB provided the continent's banks with 3-year loans and allowed the banks to use sovereign debt as collateral.

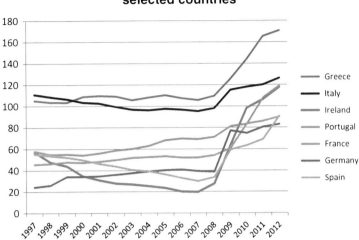

Fig. 12.12   European Gross Debt to GDP 1997–2012, selected countries (*Data Source: IMF*)

of extensions and concessions on previously negotiated terms with bailout recipients, has allowed the euro "to be kicked down the road" much longer than many analysts and economists anticipated. The precariousness and uncertainty surrounding these interventions was highlighted in late 2012 when the credit rating of the ESFS itself was downgraded due to concerns about France, its second-largest contributor.

Regardless of what occurs in the short term, the overhang of debt across Europe is nearly overwhelming, and it is unclear as of this writing if and in what manner sovereign debts across the region will ultimately be restructured.

12.4.10   The Future of the Euro

This episode has exposed important shortcomings of the single European currency, which can be boiled down to:

Single currency + Independent national budgets = Massive fiscal deficits

Single monetary policy + Fixed exchange rate = Persistent trade imbalances and high unemployment[15]

With the single European currency came a uniform European monetary policy. This allowed the national governments of the smaller and weaker states on the periphery, including Greece, Ireland, Italy, Portugal, Spain, and Belgium, to borrow

---

[15] A concise contemporary debate on the euro's future may be found in "The Euro's Debatable Future," *Wall Street Journal*, March 8, 2011.

at more favorable rates of interest than would have been available to them otherwise, and these countries ran persistent deficits and accumulated huge amounts of debt.

However, the inflow of capital masked underlying economic weakness, which became exposed once the business cycle turned (in this instance, with a vengeance). The weaker countries found themselves hopelessly indebted and saddled with a currency too strong for their fiscal and economic circumstances. The result has been high unemployment and persistent export weakness. The euro regime, in its present form, makes macroeconomic recovery significantly more difficult for these states.

On the flip side of the equation are the Germans, who have benefited from the euro as it is weaker than would be the German mark floating on its own. This has boosted Germany's export sector and fueled growth and has made it that much harder for countries such as Italy and Greece to compete in world markets against their powerful neighbor (who already leads them in productivity).

A unified currency works over a large geographic area when that area is culturally uniform and economically integrated, with a highly mobile (or potentially mobile) workforce. This has been largely true of the USA since its inception[16] and especially over the last century. The Euro area, however, is united neither in language nor culture, and while travel within Europe is unrestricted, these differences form significant barriers to migration. And, while Europe's economic cycles have increasingly synchronized, the individual economies remain far more diverse than those of any of the 50 US states. Finally, labor mobility within the euro zone, while increasing, is nowhere near the labor mobility found within the USA.

Should the crisis worsen, resolution will depend on German willingness to foot the bill, as it is the only European country with the economic and fiscal clout to deal with the situation. While macroeconomic analysis can inform us what the likely results are of various policy initiatives, ultimately, as often in these cases, the final decision will be a political one.

Political policymakers and central bankers, however, are not the only players with a say in the global macroeconomy. The best laid plans of fiscal and monetary authorities often run aground as seas of capital ebb and flow around them, driven by investors perpetually scanning the world economy for any opportunity that they may exploit.

This is.the focus of our next section.

12.5   Speculative Attacks and Overshooting

12.5.1   Speculative Attacks

Global investors, particularly those managing what is considered "hot capital"— funds that move quickly to the areas of the world with the best relative

---

[16] In the 1800s, disputes often arose between the agrarian states, which preferred easier monetary policy that would lighten their burden of debt and support exports, and the eastern bankers and industrialists who preferred a "hard money" regime.

opportunities—are keen to anticipate changes in exchange rates and will shift capital at the first sign of opportunity or trouble.

With billions under management, even minor fluctuations in interest and exchange rates offer the possibility of extraordinary gains or losses to large institutional investors and "global macro" hedge funds. The biggest opportunities present themselves when a pegged currency is perceived to be weaker than the official exchange rate and is under pressure.

Speculative attacks generally begin with a currency crisis arising from a combination of an artificially strong currency, unfavorable economic factors, and poor policy decisions. Non-sustainable budget deficits, the impending bursting of speculative asset bubbles, major bank failures, changes in government, or some external shock[17] may undermine confidence in a currency.

When this happens, investors holding assets denominated in the currency run for the exits, in order to preserve their capital. Very often, the currency crisis becomes self-reinforcing and self-fulfilling, as no one wants to be left holding the currency *after* it has been devalued.

Into this environment come the currency speculators, seeking to profit from the now-inevitable revaluation. These investors will "short" the weakening currency by borrowing it and selling it (exchanging it for another currency, in which they lend at short-term rates), in the anticipation that when they repay the loan, the currency will have declined significantly in value so that it may be repurchased at a fraction of the original price.

Taking the 1992 European currency crisis as an example, the exchange rate of the British pound in August 1992 was approximately $1.90 to £1 GBP (for the UK, $e = [1/1.90] = 0.526$). This was already perceived to be a stronger rate than would prevail under floating exchange rate conditions, and with German reunification and the Bundesbank's savage increase in interest rates, questions were raised whether Britain would send itself into a deep recession simply to preserve its currency peg. Very often, the seed of doubt is all that is required to sprout a vicious cycle.

The British raised interest rates as high as 15 % and spent some $30 billion in foreign exchange reserves in an attempt to preserve the value of the pound,[18] all of which came to naught. On September 16, 1992, the UK formally left the EMU and allowed its currency to adjust. The results were dramatic. The pound immediately declined in value, falling to $1.65 in October and all the way to around $1.40 to the USD within 5 months.

A speculator operating with US $1 billion might execute these transactions:

(a) Borrow UK £526.3 million for 30 days at 15 %.
(b) Convert the UK £526.3 million to US $1 billion at the rate of 1.9:1.

---

[17] For example, the UK currency crisis of 1992–1993 was precipitated by German reunification, and the Russian Ruble crisis of 1998 was caused in part by a sharp drop in the price of oil.

[18] As we have reviewed throughout, as domestic currency holders rush to convert their currency, their selling pressure which would otherwise weaken the exchange rate must be taken up by the Central Bank that purchases the domestic M with its reserves of FX.

(c) Buy US \$1 billion short-term US T-bills at the then-prevailing rate of 3 %.

If our speculator's timing was right, she would then, upon the devaluation:

(a) Redeem the T-bills for US \$1.0025 billion.
(b) Convert US \$879.3 million of the proceeds into UK £532.9 million at the new rate of 1.65:1.
(c) Repay the UK loan with the £532.9 million.

Her profit would be US \$123.2 million.

This is, roughly speaking, what George Soros famously did in 1992, but with \$10 billion, earning more than \$1 Billion in profit.

When currency speculators enter the fray, the volume of transactions exerts additional pressure on the currency. With enough pressure, the defender's reserves will be depleted and the currency will crash. This is a speculative raid or speculative attack. While the term implies collusion, in fact these operators are all watching the same data extremely closely, and the simultaneous and seemingly coordinated raids are simply the result of individual managers smelling blood in the water, rather than the result of any overt coordination.[19]

A country facing a speculative attack basically has three choices:

1. Defend the exchange rate by buying its currency using FX reserves
2. Raise interest rates sufficiently high to retain and attract capital
3. Allow the currency to depreciate

Empirical research shows that the second option, while undertaken in almost every case as part of the defensive strategy, is uncorrelated with success or failure in repelling speculative attacks.[20] Since most currency crises resolve themselves over a very short time horizon of a few months at most, raising short-term interest rates even as high as 20 % per annum or more offers investors slight return over horizons of only few months by comparison with what they risk should a devaluation occur. To the speculator, 6 % interest to borrow the currency for three or four months is a small price to pay when the potential returns are so large. Even the extraordinary 1992 Swedish increase in short-term rates to over 500 % could only temporarily postpone devaluation, as such an unsustainable policy is perceived as a sign of desperation rather than as a sign of commitment.

The key determinant in the success or failure of a speculative attack is the central bank's reserve of foreign currency. Once a country with an artificially strong currency runs out of foreign exchange to sell (buying its own currency to prop up its price), the game is over. During the 1997–1998 Asian crisis, Hong Kong successfully defended its peg because it started with a huge \$80 billion pool of

---

[19] This is not to say that overt coordination does not happen. In many of these instances, however, overt coordination is not required in order for active market participants to all see the same potential weakness in a given currency.

[20] Aart Kray, "Do High Interest Rates Defend Currencies During Speculative Attacks?" World Bank, December 2001

FX reserves to call upon and demonstrated that it was willing to use it. Hong Kong would deploy some US $15 billion of reserves in its successful defensive operation.

The study of currency crises has advanced over recent decades. The "first generation" models of the late 1970s and 1980s predicted that investors observing deteriorating fundamentals will bet on a devaluation and assumed that the authorities would expend all their reserves in an effort to defend their currency peg. "Second-generation" models, developed in the mid-1990s, added game-theoretical implications, where generally speaking investors may attack a currency if they believe other investors are likely to do so. The currency's government is part of the equation, as these models take into account the fact that the authorities may see a threat developing, deem their reserves to be inadequate to the task, and preemptively devalue.[21]

"Third-generation" currency crisis models of the late 1990s incorporate the banking system as a key player. In these models, bank liabilities are considered by investors in evaluating a currency's fundamentals, given the likelihood that in a crisis, the central authorities are likely to assume responsibility for their banks' debts. A seminal third-generation paper from 2000 succinctly anticipated the essence of the Icelandic banking crisis of 2008, which we discussed in Chap. 8: "In a world with government guarantees, it is optimal for banks to have an unhedged currency mismatch between their assets and liabilities. When a devaluation occurs, banks simply renege on foreign debt and go bankrupt."[22]

Speculative raids generally accompany any currency crisis where capital movement is not restricted and the opportunity exists to enter into a trade. High-profile cases from recent memory include the 1994 Mexican peso crisis, the 1998 Ruble crisis, and the Argentinean crises of 2000–2002.

In fact, these actions occur with surprising frequency. A partial list of successful and unsuccessful speculative currency attacks for the period 1975–2000 reveals 192 attacks, of which 78 were successful while 114 failed (Fig. 12.13):

12.5.2   Overshooting

Very often, a successful speculative currency attack will result in a depreciation below the presumed long-run equilibrium level of the currency.

We may illustrate overshooting with a hypothetical example.

---

[21] Olson O, He M (1999) A model of balance of payment crisis: the strong currency as a determinant of exchange rate disequilibria. Nova Southeastern University, Fort Lauderdale

[22] Burnside C, Eichenbaum M, Rebelo S (2000) Hedging and financial fragility in fixed exchange rate regimes, Financial Institutions & Market Research Center, Kellogg School of Management, Northwestern University, Evanston

Speculative Currency Attacks 1975-1999

Cur	Year	Outcome	Cur	Year	Outcome	Cur	Year	Outcome	Cur	Year	Outcome	Cur	Year	Outcome
ARG	1975	Successful	BOL	1979	Successful	MUS	1982	Failed	JOR	1988	Failed	FRA	1993	Failed
BWA	1975	Successful	CRI	1979	Failed	ZAF	1982	Failed	SWE	1988	Failed	IRL	1993	Successful
DNK	1975	Failed	FIN	1979	Failed	IDN	1983	Successful	TTO	1988	Failed	NAM	1993	Failed
IDN	1975	Failed	FRA	1979	Failed	JAM	1983	Successful	DNK	1989	Failed	PNG	1993	Failed
NAM	1975	Successful	MUS	1979	Successful	KOR	1983	Failed	GRC	1989	Failed	TTO	1993	Successful
PER	1975	Successful	NLD	1979	Failed	PHL	1983	Successful	GTM	1989	Successful	URY	1993	Failed
PRT	1975	Failed	NOR	1979	Failed	BWA	1984	Successful	IRL	1989	Failed	DOM	1994	Failed
TUR	1975	Failed	NZL	1979	Failed	CAN	1984	Failed	ISR	1989	Successful	MEX	1994	Successful
ZAF	1975	Successful	TUR	1979	Successful	NAM	1984	Successful	KOR	1989	Failed	MEX	1994	Failed
ZAF	1975	Failed	USA	1979	Failed	NZL	1984	Successful	PRY	1989	Successful	MUS	1994	Failed
AUS	1976	Successful	BEL	1980	Failed	PRY	1984	Successful	BOL	1990	Failed	PNG	1994	Successful
BEL	1976	Failed	DOM	1980	Failed	THA	1984	Successful	CAN	1990	Failed	THA	1994	Failed
CAN	1976	Failed	FIN	1980	Successful	THA	1984	Failed	DOM	1990	Successful	TTO	1994	Failed
DNK	1976	Failed	ITA	1980	Failed	VEN	1984	Successful	FIN	1990	Successful	ARG	1995	Failed
DOM	1976	Failed	KOR	1980	Successful	ZAF	1984	Successful	ITA	1990	Failed	COL	1995	Failed
FIN	1976	Failed	KOR	1980	Failed	ECU	1985	Successful	PRT	1990	Failed	ESP	1995	Successful
JAM	1976	Failed	MAR	1980	Failed	PRT	1985	Failed	SWE	1990	Failed	VEN	1995	Successful
MEX	1976	Successful	MYS	1980	Failed	THA	1985	Failed	THA	1990	Failed	FIN	1996	Failed
MUS	1976	Failed	SWE	1980	Failed	TTO	1985	Successful	FIN	1991	Successful	KOR	1996	Failed
NLD	1976	Failed	ZAF	1980	Failed	BEL	1986	Failed	FIN	1991	Successful	BRA	1997	Failed
NOR	1976	Failed	ARG	1981	Successful	IDN	1986	Successful	HKG	1991	Failed	GRC	1997	Failed
SGP	1976	Failed	BOL	1981	Failed	IRL	1986	Successful	IDN	1991	Failed	GTM	1997	Successful
SWE	1976	Failed	CAN	1981	Failed	IRL	1986	Failed	SWE	1991	Failed	IDN	1997	Failed
SWE	1976	Failed	CRI	1981	Successful	ITA	1986	Failed	TUN	1991	Failed	KOR	1997	Successful
ZAF	1976	Failed	ITA	1981	Failed	MYS	1986	Failed	ARG	1992	Failed	PHL	1997	Successful
ESP	1977	Successful	MUS	1981	Successful	NOR	1986	Successful	BEL	1992	Failed	THA	1997	Successful
FIN	1977	Successful	MYS	1981	Failed	PHL	1986	Failed	BOL	1992	Failed	BWA	1998	Successful
ISR	1977	Successful	NLD	1981	Failed	PRY	1986	Successful	BWA	1992	Successful	DNK	1998	Failed
PER	1977	Successful	ZAF	1981	Failed	TUN	1986	Failed	ECU	1992	Successful	FIN	1998	Failed
SWE	1977	Successful	AUS	1982	Failed	VEN	1986	Successful	GBR	1992	Successful	GRC	1998	Successful
TUR	1977	Successful	BEL	1982	Successful	BOL	1987	Failed	ITA	1992	Successful	HKG	1998	Failed
AUT	1978	Failed	BOL	1982	Successful	DNK	1987	Failed	NOR	1992	Failed	MEX	1998	Successful
CAN	1978	Failed	DOM	1982	Failed	DOM	1987	Successful	SWE	1992	Successful	NAM	1998	Successful
IDN	1978	Successful	ECU	1982	Successful	ESP	1987	Failed	THA	1992	Failed	PNG	1998	Failed
JAM	1978	Successful	ESP	1982	Successful	ITA	1987	Failed	DNK	1993	Successful	SWE	1998	Failed
THA	1978	Successful	FIN	1982	Successful	JOR	1987	Failed	DNK	1993	Failed	URY	1998	Failed
AUS	1979	Failed	GTM	1982	Failed	PER	1987	Successful	FRA	1993	Failed	ZAF	1998	Successful
AUT	1979	Failed	MAR	1982	Failed	GRC	1988	Failed	IRL	1993	Successful	BRA	1999	Successful
BEL	1979	Failed	MEX	1982	Successful	IDN	1988	Failed	NAM	1993	Failed	MUS	1999	Failed

Fig. 12.13 Speculative currency attacks, 1975–1999. **Successful attacks** are defined as large depreciations preceded by a period of stable fixed exchange rates. **Failed attacks** are defined as downward spikes in reserves accompanied by upward spikes in short-term default risk, which are not followed by devaluation within 3 months (*Source: "Do High Interest Rates Defend Currencies During Speculative Attacks?" Aart Kray, World Bank, December 2001*)

The Belize (BZD) dollar has been pegged to the US dollar since 1978 at the rate of 2:1. The currency is generally considered to be slightly stronger than the rate implies and trades in range of BZ$1.90 to BZ$2.00 to US $1.

Let's say that a combination of a steep worldwide drop in the price of sugar, the country's main export, the threat of a change in government over to a radical party with an uncertain outcome, and a sharp decline in tourism due to this political uncertainty puts the BZD's 2:1 USD peg under pressure. Market experts evaluating the situation estimate the fair value of the BZD at perhaps 2.6–1 USD, were it permitted to float. Nervous investors sell their BZD-denominated financial assets where they can and undertake expensive hedges where they can't. Speculators pile in, adding to the pressure.

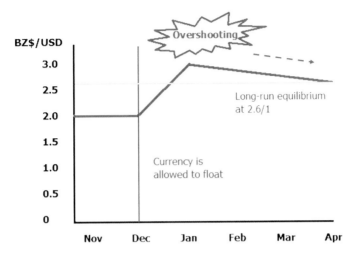

Fig. 12.14 Overshooting

For a while the central bank valiantly defends the peg, raising short-term interest rates as high as 25 %; alas, the country's reserves are insufficient and ultimately the BZD is allowed to float. The exchange rate skyrockets as there are no buyers; no one wants to hold BZD until the dust settles and the exchange rate moderates. In a few weeks, the BZD is trading at 3:1 USD.

At this point, speculators come in to take their profits, bringing demand, and the exchange rate stabilizes. Seeing some measure of stability, investors and those doing business in Belize return to BZD-denominated assets and slowly drop their costly hedging transactions. The increased demand boosts the currency toward its long-run equilibrium level of 2.6:1 USD.

This is a practical example of **Overshooting**, which occurs whenever a change in circumstances results in a shift from one disequilibrium point to another disequilibrium point in the opposite direction, which eventually moderates toward long-run equilibrium (Fig. 12.14).

The cause of overshooting in this example was the tremendous *uncertainty* of the expected exchange rate (e^e) prior to the devaluation, as expectations of an imminently bursting peg ratcheted up selling activity. While there may be a consensus on the currency's long-run "fair value," this means little to the businessperson who needs to operate in Belize next month or the investor who is responsible for generating quarterly returns. In a crisis, people generally seek to "play it safe"—and this means abandoning the currency where possible. However, "momentum-based" overshooting, while supported by recent research in behavioral economics, is not the only type.

Rudiger Dornbusch, in his seminal 1976 paper "Expectations and Exchange Rate Dynamics," explained how overshooting may occur *as a necessary result* when certain variables in a mathematical identity are "stickier" than others; that is, some variables may adjust instantly, while others take time to adjust. We discussed

Fig. 12.15 Currency
depreciation followed
by inflation

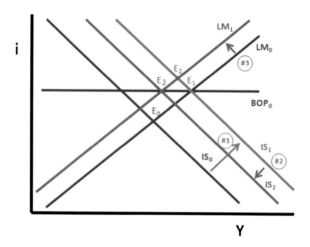

this when comparing the relative slopes of the LM curve and the BOP curve—the
difference in slopes being due to the faster speed at which variables related to
capital (KAB) adjust compared with the slower movement of variables related
to goods and services (CAB).

Recall the formula for the real exchange rate: $R = (P^*e)/P$. We know that real
exchange rates will generally tend toward parity (while rarely, if ever, meeting
strict parity of $R = 1$). So, a large change in one of the variables will be followed by
a change in another, compensating variable, over time, to return the real exchange
rate to equilibrium. A sudden change in the exchange rate, e, will therefore require a
compensating change in the price level, P. However, exchange rates change near
instantly, while prices are sticky and move much more slowly.

Overshooting due to the difference in the timeliness of movement between the
price of currency and the prices of goods can be illustrated through an ISLM-BOP
example:

Let's take a country that loses a fight to defend its currency following a BOP
crisis.

Here in Fig. 12.15 we start with Country A, with a currency peg of 5:1 USD,
under speculative attack with the BOP in disequilibrium (E_0 is in BOP deficit).
When the currency peg breaks despite A's best efforts to preserve it, the currency
weakens ($e\uparrow$) from 5:1 to 8:1 USD and the IS shifts from IS_0 to IS_1. This adjustment
happens over a short period of weeks or months as the speculative pressures built up
during the currency attack blow themselves out. The economy settles at a new
short-term equilibrium at E_1.

Over time, however, the weaker currency makes imports more expensive,
increasing the price of key raw imports and consumer staples, leading to inflation.
As the price level increases ($P\uparrow$), this causes a shift in the **LM** curve from **LM_0** to
LM_1. This process takes more time than the exchange-rate adjustment, however, as
even instantaneous price increases from overseas suppliers take weeks or months to
reach consumers.

We are once again in disequilibrium as the new goods market–money market equilibrium E_2 (where IS_1 and LM_1 intersect) is in BOP surplus (SFX>DFX). As our currency is freely floating, the IS curve does the adjustment into equilibrium, with the currency exchange rate strengthening ($e\downarrow$) from 8:1 to 7:1 USD. The IS curve shifts from IS_1 to IS_2, and our new equilibrium point is at E_3.

So, this example of overshooting saw our exchange rate initially shoot upward, from 5:1 to 8:1, then strengthen back to a new equilibrium at 7:1, due to a delay between the adjustments to the numerator and denominator of the real exchange rate $R = (P*e)/P$. "Momentum" based on the herd behavior of investors had nothing to do with it.

In practice, overshooting likely involves both behavioral and structural forces, though these may be difficult to distill from the data.

In either case, it is important to note that it is independent (primarily institutional) investors and businesspeople, rather than governments or monetary authorities, who are driving these massive macroeconomic shifts. Often the final results are exactly counter to what authorities seek to achieve. Just how much power do the authorities have versus independent financial and business actors in the global macroeconomy? We turn next to address this question.

12.6 Bigger Than Central Banks? Global Investors and the Balance of Financial Power

We generally take the power of the central bank for granted. It is "in charge" of our money, on which its name, and often its image, appear. It sets interest rates, controls the quantity of money in circulation, and establishes the rules by which the banks operating under its authority maintain their reserves. When central bankers issue their often obscure pronouncements, politicians, economists, and investors the world over parse their every word for hidden meaning. And no matter what else happens, the central bank can always simply "print" as much (or as little) money as it wants.

After all, "You can't fight the Fed!" But then...

- How was it possible during the EMU crisis of 1992 for a few global investors to overwhelm the power of the Bank of England, one of the oldest and most powerful financial institutions in the world?
- Why, despite two decades of easy monetary policy from the 1980s into the 2000s, was the Bank of Japan unable to spur economic growth?
- How were entire economies in Southeast Asia overwhelmed by flows of hot capital in the late 1990s?
- And why was the ECB unable to contain the spread of the European sovereign crisis of 2010–2011?

At the time official central banks were first established in the West, beginning in the late seventeenth century, they did in fact represent a significant concentration of financial power. So much so that the United States, with distrust of central authority built into its DNA, launched, then closed, two official banks over its first hundred years of existence before finally establishing the Federal Reserve in a peak era of progressive activism in 1913, the last major economic power of the era to do so. Central banks do not lack for power; they typically have independent control over monetary policy, intervene in foreign exchange markets at will, are the lenders of last resort to the banking system, and in many countries play a large regulatory role as well.

And let us not forget that the central bank can, actually, create money at will.[23]

However, just like the Wizard of Oz, central banks often rely more on their reputation and image than on actual brute financial force. Their raw power is in fact more limited than many would assume.[24]

12.6.1   Size

We can begin by simply looking at the size of the balance sheets of the world's monetary authorities relative to those of the world's private pools of capital.

---

[23] Or at least out of electrons in the form of bytes of information in electronic transactions.

[24] For the likening of central bankers to the Wizard of Oz we are indebted to John Hussman, Ph.D., who wrote that "Alan Greenspan isn't 'The Maestro.' He's Oz," in *Why the Federal Reserve is Irrelevant*, Hussman Funds Research & Insight, August, 2001, accessed November 18, 2011, http://www.hussmanfunds.com/html/fedirrel.htm. See also "Superstition and the Fed", October, 2006, accessed November 18, 2011. http://www.hussmanfunds.com/wmc/wmc061002.htm. Dr. Hussman's writings, available at the aforementioned site, are indispensable to those seeking to understand contemporary financial markets from an analytical and historical perspective.

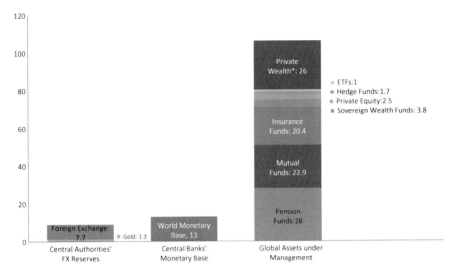

Fig. 12.16 World FX reserves, monetary base, and private assets under management 2009–2010 (in trillions of USD). Private wealth is a net figure of the $39 trillion in privately managed assets of high net worth individuals less $13 trillion which falls under other categories in the chart. Foreign Exchange Reserves are held by central banks or government treasuries, depending on the country. The majority (>60%) are held in US-Dollar denominated assets, with ~30% in Euro, and 10% in other currency-denominated assets, primarily Japanese Yen and British Pounds. The world monetary base is a fair proxy for the scale of the world's central banks in the global financial picture. Total assets of the world's central banks are perhaps 30% to 50% higher than this figure as central bank debt and other liabilities add to the total. Nevertheless, the scope of credible monetary policy does bear a relation to the current monetary base at any given time. (*Data sources: Natixis, Credit Suisse, Boston Consulting Group, TheCityUK*)

The world's central banks and government treasuries held a combined total of roughly US $9 trillion in foreign exchange reserves in 2010, of which $1.3 trillion was in gold, and $7.7 trillion was in foreign currency and bonds. The combined monetary base of the world's central banks totaled some US $13 trillion.[25] These are impressive figures. The combined assets under management (AUM) of the world's investors, on the other hand, totaled around $106 trillion.[26] Comparing the scale of the resources at the disposal of official monetary authorities versus global investors is illustrative (Fig. 12.16).

Clearly there are pools of assets that dwarf the combined resources of all the world's central banks. Blackrock, the world's largest asset manager as of December

---

[25] Artus P (2011) Do central banks withdraw liquidity they have created? Natixis Flash Markets Economic Research, February 4, 2011 (Paris: Natixis, 2011)

[26] Marko Maslakovic, *Fund Management 2010* (London: UK, October 2010_. See also *BCG Report, Global Asset Management 2010: In Search of Stable Growth* (Boston: Boston Consulting Group, July 2010).

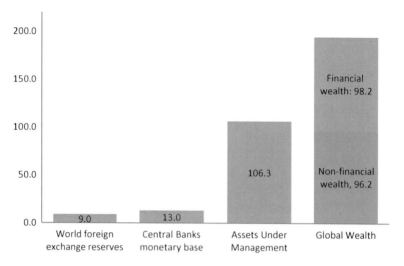

Fig. 12.17 World FX reserves and monetary base versus private assets under management and total global wealth, 2009–2010, USD trillions (*Data sources: Natixis, Credit Suisse, Boston Consulting Group, TheCityUK*)

31, 2010, had some $3.6 trillion under management.[27] The sum of the assets managed by this single private entity is greater than that of the People's Bank of China, the world's largest central bank by total assets, as well as that of the (bloated, as of 2010) US Federal Reserve.

New entities have entered the picture, whose effect on the world's financial markets is as yet uncertain. Sovereign wealth funds, pools of government capital held outside the central bank and deployed for financial gain, have proliferated since the 1990s. The funds held by the Abu Dhabi Investment Authority (US $627 billion), Norway's Government Pension Fund Global ($443 billion), and Saudi Arabia's SAMA Foreign Holdings ($415 billion) exceed those of all but the world's largest central banks.

And, counting "assets under management" only conveys part of the picture. Global wealth, including both financial assets and nonfinancial wealth such as housing, real estate, and small business assets, totaled $194 trillion in 2010[28] (Fig. 12.17).

---

[27] Blackrock, "About Us," accessed March 27, 2011. www2.blackrock.com. http://www2.blackrock.com/global/home/AboutUs/index.htm.

[28] *Global Wealth Databook*, Credit Suisse Research Institute (Geneva: Credit Suisse Group AG), August 2010. Note: Figures for global wealth vary significantly depending on how the studies' authors accounted for currency effects. While Credit Suisse arrives at a figure of $194 trillion for 2010, the Boston Consulting Group, using a methodology that eliminates certain currency effects, comes up with a figure of $114 trillion.

Should a government or central bank seek to "defy gravity" by maintaining a policy that runs counter to market forces (e.g., by maintaining an artificially strong exchange rate), it is clear that the market of global investment funds is sufficiently large so as to overwhelm such efforts if they persist for long.

In the words of economist Herbert Stein, "If something cannot continue, it won't."

However, despite being outgunned, the central authorities do hold powerful tools that are denied to non-state actors. Let's examine the tools at the central bank's disposal.

12.6.2   FX Intervention

The "FX" lever is a powerful tool by which the central bank may manage the domestic currency's exchange rate.

The central bank can artificially create a "strong" exchange rate by selling foreign exchange and buying up domestic currency. However, this policy is limited by the bank's finite reserves of foreign exchange. When it runs out of FX, it's "game over" for a strong-currency policy. This scenario has played out in countless speculative attacks. The bank may borrow FX from other central banks to continue for a while, but once investors see this happening, the full fury of market forces will be unleashed against the bank's efforts. Unless the authorities have sufficient resources to credibly maintain a defense, as Hong Kong did in the 1997–1998 crisis, their efforts must eventually fail.

A "weak" currency may generally be maintained for a longer period of time, as has been the case with China for the first decade-plus of this century. This is accomplished by buying up FX with newly issued domestic currency. The limits of this policy are eventually reached, however, as the increase in domestic money stock leads inevitably to inflation and an appreciation of the real exchange rate. "Sterilization," which we explore in the next chapter, involves the central bank removing this money through open-market operations or adjustment to the RRR. This may hold inflation at bay for a time. Such a policy, however, is highly distortive if maintained for an extended period as it leads to overinvestment in export-related manufacturing, atrophy among domestic-focused manufacturers, underdevelopment of the service sector which is a key component of an advanced economy, and impoverishment of domestic consumers through the significant dilution of their purchasing power.

12.6.3   Monetary Policy

The "M" lever is another powerful tool, which unlike FX intervention, is not limited by a finite stock of reserves. Surely such power tilts the playing field in the central bank's favor—after all, the authorities can "print money" at will!

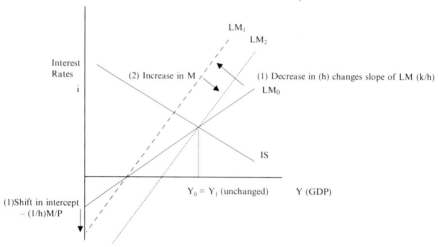

Fig. 12.18 Liquidity trap

The central bank uses three standard tools to alter the quantity of money in circulation: open-market operations, adjusting the required reserve ratio, and setting the discount rate. Unconventional policies, many of which were unleashed during the post-2007 period, include lending programs to non-bank institutions, the purchase of longer-dated government bonds, the purchase of government-sponsored agency securities, and the purchase of private-sector assets.

The central bank may also resort to outright monetization—the direct purchase of new on-the-run government debt.

There are key limitations to monetary policy, however. These include:

(i) The central bank can influence the supply of money and credit, but it has no direct influence over the *demand* for money or credit. We saw this in the "liquidity trap" example which we briefly examined in Chap. 9. When money demand becomes insensitive to changes in interest rates, even a significant increase in money supply will fail to affect output (Fig. 12.18).

Recall the LM equilibrium equation:

$$i = \left[\frac{k}{h}\right]Y - \left[\frac{1}{h}\right]\left[\frac{M}{P} + FX\right]$$

The decrease in the sensitivity of money demand to changes in interest rates ("h") both increases the slope and drops the intercept of the LM line. This renders an increase in "M" impotent to generate an increase in output from its original level. These scenarios normally include a drop in the IS line due to collapsing confidence, which we have not shown here; this further exacerbates the effect,

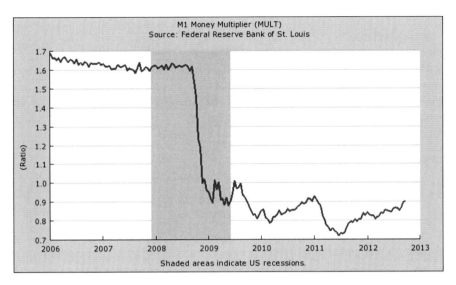

Fig. 12.19 M1 money multiplier 2006–2012 (*Source: St. Louis Fed*)

pushing Y lower. A real-world example was evidenced by the severe drop in the "money multiplier" in advanced countries following the financial crisis of 2007–2009. A huge increase in base money simply sat as idle bank reserves with few takers among commercial borrowers. The overall total of money and credit in the economy actually declined despite the explosion in base money (Fig. 12.19).

Essentially, under certain circumstances, active monetary policy becomes useless.[29]

(ii) "Seigniorage" is the term used to denote the value gained by the central government by the issuance of new currency into existence. At the time the currency is first issued, the overall economy has not yet adjusted itself to the fact of an increased quantity of money in circulation. Thus, the first to have their hands on this newly issued money (banks, under open-market operations, or the central government under monetization) will enjoy real purchasing power which dissipates as the market adjusts its expectations to the new level of money supply.[30]

---

[29] See James Bullard, "Seven Faces of 'The Peril," *Federal Reserve Bank of St. Louis Review*, September–October 2010 St. Louis: St. Louis Fed, 2010) for a thorough discussion of the effectiveness of monetary policy during and after the 2008–2009 crisis.

[30] The similarity of these operations to counterfeiting has long been remarked upon. The counterfeiter, having his hands on the newly printed money before anyone else, gains real value; as the volume of his notes enter circulation, they add to the money stock and ultimately dilute everyone's purchasing power. However, by the time this happens, the counterfeiter, like the legitimate currency issuer and those closest to it, has already made his gain. For a lengthy treatment from this perspective, see Murray N. Rothbard, *The Case Against the Fed*, Ludwig von Mises Institute, 2007.

This is an ancient practice with a long tradition. In past millennia, seigniorage was accomplished by diluting the gold content in various coins or "clipping" the edges by some percentage and using the clipped portion to create new coins.

However, while the monetary authorities can theoretically "print" as much money as they want, the utility of this exercise quickly becomes limited as the public learns to expect a depreciation in the currency's purchasing power. A limit is eventually approached in the real value gained through seigniorage,[31] beyond which the policy is self-defeating and leads to monetary and financial collapse.

12.6.4   The Limits of Active Policy in an Open Economy

We have seen in Chaps. 8 and 10 how interest parity and purchasing power parity dictate that manipulation of the exchange rate will be mitigated, in real terms, by endogenous adjustment of interest rates and price levels—returning the real exchange rate back to parity or near-parity.

And, in Chap. 11, we saw how active monetary policy may be counteracted by both inflation and exchange-rate adjustments (under floating rates) and an outflow of foreign exchange (under fixed rates).

Thus, the world's monetary authorities, though backed by the power of their sovereigns and with seemingly unlimited ability to call money into and out of existence, are both severely outgunned by global investors with respect to total financial resources in the marketplace and are in practice somewhat constrained in their actual ability to directly affect outcomes.

12.6.5   The Source of a Central Bank's Power

> We knew how much of banking depended upon make-believe or, stated more conservatively, the vital part that public confidence had in assuring solvency.
>
> *Raymond Moley, FDR Presidential Advisor 1932–1936*

> "Pay no attention to that man behind the curtain! The Great Oz has spoken!"
>
> *- The Wizard of Oz (1939)*

---

[31] The limit is a function of nominal interest rates, inflation, and GDP growth. A discussion may be found in Willem H. Buiter, "Can Central Banks Go Broke?" London: Centre for Economic Policy Research, May 2008.

Raymond Moley (1886–1975), Associated Press

The most powerful weapons in a central bank's arsenal are its credibility and the confidence that the public has in its prudent management of monetary policy. We have seen the power of confidence to affect economic outcomes in our models, as shifts in $\underline{C}$ and $\underline{I}$ may cause large moves in the **IS** curve. A central bank's credibility is built over time through sound management of the currency and banking system and by keeping inflation contained.

Central bankers know better than anyone the actual limitations of their policy tools when deployed against the vast forces of the market. Their efforts therefore are largely directed toward managing *expectations*, in the hope of affecting market sentiment—so that the market will voluntarily move in the desired direction or at least soften its resistance. The pronouncements of central bankers are deliberately obscure, leaving room for interpretation, as explicit statements may "pin down" the monetary authorities, reducing their flexibility for action and potentially harming their credibility should events move in a manner contrary to their statements.

The veil of secrecy over many of the activities of the central bank aids its efforts. The exact nature of its foreign exchange interventions, discount-window lending, and internal deliberations are often kept secret from the public, who are left to parse every utterance of the bank's representatives in the manner of Sovietologists of old studying the position of various Politburo members in the parade stand on Red Square.

When a central bank telegraphs its intention to hold interest rates low "for an extended period," for example, investors will hesitate to bet against that outcome. A "crawling peg" works in much the same way—if the authorities indicate a planned, gradual depreciation of a strong currency, investors will be less likely to bet on a sharp break, even if the planned depreciation still leaves the currency stronger than market rates would dictate.

Confidence is a fragile thing and takes years to build. And it can be destroyed very quickly.

12.6.6   *The Straw That Breaks the Camel's Back*

Despite the vast aggregate sum of financial resources commanded by the world's investors, only a small fraction consists of "hot money" or potential hot money.

The world's 7,000 or so hedge funds, which represent a significant portion of the world's potential "hot money," only manage around US $2 trillion combined, with "global macro" strategies representing perhaps 20 % of the total.[32]

Speculative attacks, discussed in the section above, are generally spearheaded by this relatively small pool of capital. How then are they so often successful?

The key is the asymmetry in the way people evaluate potential gain and loss. Positive feelings, including the confidence which the central bank seeks to build brick by brick, take a long time to develop. Investors are constantly on the lookout for threats to their capital—this is why, for example, stocks are said to climb "a wall of worry" when they are rising. Fear, however, is powerful and contagious, and market declines are almost invariably much sharper and more severe than gains.[33] Relatively small amounts of hot money piling on against a currency peg can have the same effect as yelling "fire" in a crowded theater; investors tend to run for the exits to avoid even the chance of being burned.[34] Larger, slower-moving pools of capital, observing the speculative bets, will check their risk exposure and may take action to protect themselves. Even long-term investors in the domestic economy may become concerned enough to hedge their currency and other exposure, and global firms may begin to shift production and resources to other countries.

A central bank attempting to maintain a policy at odds with these movements, whether in exchange rate or monetary policy, will quickly find itself facing an increasing number of forces arrayed against it.

In the long-run, market forces invariably prevail, though prudent fiscal and monetary policy and deft management of expectations can successfully ward off the adjustment for long enough that other factors come to reshape market pressures. Moreover, extremes of euphoria and fear are fleeting, and the monetary authority may successfully maintain its policy long enough for passions to cool and reason to reassert itself. A country might "buy time" for its domestic industry to recover from a sharp recession with a period of normally non-sustainable monetary policy; likewise, the disruption from an impending currency crash may be held off long enough for a country to get its fiscal house in order to provide underlying strength to the currency. And, at times, investors may simply be wrong about a perceived

---

[32] As of 2008 per RaisePartner Quantitative Portfolio Management, "Global Macro Strategies: Fundamental Expertise and Quantitative Modeling," The Quant Corner November 2008 (Paris: Raisepartner, 2008), accessed March 27, 2011, http://www.raisepartner.com/lexique/files/488344.pdf.

[33] The best treatment ever on this subject is Charles Mackay's 1841 classic *Extraordinary Popular Delusions and the Madness of Crowds*, which we mentioned in Chap. 11. A modern classic is Charles Kindleberger and Robert Aliber's *Manias, Panics and Crashes: A History of Financial Crises*, Sixth Edition (Palgrave Macmillan, 2011).

[34] The old adage applies: "If there is going to be a panic, it's best to be first!"

weakness, and the bank may succeed in holding off the onslaught for long enough for these misperceptions to correct themselves.

Central bank efforts to implement and maintain their desired policies are part of a battle that plays out every day in the marketplace through hundreds of billions of dollars' worth of transactions.

Articles

Article 12.1. The Sarangam Economy: A Retrospective

Dr. Peter Parks, *East Brunswick Economic Review*

The "happy years" were indeed happy. Things were good all over for the Sarangam economy with its openness to foreign capital and fixed exchange rates; housing, jobs, the stock market, interest rates, food prices, even the weather had cooperated. But then after about four euphoric years in which books such as "The Sarangam Century", "Behold the Sarangam Economic Miracle", and the enticing, "100 Ways to Invest in Sarangam and Get a Slice of the Pie" dominated the best-seller lists, cracks began to appear.

At first the warnings sounded like a peevish naysayer's ramblings against an economy that was the poster child for macroeconomic growth. But then the lone sirens began to have company. More and more analysts began to notice the cracks that mysteriously appeared and then grew quickly into myriads of fault planes. Suddenly the "growth" was being dismissed simply as "not real" and mainly as asset price bubbles. Sarangam's exceptionally tall Paradise Tower was lambasted as the "Tower of Babel—an unintelligible project." The country's new aircraft carrier program was derided as "the fleet built for tourism," and President Me King Ling's fourth palace—this one made of exquisite malachite imported in special barges from the Ukraine—was fodder for late-night talk shows.(a)

The macro outlook suddenly crumbled when it became evident from Finance Minster Me Noking's comments that the peg would be difficult to sustain if foreign investors and foreign investment houses kept frantically pulling their money out of Sarangam. It was even rumored that the legendary financier Jorge Sideous was placing massive one-way bets against the currency.(b) With the currency under severe pressure, and with the economic outlook dropping remorselessly, the Central Bank of Sarangam finally de-pegged the local currency, the Mekong, and saw it depreciate immediately by 35 %. (c)

It seemed that the rapidly depreciated currency would actually pull the country out from its self-made mess by stimulating its exports, (d) but then after about 4 weeks the inflation became impossible to ignore—in fact, it was crippling. Output slumped back down as the currency appreciated by roughly 15 %, and interest rates that had shot up with the rise in prices following the devaluation subsided to some degree.(e)

By the time the dust had settled, final output growth was pretty much where it was before the big devaluation, but interest rates remained stubbornly high along with the residual inflation, which seems to be a legacy of the "Happy Times" that Saranganians are now trying to forget.

Hints and Solutions

Article 12.1

(a) Sarangam has obviously enjoyed an economic boom that has gone too far and has included speculative asset price bubbles. Generally such a boom would include "cheap money," interest rates maintained too low for too long, and a surfeit of hot capital flows finding their way into riskier and riskier assets.

At the point where the imminent collapse of the bubble becomes obvious, as it has here, we will see a significant drop in the long-term macroeconomic outlook for Sarangam (**Pr↓**).

The BOP rises as Pr falls—we find ourselves in BOP deficit (DFX>SFX) at point E_0 in Fig. 12.20 below.

Here, we face the prospect of a hard landing as FX flees the country, pushing the LM line back to LM_1.

(b) Jorge Sideous is launching a speculative attack on the currency—which he would undertake by:

(i)   Borrowing in Sarangam's currency
(ii) Selling the borrowed currency at its present conversion rate and investing the proceeds in his domestic currency

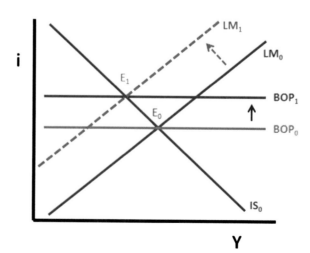

Fig. 12.20 Declining macro outlook (Pr↓), fixed rates, PMK

Fig. 12.21 Given declining macro outlook (Pr↓), fixed rates, PMK: proceed to weaken the currency

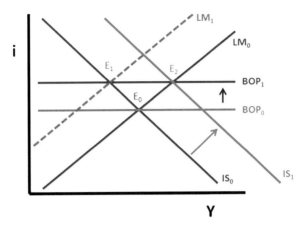

(iii) Waiting for Sarangam's monetary and political authorities to succumb to the pressure and break their peg, or at a minimum revalue at a weaker exchange rate

(iv) Upon the devaluation, convert his domestic currency into Sarangam currency and repay the original loan

Sideous' profit would come from the gain made on the devaluation (iv), plus whatever interest he earned on his invested funds from (ii), less whatever interest he had to pay on the borrowed funds (iv).

(c) The central bank's move will ensure that the shift into general equilibrium will be done by the IS curve through the weakening of the exchange rate (**e**↓), rather than by the LM curve as was the only option under fixed rates (see [a], above).

So, the IS curve shifts from IS_0 to IS_1 to attain E_2 as we see in Fig. 12.21. Here, we have avoided the hard landing (for now) and spurred exports, but we have also activated the forces of inflation.

(d) As the currency depreciates, exports become cheaper and output, therefore, increases. We can see this if we drop the X and V curves below the ISLM-BOP curve, as we do in Fig. 12.22.

We started the X and V curves in hypothetical positions where Sarangam initially had a current account deficit ("**CAB-**"on the graph), and with exports growing and imports shrinking in response to the weakening exchange rate, the current account deficit has been erased and is now a surplus. (This is not a necessary result—it would depend on the initial positions of the X and V curves. The consistent result, however, will be an increase in the CAB from its starting point).

(e) Here we have prices increasing (**P**↑) so LM snaps back to LM_1 to a new IS–LM intersection at E_3. The BOP surplus condition (SFX>DFX) is resolved by a strengthening of the now-floating currency (**e**↓), and the IS then drops back to IS_2. The economy ultimately comes to rest at equilibrium point E_4 (Fig. 12.23). Sarangam is left with reduced output from the exorbitant levels seen immediately after the depreciation at Y_1, but still higher than it was originally.

Fig. 12.22 Given declining macro outlook (Pr↓), fixed rates, PMK: results from weakening the currency, including effects on imports and exports

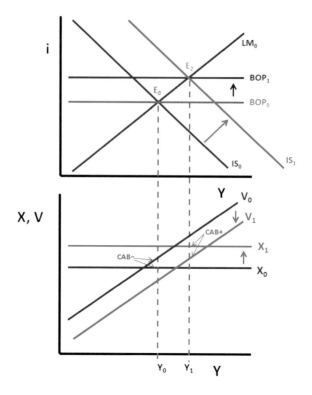

Fig. 12.23 Given floating rates, PMK: inflation and strengthening currency following a sharp depreciation

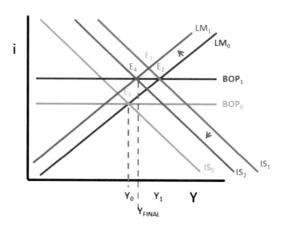

Thanks to the modest rebound in the strength of the currency—a classic example of "overshooting"—interest rates moderate from where they would have been at E_3. Interest rates and prices, however, remain elevated from what they were before the episode began in (a) above.

Chapter 13
The Global Monetary System

Summary In the last chapter, we began to explore major aspects of the global monetary system in the early decades of the twenty-first century: fiscal sustainability in the face of large public deficits, the euro, speculative attacks and the role of huge pools of capital in driving market forces which often frustrate the designs of macro policymakers.

In this chapter, we deepen our discussion of the global monetary system. Foreign exchange sterilization is explained in detail. It emerges through careful exposition that this can only be an effective policy over the short run.

What do we make of the dollar–yuan and the euro–yuan sagas? How crucial is China's "managing" of its exchange rate to US–China trade imbalances, and what is the effect of this currency intervention on China's economy? And as the yuan has progressively appreciated since 2005, how relevant is the yuan intervention saga? Answering these questions provides an excellent opportunity to further develop our understanding of the relationship between exchange rates, trade policy, fiscal and monetary policy, and global capital flows.

The US dollar's role as the world's "reserve currency" has come to be questioned by many observers since the global financial crisis of 2007–2008 whose epicenter was the USA. What does reserve currency status mean for the US dollar and the US economy? What are the alternatives to the dollar? We explore these issues in depth in this chapter.

Finally, a question that has been raised with increasing frequency lately, not just by academic economists but also practitioners such as investment bankers and senior central bank officials, is: Will the gold standard return? Why are such a wide range of policymakers and economists calling for the return of some gold-based standard? And why was it abandoned anyway?

F. Langdana and P.T. Murphy, *International Trade and Global Macropolicy*, 343
Springer Texts in Business and Economics, DOI 10.1007/978-1-4614-1635-7_13,
© Springer Science+Business Media New York 2014

Fig. 13.1 China macro
outlook is great ☺ (**Pr**↑),
fixed rates, perfectly mobile
capital

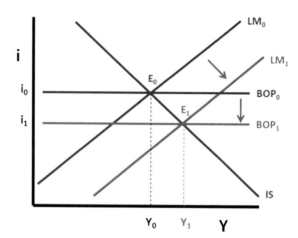

13.1   Foreign Exchange Sterilization

Earlier, in examining the Southeast Asian crisis of 1997–1998, we discussed the
situation wherein a very positive economic outlook (**Pr**↑) in a regime of fixed
exchange rates can attract a flood of overseas capital and overheat the economy.
Singapore's Dr. Hu inoculated the country's economy from the worst of the
inevitable crisis by prudently adjusting the exchange rate over time, allowing the
currency to gradually strengthen during the boom (**e**↓). Some of the boom growth
was thus sacrificed in return for reduced exposure to overheating.

A country may desire, for whatever reason, to maintain its peg despite a flood of
incoming foreign exchange (FX). China, particularly from 2004 to 2010, provides a
good example of such a scenario characterized by exuberant growth and an
inundation of foreign capital seeking to get in on the action.

We know the story: A huge increase in long-term outlook (**Pr**↑) pushes the **BOP**
line down↓. The **LM** also adjusts down↓ (as **FX**↑). Output soars, interest rates are
low, and before long, the pressure on the economy to overheat, with the usual
attendant speculative asset bubbles, is overwhelming (Fig. 13.1).[1]

1. **Pr** ↑ (☺ long-term macro outlook) →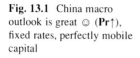
   BOP₀↓ to **BOP₁**
2. **E₀** is in BOP surplus, S̲FX > DFX, fixed rates → **FX**↑
3. Fixed rates: **LM₀** adjusts↓ to **LM₁** and new equilibrium is found at **E₁**
4. Result

   Y↑, **i**↓, overheating, SAP bubbles forming…

---

[1] China's capital mobility is imperfect; we use the horizontal BOP here to keep the graph simple.
The results are not meaningfully affected.

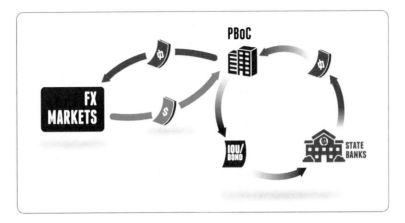

Fig. 13.2 Sterilization of FX intervention to maintain a weak currency (*Illustration by Ricardo Paredes.* (#1) Central bank buys FX with domestic currency, increasing **M**. (#2) Central bank then sells domestic bonds to state banks, decreasing **M** back to its starting point)

Since China was intent on holding its currency within a very tight exchange rate range during the period in question, and hence, would not allow e to adjust meaningfully, some other mechanism was needed to diffuse the effects of the vast sums of hot capital and FX flowing in for the country to avoid overheating.

China's FX comes from four sources:

1. Its trade surplus with the rest of the world—and the attendant capital inflow, per our discussion of the NSI in Chap. 7
2. Foreign direct investment (FDI)
3. FX intervention to maintain the peg
4. Hot capital inflow, especially during times when the world is "shorting" the US dollar

China uses a technique known as **foreign exchange sterilization** to mitigate the effects of the FX inflow.

The process begins with the FX intervention by the People's Bank of China (PBoC), China's central bank (see Fig. 13.2). Every morning (so to speak), the PBoC buys up the incoming foreign exchange and sells RMB (the Chinese currency) to prevent the currency from appreciating. The intervention replaces FX with domestic currency in the economy, which effectively increases **M**. This is what drives the LM curve downward under a fixed, weak currency peg.

There is now a flood of **M** in the domestic economy. That afternoon (to continue the metaphor), the PBoC **sterilizes** the effects of its earlier FX intervention by selling bonds to the state banks and accumulating the extra **M** that it had previously injected.

In Fig. 13.3, we start at the final equilibrium point E_1 from Fig. 13.1. The FX sterilization described above has the effect of lowering **M** back down, which moves the LM curve up to LM_2, with the IS–LM equilibrium now at E_2 near Fig. 13.1's original starting point E_0.

Fig. 13.3 Sterilization
operations (**M↓**), fixed rates,
perfectly mobile capital

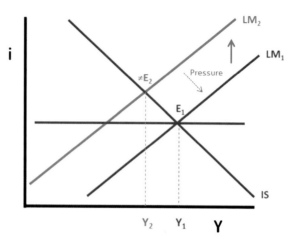

However, we see that sterilization does not resolve the BOP imbalance. E_2 is not a *general* equilibrium, as it remains above the **BOP** line. Thus, sterilization has only a temporary moderating effect. Because the goods market–money market equilibrium is in BOP surplus, the pressure remains for **LM** to adjust back down to LM_1, reversing the sterilization (the pressure *could* be relieved if the **IS** were to shift, if the peg were eased or adjusted). The same process of intervention and sterilization must be continuously repeated if the country insists on remaining in BOP disequilibrium.

Foreign exchange sterilization may involve changing the **required reserve ratio (RRR)** of domestic banks, rather than open-market operations. By increasing the RRR, the central bank can just as effectively withdraw money from circulation. China has taken to using this method in recent years—drastically increasing the RRR in attempting to deflate bubbles in the property market (as in 2005) and, more recently, in the wake of the global subprime crisis.[2] The ISLM-BOP analysis would yield basically the same results as given above, with the **LM** curve being artificially propped up by the exercise, although changes to reserve requirements are typically large, infrequent adjustments rather than daily interventions.

There are certain unwelcome effects associated with sterilization operations. As long as the currency is kept artificially weak, the central bank continues to accumulate FX reserves, which exposes it to interest rate and default risk on the sovereign bonds it typically purchases with the FX. Meanwhile, the process of selling domestic bonds to soak up the **M** created by its FX intervention artificially raises

---

[2] The RRR was, for example, increased from 18.0 % to 18.5 % in November 2010, effectively taking 350 billion yuan out of circulation. Source: Aileen Wang and Simon Rabinovitch, "China Raises RRR Again as Inflation Fight Intensifies," *Reuters*, Nov 19, 2010, 7:34 ET

the government's borrowing costs and interest rates overall. And the central bank often takes a loss on its sterilization operations, as it generally pays out more interest on the domestic bonds issued to the primary/state banks than it earns on the foreign sovereign bonds that it buys in its FX operations.

There are other distortions as well.

1. By removing FX from the banking system, the central bank takes away funds that may instead be invested in higher yielding real and financial assets, such as overseas companies, factories, and real estate, and instead stuffs the banks with lower-yielding government bonds or piles of idle reserves.
2. Export-related industries are artificially encouraged to grow, while other industries face a relative scarcity of resources. For emerging economies, prolonged sterilization operations may delay advancement to a higher level of development, which generally involves transition from low-skilled manufacturing into higher-end manufacturing and services (recall the PLC from Chap. 5).
3. By holding a currency artificially weak, the central bank diminishes domestic consumers' purchasing power, and they end up paying higher real prices for any merchandise with an imported component. Conversely, an artificially strong currency weakens the export sector and may encourage overconsumption.

Sterilization is today most commonly employed by exporting countries with a BOP surplus who seek to maintain a weak currency to bolster exports, in the manner described above.

Sterilization may also be used by a country that seeks to keep its currency strong, for example, a country whose currency has fallen under speculative attack. In this case, the central bank would be *selling* FX to maintain its artificially strong currency and in doing so would be taking **M** out of the economy. To negate the deflationary effects of this operation, the central bank would pump **M** back into the economy by buying domestic bonds from primary/state banks.

The maintenance of a strong currency through sterilization operations will artificially weaken the export sector and may encourage overconsumption of imported goods, harming domestic industry.

The main weakness with this approach, however, is that an artificially strong peg cannot be maintained forever. Eventually the central bank will run out of FX reserves, as we discussed in detail in Chap. 12. Owners of domestic assets may anticipate an eventual devaluation and sell or hedge their holdings, exacerbating the BOP imbalance.[3] When speculators sense that a central bank may be engaged in a battle against currency depreciation that it cannot win, they will pile on, accelerating the process. It can require vast reserves to maintain a credible defense of a strong peg under attack.

---

[3] Neely, "Capital Controls," 6

13.2   The Chinese Yuan

US Treasury Secretary Timothy Geithner, March, 2009 Getty Images for Meet the Press; Chinese
Premier Wen Jaibao, November, 2009 Bloomberg via Getty Images

"President Obama—backed by the conclusions of a broad range of economists—believes
that China is manipulating its currency."

–US Treasury Secretary Timothy Geithner, January 25, 2009

"The responsibility does not lie with the Chinese side, but the United States."

–Chinese Premier Wen Jaibao, March 14, 2010

So... who is right?

Starting around 2004, concerns began to arise among US policymakers regarding China's undervalued exchange rate, trade surplus, and rapidly growing foreign exchange reserves. China was not the only country about which these issues of "global imbalance" were being raised, but it was the largest, and over time its trading relationship with the United States grew so rapidly that it came to dominate concerns about US trade (Fig. 13.4).

To understand the controversy surrounding the yuan's peg and its relationship to the US trade deficit, we must start by reviewing the relationship between the exchange rate and the balance of payments.

A currency that is weaker than its equilibrium level implies a balance of payments surplus. Normally, when a currency is too weak, one of two results will follow (we assume capital mobility in our examples, for simplicity).

Under freely floating exchange rates, the incoming flood of foreign capital will, through market forces, drive the currency to strengthen (**e↓**), and BOP equilibrium will be restored as the **IS** curve adjusts (Fig. 13.5).

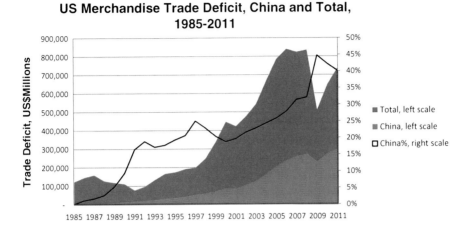

Fig. 13.4 US merchandise trade deficit, china and total, 1985–2011. *Data Source:* US Census Bureau

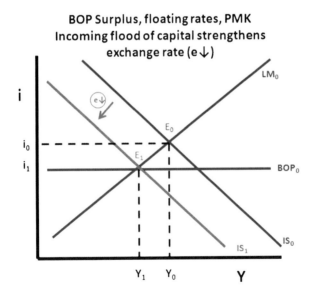

Fig. 13.5 Weak currency under floating exchange rates, perfectly mobile capital

Under fixed exchange rates, the incoming foreign exchange (**FX**↑) is purchased by the monetary authorities as they intervene in the foreign exchange markets. The LM curve adjusts to a new **BOP** equilibrium (Fig. 13.6).

There are follow-on effects from both policies. Under floating rates, the strengthening of the exchange rate harms exporters, as their products are now

Fig. 13.6 Weak currency
under fixed exchange rates,
perfectly mobile capital

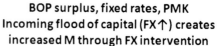

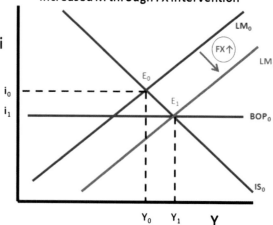

more expensive in world markets. To an economy like China's, where exports
account for roughly 30 % of GDP,[4] such an outcome would be destabilizing.

Under fixed rates, a big inflow of unsterilized FX will create severe inflation. The
resulting increase in the domestic price level eventually makes domestic goods just
as expensive to other countries as they would have been had the nominal exchange
rate been allowed to strengthen. Such an outcome is also destabilizing to a developing country like China where typically 30 % of household consumption is spent
on food.[5]

Essentially, in either case, the **real exchange rate** strengthens.

	Floating rates "e" _strengthens_	Fixed rates "P" _increases_	_Same result_
Real exchange rate	$r = \dfrac{P^*e\downarrow}{P}$	$r = \dfrac{P^*e}{P\uparrow}$	$r\downarrow$

This example illustrates the self-correcting nature of the balance of payments.
When goods and services in Country A (China) become "cheap" in real terms, the
result is a surge in demand for the country's products from Country B (USA). This
creates a current account surplus in Country A (exports > imports) and a current
account deficit in Country B (exports < imports).

---

[4] Exports of goods and services accounted for 31 % of China's GDP in 2011 (source: World Bank).
Among the world's ten largest economies (taking the EU as a unit), China's export-to-GDP ratio is
only matched by Mexico, at 31 %. Others: Canada (29 %), Russia (28 %), India (25 %), Australia
(21 %), Japan (15 %), European Union (14 %), United States (13 %), and Brazil (12 %)

[5] Food consumption in China accounted for 32.9 % of household expenditure in 2009. Compare to
6.2 % in the US, 11.4 % in Germany, 14.9 % in Japan, 24.7 % in Brazil, and 35.4 % in India.
Source: _USDA Food CPI and Expenditures: 2009_

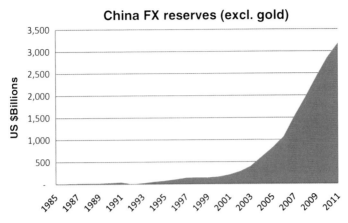

Fig. 13.7 China foreign exchange reserves (excl. gold) 1985–2011. *Data source:* State Administration of Foreign Exchange, People's Republic of China

The surge in demand for A's exports ultimately causes real exchange rate appreciation (through nominal exchange rate appreciation or domestic inflation). Once the real exchange rate has appreciated sufficiently, A's domestic goods will no longer be so "cheap" relative to B's. Country A will begin importing more from Country B, which reverses some flow of foreign exchange back to B. The current account balances of both countries will moderate back toward zero.

This is how the balance of payments and its component trade and capital flows tend over time toward equilibrium.

However, to prevent inflation and real exchange rate appreciation, China sterilizes some 90 % of FX inflows,[6] primarily through changes to the reserve requirement at state banks and the issuance of special "sterilization bonds" directly from the central bank (Fig. 13.7).[7]

China's sterilization effort defeats the self-correcting mechanism of the BOP and has resulted in a massive buildup of foreign exchange over the 2002–2011 period. China's FX reserves in 2011 accounted for roughly 1/3 of the world's total.

Through foreign exchange sterilization, China suppresses real exchange rate appreciation and keeps Chinese goods artificially cheap on world markets.

This policy is not without significant negative distortions. For one, the PBoC faces the risk of loss on its sterilization operations. Estimating this cost is complicated as

---

[6] Alice Y. Ouyang, Ramkishen S. Rajan, and Thomas D. Willett, "China as a Reserve Sink: The Evidence from Offset and Sterilization Coefficients," Hong Kong Institute for Monetary Research, Working Paper 102007, October 2006, 23. http://papers.ssrn.com/sol3/papers.cfm?abstract_id = 1008194. Accessed November 12, 2012. Chenying Zhang obtains that between 79 % and 93 % of foreign exchange is sterilized. Chenying Zhang, "Sterilization in China: Effectiveness and Cost," The Wharton School, University of Pennsylvania Finance Department, September 2010, 23

[7] Other methods are also used from time to time, such as "credit ceilings." Fan Geng, "China's Monetary Sterilization," *China Daily*, November 30, 2010

several moving parts must be considered, including the spread between Chinese and US interest rates, inflation, exchange rates, and the implied capital loss in the event of significant liquidation of a huge, concentrated position in one type of asset.[8]

Additionally, by removing FX from the country's banks, the PBC has taken foreign exchange that may be invested at higher returns overseas and replaced it with lower-yielding bonds or idle reserves. This imposes another kind of cost on the Chinese economy, both directly in lost yield and indirectly in foregone opportunity for additional economic integration with the rest of the world.

Additionally, a cost is imposed on China's banks, which are forced to lock up funds in reserves and sterilization bonds that might otherwise be profitably lent out. Banks are weaker and less profitable as a result. Some ¼ of the country's money supply is estimated to be immobile as a result of these policies.

Misdirected investment is another result, as export-related industries are artificially encouraged to grow, while the industries essential to an advanced economy, such as information technology, healthcare, and services, are underdeveloped. Continued adherence to the policy only makes the eventual shift more painful.

Another important result of China's weak currency policy is that it impoverishes Chinese consumers, in real terms. The prices of foreign goods are held artificially high, which puts them out of reach for many consumers. While the vast bulk of China's citizens are in no position to consider buying a German luxury car, regardless of the exchange rate, companies like Unilever[9] have developed a portfolio of safe and high-quality consumer products geared toward the economic "bottom of the pyramid" in the developing world. These marginal consumers are shut out from these quality imports by China's currency policy and are relegated to using inferior locally made substitutes. China's weak currency also subjects its consumers to more pain from sharp price increases of imported food and energy, which are volatile commodities.

Generally, over a long period of time, large-scale sterilization efforts prove to be non-sustainable.[10]

China's weak currency lowers the "world supply" curve among its trading partners for the goods it exports; however, a supply curve on its own involves no transactions. It requires a demand curve with which to intersect. The Chinese and

---

[8] Chenying Zhang (2010), using only relative interest rates on US Treasuries and interest rates paid on Chinese bank reserves and sterilization bonds, estimates that China's net returns from sterilization between 2003 and 2010 were positive. His calculations do not incorporate the steady USD depreciation against the RMB, the illiquidity premium described above, or the effect of changes in interest rates on the market value of USD holdings. Chenying Zhang, "Sterilization in China: Effectiveness and Cost," The Wharton School, University of Pennsylvania Finance Department, September 2010, 23

[9] C. K. Prahalad and Stuart L. Hart, "The Fortunate at the Bottom of the Pyramid," *strategy + business issue no. 26 first quarter 2002*. (McLean, VA: Booz Allen Hamilton), 2002

[10] The experiences of Malaysia in the 1990s and Japan in the late 1960s illustrate the point. A discussion of these events and the various effects of PBC sterilization may be found in John Greenwood, "The Costs and Implications of PBC Sterilization," *Cato Journal 28,No. 2* (Spring/ Summer 2008): 205–217

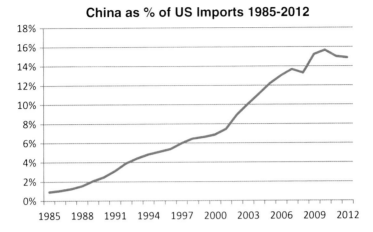

Fig. 13.8 China share of US Imports 1985–2012. *Data source:* US Census Bureau, data through August 2012

other developing exporters who keep their currencies artificially weak could not sell so many goods without willing buyers.

And here is where we find the United States, the world's #1 buyer of imported goods, playing its part in building the much-discussed "global imbalances" (which we explore later in this chapter) in several key ways.

1. *"The Great Moderation"*

The period in the USA from the mid-1980s to the mid-2000s, known as "the Great Moderation" (discussed in Chap. 11), featured a massive consumption boom driven by plentiful credit and rising incomes. A combination of the effects of globalization, asset bubbles, and financial innovation held consumer price inflation in check.

Normally, rising demand would bump up against capacity (supply) and lead to inflation. However, this consumption boom simply led to an expansion in the number and type of goods imported. We have discussed how rising national income is generally accompanied by rising imports (Chap. 10), and this period was no exception. The US current account balance turned sharply negative as imports surged, with a growing percentage coming from China (see Fig. 13.8).

It is a mathematical identity that the net importation of huge amounts of goods and services will be accompanied by a net exportation of title to real and financial assets (Chap. 9). China's holdings of US Treasury and Agency securities soared as its foreign exchange reserves grew from $300 billion in 2002 to $3 trillion in 2011.

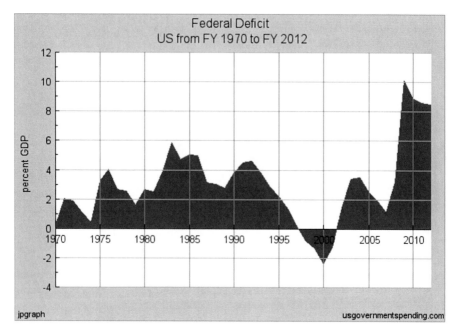

Fig. 13.9 US federal budget deficit, 1970 to 2012 (*Source:* usgovernmentspending.com)

2. *The US "Twin Deficits" and US Fiscal Policy*

There is another aspect to the USA's share of culpability for the US–China imbalance.

For decades, with the exception of a brief period at the height of the 1990s economic boom, the USA has run a large fiscal deficit. With the financial collapse of 2008 and the global recession that followed, revenues were curtailed, but US fiscal and monetary stimulus programs expanded dramatically. This caused the US budget deficit to explode to more than 10 % of GDP in 2009, and it remained elevated thereafter (Fig. 13.9).

The US Treasury is churning out $billions[11] a day in new debt, which will be purchased by *someone*. There is an interrelation between changes in the trade deficit and changes in the fiscal deficit. Under equilibrium conditions[12]:

$$- \text{CAB} = \text{KAB}$$

An increase in the fiscal deficit creates an additional demand for loanable funds, which can only be met by savings (**S**) and overseas capital (as represented by the **KAB**, which is inflows minus outflows). The resulting

---

[11] $2 billion to $4 billion per day as of 2012–2013

[12] See Chap. 9.

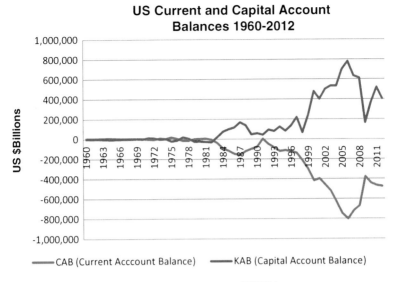

Fig. 13.10   US CAB and KAB 1960–2012. *Data source*: US BEA

inflow (↑**KAB**) in turn allows the country to increase imports, exacerbating its current account deficit.[13] A country like the USA, with a negligible savings rate, must by mathematical identity meet its financing needs by selling bonds overseas.

The interrelation between **CAB** and **KAB** runs both ways. An increase in the current account deficit (↓**CAB**) creates an additional supply of capital overseas, which returns to purchase real and financial domestic assets and also drives down interest rates, making it easier for the fiscal authorities to perpetuate an otherwise non-sustainable budget deficit (Fig. 13.10).

3. *US Monetary Policy and "Exported Inflation"*
The Federal Reserve pulled out every tool in its arsenal to combat the effects of the financial crisis that began in 2007. In addition to driving interest rates to zero, it initiated an alphabet soup of lending facilities to the financial system, provided lifesaving credit guarantees and support to the world's largest financial institutions, facilitated the fire sale of two of the biggest Wall Street firms, loaded up its balance sheet with a host of nontraditional assets, and increased the money supply at the fastest rate in its history (Fig. 13.11).

When the economy remained mired in recession despite interest rates at the zero bound, the Federal Reserve resorted to the unconventional policy that came to be known as "quantitative easing." This policy involves the expansion of

---

[13] It should be noted that some, including Fed Chairman Ben Bernanke, reject the "twin deficits" hypothesis that budget deficits cause current account deficits, pointing to Germany and Japan which run trade surpluses and fiscal deficits.

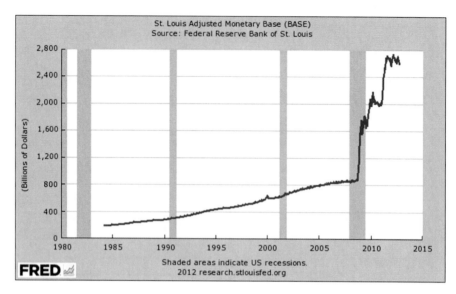

Fig. 13.11 US Monetary Base, 1984–2012 (*Source:* St. Louis Fed)

the money supply through the purchase of longer-term government bonds and other assets, rather than through open-market operations which generally involve only short-term instruments. The purpose is to drive longer-term interest rates down, spurring economic activity as well as creating a positive wealth effect by driving stock and other asset prices higher.

Inflation generally lags money creation by 12–36 months[14] and can lag even longer in a severe and prolonged downturn. In the US, a generally dour outlook and lack of appetite for credit among businesses and consumers largely defeated all the Fed's best efforts to spur growth,[15] as the expansion in the money supply was offset by a collapse in the money multiplier. However, the vast amounts of liquidity created by quantitative easing and other Fed policies created side effects overseas:

(a) Many critics claimed that huge pools of Fed-created "hot money," seeking attractive returns unavailable under near-zero interest rates in the United States, flooded into commodities and emerging markets.

(b) Loose monetary policy combined with large fiscal deficits further depreciated an already chronically weak dollar, which exacerbated inflation in countries on dollar pegs (Fig. 13.12).

---

[14] Mark J. Perry, Ph.D., Chap. 14:*Modern Macroeconomics and Monetary Policy*, ECONOMIC$ 201 - PRINCIPLES OF MACROECONOMIC$ (Flint: University of Michigan). Accessed March 31, 2011, http://spruce.flint.umich.edu/~mjperry/macro14.htm

[15] This is the "liquidity trap," which we have discussed in earlier chapters.

Fig. 13.12 Trade-weighted index of US currency purchasing power (e' = foreign/1 USD) 1973–2012 (*Source:* St. Louis Fed)

Inflation in food and other commodities surged during the same period the Federal Reserve held the monetary spigots open; whether correlation implies causation was a hotly debated topic, with economists and foreign ministries pointing to the Fed[16] and Fed Chairman Bernanke pointing directly back at foreign critics (Fig. 13.13):

> *"I think it's entirely unfair to attribute excess demand pressures in emerging markets to US monetary policy because emerging markets have all the tools they need to address excess demand in those countries. It really is up to emerging markets to find the appropriate tools to balance their own growth."*

–Federal Reserve Chairman Ben Bernanke, February 3, 2011[17]

Price surges like these are felt most severely in the world's developing economies, where food accounts for a major share of the average person's budget (Fig. 13.14).

---

[16] Ronald McKinnon, "The Latest American Export: Inflation", *Wall Street Journal,* January 18, 2011, accessed November 18, 2012. http://online.wsj.com/article/SB1000142405274870 4405704576064252782421930.html

[17] Phil Flynn, "Bernanke Says Unfair to Blame Inflation on QE," *Futuresmag.com,* February 4, 2011, accessed March 31, 2011, http://www.futuresmag.com/News/2011/2/Pages/Bernanke-says-unfair-to-blame-inflation-on-QE.aspx

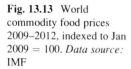

Fig. 13.13 World
commodity food prices
2009–2012, indexed to Jan
2009 = 100. *Data source:*
IMF

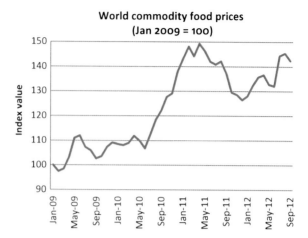

China, where food accounts for more than 20 % of household expenditures, saw inflation exceed its targets in early 2011,[18] with January food prices climbing 10.3 % from a year earlier. Fruit prices surged 35 %, and grain increased by 15 %.

This trend presented a quandary for Chinese authorities, who had seen bouts of inflation accompanied by social disturbances during the 1988–1989 and 1993–1995 periods.[19] Inflation normally strengthens the exchange rate, and for a country intent on maintaining a weak currency, inflation brings an adjustment in the real exchange rate anyway.

To control both the exchange rate and inflation and maintain a weak currency in both nominal and real terms, aggressive FX intervention and monetary tightening (sterilization) are required. The result is an even more distorted financial system with even greater buildup of foreign exchange and a massive accumulation of "frozen" reserves of yuan in the banking system.

13.2.1   So, Who is Responsible for the US–China Trade and Currency Imbalance?

China is certainly managing its exchange rate—this is true by definition of any fixed- or managed-rate regime.

Despite permitting some flexibility beginning in 2005 and allowing the yuan to strengthen by more than 25 % since that time, China continues to maintain an artificially weak currency (Fig. 13.15).

---

[18] Li Yanping, "China's Inflation Exceeds Target for Fourth Month, Adding Rates Pressure," Bloomberg.com, February 15, 2011, accessed March 31, 2011, http://www.bloomberg.com/news/2011-02-15/china-s-january-consumer-prices-increase-4-9-producer-prices-climb-6-6-.html

[19] Greenwood, "The Costs and Implications of PBC Sterilization," 208

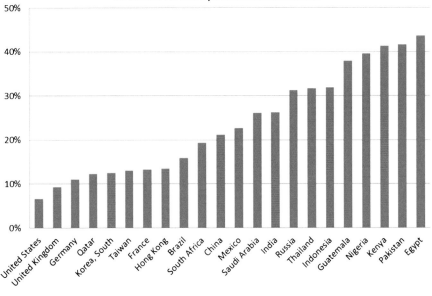

Fig. 13.14 Food as % of household expenditures consumed at home in 2011, selected countries. *Data source:* USDA Economic Research Service

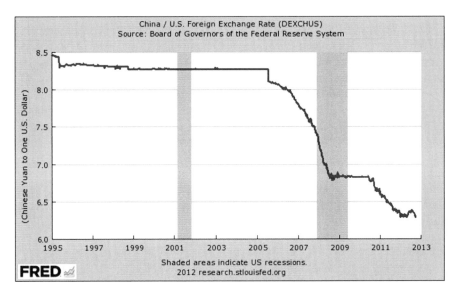

Fig. 13.15 China/USD exchange rate 1995–2012 (*Source:* St. Louis Fed)

Min. Hourly Wage (2008, in USD)

Fig. 13.16 *Source*: The National Labor Committee (*Bangladesh Garment Wages the Lowest in the World–Comparative Garment Worker Wages*, (The National Labor Committee: August 19, 2010). Figures from field research, news reports, and the 2009 Country Reports on Human Rights Practices of the Department of State (Sabrina Liu, National Labor Committee). Note that these costs do not include social costs, which can be a significant portion of wages in developing countries. Also, the prevailing wage may differ from the minimum wage. Apparel being among the lowest-skilled manufactures, prevailing wages are unlikely to be significantly higher than the minimum)

Meanwhile, the USA has clearly contributed to the situation: A consumption boom driven by chronically easy money, perpetually large twin deficits, and exported inflation pressures are all the result of fiscal and monetary policy choices made by US authorities over many years. Many of the pressures driving the US–China trade imbalance and Chinese FX-reserves buildup are within the US's ability to ameliorate through the adoption of prudent fiscal and monetary policies.

And there is a key question one must ask when considering this situation: *If China were to freely float the yuan, and it appreciated dramatically—say, from 6¼ down to 5 RMB to 1 USD—would the USA reduce its imports?*

Are there not other countries factor abundant in low-skilled labor to which production of those goods now made in China would quickly shift? This has already been seen in shoe manufacturing, where a huge share of China's production base has moved to Vietnam and elsewhere, and in several areas of apparel production, which is easily shifted and highly responsive to currency and labor-cost differentials.

A comparison of the minimum hourly wage across several countries from 2008 provides a good indication that alternatives to China would likely emerge (Fig. 13.16):

Thus, even without China, it would appear that the USA would quickly seek and find sources to feed its near-insatiable demand for inexpensive consumer goods.

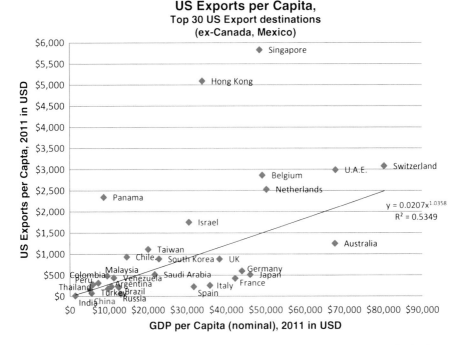

Fig. 13.17   US Exports per Capita versus GDP per Capita among top 30 US export destinations, 2011. Excludes Canada and Mexico. *Data source:* US Census Bureau, CIA World Factbook, authors' calculations

A more valid complaint may be made that China's weak currency policy reduces its demand for US exports.

The USA is comparatively advantaged in many products that may be out of reach for the typical developing country consumer. As such, US exports generally expand with the GDP per capita of the destination country. A look at the top 30 US export destination countries illustrates the relationship.[20]

We can see in Fig. 13.17 how US exports per capita of the importing country grow as GDP per capita of the importing country increases. Limiting the analysis to only developing countries in Asia narrows the scope and controls for geography and other variables. A similar picture emerges (Fig. 13.18).

China's 2011 imports from the USA would be 47 % to as much as 70 % higher if China followed the trends among other US trading partners based on per-capita GDP. Though countries vary from the trend, this analysis provides inferential

---

[20] Mexico and Canada are excluded as their proximity and volume of interindustry trade are atypical among US trading partners. Data from US Census Bureau and CIA World Factbook, calculations by authors. Exponential regression is used in Fig. 13.17 as this method provides a better fit given the great heterogeneity between developing and advanced countries. Fig. 13.18, which includes only developing Asia, uses a linear regression with an intercept of zero, as these countries are more homogenous.

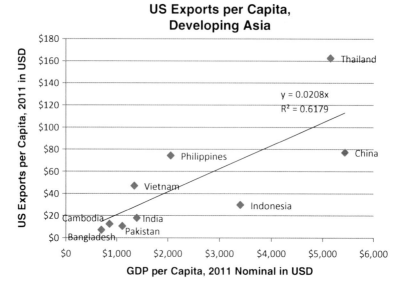

Fig. 13.18 US Exports per Capita versus GDP per Capita, Developing Asia, 2011. *Data source:* US Census Bureau, CIA World Factbook, authors' calculations

evidence that, in fact, US exports to China may be suppressed by the dollar's artificial strength against the Yuan, by perhaps $50 to $70 billion using 2011 figures.[21] While not insignificant, this represents a mere 3 % or 4 % of total US exports and would only close the 2011 US–China trade deficit from −$295 billion to (at best) −$225 billion, which would remain a staggering sum considering the next largest gap—with Mexico—of just −$64 billion.

And here, too, one must be careful in applying data and analysis to the real world in which we live. Any change in the USD–RMB exchange rate that is not very gradual may result in severe distortions in China's export-based economy. Running out to the Apple Store to buy the latest iPad would probably be low on the list of priorities for the hordes of suddenly out-of-work laborers from export-sector factories, following a shock revaluation.

For this reason, China's go-slow approach may be prudent, assuming the crawling peg is permitted to continue moving toward its natural equilibrium.

It should be remembered as well that currency issues tend to be resolved, over time, by market forces, despite the most earnest efforts by policymakers to ward them off. This process may have already begun, as we see in Fig. 13.8, with the moderation in China's share of US imports starting around 2011. The public outcry over China's policies during the early part of this century is reminiscent of the obsession over

---

[21] Per-capita exports to China following the regression lines in Figs. 13.18 and 13.19 would be $133 and $113, respectively, instead of the actual $77. This equates to a potential increase of 47–70 % if China followed the trend. US Exports to China in 2011 were $103.9 billion. Imports were $399.4 billion.

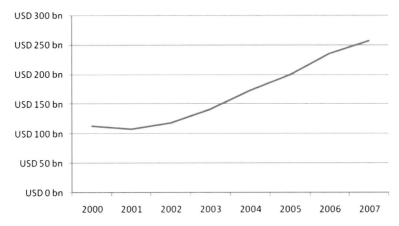

Fig. 13.19 Evolution of trade in counterfeit and pirated products (upper limit) *Source:* OECD (*Magnitude of Counterfeiting and Piracy in Tangible Products: An Update* (OECD: November 2009), 1)

"Japan, Inc." during the late 1980s and, if history is any guide, will likely prove as transitory. In fact, as recently as 2002, China's exchange rate was generally thought to be *overvalued* and had been chronically so going back many years![22]

13.2.2 Something for Nothing: IP Theft, Economic and Industrial Espionage, and Technology Bleed

There is an important but less-commented-upon aspect to the US trade deficit with China.

The Stolper–Samuelson theorem[23] holds that each trading country's abundant factor will benefit as a result of open trade. Clearly this has been true of China, where manufacturing has expanded steadily, particularly in the wake of the WTO's elimination of many quotas and tariffs in 2005. The shift overseas of manufactured products that intensely utilize low-skilled labor to countries where these factors are abundant adheres to everything we learned in Part 1 of this book.

The USA is capital abundant as well as factor abundant in highly educated knowledge workers, and it holds significant comparative advantage in areas relating to high-tech manufacturing, nanotechnology, advanced design, biotech and pharma, innovation, sophisticated data collection and analytics, and intellectual property (including the entertainment industry). These areas share the characteristic of being knowledge based and are thus heavily reliant on strong patent and copyright protection. In much of the developing world, particularly Asia, such protections are weak (Fig. 13.19).

---

[22] Greenberg, "The Costs and Implications of PBC Sterilization," 206

[23] See Chap. 4.

Worldwide trade in counterfeit and pirated goods reached an estimated $250 billion in 2007, growing steadily by 12 % per year.[24] Asia accounted for some 69 % of customs seizures in such goods, with China representing a significant share.[25] This trade spans a wide range of products, including software, music, film, video games, books, branded apparel, pharmaceuticals, tobacco products, and chemicals.[26] These figures relate to internationally traded goods and do not even count the counterfeit and pirated goods that are produced and consumed *within* a given economy, or over the internet, which might result in a figure *several hundred billion* dollars higher.[27]

Estimates vary about the amount of revenue lost to US firms from intellectual property theft, but given the US intensity in the types of products affected, the figure is probably much higher—perhaps as much as $400 billion[28]—which would erase most of the US trade deficit.

---

[24] *Magnitude of Counterfeiting and Piracy in Tangible Products: An Update* (OECD: November 2009), 1. Other estimates range higher, for example, the International Chamber of Commerce put the value at $600 billion. The OECD study remains as of early 2013 the most authoritative, comprehensive, and rigorously documented effort to determine the scope of counterfeiting and piracy.

[25] The OECD's GTRIC-e index is a measurement of the relative intensity of counterfeit and pirated exports of a given economy. The highest ratings for the 1999–2005 period went to China–Hong Kong SAR (2.86), Laos (2.85), Afghanistan (2.35), the United Arab Emirates (2.06), North Korea (1.94), Togo (1.92), Kyrgyzstan (1.77), Tokelau (1.76), Lebanon (1.73), Pakistan (1.66), and Cyprus (1.54). China's economy dwarfs the others on the list (Hong Kong is included in the figure as it is a significant passageway for goods moving in and out of China). By way of comparison, the GTRIC-e ratings for several other large economies include the USA (0.14), Japan (0.05), Germany (0.04), Brazil (0.13), India (0.64), Russia (.0.26), Australia (0.09), and Mexico (0.07). Source: OECD *Magnitude of Counterfeiting and Piracy*, 6. The majority of customs seizures in the USA for counterfeit and pirated goods each year originate in China (source: U.S. Customs and Border Protection and US Immigration and Customs Enforcement, Report on 2011 Counterfeit Seizures).

[26] *The Economic Impact of Counterfeiting and Piracy* (OECD: 2007), 29. Note that while many of these items are manufactured overseas for US firms, royalty and license fees, which flow to the US patent and copyright holders, are an export item within the current account.

[27] *The Economic Impact of Counterfeiting and Piracy* (OECD: 2007), 15

[28] With growth at the 12 % trend from $250 billion in 2007, the 2012 figure would be $440 billion. Assuming at least an equal amount is lost from domestic and internet theft and piracy *outside* of the United States, this brings the total figure to $880 billion. Given the USA's economic leadership in most of the areas subject to the most severe losses, it is not unreasonable to assume the USA bears at least 50 % of the total loss, or $400+ billion. The 2011 US trade deficit was $466 billion. (At a *minimum*, the US share of the theoretical $880 billion figure should equate to its share of world GDP, which would put the US loss at $190 billion.)

Related, but impossible to reliably measure, is the technology bleed out of the USA through economic and industrial espionage,[29] as well as through more indirect means, such as industrial policies crafted to glean proprietary information from US firms operating abroad, all of which result in the uncompensated transfer of technology and know-how—the things that form the core of US comparative advantage.[30]

Unlike the issue of "currency manipulation," in which the responsibility of each party may be analyzed with the standard tools of macroeconomics, the issues of intellectual property theft and technology bleed are not even contemplated in the classical treatments of international trade. The economic effects on the USA of the billions in lost revenues due to weak IP enforcement abroad are no different from the effects on its trading partners if US firms broke into overseas factories undetected each night and removed billions in valuable inventory. In both cases, one trading partner is benefitting from the comparative advantage of the other without compensation.

Here, there may be a stronger case for remedial action, whether in the form of countervailing duties, or other restrictions, as a means of encouraging a fair and transparent international playing field. However, the weakness of the US fiscal position limits its options in this regard, as the treasury relies heavily on flows from countries with large current account surpluses with the USA—many of which are the most significant offenders.

Preferable to any form of escalation, however, would be the embrace of a strong IP regime today by all parties. Ultimately, migration through production life cycle from low-skilled labor to knowledge-based economies will lead China and other developing countries into the role of innovators—this is not only the natural progression of events but reflects the aspirations of an increasing number of educated citizens in these countries. As this evolution progresses, it will be very much in these countries' interests to have robust IP protection. Forward-thinking leaders on all sides would be well advised to work together today to ensure that result.

---

[29] China, Russia, and a core handful of nations account for the vast bulk of the activity in collecting US information and technology. It is notable that the USA runs a trade deficit with the largest of these countries. See *Annual Report to Congress on Foreign Economic Collection and Industrial Espionage FY07* (Office of the National Counterintelligence Executive, 10 September 2008). It should be noted that information gathering of this nature is a near-universal practice.

[30] See James McGregor, *China's Drive for Indigenous Innovation, a Web of Industrial Policies*, US Chamber of Commerce, 2009, which analyzes China's policies of "assimilation, absorption, co-innovation and re-innovation" in this context. It should be noted however that the historical evidence is fairly clear that the USA itself engaged in wholesale appropriation of intellectual property without compensation during the post-Revolutionary era, primarily from Great Britain. At the time, the British were just as indignant at the violation of their patent rights and theft of their trade secrets as the USA is today. Peter Andreas makes a convincing argument that this activity was central to the extraordinary pace of development during the USA's early years in Peter Andreas, *Smuggler Nation: How Illicit Trade Made America*, Oxford University Press, 2013.

13.3   Global Imbalances and the "Savings Glut"

The US–China trade and currency controversy is the primary but not the only component in a larger saga, that of "global imbalances." These include a growing differential between the developed and developing world, and primarily between the United States and developing Asia, with respect to current accounts, savings patterns, external accounts, and fiscal position. In all four categories, the US trend has been negative, and the trend in developing Asia has been positive.

One of these "imbalances" has come to be known as the worldwide "savings glut."[31]

The notion of the **"savings glut,"** which was first put forth by Ben Bernanke in a 2005 speech, primarily refers to the large discrepancy between US and Asian savings rates and resulting net investment positions. With historically low US savings rates, foreign savings have increasingly come to fund US investment and fiscal deficits. A key component in the savings glut scenario has been the reversal of the role of advanced and emerging economies: For decades prior to the 1990s, emerging countries were net borrowers and advanced economies were net lenders. This change was driven in part by policy choices among the Asian economies that had been affected by the crisis of the late 1990s (see Chap. 11). Many of these countries reoriented themselves to prevent a future, similar crisis by (1) gaining control over their fiscal budgets, (2) paying down foreign debt, (3) setting a weak exchange rate and promoting exports, and (4) building up piles of foreign exchange reserves. The result has been a surplus of savings over the investment needs of the domestic Asian economies, which has flowed out seeking investment opportunities abroad (i.e., capital account deficits).

We may summarize here the main sources of the **"global imbalances"** from both sides:

Developing Asia

- Export focus
- Artificially weak currencies
- High savings rates
- Growing piles of foreign exchange reserves

---

[31] Ben Bernanke coined this term in a 2005 speech, "The Global Saving Glut and the U.S. Current Account Deficit." Remarks by Governor Ben S. Bernanke at the Sandridge Lecture, Virginia Association of Economists, Richmond, Virginia, March 10, 2005, accessed November 18, 2012. Bernanke blamed high savings rates worldwide for a global savings glut; the authors agree here with economist John Taylor's critique that the empirical evidence rather points to a savings glut of sorts in developing Asia *and* a concurrent savings deficit in the United States. We present this interpretation of the "savings glut" here. See John B. Taylor, "The Financial Crisis and the Policy Responses: An Empirical Analysis of What Went Wrong," November 2008, 5, accessed November 18, 2012. http://www.stanford.edu/~johntayl/FCPR.pdf

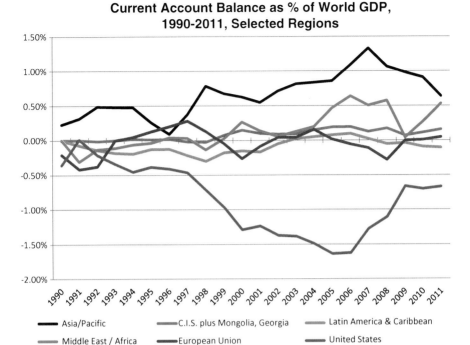

Fig. 13.20   CAB as % of World GDP, 1990–2011, by region. *Data source*: IMF

United States

- Low savings rates and overconsumption
- Easy monetary policy, low interest rates
- Large fiscal deficits
- Growing piles of fiscal debt

These causes feed back into each other and have formed a dynamic which has thrown previously predictable economic relationships far out of balance.

In the previous section, we discussed the self-correcting nature of the balance of payments: A large current account surplus will bring foreign exchange into the country, which will cause an appreciation of the real exchange rate through either (1) nominal appreciation, under floating rates, or (2) inflation, under fixed rates.

This adjustment keeps a country's current account from going too far from balance—the larger the surplus or deficit, the stronger the forces pushing the real exchange rate back toward parity.

Historical observation supports this notion. While countries run current account surpluses and deficits over time, often chronically, generally the variations do not grow beyond a limited range. In Fig. 13.20 we show the current account balances as a percentage of world GDP for various regions over time. We can see that starting in the late 1990s, the normal fluctuations came unglued, particularly between Asia and the United States.

Amelioration of these imbalances is in the hands of the worlds' policymakers if they can gather the will to make the necessary adjustments. Prescriptions would include:

Developing Asia

- Allow appreciation of weak currencies.
- Limit or eliminate sterilization operations.
- Develop transparent financial markets and consumer protections to create a climate where savers feel free to consume and invest.

United States

- Regain control of the fiscal deficit, bringing it back to a sustainable level.
- Stop the printing presses.
- Focus its trade policy on equitable treatment for all in world markets (rather than currency differences) including, importantly, intellectual property.
- Nurture the comparative advantages of the USA by clearing away onerous taxes and layers of regulations that stifle innovation and growth.

13.4   The US Dollar's Role as the World's Reserve Currency: Past, Present, and Future

Foreign exchange reserves are assets held by central banks which may be used for international settlements and transactions. Foreign exchange generally takes the form of foreign currency and government liabilities,[32] plus gold. Almost all countries hold foreign exchange reserves. Foreign exchange reserves are held for a variety of purposes,[33] with the most common being:

- Servicing international liabilities and debt obligations
- For use as tools of exchange rate policy

  Additional reasons for holding foreign currency reserves include:

- Formal backing for the domestic currency
- As a tool of monetary policy

---

[32] Currency and Government Debt may be seen simply as two forms of Sovereign Liabilities, the difference being that the former pays no interest. See John Hussman, Ph.D.,"Why the Federal Reserve is Irrelevant,", *Hussman Funds Research & Insight*, August, 2001, accessed November 18, 2011, http://www.hussmanfunds.com/html/fedirrel.htm

[33] A thorough exposition of the topic is given in John Nugeé (2000). *Foreign Exchange Reserves Management*, Bank of England Centre for Central Banking Studies Handbooks in Central Banking No. 19.

- As a source of funds for paying government liabilities overseas
- As a contingency against emergencies or disaster
- As an investment fund for pecuniary gain

It is sometimes suggested that reserves are also held as a means of settlements in commodities denominated in the reserve currency. However, this is simply an accounting function, and such commodities are actually purchased using any number of currencies.[34]

For several decades, the US dollar has been the world's primary reserve currency. The dollar's role as the primary reserve currency (and, more generally, as the primary international currency) was not established by decree but, rather, because of the emergence of the US as the world's major economy.[35] Several factors contribute to determine the use of a currency for reserves:

- Size of the economy
- Importance of the economy in global trade
- Size, depth, and liquidity of currency and government bond markets
- Size, depth, openness, and transparency of financial markets generally
- Freedom of movement of goods and capital
- Convertibility of the currency
- The use of the currency as a currency peg
- Sound fiscal policies, monetary discipline, and price stability
- Stable, democratic political system
- Strong institutions, rule of law, and property rights
- Ownership segment which exerts constraints on policymakers

An additional reason sometimes offered for the predominance of a reserve currency involves network effects[36] (the incentives to adopt the dominant choice in the market, for example, the Windows computer operating system). However, with deep and liquid markets, network effects are largely irrelevant.[37]

---

[34] Mike Shedlock. "US Dollar About to Lose Reserve Currency Status–Fact or Fantasy?" *Mish's Global Economic Trend Analysis*, February 28, 1011, accessed November 18, 2012, http://globaleconomicanalysis.blogspot.com/2011/02/us-dollar-about-to-lose-reserve.html

[35] United States Treasury Office of International Affairs, "Appendix 1: An Historical Perspective on the Reserve Currency Status of the US Dollar," *Report to Congress on International Economics and Exchange Rate Policies*, October 15, 2010

[36] Craig Elwell, "The Dollar's Future as the World's Reserve Currency: The Challenge of the Euro," Congressional Research Service Report for Congress, July 10, 2007, 7

[37] Barry Eichengreen, "Sterling's Past, Dollar's Future: Historical Perspectives on Reserve Currency Competition" (Tawney Lecture delivered to the Economic Historical Society, Leicester, United Kingdom, April 10, 2005), 7

13.4.1   History

Greek Silver Tetradrachm, ~494–404 B.C. (*Source*: Ancient Coins, "Coin Collecting Guide for Beginners." Accessed April 6, 2011, http://www.coin-collecting-guide-for-beginners.com/ancient-coins.html)

The notion of a reserve currency itself is relatively new, historically speaking. While history has seen a number of *international currencies* rise and fall over the centuries, these currencies were circulating coins, not paper (or electronic) money held as reserve assets in the world's central banks.[38] Most notable among these were[39]:

- The Chinese ban liang (~378–118 B.C.)
- The Greek drachma (~600–100 B.C.)
- Indian silver punch-mark coins (~500 B.C.)
- The Roman denari (269 B.C.)
- The Byzantine gold solidus (498–1030 A.D.)
- The Islamic dinar (697 – ~1100 A.D.)
- The Venetian ducat (1284 – ~1800 A.D.)
- The Dutch guilder (1680 – ~1900 A.D.)

The emergence of *reserve currencies* came about with the rise of central banking, in the eighteenth and particularly nineteenth centuries. The world's first central bank was the Riksbank of Sweden, established in 1668. This innovation was soon duplicated by Britain with the establishment of the Bank of England in 1694 and would be adopted on a widespread basis during the nineteenth century starting with France (1800), followed by the Netherlands (1814), Belgium (1850), Germany (1878), Japan (1882), Italy (1893), and after two earlier abortive attempts, the United States (1913).

---

[38] Eichengreen, "Sterling's Past, Dollar's Future: Historical Perspectives on Reserve Currency Competition," 3

[39] Avinash Persaud "When Currency Empires Fall,", October 11, 2004, www.321gold.com. Accessed February 18, 2011

Central banking emerged during the period of the gold standard, where paper currency was redeemable for a specific quantity of gold. Central bank reserves thus consisted primarily of gold deposits, with relatively small quantities of foreign currency-denominated assets (cash and government liabilities). As trade expanded through the nineteenth century, foreign exchange rose steadily as a percentage of central bank assets, reaching approximately 1/7th of global international reserves by the end of 1913. Today, foreign-denominated currency and debt account for 85 % of the world's estimated US $9 trillion in foreign exchange reserves, with $1.3 trillion in gold reserves making up most of the difference. Overall, foreign exchange represents more than ½ of global central bank assets and has grown especially rapidly over the 2002–2011 period.[40]

13.4.2 *Reserve Currencies over Time*

Britain was the dominant world economic power of the nineteenth and early twentieth centuries. It was natural that the pound sterling would arise as the primary currency held as foreign exchange reserves among the world's central banks. World War I greatly disrupted the international monetary order, as France, Germany, and the UK all suspended or restricted gold convertibility and capital mobility and engaged in inflationary war financing.

The USA, already a major economic power at the outbreak of the war, had heretofore been limited in its appeal as a financial center without a central bank. The establishment of the Federal Reserve in 1913 removed this constraint, and the dollar's role as a reserve currency began to grow. The dollar's rise was aided by the fact that during the war and after, unlike the European powers, the USA maintained gold convertibility and the generally free movement of goods and capital (with restrictions applied to the Central Powers).

The German hyperinflation and postwar turmoil took the Mark out of use as a reserve asset, with the dollar filling an increasingly important role. The USA's suspension of gold convertibility and the -38 % dollar-gold devaluation in 1933 only temporarily delayed the dollar's rising international status.

France, beginning in the 1920s, accumulated vast quantities of gold and was a natural candidate for reserve currency status but shunned the volatility that accompanies freely mobile capital. France imposed capital controls of various forms and actively discouraged the use of the franc as a reserve currency. Germany,

---

[40] Data sources: $9 trillion in total foreign exchange reserves as of December 2010 per IMF; $1.3 trillion in gold reserves as of December 2010 per World Gold Council, calculated from 29,978 tons at US $1,400 per ounce; $13 trillion global monetary base per Natixis implies a ratio of 9/13 foreign exchange to total central bank assets.

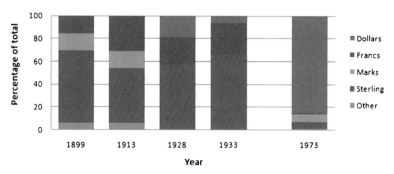

Shares of currencies in known foreign exchange reserves

Fig. 13.21 Evolution of the mix of currencies held as foreign exchange reserves, 1899–1973. *Data source:* Eichengreen 2005

with the 1920s hyperinflation still fresh in its collective memory, discouraged the use of the Deutsche mark as a reserve currency as it believed such a development would constrain its ability to control inflation (Fig. 13.21).[41]

Following World War II, the establishment of the Bretton Woods system in 1945 ensured the dollar's eventual dominance, as the major global currencies were to be pegged to the USD, which would remain convertible into gold. However, the shift away from pounds and into dollars as the primary reserve currency took a surprisingly long time. In 1949, 4 years after Bretton Woods, sterling still accounted for more than half of global reserves, and even as late as 1957, sterling represented a full one-third of the world's total.[42]

The late 1960s brought to light a key problem for issuers of reserve currencies: While the rest of the world is dependent on the issuer's monetary policy, the issuing authority is generally answerable only to domestic mandates, and not to international concerns. This problem is known as the **Triffin dilemma,**[43] which predicts that the reserve currency's bank will focus first and foremost on its domestic economic objectives (often as required by domestic law), which will supersede those of the international community if they conflict.

As the USA financed its Vietnam War and burgeoning social programs from the late 1960s forward, fiscal recklessness brought monetary expansion and inflation,

---

[41] Eichengreen, 2005, "Sterling's Past, Dollar's Future: Historical Perspectives on Reserve Currency Competition," 10

[42] Eichengreen, 2005 "Sterling's Past, Dollar's Future: Historical Perspectives on Reserve Currency Competition," 10

[43] After Belgian-American economist Robert Triffin (1911–1933), who predicted the failure of the Bretton Woods system based on this inherent conflict

Currency Composition of foreign exchange reserves, percent of allocated world total 1995-2011

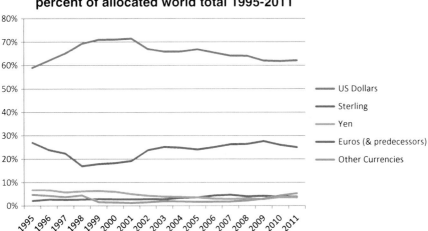

Fig. 13.22 Currency composition of foreign exchange reserves, % of allocated world total, 1995–2011. *Data source:* IMF COFER database

and the USA slacked in maintaining its gold-cover ratio as agreed under Bretton Woods. The Bretton Woods system collapsed in 1971 when the USA formally abandoned its gold-exchange responsibilities, with President Nixon's closing of the "gold window."

With US economic policy in disarray in the 1970s, the dollar's share of reserves fell as European currencies, particularly the German Mark, gained. From 1979 to the present, the composition of global foreign exchange reserves has remained remarkably stable, with the dollar ranging slightly above 60 % of global foreign exchange reserves (Fig. 13.22).

13.4.3 The Future of the US Dollar as the World's Reserve Currency

The financial crisis of 2008–2009 and its aftermath shook the foundations of the world economy, with the USA at the epicenter. American private financial institutions crumbled, and the US government abandoned fiscal discipline in its efforts to mitigate the economic effects of the crisis, with the Federal budget deficit reaching nearly 10 % of GDP for the years 2009–2011. In addition, monetary discipline was severely relaxed as the Federal Reserve expanded its balance sheet more than threefold in an effort to support the financial system and spur the economy back toward growth.

The extraordinary level of fiscal and monetary expansion exacerbated chronic US imbalances, particularly the growth of the United States' net foreign debt, which had climbed substantially over the previous two decades (Fig. 13.23).

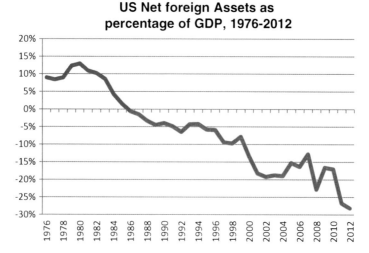

Fig. 13.23 US Net Foreign Investment position (net foreign assets as % of GDP), 1976–2012.
Source: US Bureau of Economic Analysis

While there is no theoretical reason why the reserve currency country cannot be a net debtor,[44] history gives us no example of the world's reserve currency country being in debt to the rest of the world at the level of 25 % of its GDP.[45]

These developments have led many to question the future of the US dollar as the world's primary reserve currency, with various monetary officials openly speculating about replacing the dollar with another currency or group of currencies.[46]

Certainly, over long periods of time, the world's political and economic picture changes, and some time in the future, it is likely that the present dominance of the US dollar will come to an end. However, as we noted above regarding the British pound, such changes are most likely to occur gradually. While sudden deterioration in a currency's relative position can occur, such as the German Mark's fall after World War I, such seismic shocks are generally the result of large-scale military defeat, an unlikely outcome for the United States for the foreseeable future.

---

[44] The United Kingdom was a net debtor following World War I while sterling retained its prominence for a long time after.

[45] Eichengreen, "Sterling's Past, Dollar's Future: Historical Perspectives on Reserve Currency Competition," 1

[46] "China and the Dollar," *Wall Street Journal*, March 26, 2009. US Treasury Secretary Geithner offered that he was "quite open" to the suggestion of Chinese Central Bank Governor Zhou Xiaochuan that an international currency supplant the dollar as the world's reserve currency.

WORLD GDP 2011	GDP (Nominal)
Top 10 Economies	in US $Trillions
1 European Union	17.33
2 US	15.09
3 China[1]	7.30
4 Japan	5.87
5 Brazil	2.49
6 Canada	1.74
7 Russia	1.85
8 India	1.68
9 Australia	1.49
10 Mexico	1.16
World Total	69.99

WORLD TRADE 2011	Trade in US $Trillions		
Top 10 Economies	Exports	Imports	TOTAL TRADE
1 European Union[2]	1.79	2.00	3.79
2 US	1.50	2.24	3.73
3 China	1.90	1.74	3.65
4 Japan	0.79	0.81	1.60
5 South Korea	0.56	0.52	1.08
6 Canada	0.46	0.46	0.92
7 Hong Kong	0.43	0.48	0.91
8 India	0.30	0.46	0.76
9 Singapore	0.41	0.37	0.78
10 Russia	0.52	0.32	0.84
World Total[3]	19.76	19.82	39.58

Fig. 13.24 Top Economies by GDP and Trade, 2011. Notes (1) China's GDP may be better measured in PPP terms at $11.44 trillion, as its artificially weak currency distorts the nominal GDP measure here; (2) European Union figures exclude internal trade, EU exports & imports are 2010 estimates. All other country figures are for 2011; (3) "World Total" trade is half the 39.58 figure, as A's export is B's import. *Data Source:* CIA World Factbook

The most important point to remember when thinking about this issue is that *reserve currencies are not established by decree*. Rather, a currency *emerges* as the preferred component of international central banks' foreign exchange holdings due to its attractiveness with regard to the several requirements mentioned at the beginning of this section. No international agreement or cartel arrangement can artificially prop up one currency above others if it does meet those criteria better than the alternatives (Fig. 13.24).

Let's take a look at the top candidates that have been put forward as potentially supplanting the US dollar.

13.4.4   The Chinese Yuan

China's economy was the world's third largest as of 2011,[47] and the country appears poised to become an even greater global economic and political power in the decades ahead. China has also enjoyed sound macroeconomic management for many years. However, there are several factors which proscribe the yuan's widespread acceptance as a reserve asset for the foreseeable future.

China's financial markets lack transparency, and trading in its currency and government bonds is negligible in world markets (Fig. 13.25).

---

[47] We count the euro area as a single economy. China ranks #2 among sovereign nations after the United States.

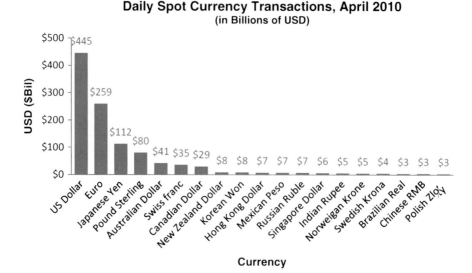

Daily Spot Currency Transactions, April 2010
(in Billions of USD)

Fig. 13.25 Daily Spot Currency Transactions, April 2010 (in billions of USD). *Data Source:* Bank for International Settlements. (Bank for International Settlements, "Report on Global Foreign Exchange Market Activity in 2010," *Triennial Central Bank Survey* (Basel, Switzerland: December, 2010), accessed September 15, 2012, http://www.bis.org/publ/rpfxf10t.pdf)

The nonconvertibility of the Chinese currency and the country's restrictive capital controls also limit the appeal of the yuan as a reserve asset. The lack of a representative political system and legal transparency, as well as an often arbitrary approach to property rights, have also been cited as significant barriers to the yuan's widespread adoption.

Over many years, several of these factors are likely to change. However, such change is measured on a scale of decades, rather than years. Today, and for the foreseeable future, the yuan's use as a reserve asset may be limited to transactional requirements with large commodity trading partners.

13.4.5   The Japanese Yen

The Japanese yen enjoys many of the advantages required of a reserve currency, including the world's third largest economy, a significant share of global trade, and a large and liquid market for government debt. However, the yen has seen its peak as a reserve asset for the foreseeable future. The yen topped out at about 9 % of central bank reserve assets in the late 1980s and early 1990s but has declined along with Japan's economy over a protracted period since. Japan, with its aging population and public indebtedness exceeding 200 % of GDP, is likely to continue to fall behind relative to other economies in the years ahead.

13.4.6 Developing and Growing Economies: India, Brazil, and South Korea

Certain countries, most notably India and Brazil, appear headed for a much larger role in the international economy in the years ahead. However, while these countries are growing and enjoy prudent economic and fiscal policies, they have a long way to go on the path to meeting the requirement of a dominant reserve currency. The primary impediment today is simply the size of their economies and their share of world trade, which although growing quickly, are still a very small portion of world totals. Over-reliance on the currency of a small country can result in disaster, as we have already seen in the case of the Icelandic Króna in Chap. 8.[48]

In addition to strong economic expansion, which is expected to continue, several other developments will need to occur as these countries grow. Most notable are increased transparency in financial markets, expansion of the market for their government bonds, and the free movement of goods and capital, including freely floating exchange rates.

More recently, the "hard landing" of the Indian economy in the wake of rapidly deflating asset price and housing bubbles, and a slowdown in the Chinese economy, have taken both of these emerging powers out of serious contention for global reserve currency status.

13.4.7 SDRs

The SDR, or "special drawing right," is an accounting entity which comprises a basket of international currencies. SDRs were created in 1969 by the International Monetary Fund (IMF) as a vehicle for easing frictions in the international monetary system arising from periodic disruptions in the gold and US dollar markets. The collapse of the Bretton Woods system 2 years after the SDR's introduction left the unit in limbo; it is today used in settlement of IMF obligations and as a means of adjusting the composition of central bank reserves. Total SDRs outstanding were 204 billion as of 2011, equivalent to US $308 billion.[49]

The attraction of the SDR to its proponents is that it is a global currency with no dominant component and as such might be seen as a more stable unit of account with which to facilitate international transactions.

However, this is a fiction. SDRs suffer from several drawbacks which cannot be overcome. The SDR is not a circulating currency and suffers from many of the same problems as the ECU before it—the individual component currencies cannot be counted on to maintain their trading bands when under pressure, and if put into

---

[48] This insight is attributed to Shedlock, "US Dollar."

[49] "Special Drawing Rights (SDRs) Factsheet," International Monetary Fund, December 9, 2010, accessed November 18, 2012, http://www.imf.org/external/np/exr/facts/sdr.htm

general use, the SDR would only be as strong as its weakest link. Further, as the SDR is an accounting entity, not a circulating currency, no one trades goods or services in SDRs[50]; there is as yet no market for SDR-denominated bonds, and a market for such bonds, once created, would take a long time to mature. Finally, without a fiscal or political authority standing behind it, SDR monetary policy cannot exist.

While a pleasant dream to the more utopian-minded, the notion of the world adopting the SDR as its reserve currency is about as likely as Esperanto becoming the world's common language: *Tio will ne okazi tre baldaux*.

13.4.8   The Euro

Until the 2010 Eurozone crisis, the euro was generally regarded as the most likely candidate to supplant the US dollar as the primary reserve currency. The euro confers nearly all the advantages of the US dollar in terms of the size of the economy and share of world trade, transparency and liquidity of currency and financial markets, freedom of movement of goods and capital, a stable and representative political system, and among its largest members, generally sound fiscal and monetary policies.

However, the main disadvantage of the euro has become quite visible as the 2010- European Sovereign Debt Crisis has unfolded: Without a single fiscal authority closely affiliated with the currency, euro government bond markets lack the necessary size, depth, and liquidity necessary to support a primary reserve currency. Furthermore, as of late 2012, only four of the 17 euro area states earned an AAA credit rating.[51]

The crisis has brought a consensus among European policymakers that the lack of a unified fiscal authority backing the currency is a problem to be addressed; however, a solution will require a much closer level of political and economic integration than prevails at present or is likely to occur in the next few years.

13.4.9   The US Dollar's Future

The privilege of reserve currency status confers important benefits to the currency's home country. The country is free to borrow in its own currency, which puts it largely in control of its own debt service and eliminates exchange rate risk as a factor in servicing its debt obligations.

The ability of the USA to perpetually borrow in its own currency while lending and investing overseas in foreign currencies was famously dubbed the "exorbitant

---

[50] Shedlock, "US Dollar"

[51] Source: Standard & Poor's. See also "Hopes Raised, Punches Pulled," *The Economist*, February 10, 2011

privilege" by a French official[52] in the early 1960s. Because US assets overseas are generally foreign currency-denominated and US liabilities are in dollars, when the dollar depreciates, the US enjoys a capital gain on its investments.[53]

The demand for US dollars from central banks and other economic actors reduces US interest rates. US long-term borrowing rates are estimated to be 0.5–1 % lower than they would otherwise be without demand from the world's central banks.[54] The currency is also less subject to exchange rate shocks as the currency flows among central banks are far less volatile than those of private entities.[55] Furthermore, reserve currency status raises the level of participation of foreign investors in the home country's financial markets, increasing their breadth and liquidity and attracting additional foreign investment.

For these reasons, it behooves the United States to do what it can to preserve the US dollar's status among global currencies. Certainly, as formerly poor, agrarian countries continue to develop, many of their currencies will gain stature and eventually compose some portion of global reserves. And eventually, one way or another, the Eurozone and/or its constituent nations will purge their fiscal and monetary excesses and perhaps contend for currency preeminence.

Competing claims to global reserve currency status do not represent a threat to the USA or its currency, however. The entire first part of this book was devoted to demonstrating how international trade is not a zero-sum game; the growth of developing countries and the increased soundness of global macroeconomic policies benefit all countries. Furthermore, there is nothing that prohibits several currencies from each representing a significant share of the world's foreign exchange reserves. We have seen (see Fig. 13.21) that this was the case for many decades prior to the current dollar era. Such an arrangement, while implying a reduction in the dollar's relative share of reserve assets, would not necessarily involve a deterioration of the dollar's stature, or even the loss of its preeminence.

The main challenge to the dollar's reserve currency position arises from the United States itself, with the paramount issues being fiscal and monetary discipline, and its huge regulatory overhang that impedes growth. Without significant adjustment to regain control of its monster-sized deficits, the US fiscal position will eventually deteriorate beyond the point at which its debt obligations are considered safe haven assets. US monetary policy must grapple with the unprecedented expansion of Federal Reserve liabilities over the 2007–2013 period. Moreover, the persistent erosion of the US dollar as a store of value is an unattractive feature to central banks and investors alike (Figs. 13.26 and 13.27).

---

[52] The phrase was originally credited to Charles De Gaulle, but recently has been attributed to Valery Giscard d'Estaing. Brad De Long, "Exorbitant Privilege," February 22, 2005

[53] Richard Clarida estimates that the dollar's decline from 2002 to 2007 reaped the USA a capital gain of $1 trillion in this manner. Richard Clarida, "With Privilege Comes..?" *Global Perspectives*, Pimco, October 2009

[54] Elwell, "The Dollar's Future," 2

[55] Elwell, "The Dollar's Future," 4. See also Barry Eichengreen and Donald J. Mathieson, "The Currency Composition of Foreign Exchange Reserves: Retrospect and Prospect," IMF Working Paper, July 2000, 6

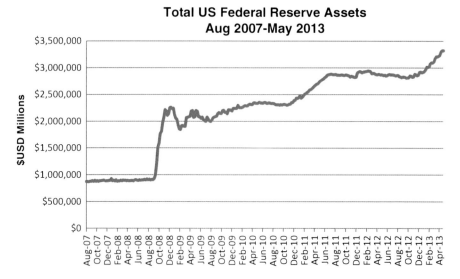

Fig. 13.26 Total Assets of the US Federal Reserve, August 2007 to October 2012. *Source:* US Federal Reserve

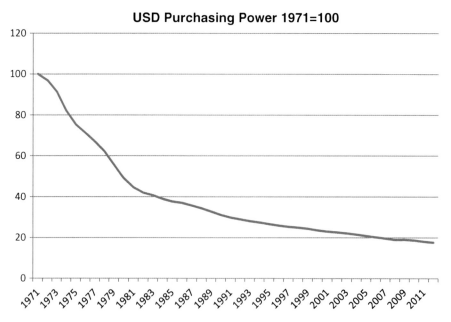

Fig. 13.27 US dollar purchasing power 1971–2012, indexed to 1971=100. *Data Source:* US Bureau of Labor Statistics, data through Oct 2012

The USA must also face long-term structural challenges including its educational system, infrastructure, and regulatory environment, as well as a looming mountain of entitlement liabilities, in order to maintain its preeminence in global productivity and competitiveness among large economies.[56]

However, decline is not inevitable. Given that the challenges all stem from policy choices, rather than from external forces, all are addressable. As recently as 2000, the US fiscal deficit was in surplus, demonstrating that fiscal prudence is not out of reach. The USA also enjoys an unparalleled endowment of human and physical capital which provides a vast resource to be leveraged into future economic growth.

America is unique among developed Western countries, among which populist anger often erupts over the hint of reductions in government spending, in that the USA has a long tradition of populist enthusiasm for fiscal restraint and monetary discipline that rises from time to time in response to government profligacy. Decline for the US dollar is a choice, not an inevitability, and the choice is in the hands of the USA itself.

From left: Americans protest against spending increases in Sacramento, CA (MCT via Getty Images) and Madison, WI (Associated Press), April 15, 2009; People march against retirement benefit changes during a protest in Marseille, southern France, September 23, 2009 (Associated Press)

Despite the challenges that we have chronicled for the US Dollar, we have seen that there are few credible currencies ready to step up and challenge the dollar's primacy.

Is there no alternative then to a global "dollar standard"?

In fact, there is an alternative with which mankind has centuries of experience. Its proponents argue that it can impose monetary discipline and foster stable and durable economic growth. Its detractors rue its inflexibility and the constraints that it places on policymaking.

---

[56] The US ranks 4th in competitiveness behind Sweden, Switzerland, and Singapore but is 1st among large economies. The next five large economies are Japan (6th), Canada (10th), Taiwan (13th), Australia (16th), and the EU (20th overall by weighted GDP as calculated by the authors). Data source: Klaus Schwab, ed, *The Global Competitiveness Report 2010–2011* (Geneva: World Economic Forum, 2010), 15

With the increased interest that this topic has garnered since the financial crisis of 2007–2008, there is value in exploring it in some detail.

For this discussion, we must start at the very beginning, with the foundations of money itself.

13.5   The Gold Standard

Nearly all currencies today are fiat paper currencies. This means that (a) they are issued by "fiat," in other words, simply at the discretion of the monetary authority, and (b) as they are made of paper, they have no intrinsic value of their own.

Printed across the top of any US dollar bill are the words "Federal Reserve Note", identifying the issuer: the US Federal Reserve. This wording confers upon the bearer the right to take that dollar to any Federal Reserve Bank and exchange it for. . . another dollar bill.[57]

So, we have a piece of paper that cannot be exchanged for anything other than itself if we bring it to the entity who issued it. What, then, gives the dollar bill its value?

To answer this question we need to start with fundamentals and ask another question: What is money?

13.5.1   Money

Before there was money, people living in early civilizations bartered goods directly. When the number of traded goods increased beyond a very small scale, it became necessary to relate the value of goods to each other in terms of some standard unit.

---

[57] Hussman, "Why the Federal Reserve Is Irrelevant,", *Hussman Funds Research & Insight*, August 2001

Gold and silver jewelry had been valued by ancient peoples due to the scarcity[58] and durability of these metals, so it was natural that they would often be exchanged for goods and services. These metals fill the first of the three main criteria for money: They serve as a **store of value**.

As the scale of barter transactions grew, some method of keeping track of the goods traded and owed between parties was needed. The Sumerians, 2,600 years ago, solved this problem by using special clay tablets to record their accounts. These tablets reveal that transactions were conducted using quantities of silver to indicate the value of traded goods. In fact, the evidence suggests that the first writing was developed for accounting purposes![59] Thus did gold and silver fulfill the second requirement of money: that it be a **unit of account**.

However, while transactions were valued and recorded using quantities of gold and silver as the standard, the practice was generally ad hoc, and the seller and buyer would need to carefully measure what they were giving and receiving.

Enter the Lydians, who around 600 B.C. began minting gold and silver alloy into coins of specific weights, which quickly entered widespread use due to their convenience. These coins were portable and universally recognized as being of the indicated purity and weight, which greatly facilitated transactions. Thus did gold and silver coins fill the third and last primary criterion of money: that they be a **medium of exchange**.

Lydian coins, circa 600 B.C.

In addition to the three primary criteria, there are other properties which are necessary for money. The medium serving as money must be:

• Durable
• Scarce

---

[58] Gold remains quite scarce—consider: if the entirety of the world's outstanding 187,000 t of gold were divided equally among the world's 8 billion people, each would receive but 0.75 oz of gold (total tonnage of 187,000 per World Gold Council, 2011).

[59] Richard Brown, *A History of Accounting and Accountants* (New York: Cosimo, Inc.), 2004. Originally published by Augustus M. Kelley Publishers, 1905

- Uniform
- Divisible
- Transportable

Among anything mankind has found or invented on earth, gold and silver, and also platinum and copper, fill all the criteria better than any other substances. It was natural then that the Lydians' innovation of coins minted from precious metals would endure as the primary money type in human civilization for more than two millennia.

13.5.2   Paper Money Backed by Precious Metal

Coins made of precious metals do, however, present their own problems. Primarily, for large transactions it is inconvenient, expensive, and possibly dangerous to transport and exchange large quantities of metal coins. Furthermore, from early times sovereigns learned that they could "clip coins," shaving off the edges and reminting additional coins, or alternatively alter the purity of the metal and pocket the gain (which was inevitably discovered by the public, leading to inflation, more coin clipping, etc.).

The Chinese, around 750 A.D., began using paper as a convenient means of recording the funds entrusted to "money shops," where the paper might be redeemed for coin at locations throughout China.[60] This solved the transport problem for merchants doing volume business over long distances. This fei ch'ien, or "flying money," was a credit instrument: not money per se but it was the basis for the development of the first paper money, which emerged in the eleventh century A.D. in Szechwan, China. Around 1000 A.D., a shortage of copper forced the authorities to adopt iron as a substitute currency. However, at 1/9th the value of copper, unwieldy amounts of iron coin were required for even the simplest of transactions. To solve this problem, the sixteen largest merchant houses coordinated to establish a system whereby they would accept deposits of iron and copper coin and issue uniform paper notes, redeemable at any of the cooperating merchant houses, for the specified quantity of coin.

This was the first example of a currency backed by precious metals. A precious metal-backed currency allows the bearer of a paper note to redeem it at any participating institution for a specified quantity of precious metal coin.

---

[60] The authors are deeply indebted to Ralph T. Foster, whose indispensable *Fiat Paper Money: The History and Evolution of our Currency* (Berkeley: Ralph T. Foster, 1991) provided much of the historical information presented in this section.

Paper money backed by precious metal would eventually make its way from China to the West, with the first issue made by Johan Palmstruch and the Bank of Stockholm in 1661. The innovation was quickly adopted throughout Europe and would be the dominant form of money for some 300 years.

13.5.3   The Gold Standard

Stockbyte/Getty Images

Under a gold standard, paper notes are issued which are redeemable at the issuing bank for a specified quantity of gold. Such systems will often include silver-denominated notes as well. Over time, banks formally chartered by governments came to dominate money issuance. By the nineteenth century, the money of the world's largest economies was all based on paper notes convertible into gold. The issuing authorities pledged to buy gold and sell gold at specific conversion rates—in the USA, $20.67 an ounce.

With worldwide trade and communication increasingly fast and efficient, the proliferation of gold-backed currencies tended to check the ability of governments to over-issue notes. Any attempted inflation of the quantity of currency in circulation beyond its backing would result in price inflation for goods and services, which would change the currency exchange rate. Gold would still be at its original, and now too-low, official conversion price, however. This would permit an arbitrageur to purchase gold at the artificially low official price and redeem it in another country, earning a profit on the transaction. The central bank's supply of gold would quickly be depleted, as domestic currency was redeemed for gold. The original inflation would thus be reversed as the quantity of currency in circulation constricted.

Each country's monetary authority would maintain its peg to gold through market operations, buying gold with its currency if the price had fallen too low, and selling gold to take its currency out of circulation if the price had risen too high. Exchange rates between currencies (e = domestic currency/foreign currency, e.g., $/£) were quite stable during this period as a result, since each country's currency was fixed against the same commodity.

Despite including its share of financial crises and recessions, the era between the 1870s and the onset of World War I in 1914 was characterized by a remarkable level of monetary stability and saw world trade explode in a way that would not be repeated until the globalization era of the 1990s. This stability bred a level of confidence among the citizenry of each country, and actual redemptions of gold were exceedingly rare.

From an international trade perspective, if a country ran a current account deficit (imports > exports), this meant that gold would flow out of the importing country into the exporting country. An importer would effectively need to convert his domestic currency into gold, then use the gold to purchase currency in the sourcing country, where he would pay the supplier in that local currency.

This process would over time tend to make goods produced in the importing country less expensive as the domestic money supply constricted the more of it was redeemed out of circulation into gold. Likewise, as gold accumulated in the exporting country, money in circulation in that country would increase, raising prices for goods and services. Eventually, the difference in relative prices would make imports less attractive to the originally importing country and would result in a reversal of the flow of goods. The balance of payments was thus self-correcting under this system.

This of course assumes that each country adheres to the "rules of the game" and refrains from sterilizing gold inflows. A country may decide to sterilize its gold inflows out of a desire to maintain a weak exchange rate for the promotion of exports or as a tool of monetary policy to prevent gold inflows from causing inflation. Should a country determine to sterilize gold inflows, that country will accumulate gold reserves that effectively drop out of the international gold-standard system, creating a "gold sink" which causes money contraction and deflation in the rest of the world due to a scarcity of circulating gold.[61] During the prewar period, this did not occur, and the gold standard functioned well.

For the sake of convenience, it developed that central banks began keeping deposits of gold for foreign central banks within their own vaults to obviate the need for the movement of physical specie. Essentially, under this system, international shipment of physical gold and silver was replaced by simply taking the label that said "Country A" on a particular quantity of gold in the central bank's vault and replacing it with a label that said "Country B." In this way, specie could be

---

[61] Douglas Irwin presents a convincing case that the sterilization activities of the United States and especially France in the late 1920s and early 1930s were the trigger that initiated the massive world deflation and ensuing Great Depression. Douglas A. Irwin, "Did France Cause the Great Depression?" Dartmouth College and NBER, November 15, 2010

transported only when necessary to ensure that Country B had sufficient gold reserves on hand to meet domestic physical demand.

A central banker "ships" gold from Britain to France (Photo "Gold bars stacked in a pyramid shape": Jon Boyes/Photographer's RF/Getty Images. Drawing by the authors)

Discretionary monetary policy is greatly constrained under such a system. Should a central bank attempt to put more currency into circulation by buying gold, the price of goods and services in the economy will inflate, which will result in consumers and merchants switching to less-expensive imported goods. These buyers of foreign goods will redeem their currency for gold to use in purchasing goods with foreign currency—thus returning the domestic money stock back to where it started! (Note that when we talk about people "redeeming their currency for gold" to use in foreign purchases, in practice, this means simply buying foreign currency from their bank, who executes the "movement" of gold in the manner described above.)

There are several advantages of the gold standard:

1. It severely limits discretionary monetary policy and thus takes inflation as a policy tool largely off the table, limiting the sovereign's ability to confiscate wealth through the "inflation tax."
2. It limits fiscal profligacy since monetization is impossible; a country may run a bond-financed deficit but is constrained from printing money should the bond market not offer a bid for the country's debt.
3. While inflation and deflation will occur as the worldwide supply of gold inevitably grows at a different rate than the economy, these fluctuations are exogenous; hyperinflation, which is always man-made, is impossible.[62]

---

[62] As few things said to be "impossible" remain that way over the long term, we note that the exception would be, of course, if someone were to discover the legendary "Philosopher's Stone" (or its equivalent inside a fusion reactor), which turns lead into gold, rendering gold intrinsically worthless.

4. It provides citizens with confidence in the banking system, which greatly enhances trade and commerce, fosters capital formation which in turn raises productivity, and reduces transaction costs.
5. Currency exchange rates are exceedingly stable over time.

The gold standard does, however, present several problems:

1. The quantity of money in circulation worldwide ultimately depends on the amount of gold mined each year, which can be extremely volatile. This causes heightened and unpredictable fluctuations in prices.
2. Gold discoveries are intermittent; during long periods, the economy may grow faster than the supply of gold, meaning that the money supply will not keep up with the demands of the economy. This will bring about prolonged periods of price deflation. Deflation is neither good nor bad in itself; however, a deflationary environment, by discouraging borrowing (since the future dollars needed for repayment will be worth more than the dollars borrowed), tends to limit business expansion and the pace of economic activity, and development in general.

    But most importantly,
3. **It is operated by human beings**.

Ultimately, the prewar gold standard blew apart in a time-honored tradition first developed, like paper money itself, in eleventh-century China.

Returning to our innovative Chinese merchant houses of 1000 A.D., we find that by 1022, while having agreed to issue currency only for actual deposits, the issuers soon discovered that they could print more currency than could actually be redeemed for coin, as depositors would not conceivably come to redeem their coin all at once. Abuse of the system proliferated, and for the first, but not nearly the last time in history, the system broke down in 1022 from over-issuance.

Paper money was resurrected, however, by the ruling Sung Dynasty a mere 2 years later in 1024 as a formal government issue. The Sung were disciplined in their management of the money—the "*chiao-tsu*"—which even as late as 1090 still retained 85 % of its original value.

It is in the nature of human beings, however, that from time to time they feel the need to kill each other on a grand scale, and when they get this idea, the notion of monetary discipline is not going to stand in their way. Conflict with the Chin Tatars led to massive over-issuance for war finance starting around 1100 A.D. By 1127 the currency had depreciated to the point of utter worthlessness. Thus did China make yet another seminal discovery in monetary policy: hyperinflation brought about by war finance (Fig. 13.28).

Paper currency would continue to be used in China for another 600 years, with five dynasties going through the same cycle of issuance, over-issuance, and hyperinflation, as often as not a consequence of war funding. Paper money would ultimately be abandoned in China in the year 1661, which, proving that fate has a

Fig. 13.28 The Value of the
Chiao-Tsu, paper currency of
the Sung government.
Courtesy of Ralph T. Foster,
Fiat Paper Money:
The History and Evolution
of our Currency

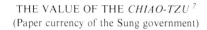

THE VALUE OF THE *CHIAO-TZU* [7]
(Paper currency of the Sung government)

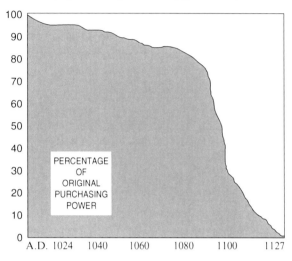

Fig. 13.29 Inflation
1914–1918

	1914	1918	Annualized Inflation
USA	100	202	19%
UK	100	246	25%
France	100	355	37%
Germany	100	240	24%

sense of humor, was the same year that Johan Palmstruch introduced the first gold-backed paper currency in the West.[63]

The pre-World War I monetary order completely disintegrated between 1914 and 1919 as the main combatants (except for the United States) suspended gold redemptions, allowed currency exchange rates to float, and once the saturation point for debt had been reached, like the Sung 800 years before them, turned to money printing to pay for their war effort.

Taking 1914 as a base for price levels (P = 100), by 1918, price levels among the major parties to the conflict had risen dramatically (Fig. 13.29).[64]

---

[63] Johan Palmstruch managed to make it a full 2 years, to 1663 A.D., before his bank failed from overprinting of notes, and he died in prison in 1670. Nevertheless, his introduction of gold-backed paper money laid the foundation for the dominant monetary system in the West for the next 300 years.

[64] Eichengreen, "Sterling's Past, Dollar's Future: Historical Perspectives on Reserve Currency Competition"

The German situation would deteriorate completely after the war. By 1923, the currency had fallen to *one trillionth* of its 1914 value, and the central bank became more involved with pioneering high-speed printing technologies to keep up with the need for new notes than with any notion of monetary stewardship.[65]

An attempt was made by the UK, France, and the United States to return to the gold standard in 1925, but the effort was ill-fated. The war had disturbed the prewar rates of exchange, and countries returning to gold faced the choice of either:

(a) Returning to gold at prevailing market rates, which would represent a severe loss to anyone earning fixed interest or rent or receiving pension payments, impoverishing retirees and pensioners and potentially rendering many financial institutions insolvent, or

(b) Returning to gold at or near the prewar rate of exchanges, which would drastically constrict the quantity of currency in circulation, cripple exports, and engender a brutal deflation and depression

France chose option (a),[66] while the UK, largely out of a desire to maintain Sterling's prominence among currencies, chose option (b). Ultimately the UK's artificially strong exchange rate put strains on its gold reserves and proved unsustainable. Germany, meanwhile, saddled with the seizure of a huge proportion of its productive assets including ships, trains, and raw materials and burdened with infeasible reparations payments, chose option (c): Fire up the printing presses and abandon all pretense of monetary discipline.[67]

These shaky foundations would set the stage for the gold standard to fall apart again with the onset of the Great Depression. It would not return.

13.5.4   The Gold-Dollar Standard

In the aftermath of World War II, a negotiated international system was established based on the US dollar, which would be the sole currency convertible into gold. The Bretton Woods system, initiated in 1945, fixed the rate of exchange of the world's major currencies to the US dollar. The US dollar would be convertible into gold upon demand to other central banks at $35 per ounce.

---

[65] Please see Chap. 7 of Langdana, *Macroeconomic Policy: Demystifying Monetary and Fiscal Policy*, for a discussion of the German hyperinflation during the Weimer Republic.

[66] France actually chose a rate that proved to be undervalued; its weak exchange rate led to an accumulation of gold which would be the cause of serious conflict between finance ministers in the interwar period and may even have caused the Great Depression. See Irwin, *Did France Cause the Great Depression?*, Dartmouth College and NBER, November 15, 2010.

[67] Keynes' prophetic *The Economic Consequences of the Peace* (1919) discusses the impossible conditions imposed on Germany, and their inevitable results (written before the fact), in excellent detail.

The USA committed itself to maintaining an adequate gold reserve to support the currency it issued, and the central banks of the world committed to maintain sufficient US dollar reserves to maintain their pegs.

Thus did the US dollar become the world's **reserve currency**, a status it retains today, along with, to a degree, the euro. The gold-exchange system lasted for some 26 years until a familiar story, now nearly a full millennia old, replayed itself as the financing needs of the Vietnam War (and that of the huge social programs initiated in the 1960s) led the US government to print money beyond what its reserves could support.[68] In 1971, facing up to this reality, the US formally suspended gold convertibility.

The world's reserve currency was now backed by... nothing!

13.5.5 Fiat Paper Currency

Thus was ushered in the era of fiat paper currency. Its value comes solely from the confidence of the people who use it as money. So long as it is generally accepted as a unit of account, a medium of exchange, and representing, thanks to its enduring purchasing power, a store of value, fiat money functions just as gold-backed money did before it.

Generally, legal sanction also requires the acceptance of a country's fiat currency in all transactions, as our dollar bill makes clear.

"THIS NOTE IS LEGAL TENDER FOR ALL DEBTS, PUBLIC AND PRIVATE"

However, legal sanction is never sufficient to uphold a currency's value as money. China's various dynasties enforced similar requirements, and every currency came to the same end. Once the government's issue of notes became irresponsible, confidence was lost, and the currency quickly became worthless.

---

[68] The inherent conflict between acting as a responsible manager of the world's currency standard while simultaneously pursuing domestically driven monetary policy objectives became known as the Triffin dilemma.

Fig. 13.30 US dollar purchasing power 1913 to 2012, indexed to 1913–100. *Data Source:* US Bureau of Economic Analysis

A look at the purchasing power of the US dollar over time is illustrative (Fig. 13.30).

While the US dollar has obviously struggled with its role as a *store of value*, it has fared no worse than other paper currencies in this regard, and it has, since its introduction in 1792, served quite well as a *medium of exchange* and *unit of account*.

As the US dollar remains the primary reserve currency, the global economy today is based largely on the world's confidence in (a) the US government's ability to meet its debts without resort to monetization and (b) the US Federal Reserve's responsible stewardship of monetary policy.

Forty-plus years on as of this writing, the new fiat-money system endures, though strains on the credibility of US fiscal and monetary policy have emerged since the onset of the 2008 crisis.

13.6   A Return to the Gold Standard?

In the aftermath of the financial crisis and global recession of 2008–2009, and the unprecedented fiscal and monetary expansion that followed, the idea of a return to the gold standard has gained adherents, although it remains a minority view. Demand for the resurrection of the gold standard is not an unreasonable response to the excessive monetization of the US runaway deficits. The Federal Reserve in its unrelenting zeal to flood the economy with liquidity since the 2008–2009 crisis has

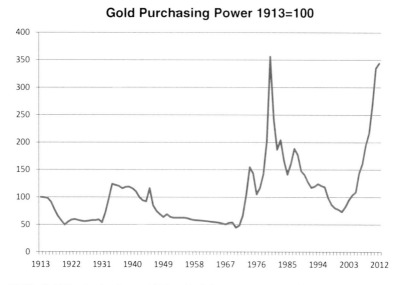

Fig. 13.31   Gold Purchasing Power 1913 to 2012, indexed to 1913=100. *Data sources*: US BEA, kitco.com

indulged in an unprecedented (for the USA) amount of monetization. Adherents of the gold standard believe that it is the only discipline that might constrain the Fed from further rounds of monetization (including "quantitative easing").

The main attraction of the gold standard is that it takes money creation out of the hands of policymakers; of the two evils, the vicissitudes of gold discovery are seen as preferable to the machinations of politicians and central bankers.

Gold, the metal itself, has in fact succeeded where the US dollar and virtually all the world's currencies have fallen short—as a *store of value* (Fig. 13.31).

However, one cannot escape the fact that a common feature of all monetary regimes preceding the current era, whether based on coins of minted precious metal, or gold-backed paper, is that they *came to an end*, generally as the result of an inflationary collapse.

Whether by "coin clipping," fiddling with the purity of minted metals, printing more notes than can be redeemed for their promised gold, or electronically creating bank reserves out of thin air, the essential element is the same—a government that manipulates the currency to its own ends.

Ultimately, hard precious-metal money, gold-standard money, and fiat money all rely on one thing only in the final analysis, and that is *confidence*. History shows that "gold-standard" currencies inevitably collapse in the same way that fiat currencies do. Issuers finally succumb to the temptation of printing unsupportable quantities of money, confidence disappears, and an inflationary spiral reduces the monetary unit to worthlessness.

The problem with monetary systems is neither the physical composition of the money unit, nor the standard of value against which a currency is redeemable, nor even whether the currency is redeemable at all, but the inescapable fact that all such systems must be run by *individual policymakers*. In periods of crisis, since time immemorial, these policymakers, unfortunately, often resort to the most expedient solution, without reference to constraints designed in "normal" times.

It is perhaps appropriate that we have concluded our studies at the beginning, in a sense, with a discussion of gold—the most ancient form of money—and its benefits and pitfalls. In the post-financial crisis world of 2013 and beyond, the most fundamental economic assumptions, long taken for granted, are being reexamined. We hope that we have equipped you, dear reader, with the knowledge and tools that will enable you to successfully navigate the uncertain economic waters ahead.

References

1. Ancient Coins Coin collecting guide for beginners. http://www.coin-collecting-guide-for-beginners.com/ancient-coins.html. Accessed 6 Apr 2011
2. Andreas P (2013) Smuggler nation: how illicit trade made America. Oxford University Press, Oxford
3. Annual Report to Congress on Foreign Economic Collection and Industrial Espionage FY07. Office of the National Counterintelligence Executive. http://www.ncix.gov/publications/reports/fecie_all/fecie_2007/FECIE_2007.pdf. Accessed 10 Sept 2008
4. Annual Report to Congress on Foreign Economic Collection and Industrial Espionage FY08. Office of the National Counterintelligence Executive. http://www.dtic.mil/cgi-bin/GetTRDoc?AD=ADA506093&Location=U2&doc=GetTRDoc.pdf. Accessed 10 Aug 2009
5. Artus P Do central banks withdraw liquidity they have created? Natixis Flash Markets Economic Research, February 4, 2011. Paris: Natixis, 2011. http://cib.natixis.com/flushdoc.aspx?id=56578. Accessed 4 Apr 2011
6. Artus P, Chardon S The correlation between equities and bonds in the Eurozone: how many regimes? Natixis Flash Markets Economic Research, August 6, 2010. Paris: Natixis, 2010. http://cib.natixis.com/flushdoc.aspx?id=54224. Accessed 20 Sept 2012
7. Balzli B How goldman Sachs helped Greece to mask its true debt. Der Spiegel, February 8, 2010. http://www.spiegel.de/international/europe/0,1518,676634,00.html. Accessed 6 Apr 2011
8. Bangladesh Garment Wages the Lowest in the World–Comparative Garment Worker Wages. The National Labor Committee, August 19, 2010. http://www.nlcnet.org/alerts?id=0297. Accessed 6 Apr 2011
9. Bank for International Settlements. Report on global foreign exchange market activity in 2010. Triennial Central Bank Survey, December 2010. http://www.bis.org/publ/rpfxf10t.pdf. Accessed 20 Feb 2011
10. Barbosa D As China's wages rise, export prices could follow. New York Times, June 7, 2010. http://www.nytimes.com/2010/06/08/business/global/08wages.html. Accessed 6 Apr 2011
11. Barro R Macroeconomic effects from government purchases and taxes. Mercatus Center, Georgetown University, July, 2010. http://mercatus.org/publication/macroeconomic-effects-government-purchases-and-taxes. Accessed 9 Sept 2011
12. BCG Report, Global Asset Management 2010: In Search of Stable Growth. Boston: Boston Consulting Group, July 2010. http://www.bcg.com/documents/file53448.pdf. Accessed 15 Mar 2011
13. Behera HK, Narasimhan V, Murty KN Relationship between exchange rate volatility and central bank intervention: an empirical analysis for India. South Asia Economic Journal, Research and Information System for Developing Countries, New Delhi, India and Institute of Policy Studies, Colombo, Sri Lanka, June 2008. http://www.igidr.ac.in/~money/mfc_08/

F. Langdana and P.T. Murphy, *International Trade and Global Macropolicy*,
Springer Texts in Business and Economics, DOI 10.1007/978-1-4614-1635-7,
© Springer Science+Business Media New York 2014

Relationship%20bet%20Exchange%20rate%20Volatility...%20Behera,%20Narsimhan%
20&%20Murty.pdf. Accessed 4 Apr 2011

14. Bernanke B Asset-price "Bubbles" and monetary policy. Remarks by Governor Ben S.
    Bernanke before the New York Chapter of the National Association for Business Economics,
    New York, New York, October 15, 2002. Source: Federal Reserve Bank of New York.
    http://www.federalreserve.gov/BoardDocs/speeches/2002/20021015/default.htm. Accessed
    11 Feb 2011

15. Bernanke B The economic outlook. Speech presented before the Joint Economic Committee,
    US Congress, March 28, 2007. Source: New York Fed. http://www.federalreserve.gov/
    newsevents/testimony/bernanke20070328a.htm. Accessed 18 Nov 2012

16. Bernanke B The global saving glut and the U.S. current account deficit. Remarks by
    Governor Ben S. Bernanke at the Sandridge Lecture, Virginia Association of Economists,
    Richmond, Virginia, March 10, 2005. http://www.federalreserve.gov/boarddocs/speeches/
    2005/200503102/. Accessed 18 Nov 2012

17. Brown R A history of accounting and accountants. New York: Cosimo, Inc., 2004. Originally
    published by Augustus M. Kelley Publishers, 1905

18. Buiter WH Can central banks go broke? London: Centre for Economic Policy Research, May
    2008. www.cepr.org/pubs/dps/DP6827.asp. Accessed 18 Nov 2012

19. Bullard J Seven faces of 'The Peril', Federal Reserve Bank of St. Louis Review, September-
    October 2010. St. Louis: St. Louis Fed, 2010. http://research.stlouisfed.org/econ/bullard/pdf/
    SevenFacesFinalJul28.pdf. Accessed 18 Nov 2012

20. Burnside C, Eichenbaum M, Rebelo S Hedging and financial fragility in fixed exchange rate
    regimes. Evanston: Financial Institutions and Market Research Center, Kellogg School of
    Management, Northwestern University. October 2000. http://www.kellogg.northwestern.
    edu/faculty/rebelo/htm/bank50000.pdf. Accessed 18 Nov 2012

21. Bussey J (2011) US firms, China are locked in major war over technology. Wall Street J,
    February 2, 2011

22. Chin M, Frankel JA (2007) Will the euro eventually surpass the dollar as leading international
    reserve currency? In: Clarida RH (ed) G7 Current account imbalances: sustainability and
    adjustment. University of Chicago Press, Chicago. http://www.nber.org/chapters/c0126.pdf.
    Accessed 18 Nov 2012

23. China and the dollar. Wall Street J, March 26, 2009. http://online.wsj.com/article/
    SB123802521198942455.html. Accessed 21 Mar 2011

24. China's foreign exchange reserves, 1977–2010. chinability.com. http://www.chinability.
    com/Reserves.htm. Accessed 26 Mar 2011

25. Clarida R With privilege comes..? Global Perspectives, Pimco, October 2009. http://www.
    pimco.com/EN/Insights/Pages/With%20Privilege%20Comes%20Clarida%20Oct%202009.
    aspx. Accessed 18 Nov 2012

26. Completing the Internal Market: White Paper from the Commission to the European Council.
    (Milan, 28–29 June 1985) COM(85) 310, June 1985. (Commission of the European
    Communities, Brussels), June 1985. http://europa.eu/documents/comm/white_papers/pdf/
    com1985_0310_f_en.pdf. Accessed 12 Oct 2012

26. The Conference Board Leading Economic Index® February 2011. New York: The Confer-
    ence Board, March 17, 2011. http://www.conference-board.org/data/bci.cfm. Accessed
    17 Mar 2011

28. Costinot A (2009) An elementary theory of comparative advantage. Econometrica
    77:1165–1192

29. De Long B Exorbitant privilege, February 22, 2005. http://www.j-bradford-delong.net/
    movable_type/2005-3_archives/000397.html. Accessed 5 Mar 2011

30. Deardorff AV (1980) The general validity of the law of comparative advantage. J Polit Econ
    88(5):941–957

31. Devika J, Miller M Devaluation of the rupee: tale of two years, 1966 and 1991. CCS Working Paper No. 0028. New Delhi: Centre for Civil Society, 2002. http://www.ccsindia.org/ccsindia/policy/money/studies/wp0028.pdf. Accessed 18 Nov 2012

32. Dornbusch R, Fischer S, Samuelson P (1977) Comparative advantage, trade, and payments in a Ricardian model with a continuum of goods. Am Econ Rev 67:823–839

33. Dunkelberg WC, Wade H NFIB Small Business Economic Trends, March 2011. New York: National Federation of Independent Businesses, March, 2011. http://www.nfib.com/research-foundation/surveys/small-business-economic-trends?
utm_campaign=SBET&utm_source=   Releases&utm_medium=Releases.   Accessed 18 Nov 2012

34. Eaton J, Kortum S (2002) Technology, geography, and trade. Econometrica 70:1741–1779

35. ECRI Weekly Leading Index. Economic Cycle Research Institute, New York. http://www.businesscycle.com/resources/. Accessed 26 Mar 2011

36. Eichengreen B Sterling's past, dollar's future: historical perspectives on reserve currency competition. Tawney Lecture delivered to the Economic Historical Society, Leicester, April 10, 2005. http://www.econ.berkeley.edu/~eichengr/research/tawney_lecture2apr29-05.pdf. Accessed 18 Nov 2012

37. Eichengreen B (1999) Toward a new international financial architecture: a practical post-Asia agenda. Peterson Institute for International Economics, Washington, DC

38. Eichengreen B, Mathieson DJ The currency composition of foreign exchange reserves: retrospect and prospect. IMF Working Paper, July 2000. http://www.imf.org/external/pubs/ft/wp/2000/wp00131.pdf. Accessed 18 Nov 2012

39. Elwell C The dollar's future as the world's reserve currency: the challenge of the euro. Congressional Research Service Report for Congress, July 10, 2007. http://assets.opencrs.com/rpts/RL34083_20070710.pdf. Accessed 18 Nov 2012

40. Fan G China's monetary sterilization. China Daily, November 30, 2010. http://www.chinadaily.com.cn/opinion/project/2010-11/30/content_11628774.htm. Accessed 18 Mar 2011

41. Fitch confirms rating of Icelandic banks. Iceland Review Online. February 24, 2006. http://www.icelandreview.com/icelandreview/daily_news/?cat_id=16567&ew_0_a_id=186790. Accessed 12 Feb 2011

42. Flynn P Bernanke says unfair to blame inflation on QE. Futuresmag.com, February 4, 2011. http://www.futuresmag.com/News/2011/2/Pages/Bernanke-says-unfair-to-blame-inflation-on-QE.aspx. Accessed 31 Mar 2011

43. Foster RT (1991) Fiat paper money: the history and evolution of our currency. Ralph T. Foster, Berkeley. This thoroughly researched and entertaining work is available from Ralph T. Foster, 2189 Bancroft Way, Berkeley, CA 94704, or by email at tfdf@pacbell.net.

44. Fujioka T, Otsuma M G-7 sells yen in first joint intervention since 2000 to Ease Japan Crisis. Bloomberg, March 18, 2011. http://www.bloomberg.com/news/2011-03-18/g-7-intervenes-to-weaken-yen-as-surging-currency-threathens-quake-recovery.html. Accessed 18 Nov 2012

45. Generational Dynamics. Sudden collapse of Iceland krona portends bursting of "carry trade" Bubble. generationaldynamics.com, February 27, 2006. http://www.generationaldynamics.com/cgi-bin/D.PL?xct=gd.e060227. Accessed 31 Mar 2011

46. Giddy I An integrated theory of exchange rate equilibrium. University of Michigan, May, 1975. http://quod.lib.umich.edu/b/busadwp/images/b/1/3/b1372506.0001.001.pdf. Accessed 18 Nov 2012

47. Global Wealth Databook. Credit Suisse Research Institute. Geneva: Credit Suisse Group AG, August   2010.   https://www.credit-suisse.com/news/doc/credit_suisse_global_wealth_-databook.pdf. Accessed 20 Feb 2011

48. Greenwood J (2008) The costs and implications of PBC sterilization. Cato J 28(2) (Spring/Summer 2008): 205–217. Cato Institute, 2008. http://www.cato.org/pubs/journal/cj28n2/cj28n2-4.pdf. Accessed 18 Nov 2012

49. Hicks JR (1937) Mr. Keynes and the "Classics"; a suggested interpretation. Econometrica 5 (2):147–159. http://www.jstor.org/stable/1907242. Accessed 8 May 2013

50. Historical Tables, Budget of the U.S. Government, Fiscal Year 2010. US Office of Management and Budget, www.budget.gov. http://www.gpoaccess.gov/usbudget/fy10/pdf/hist.pdf. Accessed 18 Mar 2011

51. Hopes raised, punches pulled. The Economist, February 10, 2011

52. Hussman J, Ph.D. Why the federal reserve is irrelevant. Hussman Funds Research & Insight, August 2001. http://www.hussmanfunds.com/html/fedirrel.htm. Accessed 18 Nov 2012

53. Hussman J, Ph.D. (2006) Superstition and the fed. Hussman Funds Research & Insight. http://www.hussmanfunds.com/wmc/wmc061002.htm. Accessed 18 Nov 2012

54. International Monetary Fund. Special drawing rights (SDRs) factsheet. December 9, 2010. http://www.imf.org/external/np/exr/facts/sdr.htm. Accessed 18 Nov 2012

55. Irwin DA Did France cause the Great Depression? Dartmouth College and NBER, November 15, 2010. http://www.dartmouth.edu/~dirwin/Did%20France%20Cause%20the%20Great%20Depression.pdf. Accessed 18 Nov 2012

56. Jones RW (1961) Comparative advantage and the theory of tariffs: a multi-country, multi-commodity model. Rev Econ Stud 28(3):161–175

57. Komulainen T (1999) Currency crisis theories–some explanations for the Russian case. BOFIT Discussion Papers 1999 No. 1. Bank of Finland Institute for Economies in Transition, Helsinki. http://www.suomenpankki.fi/bofit/tutkimus/tutkimusjulkaisut/dp/Documents/dp0199.pdf. Accessed 18 Nov 2012

58. Kray A Do high interest rates defend currencies under speculative attack? World Bank, December 2001

59. Keynes JM (1936) The general theory of employment, interest, and money. Macmillan, London

60. Kindleberger C, Aliber R (2011) Manias, panics and crashes: a history of financial crises, 6th edn. Palgrace Macmillan, New York

61. Langdana FK (2006) Macroeconomic policy: demystifying monetary and fiscal policy, 2nd edn. Springer, New York

62. Langdana FK (1989) Sustaining domestic budget deficits in open economies. Routledge, Oxford

63. Lindert P, Pugel T (1996) International economics, 10th edn. Irwin/McGraw-Hill, New York

64. Mackay C (2003 [1841]). Extraordinary popular delusions and the madness of crowds. Harriman House, Hampshire

65. Mackenzie M Short-term US interest rates turn negative. Financial Times. London. November 20, 2009

66. Magness PW (2009) From tariffs to the income tax: trade protection and revenue in the United States Tax System. http://digilib.gmu.edu/xmlui/bitstream/handle/1920/5642/Magness_Phillip .pdf?sequence=1. Accessed 18 Nov 2012

67. Magnitude of counterfeiting and piracy in tangible products: an update. OECD, November 2009. http://www.oecd.org/dataoecd/57/27/44088872.pdf. Accessed 17 Oct 2012

68. Maslakovic M Fund management 2010. TheCityUK, London, October 2010. www.thecityuk.com/assets/Uploads/Fund-management-2010.pdf. Accessed 18 Nov 2012

69. McGregor J (2009) China's drive for indigenous innovation, a web of industrial policies. U.S. Chamber of Commerce, 2009. http://www.uschamber.com/reports/chinas-drive-indigenous-innovation-web-industrial-policies. Accessed 18 Nov 2012, document link at http://www.uschamber.com/sites/default/files/reports/100728chinareport_0.pdf

70. McKinnon R The latest American export: inflation. Wall Street J, January 18, 2011. http://online.wsj.com/article/SB10001424052748704405704576064252782421930.html. Accessed 20 Feb 2011

71. Neely C An introduction to capital controls. Federal Reserve Bank of St. Louis Review (November/December 1999), 13–30. http://research.stlouisfed.org/publications/review/99/11/9911cn.pdf. Accessed 18 Nov 2012

72. New York Federal Reserve Fedpoint: balance of payments. May 2009. http://www.newyorkfed.org/aboutthefed/fedpoint/fed40.html. Accessed 18 Nov 2012

73. Nugeé J Foreign exchange reserves management. Bank of England Centre for Central Banking Studies Handbooks in Central Banking No. 19, 2000. http://www.bankofengland.co.uk/education/CCBS/handbooks/pdf/ccbshb19.pdf. Accessed 18 Nov 2012

74. OANDA Corporation Historical exchange rates. http://www.oanda.com/currency/historical-rates/. Accessed Feb-Mar 2011

75. Olson O, He M (1999) A model of balance of payment crisis: the strong currency as a determinant of exchange rate disequlibria. Nova Southeastern University, Fort Lauderdale. http://www.econ.cam.ac.uk/cjeconf/delegates/olson.pdf. Accessed 18 Nov 2012

76. Ouyang AY, Rajan RS, Willett TD China as a reserve sink: the evidence from offset and sterilization coefficients. October 2006. http://www.cgu.edu/PDFFiles/SPE/Willett/Papers/Chinaterilatest03-9-1.pdf. Accessed 18 Nov 2012

77. Perry MJ Chapter 14. Modern macroeconomics and monetary policy. University of Michigan-Flint. http://spruce.flint.umich.edu/~mjperry/macro14.htm. Accessed 31 Mar 2011

78. Persaud A (2004) When currency empires fall. www.321gold.com (October 11, 2004). http://www.321gold.com/editorials/persaud/persaud101204.html

79. Peston R Markets call time on Iceland. BBC News, October 4, 2008. http://www.bbc.co.uk/blogs/thereporters/robertpeston/2008/10/creditors_call_time_on_iceland.html. Accessed 31 Mar 2011

80. Pettis M (2013) A brief history of the Chinese growth model. Michael Pettis' China Financial Markets. http://www.mpettis.com/2013/02/21/a-brief-history-of-the-chinese-growth-model/. Accessed 5 May 2013

81. Prahalad CK, Hart SL (2002) The fortunate at the bottom of the pyramid. strategy+business issue no. 26 first quarter 2002. Booz Allen Hamilton, McLean. http://www.cs.berkeley.edu/~brewer/ict4b/Fortune-BoP.pdf. Accessed 18 Nov 2012

82. Regulators tackle 'carry trades'. Dealbook, New York Times, February 11, 2010. http://dealbook.nytimes.com/2010/02/11/regulators-tackle-carry-trades/. Accessed 5 Apr 2011

83. Romer C, Bernstein J The job impact of the American recovery and reinvestment plan. January 9, 2010. http://www.economy.com/mark-zandi/documents/The_Job_Impact_of_the_American_Recovery_and_Reinvestment_Plan.pdf. Accessed 18 Nov 2012

84. Ricardo D (1817) On the principles of political economy and taxation

85. Samuelson P (2004) Where Ricardo and Mill Rebut and confirm arguments of mainstream economists supporting globalization. J Econ Perspect 18(3)   135–146. http://www.wilsoncenter.org/sites/default/files/SamuelsonJEP042.pdf. Accessed 18 Nov 2012

86. Schwab K (ed) (2010) The Global Competitiveness Report 2010–2011. World Economic Forum, Geneva. http://www3.weforum.org/docs/WEF_GlobalCompetitivenessReport_2010-11.pdf. Accessed 18 Nov 2012

87. Scott RE The hidden costs of insourcing: higher trade deficits and job losses for U.S. workers. EPI Issue Brief #236. Economic Policy Institute, Washington DC, August 23, 2007. http://www.epi.org/publications/entry/ib236/. Accessed 18 Nov 2012

88. Shedlock M US dollar about to lose reserve currency status – fact or fantasy? Mish's Global Economic Trend Analysis, February 28, 2011. http://globaleconomicanalysis.blogspot.com/2011/02/us-dollar-about-to-lose-reserve.html. Accessed 31 Mar 2011

89. Sierminska E, Takhtamanova Y Wealth effects out of housing and financial wealth: cross country and age group comparisons. Federal Reserve Bank of San Francisco, January 2007. http://www.frbsf.org/publications/economics/papers/2007/wp07-01bk.pdf. Accessed 18 Nov 2012

90. Slaughter MJ (2004) Infant industry protection and trade liberalization in developing countries. Nathan Associates, Arlington

91. Smith A (1776) An inquiry into the nature and causes of the wealth of nations

92. Smith A (1996) Strategic policy in the European car market. In Krugman P, Smith A (eds) Empirical studies of strategic trade policy. University of Chicago Press, Chicago, pp 67–83. http://www.nber.org/chapters/c8676.pdf. Accessed 5 May 2013

93. Sousa RM Wealth effects on consumption, evidence from the euro area. European Central Bank Working Paper No. 1050 (European Central Bank, Frankfort), May 2009. http://www. ecb.int/pub/pdf/scpwps/ecbwp1050.pdf. Accessed 18 Nov 2012

94. Statement of the G6 Finance Ministers and Central Bank Governors (Louvre Accord), Paris, February 22, 1987. http://www.g7.utoronto.ca/finance/fm870222.htm. Accessed 31 Mar 2011

95. Taylor JB The financial crisis and the policy responses: an empirical analysis of what went wrong. November 2008, 5. http://www.stanford.edu/~johntayl/FCPR.pdf. Accessed 12 Nov 2012

96. The Economic Impact of Counterfeiting and Piracy. OECD, Paris, 2007. http://www.oecd. org/dataoecd/13/12/38707619.pdf. Accessed October 17, 2012. Main site: see www.oecd. org/sti/counterfeiting

97. United States Census Bureau, US Bureau of Economic Analysis. US International Trade in Goods and Services, Annual Revisions for 2009. June 10, 2010. http://www.census.gov/ foreign-trade/Press-Release/2009pr/final_revisions/09final.pdf. Accessed 31 Mar 2011

98. United States Treasury Office of International Affairs. Appendix 1: an historical perspective on the reserve currency status of the US dollar. Report to Congress on International Economics and Exchange Rate Policies, October 15, 2010. http://www.treasury.gov/resource-center/ international/exchange-rate-policies/Documents/Appendix%201%20Final%20October% 2015%202009.pdf. Accessed November 18, 2012.

99. USDA Food CPI and expenditures Table 97. http://www.ers.usda.gov/Briefing/CPIFoodAndEx penditures/Data/Table_97/2009table97.htm. Accessed 5 Mar 2011

100. Wang A, Rabinovitch S China raises RRR again as inflation fight intensifies. Reuters, November 19, 2010. http://www.reuters.com/article/2010/11/19/none-q- idUSL3E6MJ0N820101119. Accessed 18 Nov 2012

101. Wang Pengfei, Wen Yi Speculative bubbles and financial crisis. St. Louis Fed Working Paper 2009-029B. St. Louis: Federal Reserve Bank of St. Louis Research Division, July 2009. http://research.stlouisfed.org/wp/2009/2009-029.pdf. Accessed 18 Nov 2012

102. Weerapana A Lecture 5: exchange rate systems. Presented at Wellesley College, 2003. http:// www.wellesley.edu/Economics/weerapana/econ213/econ213pdf/lect213-05.pdf. Accessed 18 Feb 2011

103. Woodford M Simple analytics of the government expenditure multiplier. Columbia University, June 13, 2010. http://www.columbia.edu/~mw2230/G_ASSA.pdf. Accessed 18 Nov 2012

104. World Trade Organization International trade statistics 2010. World Trade Organization, Geneva, March 26, 2010. http://www.wto.org/english/res_e/statis_e/its2010_e/its10_toc_e. htm. Accessed 17 Oct 2012

105. Zhang Chenying Sterilization in China: effectiveness and cost. The Wharton School, University of Pennsylvania Finance Department, September 2010. http://fic.wharton.upenn.edu/fic/ papers/10/10-29.pdf. Accessed 18 Nov 2012

Index

F. Langdana and P.T. Murphy, *International Trade and Global Macropolicy*,   401
Springer Texts in Business and Economics, DOI 10.1007/978-1-4614-1635-7,
© Springer Science+Business Media New York 2014